D1201088

Effective Management of Local Area Networks

Functions, Instruments, and People

Kornel Terplan

WITHDRAWN
IOWA STATE UNIVERSITY
LIBRARY

Second Edition

McGraw-Hill

New York   San Francisco   Washington, D.C.   Auckland   Bogotá
Caracas   Lisbon   London   Madrid   Mexico City   Milan
Montreal   New Delhi   San Juan   Singapore
Sydney   Tokyo   Toronto

Library of Congress Cataloging-in-Publication Data

Terplan, Kornel.
    Effective management of local area networks : functions,
instruments, and people / Kornel Terplan.—2nd ed.
        p.   cm.—(McGraw-Hill series on computer communications)
    Includes index.
    ISBN 0-07-063639-7 (hc)
    1. Local area networks (Computer networks)—Management.
I. Title. II. Series.
TK5105.7.T47   1996
004.6'8—dc20   96-11084
                                                              CIP

McGraw-Hill

A Division of The McGraw-Hill Companies

Copyright © 1996, 1992 by The McGraw-Hill Companies, Inc. All rights
reserved. Printed in the United States of America. Except as permitted
under the United States Copyright Act of 1976, no part of this publication may be reproduced or distributed in any form or by any means, or
stored in a data base or retrieval system, without the prior written permission of the publisher.

1 2 3 4 5 6 7 8 9 0   DOC/DOC   9 0 1 0 9 8 7 6

0-07-063639-7

*The sponsoring editor for this book was Steven Elliot, the editing
supervisor was Christine Furry, and the production supervisor was
Pamela A. Pelton. It was set in Century Schoolbook by North Market
Street Graphics.*

Printed and bound by R. R. Donnelley & Sons Company.

This book is printed on acid-free paper.

Information contained in this work has been obtained by The
McGraw-Hill Companies, Inc., ("McGraw-Hill") from sources
believed to be reliable. However, neither McGraw-Hill nor its
authors guarantee the accuracy or completeness of any information published herein and neither McGraw-Hill nor its authors
shall be responsible for any errors, omissions, or damages arising
out of use of this information. This work is published with the
understanding that McGraw-Hill and its authors are supplying
information but are not attempting to render engineering or other
professional services. If such services are required, the assistance
of an appropriate professional should be sought.

To my daughter Kornelia Terplan, whose interest motivated me to complete the manuscript on time

Contents

Introduction

This book stresses three critical factors for successful LAN management: processes, instruments, and human resources. The book itself is structured in eight segments.

Chapter 1 deals with the status of and requirements for LAN management. The status review outlines the differences between LAN and WAN management. The chapter also differentiates LAN management from applications management, and tries to quantify the impact of improperly managed LANs. After identifying the three critical success factors referred to previously, I address the LAN management framework and the most likely managed objects. I end Chapter 1 by categorizing end-user requirements for LAN management.

In order to assess potential performance bottlenecks, Chapter 2 offers a walk-through of bandwidth selection, media choices, protocols, access techniques, and the most widely used topologies. This chapter introduces also high-speed LANs, switched and virtual LANs, ATM as local switching technology, collapsed and distributed structures. I also discuss interconnected LANs, including two vital interconnecting devices and how to choose the technology for interconnection. This chapter concludes with a critical assessment of source routing as opposed to spanning tree, and the use of bridges as opposed to routers. The focus with introducing innovative technologies in LANs is always on the managability of components using open or de facto standards.

Chapter 3 gives an in-depth discussion of principal LAN management functions, such as configuration, fault, performance, security, and accounting management. When appropriate, I highlight the differences between WAN and MAN management. I also reference cross-function applications. Using principles and priorities established by LAN users, I thoroughly discuss configuration and fault management, giving a number of real-life examples. Each management function has a certain set of typical instruments, which are identified in generic terms.

I also discuss LAN administration—including interfaces, help menus, documentation tools, software distribution techniques, licensing policies, advanced tools, and expert systems. This particular function may also be seen as part of operational control, usually supported by fault management. As a summary of LAN management functions and typical instruments, I introduce a matrix that indicates which instruments apply to which LAN management functions.

Chapter 4 discusses LAN management standardization. After outlining the principal directions of LAN management support protocols. I provide a comparison between SNMP (Simple Network Management Protocol) and CMIP (Common Management Information Protocol). Despite growing popularity and support for SNMP managers and agents, CMIP offers a more complete solution with rich functionality, but at a considerably higher price and overhead. Also, migration alternatives and integrated solutions are referenced as part of leading manufacturers' LAN management strategies. In order to support the product selection process for LAN integrators, leading platform solutions are also introduced. RMON1 and RMON2 probes change the philosophy of LAN management by offering state-of-the-art continuous monitoring of LAN segments. Periodically, monitored data are collected by the management stations for further processing, report generation, and distribution.

The instrumentation section (Chapter 5) deals with various types of tools. Stand-alone monitors, analyzers, test instruments, platforms, platform-independent applications, and PC-LAN-management solutions are discussed first. Next, I address the LAN management systems of various vendors, addressing in particular the management of Ethernet and token ring segments, wiring hubs, and interconnecting devices. The final part of the chapter evaluates the leading integrator products and their role in managing enterprise LANs. Special segments are devoted to device-independent applications and application suites that are addressing security management, performance management, software distribution, asset management, software licensing, and trouble tracking. In each case, the integration capabilities with management platforms are highlighted. Database and application management becomes an integral part of LAN management in many businesses. This chapter outlines the management opportunities using SNMP. LAN performance management is addressed as a service by independent companies. This service off-loads customers by polling MIBs and RMON probes from the outside, preparing reports and distributing information over the Internet or by the use of private e-mail facilities. In order to facilitate the process of selecting tools, a detailed criteria list is included and explained at length.

In Chapter 6, I analyze LAN design and planning. After introducing the principal planning steps, I address planning criteria such as quality, performance, availability, technology and costs. As part of the final design process, the role of modeling instruments is outlined, with selected examples from leading manufacturers. In particular, the cooperation between LAN monitors and modeling packages is analyzed in more detail. But, LAN design and planning are still considered more an art than a science.

Chapter 7 offers a structure for the LAN management support organization. Two groups—planning and operations—are clearly separated. All participating groups and individuals are characterized by their responsibilities, job interfaces, qualifying experiences, training requirements, and typical salary ranges. Examples for building and maintaining the LAN management team are also given. Although still in its infancy, LAN management outsourcing options are also briefly discussed.

Chapter 8 addresses the directions in which LAN management is headed, concentrating on centralization, automation, integration, MIB support, and enhancing the quality of user administration.

This book is intended for users of LANs, network designers, capacity planners who are in charge of planning and administering LANs, and LAN operators who are in charge of operating local area networks. People involved in the selection of components and technology for WANs, MANs, and LANs will also find the book valuable.

The text, which evolved from my research and consulting work, is also easily adaptable for undergraduate college and graduate university courses.

Acknowledgments

Three principal sources helped me in writing this second edition: the Network Management and Network Management Systems services from Datapro, based in Delran (New Jersey), assisted me in determining the right depth for the overall structure of the book, and gave me also product information; my consulting business helped me the recognize the real needs of users for LAN management functions, instruments and education of the LAN management team: my LAN and Client/Server Management course, which I designed and is being sponsored by Demand Technologies in Naples, Florida, enabled me to gather several real-life cases from attendees.

I am particularly grateful to all the vendors who have supported my work by providing state-of-the-art documentation and white papers on tools.

I would also thank Jill Huntington-Lee, senior analyst from Datapro, Chuck Williams, Director for Telecommunications from Georgia Pacific, Tracy Tufillaro, Director from AT&T, Subhendu Ghosh from Stevens Institute of Technology and Professor Theresa Rubinson from Brooklyn Polytechnic University for their valuable comments on my work.

I would also like to thank Jerry Papke, Patricia Amoroso, and Christine Furry for leading the production of this second edition.

Kornel Terplan

LAN Management and Enterprise Network Management

The inadequacies of existing LAN-related network management instruments and techniques have made certain LAN-based enterprise networks practically unmanageable, and the following factors have brought this situation to light:

- The rise of multiprotocol and multimedia communication architectures
- Interconnected LANs, MANs, and WANs
- Implementation of mission-critical applications on client/server systems
- The use of various WAN technologies to interconnect LANs

Nowadays, effective enterprisewide communication is expected to address the following concerns:

- Concentration on supporting business applications
- Local interconnection between various workstations and servers supporting office automation, shop floor control, image processing, work group computing, video, and other specific applications
- Remote interconnection between LAN segments using various interconnecting devices, such as repeaters, bridges, brouters, routers, extenders, and gateways
- Support for multiple communication forms such as voice, data, image, and video

- Support for a unified user interface for various applications and for different forms of communication
- Unified network access in order to ensure interoperability
- Total connectivity for supporting any-to-any communication
- Very high availability of applications, servers, and transport facilities
- Successful integration of the management of voice, data, and image structures in the local area by providing high bandwidth to end users
- Ability to supervise LAN operations from a central site using a powerful combination of management applications and platforms

After reviewing trends and present status, this chapter defines the scope and principal driving forces for managing LANs. Emphasis has been placed on LAN management components, and on the critical success factors necessary to meet LAN management user requirements. Object classes are defined, the LAN management framework is introduced, and LAN instrumentation trends are summarized. Also, the challenge of building and maintaining the LAN management team is addressed.

When observing the LAN market, network managers may observe that there has been an over-average growth rate and very high change-request ratio. Specifically, they have determined the following:

- The number of vendors selling LAN hardware, LAN software, and interconnecting devices is increasing.
- Users are demanding peer-to-peer communication with as few hubs as possible. The number of LANs, PBXs, and interconnected segments is increasing.
- Rapidly evolving LAN technologies impact managerial decision making. In particular, fast LANs, switched LANs, and ATM are competing for market share in the local area.
- Access is extended to a large number of users by LAN extenders using wired and wireless technologies.
- Due to relatively easy access, more efficient techniques are needed to prevent security violations.
- There are a number of proprietary network management products and solutions that can't yet offer interoperability.
- In addition to special-purpose solutions, SNMP (Simple Network Management Protocol) seems to be arising as the principle upon which LAN management products and concepts are based.

- The need for integrated WAN/MAN/LAN management increases.
- There's a shift toward more centralized LAN and PBX management.
- The role of interconnecting devices of wiring hubs has changed and is considered more important than before to managing enterprise networks.
- Due to the cross applicability of platforms, many LAN management product vendors will stop designing and implementing proprietary solutions and will migrate to standard platforms.
- These platforms are expected to be offered independently from the hardware on which they run.
- Device-dependent and device-independent management applications are available to support high-priority LAN management functions such as fault and performance management.

The following are questions that can't yet be satisfactorily answered by LAN designers and planners:

- How can we optimize LAN performance?
- What's the most economical way to interconnect LANs?
- How can LANs and PBXs be meaningfully combined to manage a local site?
- How could design and planning instruments be used?
- Which routing algorithm is the first choice?
- How can we handle the administration of a large number of physical and logical LAN objects?
- Which LAN management standards will win?
- How will DME (distributed management environment) help to standardize LAN management functions and instrumentation?
- Which and how many human resources are needed to support and manage various user clusters?
- How can LANs be managed from a central—often remote—site?
- How can LAN management be combined with systems management in order to support client/server systems?
- Is desktop management part of LAN management?
- How much WAN management should be incorporated into LAN management?
- Who is responsible for MAN management?

Scope and Driving Forces
of LAN Management

The overall goal of LAN management is to ensure the continuous avail-ability of business applications on workstations connected to LANs from the perspective of local area networks. This scope is broader than just supervising status of LAN facilities and equipment. It includes information collection about status of applications in servers and work-stations. One way is to monitor the actual error messages sent between applications and underlying operating systems and communication protocols. Monitoring is usually controlled by the central management station. Assuming application know-how on the central site, corrective actions can be taken quickly, sometimes before users notice problems. Also, additional information on actual hardware and software configu-ration of the users' workstations can be collected and sent along with error messages to the central management station. This whole process is expected to be standardized as part of the distributed management interface.

LAN management means deploying and coordinating resources in order to design, plan, administer, analyze, evaluate, operate, and expand local area communication networks to meet service-level objec-tives at all times, at a reasonable cost, and with optimal combination of resources.

Figure 1.1 shows a typical network of interconnected LANs from the enterprise point of view. Local area networking segments may consti-tute metropolitan area networks supporting multiple communication forms that are interconnected using wide area networking products and services. Each entity in this WAN/MAN/LAN structure may have independent management functions and instruments. End-to-end management from the enterprise point of view requires that these management entities work together.

The scope of this book is LAN management, consisting of LAN man-agement functions, instruments, and human resources supporting functions and operating instruments. Part of the scope is to define the demarcation line and interfaces between MAN and WAN manage-ment. The obvious demarcation line is the WAN-and-MAN access point, represented by interconnecting units such as gateways, routers, brouters, and bridges. Repeaters and extenders are seen within the LAN segments.

In terms of managing networking segments, there are similarities and differences, depending on the geographical reach of the structures. Table 1.1 summarizes the major differences between managing WANs, MANs, and LANs. There are certain similarities between MAN and LAN management due to the use of the SNMP protocol. In case of WANs, SNMP is used, usually not for real-time management, but for

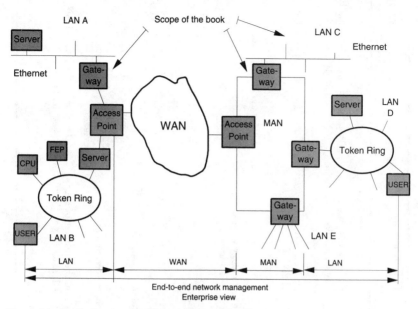

Figure 1.1   Typical network of interconnected LANs.

historical status reporting. SNMP is simply too slow to manage highly sophisticated WAN devices such as frame relay or ATM switches.

Most organizations have recognized the strategic importance of their network management. In most cases, better control ensures a higher level of performance, and this performance corresponds with higher productivity. In addition, higher productivity often translates into bottom-line financial improvements. This leads us to consider what the principal driving forces are for investing in and spending more on LAN management.

- *Controlling corporate strategic assets.*   LANs are an increasingly essential part of the enterprise's day-to-day business activity. The rapidly declining costs of personal computers, workstations, and departmental computing power is increasing the number of intelligent network elements to be connected and controlled. Completely new networking applications are available to users. But without proper control, the full power and usefulness of these new applications are barely tapped.

- *Controlling complexity.*   The constantly growing number of network components, users, interfaces, protocols, and vendors has left many managers with little or no control over what's connected to the network. In particular, LAN-based servers and stations (clients) are most frequently beyond the scope of central control.

TABLE 1.1 Differences Between WAN, MAN, and LAN Management

Criteria	Type of network		
	WAN	MAN	LAN
Number of managed objects	Medium; mostly logical components	High; mostly physical components	High; mostly physical components
Status surveillance	Active by eventing	Passive by polling; eventually eventing by traps; also individual MIBs are provided	Passive by polling, eventually eventing by traps
Management concept	Centralized and hierarchical	Decentralized; usually a customized version of SNMP	Decentralized and peer-to-peer
Standards	Proprietary and de facto; little OSI-CMIP	SNMP and SMT	SNMP (Simple Network Management Protocol)
Number of technological alternatives, protocols, and vendors	High	Mature technology with a low number of alternatives	Very high
Systems and network management	Separated becoming integrated	Integrated	Integrated
Support of network management functions			
Configuration management	Weak	Acceptable	Fair
Fault management	Architecture-specific	Good	Components-specific
Performance management	Architecture-specific	Good	Components-specific
Security management	Logical protection	Physical protection only	Physical protection
Accounting management	Host-oriented	Weak	Weak
Impacts of outages	Applications-dependent	Depends on the number of LANs connected; usually very high	Depends on the size of LAN segments
Quantification of impacts due to outages	Yes	Yes	Yes

■ *Improving service.*   Users are requesting the same and even a better service level, despite growth and changing technology. New users require support and training, and they have high expectations from advanced telecommunication solutions. Expectations are particularly high for standards, availability, and performance.

■ *Balancing various needs.*   Those who manage LANs are expected to satisfy certain business needs such as supporting new applications and customers, providing improved connectivity, and ensuring stability and flexibility. At the same time, users' needs, such as availability, reliability, performance, stability, and visibility have to be met in a LAN management environment where there's a lack of procedures and tools. Skills are limited, and there's a serious shortage of personnel.

■ *Reducing downtime.*   Ensuring continued availability of networking resources and services is the ultimate goal of enterprise communication. LAN management solutions have to ensure this capability by efficient configuration, fault, and maintenance management.

■ *Controlling changes.*   In order to increase integrity between fault, performance, and configuration management, changes have to be planned, scheduled, executed, and documented properly. Due to high flexibility requirements in LAN environments, moves and configuration changes are frequent, but their administration is still very weak.

■ *Controlling costs.*   Network management needs to keep an eye on all costs associated with data and voice communications. The network manager is expected to spend only a reasonable amount of money, which still may be considerable. Today, the average enterprise spends approximately 3 to 5 percent of the total communication budget for network management. This may grow as high as 15 to 20 percent by the late 1990s. LAN management is expected to receive an increasing portion of this money. If cost management is under control, however, the service level may be improved without increasing costs.

The interpretation of driving forces is different in each operating environment. The recommendations are as follows:

■ Use weights when considering each of the criteria defined previously.

■ Evaluate corporate LAN management strategies against all criteria.

■ Combine the evaluation result with the weights.

Table 1.2 displays the driving forces.

TABLE 1.2   Driving Forces of LAN Management

Controlling corporate strategic assets
Controlling complexity
Improving service
Balancing various needs
Reducing downtime
Controlling costs
Controlling changes

Components of LAN Management

LAN management components are grouped according to the following entities: objects to be managed, technology, management functions, standards, strategies, and costs.

MO (managed object)

Managed objects (MOs) may be further segregated by application, server, PBX, workstation, internet, subnets, and the infrastructure. The number of devices to be monitored, controlled, and managed in a typical LAN is much higher than in a WAN or even in a MAN environment. Successful LAN management requires that all objects be managed equally. In WANs and MANs, it's much easier to partition and segregate managed objects by physical and logical components, by geographical location, and by architecture.

The following gives a sense of how pervasive and how complex a presence LANs have in the market:

- Approximately 50 to 60 million personal computers are installed worldwide.

- Approximately 60 percent of personal computers are interconnected.

- Approximately 5 million local area networks are in use.

- Approximately 50 percent of the local area networks are interconnected.

- There are multiple architectures and protocols.

- There are multiple topologies.

- There are multiple transport media.

- There are multiple LAN operating systems that don't offer interoperability.

- There is use of proprietary LAN management solutions.

- There are multiple logical topologies supporting virtual LANs.

- There are many interconnecting alternatives offering a wide range of price/performance ratios.

Technology

Today, there are many different technologies, protocols, and suppliers of local area networks. Technology may be meaningfully broken down into: media, typical throughput rates, topology, and access methods. In order to consider how to allocate investments and resources, the following usage breakdown should be considered:

1. *Media*
   a. Coax, 30 percent
   b. Unshielded and shielded twisted pair, 50 percent
   c. Fiber, 20 percent
2. *Data rates*
   a. 1 Mbps, 4 percent
   b. 4 Mbps, 8 percent
   c. 10 Mbps, 40 percent
   d. 16 Mbps, 10 percent
   e. higher, 38 percent
3. *Logical topology*
   a. Bus, 60 percent
   b. Ring, 20 percent
   c. Star, 10 percent
   d. Others, 10 percent
4. *Access methods*
   a. CSMA/CD, 50 percent
   b. Token passing, 30 percent
   c. Others, 20 percent

But, always remember that LAN technology changes very rapidly. Observations show:

- Clear growth pattern for FDDI
- Uncertainty about fast Ethernet
- Great interest for full duplex and switched LANs
- Big challenge in administering virtual local area networks
- Coexistence of Ethernet and Token Ring

Network management functions, standards, and strategies

Network management functions are not yet fully supported. LAN management is an afterthought, in many cases following LAN installation by 6 to 10 months. If implemented, fault management functions are seen most frequently. Performance management is mission-driven and sporadic. Configuration management shows some progress, but it's not yet the real core function of LAN management. Security is implemented as part of the LAN operating system—usually with very few additions. Accounting management, design, and planning are not yet fully understood, and thus have been rarely implemented.

Due to the passive nature of LAN connections and some of the objects, there's no information about failing components or inoperative segments available to management. In order to gain such information, active polling of components is necessary. This is the basis for SNMP implementations. But careful consideration is needed to minimize the impact of polling on the LAN bandwidth. This problem may become severe in an interconnected LAN environment, where routers and bridges exchange status information.

Network and systems management are not yet integrated; servers, stations, hubs, and connections are managed separately. In particular, in systems management, menus, front ends, software meters, and local and remote diagnostics are rare or missing.

There are many attempts to standardize LAN management, but the use of proprietary protocols still dominates the market. SNMP has made unexpected progress at the detriment of CMOT and CMOL. But SNMP must not be considered the ultimate solution; it's simply the first step on the way to a fully open local and wide area network management architecture.

Network management strategy shows contradictory trends. At the moment, decentralized (departmental) structures dominate. But indications show a clear trend toward centralized management concepts within the next few years:

- Approximately 70 percent of customers want to manage LANs centrally (today about 35 percent).

- Approximately 20 percent of customers want to manage LANs decentrally (today about 50 percent).

- Approximately 10 percent of customers want to use a combination of both (today about 15 percent).

Plausible reasons for change are:

- Lack of human resources at the departmental level.

- Growing complexity of solutions.

- Growing number of interconnections.

- The high demand of integrated WAN/MAN/LAN management.

- Economies of scale in staffing WAN/MAN/LAN management functions.

- Availability of more powerful instruments to supervise and manage remote locations

- Availability of services from third parties to measure, analyze, and report performance

There's very little correlation between LAN and PBX management, except for wiring and equipment rooms. This fact adds another dimension to the difficulties of implementing horizontal and vertical management structures.

Costs

LAN downtime causes serious losses because a mission-critical application often runs on LAN segments. Surveys report on lost productivity, revenue, and direct expenses. LAN downtime can be quantified in certain cases. Depending on the industry, time interval of breakdown, number of impacted users, and services, $40,000 up to $130,000 may be lost during an hour of outage.

Personnel costs are increasing considerably in the LAN management area, alarming MIS and Business Units management. Observation reveals decreasing equipment costs, slightly increasing NOS costs, proportionally increasing communication costs for interconnected LANs, and overproportionally increasing costs for the people who manage LANs. Table 1.3 shows the principal facts of current LAN management.

TABLE 1.3   Facts of Current LAN Management

LAN objects
Different technologies, protocols, and suppliers
Different LAN operating systems

Network management functions, standards, and strategies
Network management functions are not fully supported
No information about failing components
Networks and systems management are not yet integrated
Proprietary protocols dominate the installations
Contradicting trends in network management
Little correlation between LAN and PBX management

Costs
LAN downtime causes serious losses
LAN downtime can be quantified
Human resources costs are increasing

LAN Management Functions, Instruments, and Human Resources

There are a few factors that determine whether a LAN is managed successfully, or whether its management fails. These factors are: processes/procedures, instrumentation, and human resources.

Processes and procedures

Processes and procedures include applications to the principal functional areas, such as configuration, fault, performance, security, accounting management, and LAN administration, design and capacity planning.

Configuration management is a set of middle- and long-range activities for controlling physical, electrical, logical, and spare-part equipment inventories; maintaining vendor files and trouble tickets; managing cables and wiring; supporting provisioning and order processing; tracking, authorizing, scheduling, and implementing changes; and managing backups and archives. Directory service and help for generating different network configurations are also provided.

Fault management is the collection of activities required to dynamically maintain network service levels. These activities ensure high availability by quickly recognizing problems and performance degradation, and by initiating controlling functions when necessary, which may include diagnosis, repair, test, recovery, workaround, and backup. Log control and information distribution techniques are supported as well.

Performance management is an ongoing evaluation of a LAN. The evaluation's purposes are to verify that service levels are maintained, to identify actual and potential bottlenecks, and to establish and report on trends for management decision making and planning. Building and maintaining a LAN's performance database and automation procedures for LAN fault management are also included.

Security management is a set of functions whose purpose is to ensure a LAN's ongoing protection by analyzing risks, minimizing risks, implementing a LAN security plan, and subsequently monitoring the success of the strategy. Special functions include the surveillance of security indicators, partitioning, password administration, and warning or alarm messages on violations. Also, the protection of the LAN management system belongs into this group of responsibilities.

Accounting management is the process of collecting, interpreting, processing, and reporting cost- and charge-oriented information on LAN resource usage. In particular, processing of raw accounting data, bill verification, software licensing, and chargeback procedures are included for data and occasionally for voice.

LAN design and planning represent the process of determining the optimal network, based on data for network performance, traffic flow, resource use, networking requirements, technological trade-offs, and estimated growth of present and future applications.

LAN administration is an evolving group of activities concentrating on LAN documentation, on the administration of user-related data, creating and distributing new operating systems and application software to servers and to clients, and maintaining the LANs.

Table 1.4 summarizes all relevant LAN management functions. Chapter 3 will address each function individually.

Such processes and procedures are designed and developed by using LAN management platforms that consist of protocols, databases, and user interfaces. Also, applications across these functional groups are expected to be implemented.

Instrumentation

Instrumentation is used for monitoring, testing, and controlling LAN media and devices by implementing remote and centrally located management devices using a network management platform and application programming interfaces. Independent of specific functions and instruments, the typical LAN management framework has three dimensions (Datapro-NM50 1989a).

1. LAN management platform
   a. LAN management applications
   b. Query languages
   c. Alarm and message displays
   d. Expert systems as an option to facilitate diagnostics and problem determination
   e. Report generators
   f. Handling of SNMP and RMON events
   g. Support of graphical user interfaces
2. Database facility with
   a. Relational or object-oriented database
   b. Query languages
   c. Database applications for configuration and performance management
3. Monitoring and control facilities with
   a. Application interfaces
   b. Diagnostic programming interfaces
   c. Test programs interfaces
   d. Analyzer device interfaces
   e. Polling mechanisms

TABLE 1.4 Overview of LAN Management Functions

Configuration management
Inventory and topology service
Change management
Naming and addressing
Cabling management
Backup and archive
Directory services

Fault management
Status supervision
Fault detection and alarming
Problem determination and isolation
Diagnostics, backup, repair, and recovery
Disaster recovery
Dynamic trouble ticketing
Tests

Performance management
Defining performance indicators
Performance monitoring
Tuning of local area networks
Modeling and performance optimization
Reporting of performance

Security management
Identifying sensitive information to be protected
Analyzing threats and defining security indicators
Reviewing and analyzing the security framework
Selection of security services
Implementing security management services
Securing the LAN management system

Accounting management
Determining resource usage
Software licensing
Billing
Bill verification

LAN administration
LAN documentation
User administration
Software distribution
LAN maintenance

Design and planning
Strategic planning
Capacity planning
Analyzing trends
Logical and physical design
Contingency planning
Installation
Testing

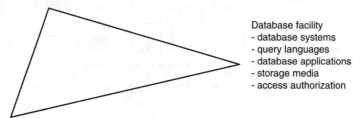

LAN management platform
- management applications
- query languages
- alarm and message displays
- expert systems
- report generators
- SNMP and RMON events
- graphical user interface

Database facility
- database systems
- query languages
- database applications
- storage media
- access authorization

Monitoring and control facilities
- application interfaces
- diagnostic programming interfaces
- test programs interfaces
- analyzer device interfaces
- polling mechanisms
- hypermedia

Figure 1.2   Management framework for LANs.

The three dimensions are shown in Fig. 1.2.

The management framework may be mapped to LAN management functions as defined by standard bodies. The matrix shown in Fig. 1.3 is intended as an aid to investment decisions. Each cell of the matrix has its own priority level. Basically, each dimension of the framework may be supported by multiple functions. Similarly, the same functions may support multiple dimensions of the framework.

The starting point for consolidating processes and instruments is a fragmented structure for managing LANs, characterized by segments for IEEE 802.3 LANs, IEEE 802.5 LANs, bridges, routers, FDDI/DQDB backbones, wiring hubs, extenders, repeaters, switches, monitors, analyzers, testers, and gateways to WANs. Figure 1.4 shows an example of this high level of fragmentation.

The database facility may help to increase the visibility of managed objects. Managed objects include:

- Applications (class, users, unattended, self-initiating).

- Servers and clients (central servers for computing, databasing and backup, local file, print, and communication servers, workstations, databases, and applications).

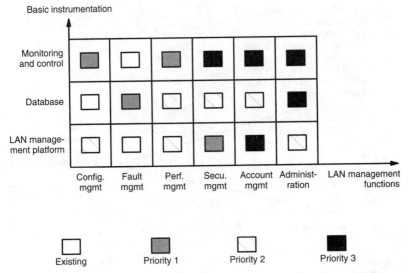

Figure 1.3 Management framework and LAN management functions.

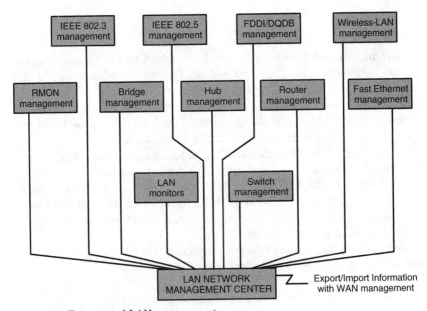

Figure 1.4 Fragmented LAN management.

- Internets (routers, bridges, brouters, multiplexers, switches, backbone links, and gateways).

- Subnets (media, adapters, extenders, modems, bridges, repeaters).

- Infrastructure (directory, application interfaces, feeder, environmental control). In particular, the object "infrastructure" requires in-depth investigation. The infrastructure includes active components, such as end-user devices, boards, network interface cards, media access units, active hubs, and also passive components such as cables and passive hubs. Additional passive components may include electrical and electromechanical parts of managed objects, such as fans, clocks, and power supplies. Moving these fault-sensitive components physically out of the main cabinet will significantly improve physical access and increase maintainability. In order to monitor passive components, external monitors have to be used.

Figure 1.5 shows the two dimensions of managed objects and LAN management functions. Future plans may concentrate on horizontal management (more functions for few objects) or vertical management (more objects, but few functions). Chapter 5 deals with the various types of instruments and offers a number of practical examples.

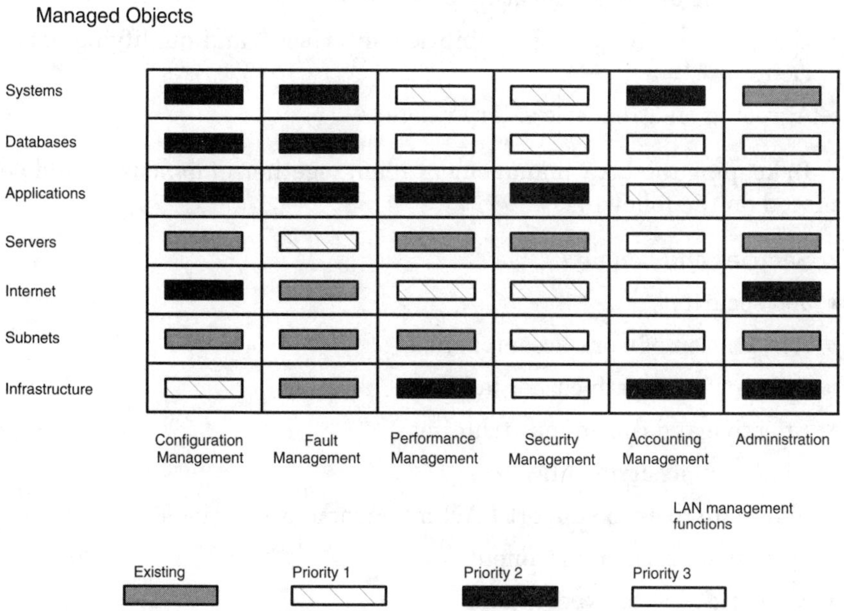

Managed Objects

Figure 1.5   Managed objects and LAN management functions.

Human resources

The third critical success factor is human resources, who execute functions using various tools. Human resources should also have a clear understanding of the responsibilities, interfaces to other organizational units, internal/external job contacts, and qualifying experiences that are required to accomplish tasks.

This third critical success factor, human resources, is currently in the evolutionary state of cross-educating users and/or WAN management staff to execute LAN management responsibilities. There are various models showing how to allocate responsibilities to human resources. The most promising one shows a combination of centralized and decentralized human resources, each with some level of distributed duties—particularly for fault and performance management. The two basic phases of building and retaining the LAN-management team are common to all management teams.

In building the LAN management team, emphasis should be on the following:

- Identifying team members
- Recruiting the right candidates
- Interviewing effectively
- Hiring new people whose presence is mutually beneficial
- Educating or cross-educating personnel
- Clearly identifying responsibilities, interfaces, and qualifying experiences
- Agreeing on a realistic salary range

In keeping the LAN management team together, emphasis should be placed on the following:

- Salaries and benefits
- Job security
- Recognition of work accomplished
- Offering dual-path career ladders
- Effective and continuous training
- Quality of assignments
- Adequate tools to support LAN management functions
- Quality of work environment
- Realistic service expectations
- Continuous employee satisfaction

Chapter 7 addresses human resources, their profiles, and the most likely levels of demands.

Requirements for Managing Local Area Networks

As critical applications have been moved to or implemented on LANs, users are increasingly demanding improved LAN management. The following details LAN management criteria:

1. Level of service
   a. Availability of statistics and historical data that may be stored in a performance or statistical database
   b. Real-time supervision of important LAN performance indicators, such as congestion, resource use, number of transmitted and rejected frames, transmit times, and access delay
   c. Low monitoring overhead through dynamically adapting polling rates to actual resource use
2. Increased productivity
   a. Maintain end-user service level despite growth and technological changes, without staff explosion.
   b. Heal, bypass, or circumvent failed LAN servers after automatically detecting and interpreting problems.
   c. Operate fully when interconnecting components have failed; this assumes the existence of powerful backup strategies and components.
   d. Coordinate remote monitoring, control, and management through centrally located instruments.
3. Flexible change management for rapid, continual response to changing LAN applications, subscribers, devices, tariffs, and services
   a. Maintain a LAN configuration database containing attributes, connectivity information, and dynamic status indicators.
   b. Automate operations, alerting, and diagnostics, using powerful filtering and fault management procedures.
4. Better platform
   a. Straightforward human interface using the most advanced technology for the graphics, called a *graphical user interface* (GUI)
   b. Horizontal and vertical integration using the most advanced solutions from hierarchical network management systems and opportunities provided by network management platforms
   c. Powerful LAN management platform for offering user-friendly solutions for problem detection, determination, and restoration
5. Migration to standards
   a. Replacing specific instruments with generic applications that address multiple LAN management areas such as fault, perfor-

mance, configuration, security, and accounting management; one popular example is trouble ticketing.

b. Migration to LAN standards that are widely used and well supported by the majority of vendors; included are SNMP, CMIP, and CMOL.

Table 1.5 summarizes the requirements, using a table format.

Summary

The most important points in Chap. 1 may be summarized as follows:

- A trend toward more interconnected LANs indicates that the number of standalone PCs and standalone LAN segments will decrease.
- The bandwidth requirements in LAN segments and in interconnected LANs will grow substantially as the convenience of total connectivity is fully recognized by users and as multimedia support is required to the desktop.
- The number of managed objects will grow and will accommodate most components of LAN segments and interconnected LANs, including servers, clients, and active and passive components.
- LAN software vendors are under increasing pressure to incorporate more management tools into the network, rather than forcing users

TABLE 1.5   Classification of Requirements

Service level
- Availability of historical data
- Real-time supervision of indicators
- Low monitoring overhead

Productivity
- High end-user service
- Efficient workarounds
- Automated switchover
- Remote monitoring
- Flexible change management
- Configuration database
- Automated operations

Platform
- Graphical user interface
- Horizontal and vertical integration
- Ease of use

Migration to standards
- Applications instead of just instruments
- Use of SNMP, CMIP, and CMOL

to purchase tools separately. This reflects the general trend toward incorporating more functionality into the NOS, such as bridging and routing capabilities, monitoring, and network management.

- Users can also expect to see an increasing number of tools that assist in tracking problems across multiple LANs in a multivendor environment. The progress of standards development will influence the effectiveness of these tools, as well as determine how quickly they and other comprehensive LAN integrated network management systems will appear on the market. In particular, the capabilities of SNMP, RMON, and DMI must be fully utilized.

- More automation in operating LANs is expected by linking LAN and WAN management systems. This trend will help to distribute management tasks by decreasing the demand for human resources at the distributed sites.

- More cross-functional applications are expected from third parties, allowing LAN-component vendors to concentrate on hardware and software features, and to leave management application design and implementation to experts.

- Future LAN management architectures and products will distribute functions, instruments of systems, and network management; however, the overall control may remain central, for various economic reasons.

- Future implementations will be based on de facto management standards, most likely SNMP versions 1 and 2, RMON versions 1 and 2; and occasionally more open, more robust network management standards, such as CMIP and CMOL, are expected to be supported.

2

Classification of Local Area Networks

In order to develop a better understanding of LAN management functions and instruments, this chapter begins with a discussion of the basic attributes of LAN topologies, protocols, access schemes, transmission media, and interconnecting devices. After addressing transmission schemes, I describe and compare physical transmission media, and I follow with a discussion of the use of hubs. A section on protocols discusses the logical-link layer and connection-oriented and connectionless alternatives. Topologies include bus, ring, star, and tree. Each is compared using a detailed list of comparison criteria.

The next section on access control techniques addresses random, centralized, and decentralized solutions and highlights the most widely used techniques. It's expected that LAN network operating systems will have an important impact on LAN management. The section also includes a brief evaluation of the existing management capabilities of leading operating systems. The section concludes by introducing interconnecting schemes and devices, such as repeaters, extenders, bridges, brouters, routers, and gateways. Also, evolving technologies, such as switched LANs, virtual LANs, the applicability of ATM for local and wide area backbones, and collapsed backbone structures are discussed.

The major emphasis in this chapter is on how to predict potential bottlenecks of certain LAN components. It's also important to analyze how LAN components can contribute to effective management by providing information on physical and/or logical status. Such information delivery may support either solicited or unsolicited management techniques. Also, the debate between the use of inband or outband management connections is raised.

LAN Transmission Schemes

In order to clarify bandwidth requirements, Fig. 2.1 shows typical data rates, distances, and the applicability of networking techniques. This graphic shows that:

- There's a wide range of typical bandwidths.
- WANs have to offer more bandwidth and more flexibility.
- Computers may easily be connected via LANs.
- The appropriateness of MANs is indicated in the high-speed LAN area.
- Using T1/T3, J1 and E1 channels, wide area networking will offer more bandwidth.
- The introduction of Sonet, B-ISDN and SMDS may further increase this bandwidth and offer more standardization.
- PC LANs will remain in the low bandwidth area, and will remain a subset of general-purpose LANs.
- It's not likely that PBX-based LANs will substantially increase the offered bandwidth.

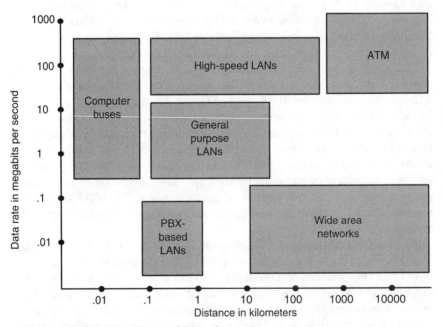

Figure 2.1   Classification of networking techniques.

Local area networks support two techniques for transmitting information over communication facilities: baseband transmission and broadband transmission. Baseband transmission uses digital signaling to transmit signals over dedicated or shared channels. Whichever channel is used, the entire channel capacity is used to transmit signals between senders and receivers. For regenerating signal forms, repeaters are used. If the channels are shared, the technique of time division multiplexing (TDM) is used to control the access rights for subscribers. Baseband has the following attributes:

- Inexpensive
- Very flexible for extensions
- Easy to handle
- Limited bandwidth
- Typically, limited distances

Broadband transmission typically uses analog transmission with wider frequencies than baseband. In this case, signals are continuous and nondiscrete. For modulation, the amplitude, frequency and phase of the signal may be used. For regenerating signals, amplifiers are used. This technique is more effective against noise and interference. The total bandwidth is usually divided into separate channels. Each channel may support different users and communication forms simultaneously by implementing the technique of frequency division multiplexing (FDM). Broadband has the following attributes:

- Technology is well proven, thanks to cable television.
- Longer distances than with baseband.
- Integration of multiple communication services due to the simultaneous use of multiple channels.
- Relatively expensive due to modems and active network elements such as headends and amplifiers.
- Limited flexibility. When new stations are connected, the whole network has to be tuned again.
- Relatively difficult access to stations connected to other communication channels. Relatively expensive bridges are required.

Baseband techniques are used for all bus- and token-based topologies. Broadband is used most frequently with bus topologies. The impact of the two techniques on LAN management may be summarized as follows:

- Fault management and error recovery techniques may be completely different with each transmission technique.

- Broadband allows the dedication of a channel to exchanging and transporting LAN management information.

- Outband management techniques may be applied in both cases.

Transmission Media

The telecommunications industry employs a variety of media for the transmission of information in wide, metropolitan, and local area networks. In the LAN area, there are three generic media types that will be described and evaluated in more detail later in this book.

- Twisted pair
- Coax
- Fiber

Twisted-pair cable is one of the most commonly used wiring materials for supporting low- to medium-speed analog and digital signal transmission. It consists of a pair of insulated copper wires, typically about 1 mm thick, with the wires twisted in a helical form in order to reduce potential electrical interference from adjacent pairs. The transmission capacity of the cable is determined by its dimension and the distance that the signal propagates. For example, for data rates in the 1 Mbps range, a transmission distance of 1 km can be achieved. For voice signals, the distance can be extended as far as 6 km without a repeater.

There are two types of twisted-pair cable: shielded twisted pair (STP) and unshielded twisted pair (UTP). STP cable has a conductive shield of metal braid, foil, or a combination of both surrounding the cable. This shield considerably reduces electrical interference, noise, and signal attenuation, but adds to the cost of the cable. The most common type of STP cable used for LANs is a 150-ohm STP referred to as Type-1 cable, which is defined by the IBM wiring system. This is high-performance cable, which carries size and cost penalties as a result. UTP cable does not have a conductive shield surrounding the core of the cable, is more susceptible to crosstalk and also has a higher signal attenuation than STP. It is therefore less suitable for transmission over long distances. UTP also radiates more electrical noise into the environment than STP. Until recently, the most common type of UTP cable used for LANs was category-3 cable, defined by the Electronic Industries Association. This cable is much lower quality than STP cables, but less bulky and also cheaper than STP. Category-3 could support 16-MHz transfer speeds. UTP category-4 increased this speed to 20 MHz with the result of supporting 16-Mbps Token Ring and 10-Mbps Ethernet. Category-5 cable is the highest-quality cable available today and is also the most popular cable for new LAN installations, even through the standard has not yet been fully ratified, leading to a fair amount of disagreement on its actual performance and characteristics. This type of cable supports 100-Mbps or faster LANs. At high frequencies, unshielded wires in the same cable are prone to crosstalk—this is basically the signal on a wire being induced onto its neighbors and is referred to as NEXT or near-end crosstalk.

A *coaxial cable* consists of a stiff copper wire as its core, surrounded by an insulation material, which is covered with a cylindrical conductor, usually in a woven braided mesh. The whole cable is then wrapped into protective plastic covering. Because of this construction, coaxial cables have an excellent noise immunity and a larger transmission capacity than twisted-pair cables. The cable length can easily be extended with a variety of cable taps, splitters, couplers, controllers, and repeaters to reach nearly all remote users.

There are two types of coaxial cables:

- *Baseband* is usually used for digital transmission and is typically less than one-half inch in diameter, with a 50-ohm impedance.
- *Broadband* is usually used in the television industry; it's normally divided into multiple frequency channels. The standard broadband cable is one-half inch in diameter, with a 75-ohm impedance.

Coax cables are less subject to crosstalk and interference than twisted-pair cables and are able to support much higher throughput rates—up to 100 Mbps. In some cases, the LAN industry uses the same cable and electronic components that are used by cable television applications.

There are two types of coaxial cables in common use: thick coax and thin coax. Thick coax is thick, yellow cable, most often used in networks that are running the 10-Base5 standard, which is one of the Ethernet family of networks. Thin coax is a type of coaxial cable that has reduced shielding and therefore has a higher signal attenuation than thick coax, but it is significantly cheaper and more flexible than thick coax. Thin coax is often used in networks that are running the 10-Base2 standard, also a member of the Ethernet family.

An *optic fiber* is a dielectric waveguide that operates at optical frequencies. The cable consists of: a single solid dielectric cylinder as its core, usually made of glass; a solid dielectric refractive coating, usually made of glass or plastic, to protect the core; and an elastic, abrasion-resistant plastic material for encapsulating the cable to add further protection from environmental contaminants. The most important consideration with fiber cables is how to keep light propagating for a longer distance without suffering a loss.

The transmission capacity of a fiber depends on the light refraction techniques used. There are two modes of light refraction: *monomode* and *multimode*. Monomode fibers require laser diodes as the light source. Multimode fibers require LEDs as the light source and are suited for shorter distances. It is cheaper than single-mode fiber. However, the dispersion of light rays inside is greater than with single-mode fiber. Multimode fiber is suitable for general-purpose networks and supports transmissions over distances of approximately 2 km. Token Ring networks almost always use multimode. Single-mode is much thinner, and it is used in long-distance networking environments such as trunk connections.

Fiber-optic cables hold considerable promise for local area networks, because they can transmit larger amounts of information over longer distances than either coax or twisted pair. They also have the lowest error rate, are immune to interferences from electromagnetic or radio sources, are extremely difficult to tap, and can be very light and thin.

Relevant to the transmission, there are two basic alternatives:

- Balanced transmission (Miller 1989)
- Unbalanced transmission (Miller 1989)

In a balanced design, the currents flowing between the generator and receiver in each of the wires are equal in magnitude, but opposite in direction. Twisted-pair and twinax cables are examples of balanced transmission lines.

In an unbalanced design, the current flowing in the signal conductor returns via a ground connection that may be shared with other circuits. Both the current and the voltage in the signal conductor are measured with respect to this signal-return conductor. Coax cable is an example of unbalanced transmission.

There are several reasons to consider wireless technology. It's predictable; wireless LANs are portable; you don't have to use cabling (a particular advantage in old buildings); and it has easy installation and maintenance. There are four choices when considering this technique:

- Microwave
- Satellite
- Infrared beams
- Radio

Infrared beams can carry traffic in the tens of megabits per second range over short distances—normally less than 2 kilometers. Dust, snow, rain, haze, and fog can lessen the ability of this transmission media to carry traffic.

Radio may be used for both short and long distances. However, this transmission technique is also subject to various types of interference. Results of recent experiments show that spread-spectrum technology is superior to FM radio due to the lower level of sensitivity to signal bouncing.

Wireless technology requires other types of transceivers for sending and receiving. Additional components, such as antennas, may also be required, increasing the number of passive devices to be managed. Wireless technology presents another alternative communication path to support outband network management. It's too early to say whether this technology will seriously compete with wire technology. But, wireless technology is definitely here to stay as an alternative or as a backup solution.

In order to help planners consider different media alternatives, Table 2.1 compares the generic alternatives using various criteria, such as the bandwidth supported, number of nodes supported, distance that can be covered without interconnecting devices, implementation and maintenance costs, the maturity of the technology, common applications, noise immunity, ability to change, key advantages, and disadvantages.

TABLE 2.1   Comparison of LAN Media

Feature	\multicolumn{5}{c}{LAN media alternatives}				

Feature	UTP	STP	COAX	Fiber	Wireless
Bandwidth	Low 100 Mbps	Low 500 Mbps	Medium-high 1 Gbps	High 1 Gbps	Low-medium 2 to 15 Mbps
Number of nodes	Low	Low	Medium-high	Low-medium	Varies
Maximum distance	100 m at 10 Mbps	100 m at 16 Mbps	600 m at 10 Mbps	2 km at 100 Mbps	Varies 50–100 feet
Noise immunity	Poor	Good	Good	Excellent	Good
Ability to change	Very good	Good	Fair	Poor	Excellent
Cost	Low	Moderate	Moderate	High	High
Technology	Mature	Mature	Mature	Emerging	Emerging
Common applications	Hub network lobe wiring	Token Ring	Ethernet	Backbone	Temporary networks
Key advantages	Low cost	Reliability	Cost/bandwidth	FDDI support	Ability to reconfigure
Key disadvantages	Noise	Cost/Performance	Cable problems	Cost	Cost and bandwidth

In order to support various LAN technologies, the importance of structured cabling is increasing. Structured cabling is a method of designing and installing communication channels within a building in such a way that cable is capable of being reconfigured to accommodate a dynamic business environment. The issues that must be addressed in cabling are:

Moves   The relocation of a user from one work area into another

Adds   Increasing the number of users on LANs

Changes   Upgrade of equipment or service

Structured cabling for voice service has been around for a long while. In the last few years, however, there has been an integration of other communication types into a central cabling infrastructure. It is now common practice to provide a single infrastructure in buildings that will eventually support voice, LANs, video, security, and also building automation. The integration of these various services into a single cabling structure is being driven by the end users, with little support from equipment manufacturers.

The ultimate purpose of each package is to provide a unique interface at the "wall" (Fig. 2.2), which can offer great flexibility to any of the cable types under consideration. This cabling converter could play an important role in managing the passive objects of a LAN infrastructure.

Each physical layout and logical topology may be completely different. The physical wiring structure is responsible for supporting the

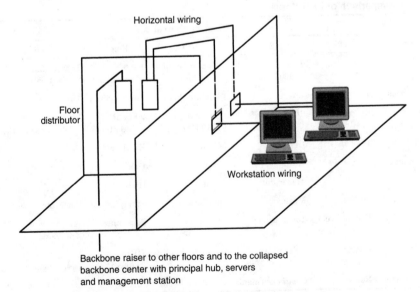

Figure 2.2 Cabling converter in the wall.

targeted logical topology. This support has different levels of sophistication, depending on the intelligence of wiring hubs. Wiring hubs are
gradually becoming the focal points of physical LAN management. Not
just cables and network interface cards, but also interconnecting
devices, may be managed from the same central place.

Intelligent, modular hubs are chassis-based, with slots that accommodate a wide choice of interface modules for connectivity to LANs,
MANs, WANs or other network devices. Intelligent hubs provide connectivity to different kinds of users, to smaller or stackable hubs, and
they offer fault tolerance for critical applications and concentrated network management applications. The architectural components include
slot capacity, backplane design, interface modules, switching architectures, upgrade capability, ATM support, and network management.

Hub flexibility and scalability are determined by the number of slots
on the chassis that are available to support different interface modules
such as Ethernet, Token Ring, FDDI, and ATM. Usual slot sizes are
between 5 and 36.

Backplane design determines the performance and flexibility to support different LAN topologies and also the capabilities of port and module switching. This design also interfaces modules supported without
connecting to backplanes, enabling support for external LANs with
media sharing.

A variety of interface modules offer access to various physical media,
such as shielded and unshielded twisted pair, fiber, thin, and thick
coax. Some vendors offer modules for bridging and routing, thus lower-
ing the price of an integrated solution. Port density on interface modules may increase cost-effectiveness, but also the vulnerability.

Packet and frame switching are more efficient solutions than port
switching. They considerably increase performance by dedicating each
port on the interface module to a single device or LAN segment. Usually, a backplane bus is providing a data path between all switching
modules. This technology enables multiple simultaneous paths to be
initiated between users. Further improvements are expected by cut-
through switching.

Upgradability guarantees that users may migrate to more advanced
features (e.g., to switching modules) without significant changes and
replacements in the hub.

ATM support addresses a new opportunity of interconnecting LANs.
It will serve as a backbone solution to support high-performance
servers, workstations and routers, and to provide hub-to-hub connections. ATM could be supported by hubs in the form of integral ATM
switches or through ATM access modules to external ATM switches.

The management systems use SNMP agents. Practically all vendors
support SNMP, but conformance to the SNMP standard may vary, and

users should verify SNMP compliance levels when evaluating products. Many vendors include RMON probes into their products. But the depth of support of RMON indicator groups may greatly vary, and only a few vendors support RMON fully.

Due to the central role of hubs, their importance in managing LAN segments and interconnecting devices will grow in the future. Figure 2.3 shows the simplistic view of a hub indicating its principal components.

The allocation of media to particular bandwidths is not apparent anymore. The 10BaseT applications have made a breakthrough on replacing coax with twisted-pair cable. Despite distance limitations, this new media allocation opens new considerations for even higher bandwidths. A fundamental problem of LANs is that at higher data rates, even with low electrical power, unshielded wiring turns into a broadcasting antenna. And at the same time, FCC antiradio emission requirements are violated.

The impact of media on LAN management may be summarized as follows:

- Each type of media has specific limitations on the practical throughput rates.

- Each type of media is sensitive to different types of environmental impacts.

- A wiring hub may be used as the physical focal point for LAN management.

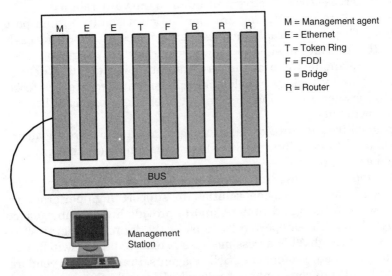

M = Management agent
E = Ethernet
T = Token Ring
F = FDDI
B = Bridge
R = Router

Figure 2.3 Simplistic structure of a hub with management agent.

■ Media emission rates may limit applicability and may impact security measures.

LAN Topology Alternatives

Network topology is defined as the way network nodes are geographically connected. Similarly, a LAN's type is determined by its topology. Depending on which technical reference you use, the type of LAN topology varies. In general, there are two types of LAN topology: constrained and unconstrained. A *constrained* topology can consist of ring, bus, and star connections. An *unconstrained* topology can consist of everything else (e.g., mesh, fully connected, etc.). Only the constrained topology is discussed here, as it represents the majority of LANs (see Chap. 1).

Star topology

In a *star topology,* all nodes are connected to a focal node, generally referred to as the *hub* or *control node,* in a point-to-point (direct) manner. All transmissions go through the control node. Therefore, the main function of the control node is to manage the network. The transmission medium for a star LAN network can be twisted-pair, coaxial, or fiber-optic cable. The star topology can be combined with other topologies, such as a ring topology, to form a hybrid network deriving advantages from both topologies. An example of a star LAN is Xerox's Fibernet II, a point-to-point topology with dual fiber-optic buses, one for transmitting and one for receiving, with a carrier-sensing multiple access/collision detection (CSMA/CD) protocol (see discussion in bus topology).

Ring topology

In a *ring topology,* nodes are connected by point-to-point links in a sequential manner to form a closed path. A signal is passed along the path one node at a time before returning to its originating node. Each node requires an interface device to recognize its own address for receiving messages, and also to act as a repeater for forwarding messages to other nodes. The transmission medium for a ring LAN can be either twisted-pair, baseband coaxial, or optic-fiber cable. A ring topology can be combined with star topology to form a star-ring LAN, thus incorporating the advantages of both topologies.

To implement a ring LAN, you need to be aware of the following conditions. First, prewiring of a ring LAN is difficult. When a node is added to the ring in order to support a new user, transmission lines must be placed between the new node and its two topologically adjacent nodes. It's difficult to anticipate the locations of the future nodes.

Second, any adding/deleting of a node or line/equipment failure will disrupt the network, causing end-user productivity losses. Third, when and where to remove transmitted data on the ring requires some intelligent design. Data will continue to circulate along the path unless it's specifically removed. One desirable design is to let the sender remove data already received since it allows an automatic acknowledgment and also allows multibroadcasting addressing when one message is simultaneously transmitted to many nodes. Wiring hubs, introduced in the previous sections, may help by offering software techniques for physically reconfiguring rings. Examples of the ring topology are IBM's Token Ring offerings, with 4 and 16 Mbps throughput rates.

Bus topology

In a *bus topology,* all nodes are connected to a common transmission medium in an open manner. Each node has its unique address; when a message is sent, it's sent to all nodes, and the receiving node must be able to recognize its own address to receive. The common transmission medium used for bus LANs is coaxial cable because of its passive nature and easy implementation without disrupting the operation. However, fiber-optic cables can be used for a bus LAN, although they require more skill to implement. Because of the bus topology's sharing nature, some type of controlling mechanism must be in place to prevent several nodes from transmitting simultaneously. The two most popular controls are polling and contention. These control techniques will be covered in more detail in the following section. An example of a bus LAN is Ethernet, which employs the CSMA/CD access control with a 10-Mbps transmission capacity. Ethernet has been studied widely, and there are many reports on its performance characteristics.

Tree topology

The bus topology can be extended to a tree topology in which multiple bus branches join at various points to form a tree LAN.

In order to aid in appropriate topology selection, Table 2.2 compares the four generic topologies using such criteria as technical reliability, complexity, flexibility, expandability, cost, and capacity.

The impact of topology choice on LAN management may be summarized as follows:

1. Each topology choice represents the following:
   a. A different fault-management solution
   b. A different built-in management capability
   c. A different single-point-of-failure consequence

TABLE 2.2   Topology Comparison

Feature	Bus	Star	Ring	Tree
Reliability	High	Moderate	Moderate	High
Complexity	Moderate	Low	Low	Moderate
Flexibility	High	Moderate	Moderate	High
Expandability	Moderate	Moderate	Moderate	High
Cost	Moderate	High	Moderate	Moderate
Capacity	Moderate	Low	High	High

2. Each topology is
   a. Associated with a different feasible throughput rate
   b. Associated with a different feasible medium
   c. Strongly associated with an access control technique that may greatly influence performance

There is a need to connect remote users to LAN-based resources. The needs are different. Everything from occasional connections up to permanent network participation can be observed in operational networks and in requirement lists. In order to meet the requirements of today's highly dispersed, often mobile workforce, several categories of remote LAN-access options are offered. These products, which give remote users access to company data, servers, network resources, and applications, include the following:

- Remote network access
- File transfer
- Application access
- Remote control

Figure 2.4 shows these alternatives symbolically.

Remote network access extends the LAN to remote workstations. Standard network packets are transferred between the LAN and the remote workstation. These servers typically support remote workstations to LAN links. Usually, multiple links are supported. Users see exactly what they would see on a workstation on the LAN. Applications are running on their own workstation, not on the other side of the link. The remote site is fully integrated. These servers employ numerous features that help network managers cope with the unique conditions of working on a LAN with telecommunication lines. Main concerns are centralized configuration management, network monitoring, and security. Features with remote access servers may include:

- Ability to create and maintain authorized user lists
- Transparent modem setup and management

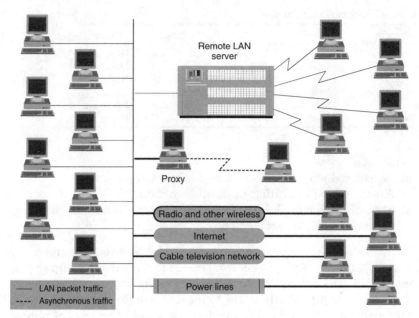

Figure 2.4 Alternatives for LAN extensions.

- Ability to configure parameters for network operating systems and protocols
- Support for built-in monitoring capabilities
- Help to identify the location of applications
- Data compression and compaction

This solution is beneficial to run the client portion on the remote site and to access central LAN resources transparently. The central site cannot afford dedicated stations when inexpensive communication services are available.

Other technologies are categorized as proxy solutions, indicating that the remote user takes control of a device connected to the LAN. In these cases, LAN packet traffic is between the proxy and other stations and servers on the LAN. Between the proxy and the remote users, asynchronous protocols are implemented. This solution is more suited for cases where LAN access is limited to single workstations or limited to periods of time. The traditional form is file transfer for occasional use. The LAN is the vehicle to access the server hosting the files. Application access means specified single-purpose, remote-access modules that allow users to dial into modems attached directly to an application server. Access is limited to a small number of applications (e.g., E-mail and servers, Mail-, or File-servers). Remote control requires a dedicated station with a LAN card, a modem, and a copy of remote-control software. Remote workers are cutting through to this dedicated station, and they control it remotely. This solution is good for large central-site database queries, sharing a single central-site application license among multiple remote users, and enabling limited-power workstations to get more CPU strength from central processors.

For the WAN part, performance and expenses are important. Basically, all WAN technologies may be applied. In most cases, dial-up solutions are selected. In more advanced cases, ISDN could play an important role due to scalability, short setup times, and reasonable cost structures.

Network management is interested in increasing channel utilization while reducing overhead due to talkative LAN protocols, management information exchange, and session establishment. Very frequently, special applications are implemented in the remote network access server and its partners at the remote site. Two applications in particular are well known. Spoofing enables remote LAN access products to maintain logical LAN links between a remote client and a central-site server by issuing and responding to keep-alive messages of the LAN operating systems' messages on either side of the link. Filtering means to keep unnecessary messages out of the WAN. Messages, events, alerts can be locally logged and transmitted only if they are needed at the other side. Filtering is still optional. Spoofing keeps the remote session active even when the WAN link is idle or temporarily deactivated. Using ISDN, the user is billed just for the traffic submitted, but not for the idle time. After reactivating the link, work can be continued immediately because the session is still alive—saving time and reducing overall traffic.

In terms of management, simple SNMP agents can be implemented into the servers; workstations are expected to be managed by using MIFs. The central manager is the same in both cases.

There is also another opportunity of LAN extension. The cable television industry has been connecting users in many buildings by a two-way cable conduit across entire cities. This infrastructure can serve as a fundamental infrastructure for two-way data communications that can connect a wide variety of computers to each other. The usual bandwidth is 10 Mbps; prices are expected to be low. There are at the present few examples, but four products from LANcity Corporation are worth mentioning. LANcity bridge helps to interconnect LAN segments over a metropolitan area. This high-speed, long-distance, MAC-layer networking product allows each computer system to make a standard, managed Ethernet connection over existing cable TV lines. The bridge is installed at each networked customer site to form a cohesive, manageable, distributed citywide network. This bridge technology requires a two-way, single, or dual data-ready cable television system.

The Internet router provides citywide Internet access using the existing cable TV infrastructure. It provides IP routing between Ethernet and cable TV networks. This product routes IP protocol packets through the cable TV networks based on IP addressing of the packets and transparently bridges all other protocol packets using the Spanning Tree Protocol standards. As a result, the cable TV infrastructure becomes part of the Internet, and shared-symmetrical, high-speed, citywide Ethernet bridge interconnectivity is also provided.

TransMaster is a customized data converter for cable TV headend use. In single-cable plant installations, the product converts the return frequency of incoming data to the forward frequency of outgoing data. Conversions take place in only 6 MHz of bandwidth and without interfering with other cable services, making this product especially well suited to cable systems in which available channels are at a premium.

In order to configure and set up the bridge and the router, an installation utility is required. It is PC-based software, which guides certified and qualified cable TV installers through site-specific, customized installation and configuration using Windows. The management solutions of the products are based on SNMP; agents that can be supervised by one of the management platforms are installed in the devices.

Another way of connecting stand-alone PCs to LANs is the use of power lines. Power lines access practically all remote offices and homes. There is noise and interference, but also a considerable bandwidth capacity over power lines. Signal amplification is absolutely necessary to eliminate noise; different types of amplifiers are available. Users in small branch offices would plug their PCs into their electric circuits using a power-line modem that would convert local area traffic into power-line traffic. That traffic goes through the power line to a bridge or router on a telephone pole or in the ground. The router or bridge would convert power-line traffic into TCP/IP or another protocol standard and deliver it to the LAN at the other end of the communication link.

In client/server systems, mainframes will not disappear. They will be used as data repositories, as powerful processors for certain applications, as backup machines for many LANs. In any of these functions, an efficient connection between the LAN and the mainframe is absolutely necessary.

The protocols supported in the LANs and by the mainframes are usually different. The location of protocol conversion is crucial for efficiency. The conversion may take place in the mainframe, in a LAN gateway, or in a special server (called an IP-host) that offloads the processing from the host. Products are available for all three of these approaches.

Channel attachment refers to a direct link between the mainframe processor and a processor capable of funneling traffic from the LAN.

This link is a parallel interface that runs at speeds of Mbps. The most established way to link a channel connection is the bus-and-tag method, which provides a direct link between a mainframe and a peripheral device. The throughput rates depend on the manufacturer. Future attachment technologies based on new bus technologies may reach the FDDI range of 100 Mbps.

In recent configurations, routers and hubs have taken over the responsibility of conversion, off-loading the mainframe, but not replacing the legacy front-end processors that are still necessary for proprietary networking solutions.

From the management point of view, mainframes and proprietary structures do have management solutions. Routers and hubs are usually managed by SNMP.

Logical Link Control (LLC) Protocols

The LLC sublayer of the IEEE 802.2 recommendation provides services to the layer above, and controls the sublayer below. Figure 2.5 illustrates the generic structure of the first three LAN layers, dividing layer 2 into two sublayers:

- Logical link control (LLC)
- Medium access control (MAC)

There are many similarities between OSI layer 2 services, implemented by HDLC (or SDLC or UDLC) and LLC. There are two types of

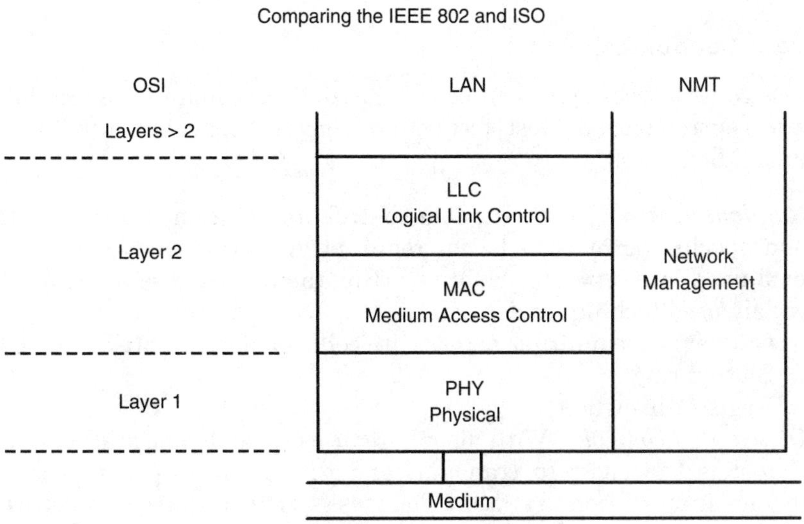

Comparing the IEEE 802 and ISO

OSI	LAN	NMT
Layers > 2		
Layer 2	LLC Logical Link Control	Network Management
	MAC Medium Access Control	
Layer 1	PHY Physical	
	Medium	

Figure 2.5 Lower layer of LAN communication structures.

operations defined between the network layer and LLC. Type 1 operation (Martin 1991) provides a facility called *connectionless service*. With type 1 operation, there's no need for the establishment of a logical connection between the communicating partners because each data unit transmitted is processed independently. Type 1 operation is sometimes referred to as a *datagram service*. This service doesn't offer sequence checking, acknowledgment on behalf of the receiver, flow control, or error recovery.

Type 2 operation is a connection-oriented service. Before transmission begins, the logical connection has to be established. The connection is maintained during transmission and will be terminated when the transmission ends. Type 2 operation offers sequence checking, flow control, error recovery, and retransmission of data units that are not correctly received (Martin 1991).

The services between LLC and MAC are well defined for the three leading MAC sublayers that control access to the physical transmission medium. These are CSMA/CD, token bus, and token ring. Slightly different rules apply for FDDI (fiber distributed data interface).

Access control techniques and FDDI will be addressed in following sections. The impact of LLC protocols on LAN management may be summarized as follows:

■ Transmission efficiency is represented by the ratio of control to data characters.

■ Error recovery and retransmission rates are significantly influenced by the selected media.

Access Control Techniques

Access control techniques can be categorized according to the location of the control entity. Most frequently, they're separated into three groups (Martin 1991):

1. *Random control.*   With random control, any station can transmit, and specific permission is not required. A station may check the medium to see if it's free before starting the transmission. The most widely used techniques are
   a. Carrier sense multiple access with collision detection (CSMA/CD)
   b. Slotted ring
   c. Register insertion
2. *Distributed control.*   With distributed control, only one station at a time has the right to transmit, and that right is passed—as a token—from station to station. The most widely used techniques are
   a. Token ring

b. Token bus

c. Carrier sense multiple access with collision detection (CSMA/CD)

3. *Centralized control.*   With centralized control, one station controls the LAN (or interconnected LANs), and other stations must receive permission from the controlling station for starting transmission. Known techniques—not limited to LANs—are

a. Polling

b. Circuit switching

c. Time-division multiplexing

The following discussion analyzes these leading access control techniques in greater depth (Infotel Systems 1990).

Figure 2.6 shows a typical example of a transmission with CSMA/CD. Device A is transmitting. B and C have data but refrain from sending because they sense activity on the channel. A finishes sending. B and C sense that the channel is idle, and both begin sending. B and C sense collision and send a jamming signal for a short period to ensure detection of the collision; then they back off. B and C start random timers. B times out first and starts sending. C senses that the channel is busy and refrains from sending. B finishes sending. C senses that the channel is idle and starts sending. This access technique is the basis of Ethernet.

Figure 2.7 displays the basic steps involved in using Token Ring. A receives the token. A sends a message to C. C copies and passes the frame on. A sees the returning frame. A issues the token to B. Token

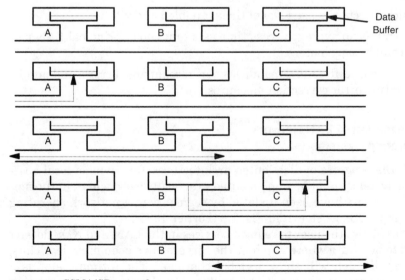

Figure 2.6   CSMA/CD example.

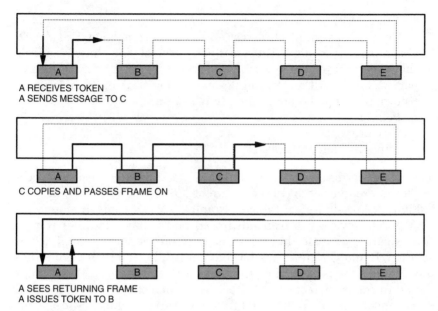

A RECEIVES TOKEN
A SENDS MESSAGE TO C

C COPIES AND PASSES FRAME ON

A SEES RETURNING FRAME
A ISSUES TOKEN TO B

Figure 2.7   Token-ring example.

Ring is the predominant architecture of IBM. A performance assessment and comparison will be presented in Chap. 3.

The impact of access control techniques on LAN management may be summarized as follows:

- Each affects the use level of the available bandwidth.

- Each has an average access time as a function of principal LAN performance parameters.

- Each has different capabilities for recognizing errors and implementing error correction measures.

Assessment of LAN Network Operating Systems

With the progress of distributed architectures, functions of local operating systems could be implemented practically everywhere in the network. Servers have been updated by segments in a network operating system (NOS), as shown in Fig. 2.8 (Fortier 1989).

NOS allows the user to request services in the LAN, and NOS doesn't need to be aware where and how the servers have been provided. Thus, this application will show a global character. The ultimate step is a global operating system (GOS) with no local autonomous operating

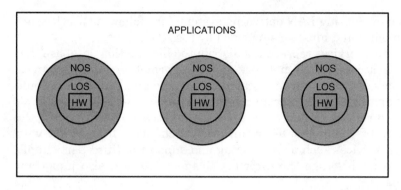

HW   Hardware
LOS   Local Operating System
NOS   Network Operating System

Figure 2.8 Network operating systems.

system or network, but one homogeneous operating system built on the available hardware (Fig. 2.9) (Fortier 1989). In general, the NOS should provide the following targeted attributes:

- The LAN should lower the costs of distributed computing by efficiently supporting client/server systems.
- The LAN should be easy to use and administer.
- The LAN should be easy to migrate to.
- The NOS should offer investment protection by providing a platform for future growth.

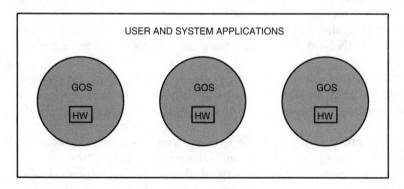

HW   Hardware
GOS   Global Operating System

Figure 2.9 Global network operating systems.

When evaluating LAN operating systems, the following services are fundamental and must be supported by the NOS.

Directory services represent a distributed information database that provides access to all network users, information, and resources, regardless of where they are located on the network. Directories should allow administrators to set up, administer, and manage networks of all sizes. A directory should have the tools necessary to manipulate the directory to accommodate organizational changes. Integration with network services such as messaging and support of third-party applications that leverage the directory's capabilities are also important features.

Messaging is a service that provides the basis for automatic data transfer across the network. This service should be open and support all of the popular mail applications from Novell, Microsoft, IBM, Lotus, and others. Basic mail management features are expected as well.

Management and administration are critical. A full-featured NOS should provide a single point-of-network administration. This will greatly simplify the administration process. In addition, easy-to-use graphical tools should be available to display status, events, and messages. Fault tolerance of components is very important to ease manageability. Management of memory, input/output devices, and names are expected as well.

Information moving across LANs must be secure. Present NOSs should provide a high level of security while maintaining the networks' performance and ease of use. Important features to look for are encryption, controlling access to servers, controlling access to applications, partitioning, auditing capability, signature dynamics, and use of other biometrics for authentication.

WAN support and routing are critical components for supporting enterprise networks. It is important to support multiple protocols, such as TCP/IP, IPX, and others. Configuring parameters is also very important for the LAN NOS. Part of this function is the support for interconnectivity.

File services should provide native file support for all client file systems, including DOS, Windows, Macintosh, Unix, OS/2, and Windows NT. In addition, file compression to reduce the storage demand, data migration to expand on-line storage by integrating cost-effective storage media into the network file system, and block suballocation to maximize disk usage are important cost-saving opportunities.

Printing support must ensure great flexibility. Directory services help to allocate printing to any printer from anywhere in the LAN. Users must not be worried about access, print file transmission, and actual printing.

Besides these key attributes, reliability, NOS maturity, installed base, number of advanced networking services, and the quality of support should be evaluated while selecting the NOS.

There are not many choices for network operating systems in LANs. Netware from Novell and Windows NT from Microsoft coexist and share approximately 85 to 90 percent of the market. The remaining market is shared by

- LAN Manager (IBM)
- Vines (Banyan)
- LANtastic from Artisoft

The impact on LAN management of network operating systems may be summarized as follows:

- Each uses the built-in capabilities of the operating systems of the network and/or servers.
- Each represents different alternatives for connecting NOS to the network management station (protocols and inband/outband).
- Each embeds external monitoring capabilities into network operating systems.
- Each vendor opens the NOS to incorporate third-party modules, such as Netware Loadable Modules.
- Each vendor tries to streamline administration services in the form of suites, such as ManageWise from Novell and SMS from Microsoft.

The Role of Private Branch Exchanges (PBXs) in LAN Management

Considering the wide distribution range of voice communication, the same physical infrastructure may be used for accommodating data, or, in the future, other communication forms. But such integration is just not happening.

Some considerations used against voice wiring and in favor of cable-oriented LANs are: voice wiring uses low bandwidths that are sufficient for voice only; voice-wiring line quality is sufficient for voice only; voice wiring has a single point of failure; voice-wiring volume is high due to central control with the star topology.

But, there also are many benefits to PBX-based solutions: availability of circuits to a large community of end users, low-risk technology, good administration, and easy migration to higher bandwidths offered by ISDN basic or primary services.

Basically, the packet-switching technology of LANs is competing against the circuit-switching technology of PBXs. New developments have brought both technologies closer to each other. Some of the facts are:

- More topological alternatives for PBXs.
- The use of wiring hubs for LANs.
- The use of voice-wiring technology for considerably higher bandwidth (e.g., 100VG AnyLAN).
- More centralized management for LANs.
- More widely used switching for LANs and interconnected LANs.
- ATM can become the local integrator of all communication forms, including voice and data.
- Not far in the future, user devices will support all communication forms using one structured cabling system.
- Some of the PBXs (e.g., Definity from AT&T) are supporting TCP/IP, opening new opportunities to manage PBXs by SNMP managers.

As a result, a number of feasible configurations can be implemented. The PBX may be considered an entry point to the campus or premises; PBXs can be connected by a LAN backbone; PBXs can be used for bridging LANs with low data traffic; data circuit switches (DCS) can be on a twisted-pair basis with LANs to economically connect low-speed terminals with each other or with hosts and their applications. In overall LAN-management architectures, PBXs are expected to provide the functionality of an element management system, working independently from or connected to LAN-management integrators.

The impact of PBXs on LAN management can be summarized as follows:

- High applicability of built-in management capabilities.
- Alternatives of connecting PBXs to the network management station (protocols and inband/outband).
- External monitoring features of PBXs.
- Use of PBXs for supervising the physical (wiring) infrastructure of premises.
- Better specification of which network management applications are needed for PBXs.
- Streamlining network management in the hubs.
- Using management features of ATM switches to incorporate PBX management.

- In environments with legacy Ethernet, Token Ring, and FDDI, management will remain separate for voice and data.

High-Speed Local Area Networks

If traditional local area networks, such as Ethernet or Token Ring, are running out of capacity, the network manager has got multiple choices to increase bandwidth.

Bridges and routers have been in operation for many years. They help to segment local area networks, offering the full original bandwidth in each segment. The result is that throughput rates are altogether higher when all segments are aggregated. Routers, bridges, and brouters will be addressed as part of the interconnecting devices segment of this chapter.

High-speed LANs include the alternatives that follow.

FDDI/CDDI (fiber or copper distributed data interface)

FDDI is an accepted standard with a wide range of available products, including bridges, routers, concentrators, wiring-hub cards, and virtually any network interface card for any bus. Throughput of 100 Mbps is standardized over two-pair category-5 unshielded twisted-pair, multimode fiber, and single-mode fiber. FDDI is coming from the LAN backbone technology and will become the Ethernet of the next decade.

FDDI is a token-passing network based on two rings of fiber-optic cable in its fullest form. The packets on each of the rings rotate around the rings in opposite directions. An FDDI network can achieve burst speeds of 100 Mbps and sustained data transmission speeds of around 80 Mbps. A full-blown FDDI network can stretch 100 km and connect over 500 stations spaced as far as 2 km apart. Even with a high cost factor, FDDI offers benefits that can't be found with any other communication medium.

Speed. First and foremost among FDDI's advantages over first-generation, copper-based LANs is the far greater speeds at which data can be transferred over the network. Ethernet's 10 Mbps and even IBM's Token Ring speed of 16 Mbps offer considerably less throughput in comparison to FDDI's speed of 100 Mbps.

Security. Security issues are always a concern for any network where critical data is readily available on the network. From the standpoint of the physical media's security, a fiber-optic medium is much more effective than a copper-based medium, which emits electromagnetic interference patterns that can be monitored. This problem is completely eliminated with fiber optics. Metal cables are also much easier to tap into than fiber-optic cables. Tapping into a coaxial cable is almost as easy as attaching a clamp to the cable. To tap into a fiber-optic cable, the cable must be cut and very precisely sliced back together or the transmission is impaired and the break detected.

Noise immunity. Metal-based (coaxial cables or twisted-pair wiring) networks are subject to EMI (electromagnetic interference), unlike lightwave communications. With the proper installation techniques, FDDI networks can stretch significantly beyond distances reached by previous networks. For example, Ethernet networks are limited to a distance no greater than 2.8 km, while FDDI can cover a distance of 100 km.

Fault tolerance. Built into the FDDI specification are certain levels of fault tolerance—a critical need in high-performance applications. In a fully configured FDDI network with two fiber-optic rings, a break or failure in one of the rings would not disable the network. An FDDI network, because of its built-in station management and network management functions, can reconfigure itself so that all nodes maintain communication at the normal speeds of the network.

Determinism. In certain real-time applications, network designers must know the time needed to transfer data from one node on the network to another, or from a supercomputer to a peripheral device, if FDDI is used as a high-speed connection to peripherals. The FDDI token-passing scheme is actually a timed token protocol that allows for just these types of applications.

The protocol is designed to guarantee a maximum token rotation time decided by a bidding process between the nodes on the network when the network is initialized. The node requiring the fastest transfer time can dictate the token rotation time for the ring. In this way, network developers can know the maximum time between a node's acquiring the token and, consequently, the maximum time needed to communicate with any other node on the network.

Many FDDI networks will actually be hybrid implementations where the type of FDDI station used—whether single or dual attachment—will depend on the application being run and the objectives of the network designer. FDDI node processors are those modules that provide connectivity to FDDI and that handle much of the protocol processing. During the early stages of implementation, it's just as important for the FDDI node processors to offer the network designer a certain degree of flexibility as it is for the node processors to support the high transmission rates of FDDI.

Because they provide that critical connection point to an FDDI network, the capabilities of node processors today and over the next several years should be of extreme importance to network implementors and OEM manufacturers who will be incorporating FDDI into their product lines. Some of the characteristics to carefully consider in a node processor are its design flexibility, internal bandwidth, host bus interface, and its ability to handle FDDI's demanding protocol processing requirements.

"Nodes" are responsible for connecting bridges, routers, computers, and other devices to the FDDI backbone. A special consideration is the use of encapsulation or transparent protocol. Protocol encapsulation limits the use of FDDI backbones to the same protocol. Transparent protocol implementation doesn't have the same restriction, enabling users to construct hybrid FDDI backbone networks.

Figure 2.10 shows the standardized FDDI layers and their mutual interfaces:

PMD   Physical medium dependent, which describes the electrical/optical link connection to the FDDI ring.

PHY   Physical layer protocol, which interfaces to PMD and handles the encoding and decoding of information.

MAC   Media access control, which connects PHY to higher OSI layers, providing packet framing and token control.

STM   Station management, which provides managing, monitoring, and configuring of the network.

Station management is still a proprietary solution, but in most cases, SNMP Agent Software is implemented. Using SNMP, management platforms can be shared with other facilities and devices.

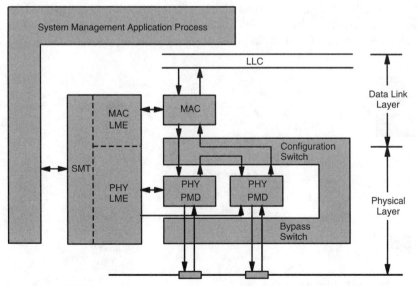

Figure 2.10   FDDI layers.

DQDB (dual queue dual bus)

DQDB uses two optical-fiber buses to connect basically the same types of objects as with FDDI. But DQDB offers a higher bandwidth (140 Mbps). These buses are separated from each other and are unidirectional. Both buses use the same frequency for signaling. Multiple slots may constitute a frame, which is generated by the frame generator at the beginning of the bus. Since network nodes are tied to each other as a logical bus, each node is located both upstream and downstream from bus nodes (Fig. 2.11).

DQDB technology revolves around the fact that all stations have knowledge of the frames queued at all other stations. Under DQDB, the end nodes continuously transmit empty data frames around each ring. Whenever a station on one of the network nodes has something to send, it generates a frame request on the bus that's carrying traffic away from its node. Stations upstream receive the request, then reserve and empty the frame for the requesting station's data; when the packet stream circles around again, the frame is sent for transmission to its destination.

If fallback security is required, a DQDB network can be configured as a looped bus in which the two ends of the buses are colocated. If a fault occurs in one of the buses, the nodes at either end of the fault become the beginning and the end. DQDB has been implemented as a typical MAN backbone alternative.

Full-duplex LANs

The throughput can be increased when transmission is supported in both directions simultaneously. In most cases, cabling does not need to be changed at all. If two cable pairs are available between stations and

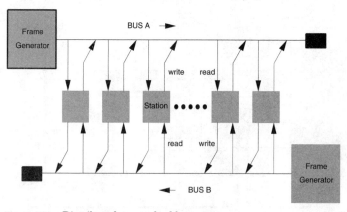

Figure 2.11 Distributed queue dual bus.

the hubs, full-duplex operation can be supported with the result of doubling the potential throughput. It is a tactical solution for network managers, but very helpful in heavily loaded segments. In particular, server hub connections can benefit from this solution. This migration needs adapter cards, hub boards, and bridge parts supporting full-duplex operations. Figure 2.12 (Kauffels 1994) shows this solution for Ethernet. But the implementation may include full-duplex fast Ethernet, full-duplex FDDI, and also full-duplex Token Ring. Using fiber, two separate cables are necessary, each supporting unidirectional transmission. The higher speed does not cause emission problems, because the individual cables are operated at the old speed. They are altogether just better utilized.

Asynchronous transfer mode

ATM promises very low latency transport of data, voice, and LAN communications over local, metropolitan, and wide area networks. Another key benefit of ATM is its ability to provide bandwidth on demand up to the committed rate for specific connections. Later in this chapter, ATM will be discussed again as a promising technology for interconnecting LANs.

The ability to integrate existing Ethernets and Token Rings is also key to ATM's acceptance. ATM is available at speeds of 44.74, 51.84,

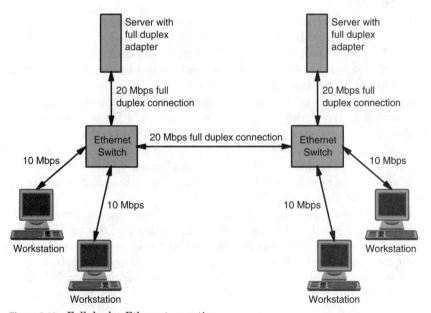

Figure 2.12 Full-duplex Ethernet operation.

100, 155, and 622 Mbps. Many users expect that 25 Mbps will also be approved. ATM supports many cabling types, including two-pair and four-pair category-3 unshielded twisted pair, multimode fiber, DS-3, and T1/E1 copper circuits.

100Base-T

100Base-T supports 100 Mbps of bandwidth using existing Ethernet media access control (MAC) sublayers operating at 100 Mbps instead of 10 Mbps. Cabling supported in the first release of this standard includes four-pair category-3 unshielded twisted pair, two-pair category-5 unshielded twisted pair, two-pair shielded twisted pair, and multimode fiber.

Standard bodies are busy modifying CSMA/CD parameters to keep and increase their efficiency at higher speeds. Cabling is star-supported by centrally located repeater hubs. But the number of hubs is limited to two between any end-user devices. Due to the length of the collision window and as a result of the round-trip delay, the distance of 100Base-T is limited to 210 meters and to 100 meters between hubs and end-user devices. The majority of market leaders are supporting this technology. This technology, however, does not offer a breakthrough; it is a combination of shared media and a less than efficient access method.

100VG AnyLAN

Ethernet and Token Ring frame formats are supported by 100VG Any-LAN at 100 Mbps. It operates over four-pair category-3 unshielded twisted pair, two-pair shielded twisted pair, and multimode fiber. The physical topology is star; stations are connected to the central hub of the segments. The hub hosts the polling authority, allowing the implementation of demand-priority access schemes. The hub polls each station whether they want to send or not. Usually, polling is implemented in a sequential order (Fig. 2.13) (Kauffels 1994). But stations and applications may receive higher priorities by changing the polling table. Hubs function as repeaters; as an additional feature, they can also support security schemes by filtering incoming and outgoing packets by source and destination addresses.

The AnyLAN indicates that the hub (intelligency is assumed) supports both Ethernet and Token Ring. The limitation of distance is again approximately 100 meters between hubs and end-user devices. Due to using demand priorities, the utilization levels are expected to be higher than in case of 100Base-T with CSMA/CD. The support on behalf of manufacturers is still very limited.

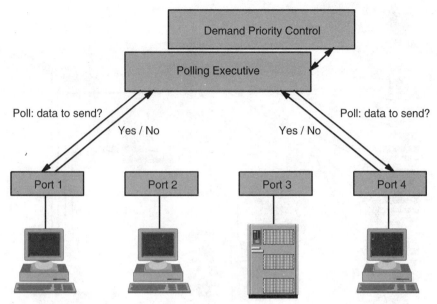

Figure 2.13   Working principle of 100VG AnyLAN.

LAN switching

Over the last few years, a new class of products has emerged that can increase bandwidth on overloaded Ethernets and Token Rings while working with conventional cabling and adapters. There are more products available for Ethernet than for Token Ring, but the technology is the same in both cases. Figure 2.14 shows the example with Ethernet and Fig. 2.15 for Token Ring.

Once switched, the connection between the hub with the switch and workstations or servers may receive the full bandwidth. In the case of Ethernet, switching may be applied for both 10Base-T and 100Base-T. But the switched bandwidth can be shared or subdivided as shown in Fig. 2.14. The practical implementation of switching is different according to vendor. There are four basic technologies used within the switch:

- Software switch with shared-memory interface (Fig. 2.16) (Kauffels 1994)
- Switch with high-speed backbone (Fig. 2.17) (Kauffels 1994)
- Switch with high-speed backplane (Fig. 2.18) (Kauffels 1994)
- Switch with high-speed crossbar (Fig. 2.19) (Kauffels 1994)

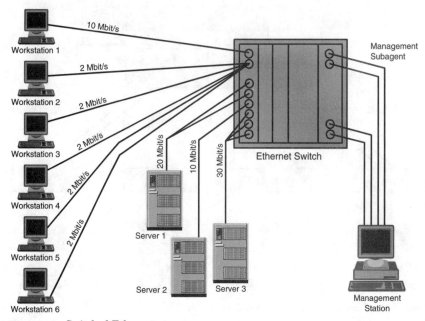

Figure 2.14 Switched Ethernet structure.

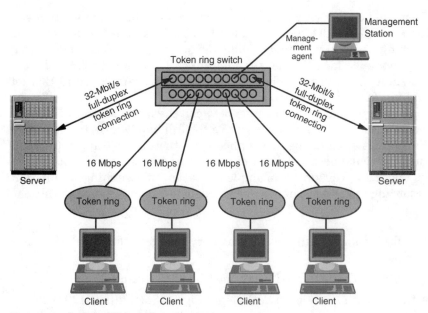

Figure 2.15 Switched Token Ring structure.

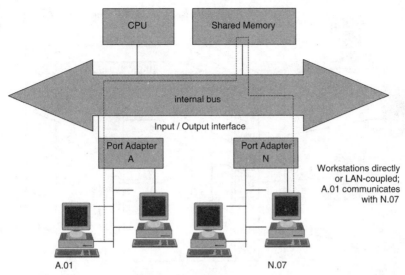

Figure 2.16   Software Switch with shared memory interface.

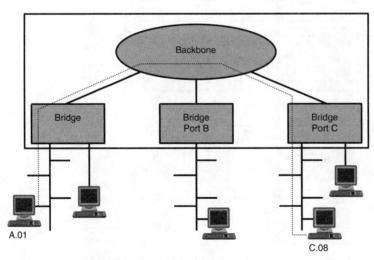

Figure 2.17   Switch with high-speed backbone.

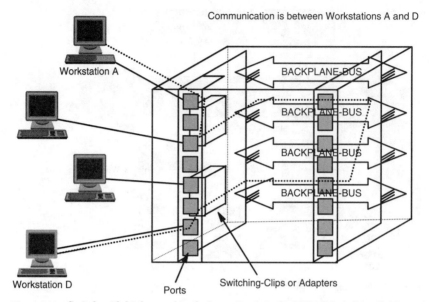

Figure 2.18 Switch with high-speed backplanes (basis is the MMAC-hub from Cabletron).

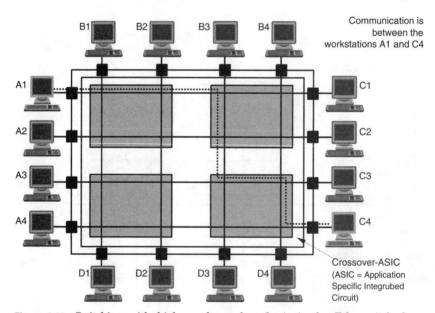

Figure 2.19 Switching with high-speed crossbar (basis is the Etherswitch from Kalpana).

There are two core technologies available for Ethernet and switching:

- Static Ethernet switching (also called *dedicated switching*)
- Dynamic Ethernet switching (also called *bandwidth on demand*)

Static switching was designed to simplify the job of change management. Automation is supported by implementing switching policies into software. The network manager is authorized to make the necessary assignments between servers, segments, and workstations. Static port switching allows network managers to move users via software from one of a hub's shared Ethernet buses to another, facilitating configuration management. Ports can be individually selected and added to different shared Ethernet buses. Selecting and moving individual ports can also maximize port usage, reducing the number of modules that need to be purchased for the hub. The static module switch also operates as a software-controlled system for implementing adds, moves, and changes to the network. However, the static module switch moves the entire hub module, including all its parts, from one shared bus to another.

Dynamic switching was designed to increase the bandwidth on an as-needed basis. Packets originating in a workstation connected to a port on a dynamic switch are examined by the switch; the switch identifies the packet's source and destination addresses; the switch then opens a dedicated circuit (10 or 100 Mbps) that carries the packet through the switching fabric from source to destination. The collisions normally associated with Ethernet LANs are substantially reduced or even eliminated, giving each user access to the LAN's full bandwidth capability. Within the switch, many source-to-destination connections may be maintained simultaneously. Once transmission requests have been fulfilled, the switch drops the circuits and dedicates its attention to other requests. In this way, bandwidth through the dynamic switch is allocated on demand. These features show similarities with ATM, but they are delivered over a standard Ethernet network consisting of standard interface cards, drivers, cabling, and applications.

Dynamic port switching allows each port to be connected to a single end station or server. Since the switch gives each port the maximal available bandwidth on demand, its function is to allocate much greater network bandwidth to individual end users and servers than is possible using shared Ethernets. Changes are requested only in hubs that accommodate the switches.

The dynamic segment switch functions internally in exactly the same way as the dynamic port switch. It allocates private, point-to-point 10- or 100-Mbps circuits to its ports on demand across the switching fabric. However, each dynamic segment switch port is able to connect to an entire network segment rather than only to an individual end station or server. The dynamic segment switch accomplishes this by being able to identify a large number of MAC addresses on each port. This ability to string entire networks from each port often allows the dynamic segment switch to be substituted for bridges and routers in segmenting LANs.

Table 2.3 (Madge-Lannet) compares and combines the core-switching solutions by identifying network problems and benefits of the solutions. A meaningful combination of all four core alternatives can be successfully utilized for virtual LANs. In summary, LAN switching offers the following unique features:

- Full bandwidth to each user, while preserving existing infrastructures

- Scalable, cost-effective solutions based on cost/performance requirements

- Standards-based connectivity and network management

- Congestion management

TABLE 2.3   Sample Switching Solutions to Solve Common Problems

The following chart puts the Ethernet switching implementations to work solving a variety of commonly encountered problems in growing and changing networks.

Network problem	Ethernet switching solution	Benefit
Frequent adds, moves, and changes to the network resulting from rapid growth, reorganization facility move, or right-sizing period	Combination: Static module switching Static port switching	Allows adds, moves, and changes to be made easily via software from the network management station Could reduce number of modules purchased to serve new users coming on the network.
Need for cost-effective LAN segmentation— many new users on the network	Dynamic segment switching	More cost-effective, easier-to-manage, and higher throughput segmentation than a bridge or router
High bandwidth needs by high-performance users	Dynamic port switching	Dynamically allocated bandwidth on demand to each end station, up to the full 10 Mbps of Ethernet
Need to create a client/ server architecture that is easy to manage and provides for high-bandwidth applications	Combination: Dynamic port switching Dynamic segment switching	Multiple dedicated 10-Mbps server connections; dedicated 10-Mbps client connections for power users; low-cost, high-throughput segmentation for clients on shared LAN segments

- High port density
- Flexibility of combining various switching techniques
- Fault tolerance
- Port prioritization
- Multicasting
- Support of port-level, multihub virtual networking

Virtual local area networks

Software control of switched LANs offers a diverse range of solutions based on the creation of virtual LANs. A virtual LAN is a secure, software-defined group of workstations and servers that function as a networked work group of users sitting logistically close together, although the nodes may actually be located in diverse places such as rooms, floors, buildings, and even sites. The virtual LAN is called *virtual* because it is defined entirely in the software of the hub and may be rapidly deleted or altered at any time by the network manager to meet business needs.

Virtual LANs constitute a new kind of network design tool created to help LAN managers quickly adapt the network to fit a competitive organization's frequently changing work-flow requirements. Figure 2.20 shows virtual LANs created as secure subnetworks in engineer-

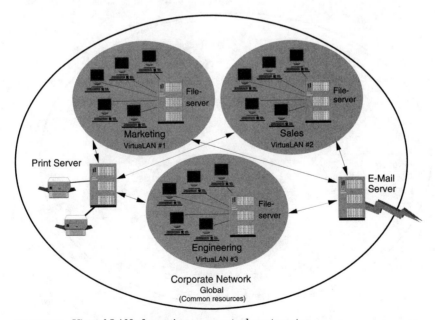

Figure 2.20   Virtual LANs for various corporate departments.

ing, sales, and marketing. These departmental virtual LANs, that may consist of many physical microsegments, ensure that only authorized employees within a department can access the departmental server, keeping the server's data secure. The interconnected virtual LAN also includes shared resources such as print servers and E-mail servers. These resources may be accessed by all subnetworks.

In Fig. 2.21 an additional virtual LAN has been created to include members of different subnetworks on the task force formed to develop a new product. Physically, the members do not move. The network manager groups them together by means of MAC addresses. This new virtual LAN allows, for example, engineering and manufacturing to perform concurrent design on the product and on the manufacturing tools needed to mass-produce it. Shared CAD and databases reside on various servers that are also included in the new virtual LAN.

The management of virtual LANs is not trivial. Not only the physical layout, but also the virtual topology must be maintained and visualized. Management instruments must be aware of virtual components and changes in real time. Segment monitoring using RMON probes must be redefined as well.

In order to reduce complexity, ATM-LAN emulation could be helpful in creating virtual LANs. Virtual LANs, using LAN emulation, consist of the ATM backbone and a number of switched virtual circuits to serve multiple workstations in different segments. Figure 2.22 shows this

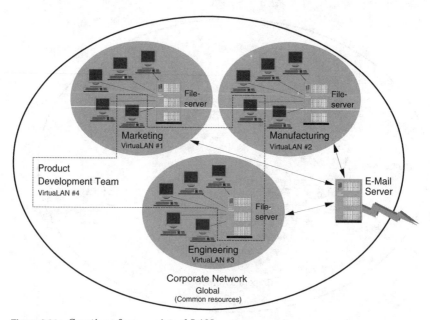

Figure 2.21   Creation of a new virtual LAN.

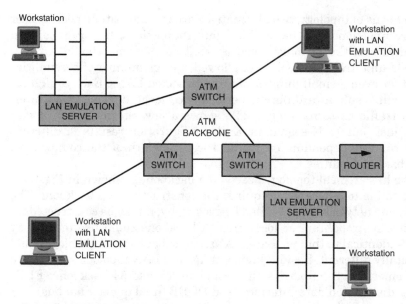

Figure 2.22 ATM-LAN emulation.

arrangement. Important components are LEC and LES that are responsible for protocol conversion. Management is usually supported by the ATM switch. This structure offers great flexibility and scalability, and can also be implemented in WAN backbones.

Interconnecting Local Area Networks

When considering the ability to ensure enterprisewide connectivity for users and local area networks, interconnectivity strategies gain importance. The following are important topics when considering interconnecting local area networks: evaluating interconnection strategies, optimizing interconnecting topologies, evaluating and selecting interconnecting devices, and evaluating and selecting interconnecting facilities.

Developing interconnection strategies includes making decisions about how and whether existing WANs may be replaced by interconnected LANs. However, this is a long process. Strategy development also includes evaluating the kind of interconnection: in other words, whether low-level or high-level gateways are required. Depending on needs, different levels of intelligence for interconnecting devices may be required. Repeaters, extenders, or bridges may be very suitable for extending the geographical reach of LAN segments; for more flexible connectivity, routers should be considered; finally, for application-level connectivity, gateways are required.

In terms of topology, two alternatives are in competition: peer-to-peer interconnections, and hierarchical interconnections. In a peer-coupled architecture, the primary issue is what connections should exist. If "mesh" and "tree" topologies are allowed, a large number of possibilities exist for even a small number of interconnected LANs. Each configuration will result in a different performance level, depending on inter-LAN traffic patterns. Figure 2.23 shows a few alternative topologies with just four LAN segments. Each configuration results in different performance, depending on traffic, the bandwidth of the connections, and backup facilities.

The hierarchical topology based on a backbone is shown in Fig. 2.24. Connecting to a backbone requires the construction of a backbone. The backbone network is not limited by geography; it may be constructed for a wide, metropolitan, or local area. A backbone could use technology that's identical to that of access LANs, or the backbone technology could be totally different. Besides known WAN and LAN topologies, there are two emerging technologies that compete for use as backbone: FDDI (fiber distributed data interface) and DQDB (dual queue dual bus).

Interconnectivity strategies include answers for the local and the wide area. In previous segments, evolving switching and virtual LAN technologies have been addressed in some depth. Both include implicit solutions for interconnecting LANs. Until now, the hubs usually took responsibility for interconnecting LANs. In this part, the book differentiates between local and wide area interconnections.

Local area interconnections

The basis is in every case the structured cabling in the building. One example for this is shown in Fig. 2.25. The central hub is the focal point

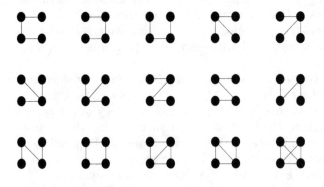

● LAN

Figure 2.23   Peer-to-peer interconnection.

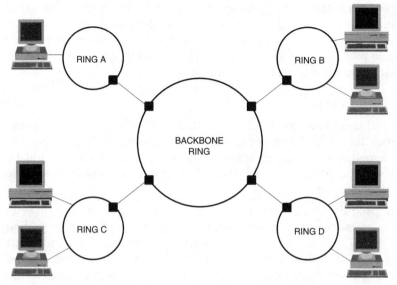

Figure 2.24 Hierarchical interconnection.

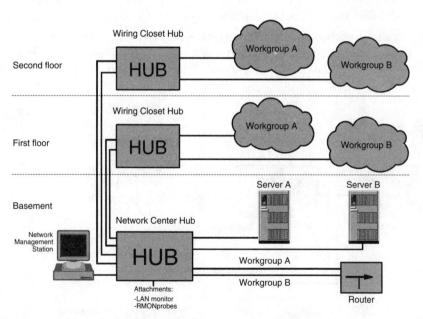

Figure 2.25 Example for structured cabling.

of supervising other hubs, preparing packets for the router, executing switching functions, and of accommodating the management station. Basically, there are two alternatives for local area interconnections: collapsed backbone and distributed backbone (Vollmer 1995). The most popular solutions will be briefly addressed.

Collapsed backbone

1. Shared bandwidth without segmenting.   It offers very basic capabilities for a small number of users. Administration is easy, but the performance depends on traffic patterns. Scalability is limited by the physics of the local area network. Figure 2.26 shows an example for this solution.

2. Collapsed backbone with bridges and routers.   A larger number of users are segmented by bridges or routers. Wiring is star-controlled by hubs. There are performance benefits within the segments that may be lost if interconnecting devices are not properly sized. A more advanced version consists of an additional central hub next to the bridge or router that controls all the wiring concentrators. Figure 2.27 shows this structure for three segments. Administration is more powerful, but also more difficult. Performance can be tuned; scalability is much better than in the previous case.

3. Parallel backbone with concentrators.   It is a more advanced version of the previous one. Each segment is connected to each hub, offering excellent switching capabilities. Bandwidth utilization is

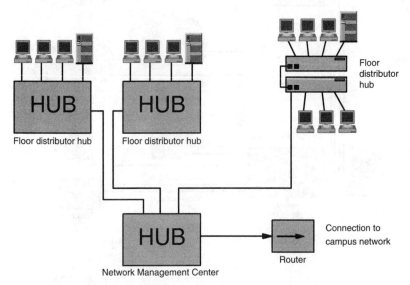

Figure 2.26   Network layout without segmentation.

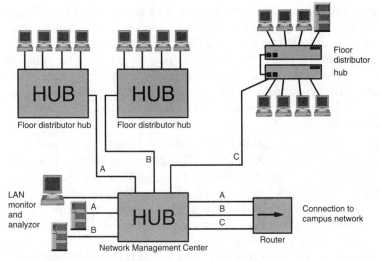

Figure 2.27 Collapsed backbone with concentrators.

good because stations and servers can receive bandwidth by being assigned to low-traffic segments. In terms of flexibility and reliability, this version has its limits. Parallel cabling is required, and multiple ports are needed in the concentrators. Within the segments, media are shared. Figure 2.28 shows this solution.

4. Collapsed backbone combined with frame switching. The structure is based on a parallel backbone, but the central concentrator is equipped with frame-relay functions. Performance is much better

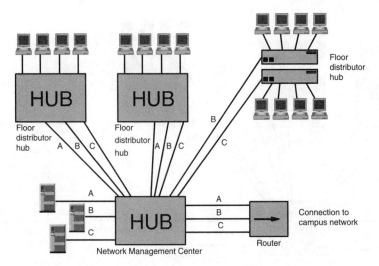

Figure 2.28 Parallel backbone with concentrators.

because multiple logical connections can be maintained simultaneously. Media sharing may be limited to low-traffic segments; dedicated connections can be reserved for central resources or for users with very high bandwidth demand. Scalability is good due to advanced switching. Administration is more powerful by using management software to implement changes. The concentration of management is targeted for the focal-point hub. Figure 2.29 shows this backbone solution.

5. Collapsed backbone combined with cell switching.   There are similarities with the previous solution. The difference is that the LAN frames must be cut into the fixed cell size of 53 bytes. Due to high speed, the performance is expected to be better. The scalability is better due to easy expandability of the matrix structure of the switches. Switching is—similarly to frame relay—at layer 2, resulting in much easier administration. Figure 2.30 shows this alternative with the central hub that may accommodate the ATM switch.

Distributed backbone

1. FDDI backbone.   It has been implemented for many years as an interconnecting technology for local and metropolitan area networks. The technology is well understood. Basically, there are two implementation alternatives. In the traditional case, interconnecting devices are directly on the ring; they are connected to the LAN segments. Software updates in the interconnecting devices may cause the ring to enter the wrap status. In case of device faults, problem determination and diagnosis are very difficult; powerful man-

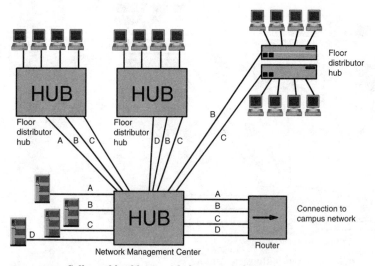

Figure 2.29   Collapsed backbone with frame switching.

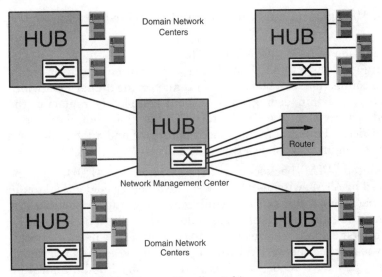

Figure 2.30 Collapsed backbone with cell switching.

agement solutions are absolutely necessary. In the more advanced case, sensitive devices will not be directly on the ring, but wired to concentrators (Fig. 2.31). In this example, the FDDI ring is built between the two concentrators. Anything else is wired to the central concentrators. In case of device faults, the ring will remain func-

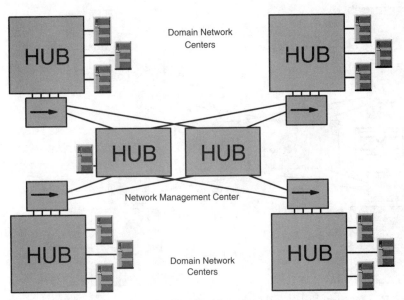

Figure 2.31 Distributed FDDI backbone with concentrators.

tional. Management applications are implemented into the central concentrators.

2. Combination of ATM and FDDI.   This alternative enables users to migrate gradually to ATM. With this combination, the user gets a second connection, can test ATM, and can provide higher bandwidth services to certain user groups without completely replacing the infrastructure. Due to different technologies, the administration is very difficult. Powerful management platforms and applications are required. Figure 2.32 shows this alternative.

3. Distributed ATM backbone with dual homing.   FDDI can be replaced by ATM switches. Otherwise the topology is identical to the FDDI backbone solution. FDDI equipment may stay for power users, but they lose the interconnecting role. The big benefit is that the shared-media solutions are pushed to the edge of the networks. Scalability is good because ATM throughput can be gradually upgraded. Routers stay for a while, causing more diversity in administration and management. Figure 2.33 shows this solution, but does not display all details for subnetworks.

4. Full ATM.   This ultimate version assumes that most end-user devices are capable of supporting ATM. Legacy-shared-media LANs can be connected by using LAN-ATM emulation. Combinations with frame relay may be supported. Routers are still present for convert-

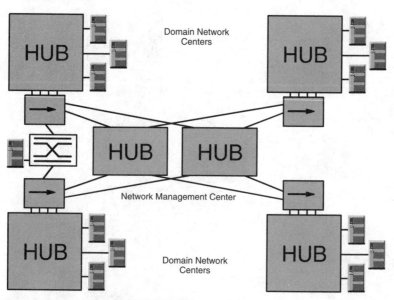

Figure 2.32 Combined FDDI/ATM backbone.

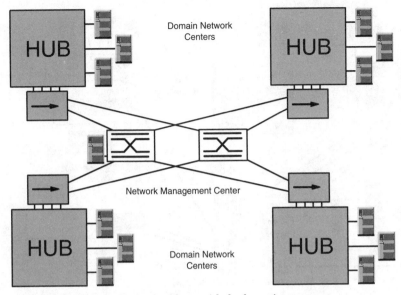

Figure 2.33   Distributed ATM backbone with dual troming.

ing protocols, traffic control between subnetworks, security firewalls, and for connecting local structures with wide area networks. In other areas, they are expected to be replaced by the switching technology. This alternative offers all the benefits of throughput and scalability of ATM solutions combined with more streamlined administration and management. Figure 2.34 gives some details about the topology of this solution.

Summarizing the attributes of the nine alternatives (five collapsed-backbone and four distributed-backbone solutions), Table 2.4 evaluates them using three key criteria, such as performance, scalability, and management.

Wide Area Interconnections

In comparison to legacy solutions, network managers have got a lot of choices, today. It is not easy to find the right choice that satisfies performance, scalability, management, and also pricing criteria. The most important alternatives include the following:

Point-to-point or multipoint leased lines.   Depending on the traffic profiles, utilization expectations, and geographic details, this is still the leading alternative. The physical implementation, whether copper or fiber, depends on the offer of the suppliers.

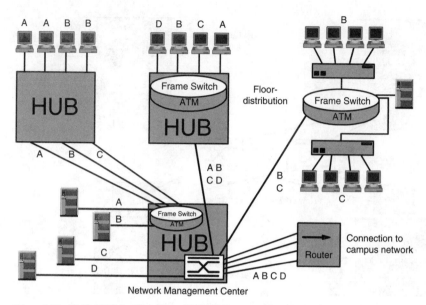

Figure 2.34   Full ATM for distributed backbone.

ISDN (integrated services digital network). In its two implementation forms, ISDN would be ideal for bursty LAN-to-LAN interconnections—in particular, when traffic does not require continuous connections.

Private or public packet switching. Due to wide geographical coverage, this choice would guarantee accessibility to each LAN segment. Performance criteria, in particular in bursty cases, may not be ideal. Broadcast storms may hopelessly overload packet-switching networks. The same is true for centralized SNMP management of multiple LAN segments.

TABLE 2.4   Evaluation of Local Area Interconnection Solutions (Vollmer 1995)

Criteria and solutions	Performance	Scalability	Management
Collapsed backbone			
Shared bandwidth without segmenting	Poor	Poor	Good
Collapsed backbone with bridges/routers	Fair	Fair	Fair
Parallel backbone with concentrators	Fair	Poor	Good
Collapsed backbone with frame relay	Good	Good	Good
Collapsed backbone with cell relay	Excellent	Excellent	Good
Distributed backbone			
FDDI backbone	Fair	Fair	Fair
FDDI and ATM	Fair	Good	Fair
Distributed ATM with dual homing	Good	Good	Good
Full ATM	Excellent	Excellent	Good

Switched multimegabit data service (SMDS). In particular, SMDS seems to be getting a lot of attention as the interconnecting technology of the future. As a MAN alternative, switched multimegabit data service (SMDS) seems to be very useful for transmitting large data files and graphics that low-speed services such as X.25 can't easily handle. And SMDS may offer an alternative to installing more expensive private-line facilities covering the speed range from 1.544 to 45 Mbps. This service will run on circuits provided by the RBOCs and connect the physical interface between a bridge or router and the SMDS network. In terms of management, the providers are expected to make network management raw data available (e.g., in MIBs). Polling the MIBs for SMDS operational and statistical data, data may be transmitted and further processed by the management station. Basically, SMDS is using short, fixed-length packet sizes for transmitting voice, data, and video.

LAN-to-LAN connections may require very broad bandwidth over the next few years. Sonet and ATM are interesting choices in this respect. *Sonet* is a set of international standards for transmission over fiber, with speeds ranging from 51.84 Mbps to over 13 gigabits per second. Synchronous digital hierarchy (SDH) is a subset of Sonet standards used in European and Asian networks.

Frame relay. Frame relay is also receiving attention. Frame relay is a network access technique that transmits data packets of variable lengths with a minimum of error checking. In interconnecting LANs, frame relay has the benefit of not force-fitting LAN applications into a specific frame size. The variable lengths of packages require minimal data conversion between frame relay and devices attached to local area networks. Frame relay has already been referenced as a local interconnection technology.

Asynchronous transfer mode (ATM). A cell-based switching technology for fast packets that uses 53-byte cells, without regard to the communication form. ATM is critical to the deployment of multimedia networks.

ATM may be the ultimate technology of unifying local and wide area interconnections. Initially, LAN-ATM emulation will be used. In the second step, larger ATM backbones will be built. And finally, a number of customized alternatives, such as ATM with edge routers, relational networks, virtual networks, and virtual relational networks will be designed and implemented.

Broadband ISDN. This offers even higher bandwidth for interconnecting LANs. But this technique is not expected to be in service before the end of the 1990s.

Microwave. Microwave circuits are useful in local and metropolitan areas. The quality is acceptable, and bandwidth requirements can be easily met. Disadvantages include weather dependency and geographical limitations.

Satellite. This technology is widely used for communications with rural locations. Bandwidth requirements can be met, but performance expectations cannot always be met due to propagation delays and transceiver processing times.

Cellular digital packet data (CDPD). This relatively new technology offers accessibility to mobile users. For interconnecting LANs over the wide area, there are serious quality, performance, throughput, and price concerns. This alternative is more suitable for wireless LAN extensions than for LAN interconnections.

Summary. Table 2.5 compares these basic wide area interconnection alternatives, using criteria such as performance, scalability, management, and price. The technical differences may be significant, but most experts believe pricing and availability will be the major factors affecting the choice between these three leading technologies.

The following is the impact of interconnecting strategies on LAN management, topologies, and facilities:

- Performance bottlenecks due to WAN-facility bandwidth
- Low processing efficiency of FDDI nodes
- Too many hierarchical steps in LAN interconnection topology

Interconnecting Devices

Depending on the interconnecting goals, different interconnecting devices can be implemented. Decisions should be based on consideration of flexibility, protocol support and transparency, processing delays, scope of functionality, and cost.

TABLE 2.5   Evaluation of Wide Area Interconnection Solutions

Criteria and solutions	Performance	Scalability	Management	Price
Point-to-point leased lines				
Copper	Fair	Good	Good	Fair
Fiber	Good	Fair	Good	Fair
ISDN	Fair	Good	Fair	Good
Packet switching	Poor	Good	Fair	Good
SMDS	Excellent	Good	Fair	Fair
Frame relay	Excellent	Good	Good	Good
ATM	Excellent	Excellent	Good	Fair
B-ISDN	Excellent	Excellent	Good	Good
Microwave	Good	Fair	Fair	Poor
Satellite	Poor	Good	Fair	Fair
CDPD	Poor	Poor	Poor	Poor

Repeaters.   Repeaters are devices with amplification, signal reshaping, and retiming functions whose purpose is to extend the cabling distance. Their attributes are as follows:

- Amplification, reshaping, and retiming to extend the cabling distance
- Connections at layer 1
- No modifications on access protocols
- No path optimization
- The possibility of media change
- Weak security features
- Number limited by higher level protocols
- Special solutions
  Buffered repeater
  Remote repeater
  Fiber repeater

Figure 2.35 shows the location of repeaters in relation to standards.

Extenders.   Extenders are devices that offer connection to local area networks for stand-alone user devices, which may be terminals or workstations. The principal attributes of extenders are as follows:

- Connections at layer 1 for both local and remote users supporting various serial interfaces (V.24, RS-232, V.35, X.21)
- Use of internal or external clocking

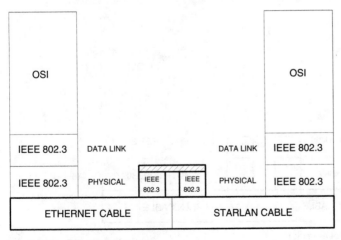

Figure 2.35   Repeater structure.

- Use of private or public communication services
- Support of rates between 1.2 to 128 Kbps
- Minimal support of higher layers—usually just support of SDLC or HDLC
- Transparency to higher-level protocols such as TCP/IP, XNS, OSI, DecNet, etc.
- Minimal network management capabilities

MAC bridges. MAC bridges are devices for offering connectivity at the layer 2 MAC level between various access protocols and media. The attributes of MAC bridges are as follows:

- Connectivity function
- Connection at layer 2A
- No change on LLC protocol
- Address analysis and filtering
- Significant reduction of collisions
- Rule-of-thumb saturation limit: 20 percent of packets bridged
- Isolation of troubles
- Media change possible
- Weak security features
- Buffering usually supported

Figure 2.36 shows the level of MAC bridges in relation to the standards.

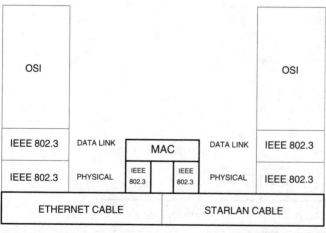

Figure 2.36   MAC-level bridge.

Bridges. Bridges are devices for offering connectivity at layer 2 between various access protocols and media. The attributes of bridges are as follows:

- Connection between various access protocols
- Connection at layer 2
- Packet deassembly and reassembly
- No path optimization
- Weak security features
- Significant "software" work for bridging Ethernet and Token Ring
- Routing bridges possible future solution, with router functions using the spanning tree algorithm

Figure 2.37 shows the scope of bridges in relation to the standards.

There are two principal alternatives for bridging LAN segments in terms of selecting the communication path. In source routing, the originating device locates the target device by sending out broadcast messages. The originator first sends a broadcast message around its own ring. If the target is on the ring, it responds to the message, a copy of which reaches every ring in the bridged token ring network. The target sends back a message containing routing information. If no messages are returned, the target is not on the network.

There are two types of source-routing broadcast messages: all routes and single routes. Figure 2.38 illustrates this process. An all-routes broadcast message takes every possible route to reach its target. In a mesh network, the target address receives several copies of the broad-

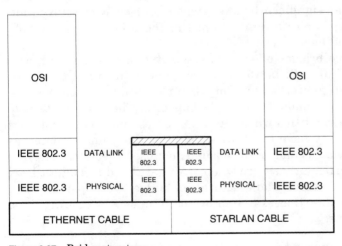

Figure 2.37 Bridge structure.

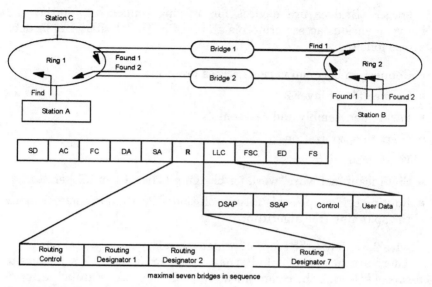

Figure 2.38   Source-routing bridges.

cast message, and it responds to each one. But the message will not be sent to the same ring twice. Thus, looping may be avoided. Single-route broadcast messages use a spanning-tree structure to guarantee that only one copy of the originated message may reach the target. In any case, the originating station may receive multiple copies of the response. On the basis of this information, the originator decides which route to choose; IBM products select the route of the first returned message. The number of source-routing messages is small, but even that number can significantly affect remote bridges. With source routing, the routing tables are maintained in the user workstation, offloading some of the bridges.

Spanning-tree bridges offer a loopless network topology with only one single logical path between the originator and target. In most cases, this topology works fine. But when there's link or node congestion, performance might be severely impacted. The use of alternate routes could prevent this when alternate routes and backup links are available, but they have to be activated after the primary route has failed. The available bandwidth is usually not used effectively. The limitations are particularly severe when WANs are used to connect LAN segments using bridges. Manufacturers of bridges with spanning-tree algorithms try nevertheless to improve performance by offering three special functions:

- Parallel line support that allows the use of multiple wide area links

- Load-balancing algorithms that distribute the load between the physical links

- Preserve-packet-sequence service that reassembles the packet at the receiver into the original sequence, which might have been lost due to parallel transmission

It's very likely that future bridges will support a combination of both techniques. More thoughts from the designers' perspective will be addressed in Chap. 6.

Routers. Routers are devices for offering connectivity at layer 3 for networks with the same protocol at layer 3 and higher. The attributes of routers are as follows:

- Connectivity for networks that operate the same protocol at layer 3 and higher

- Determining the optimal path for routing

- Addressing conversion into Internet

- Applicability for a wide variety of LANs, MANs, and WANs

- Use of a unique network protocol that's absolutely necessary

- Traffic management services such as routing, flow control, message fragmentation, and error-checking

- Brouters (bridges and routers in the same hardware) supporting multiple protocols

Figure 2.39 shows the place of routers or bridges in the connection reference model. Due to the common debates on whether routers or bridges are the right choice for certain internetworking environments, some of the manufacturers offer both on the same hardware platform, which then supports multiple protocols.

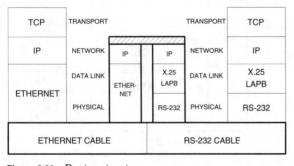

Figure 2.39   Router structure.

Gateways. Gateways are devices offering connectivity for completely different networks and architectures. Their most significant attributes are as follows:

- Connectivity between completely different networks
- Support for practically all seven layers
- Considerable development expense
- Questionable life cycle
- Possibility that performance could become a problem
- In certain cases, use of gateways unavoidable

Figure 2.40 displays communicating partners and the gateways between them. This figure emphasizes that gateways offer conversion services to all communication layers.

There are two principal conclusions concerning interconnecting devices: (1) with an increase in the intelligence level of the interconnecting devices, the expected design, development, and maintenance costs increase, and (2) the expected processing time required in the interconnecting components increases.

The following is the impact of interconnecting devices on LAN management:

- Spanning-tree or source-routing algorithms used for locating the communicating partners

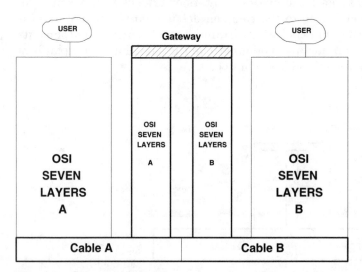

Figure 2.40 Gateway structure.

- Choosing the right interconnecting devices for the LAN segments
- Applicability of interconnecting devices for managing LANs
- Support of proprietary, de facto, or open network management protocols
- Peer-to-peer network management relationships to other managed objects, such as wiring concentrators
- The feasibility of using interconnecting devices with WAN techniques, such as frame relay, SMDS, and broadband ISDN
- Reengineering monitoring and management techniques for switches and switching hubs
- More management capabilities accommodated into hubs
- Use of intelligent management agents necessary to reduce the management overhead

Summary

This chapter has walked through the most important managed objects in the world of stand-alone and interconnected local area networks. In addition to giving an overview of how those components operate, emphasis has also been placed on what their impact is on LAN management. Details of their impact are discussed further in Chap. 3, covering LAN management functions, and Chap. 5, discussing LAN management instruments. RISC technology may dramatically change the role of interconnecting components in handling large applications, merging traffic onto high-speed pipes, and concentrating network management.

3

LAN Management Functions

Successful LAN management stems in part from the ability to manage several functions, each of which is supported by a large number of processes and procedures. These functions are categorized according to definitions of standard bodies. When considering broad definitions, those for LAN management have many similarities with the definitions that apply to managing wide area networks. LAN management functions are categorized as follows (also see Table 3.1).

Configuration management is a set of midrange and long-range activities for controlling physical, electrical, logical, and spare-part equipment inventories; maintaining vendor files and trouble tickets; managing cables and wiring; supporting provisioning and order processing; tracking, authorizing, scheduling, and implementing changes, backup, and archive. Directory service and help for generating different network configurations are also provided.

Fault management is the collection of activities required to dynamically maintain network service levels. These activities ensure high availability by quickly recognizing problems and performance degradation and by initiating controlling functions when necessary; these controlling functions may include diagnosis, repair, testing, recovery, workaround, and disaster recovery. Log control and information distribution techniques are supported as well.

TABLE 3.1 LAN Management Functions

Configuration management
Fault management
Performance management
Security management
Accounting management
Administration

Performance management involves an ongoing evaluation of the LAN. The purposes of performance management are to verify that service levels are maintained, to identify actual and potential bottlenecks, and to establish and report on trends for management decision making and planning. Building and maintaining a LAN's performance database, baselining, and automation procedures for LAN fault management are also included.

Security management is a set of functions whose purpose is to ensure a LAN's ongoing protection by analyzing risks, minimizing risks, implementing a LAN security plan, and subsequently monitoring success of the strategy. Special functions include the surveillance of security indicators, partitioning, password administration, and warning or alarm messages for violations. Also the protection of the LAN management system belongs into this group of responsibilities.

Accounting management is the process of collecting, interpreting, processing, and reporting cost-oriented and charge-oriented information on LAN resource usage. In particular, processing of raw accounting data, bill verification, software licensing, and chargeback procedures are included for data, and occasionally for voice.

LAN design and planning involve the process of determining the optimal network, based on data for network performance, traffic flow, resource use, networking requirements, technological trade-offs, and estimated growth of present and future applications. LAN design and planning are addressed separately in Chap. 6.

LAN administration is an evolving group of activities concentrating on LAN documentation, administration of user-related data, creating and distributing new operating systems and application software to servers and to clients, and maintaining the LANs.

The principal goals of this chapter are to:

- Address LAN management functions.
- Assess the present status of implementation.
- Define information demand.
- Determine the appropriate instruments for each function.
- Recommend how instruments should be allocated to functions.
- Define appropriate human-resource profiles for supporting LAN management functions.

Configuration Management of Local Area Networks

LAN configuration management is the focal point of all other LAN management functions, providing actual configuration details and receiving change requests. Figure 3.1 illustrates how information is exchanged with the other functions.

Configuration management is fragmented in most corporations at this time. There are different files or databases that maintain attributes of object groups such as modems, applications, multiplexers, hubs, repeaters, bridges, routers, switches, servers, workstations, and so on. The standards may help, assuming they don't give contradictory recommendations. The closest help is expected from SMI (structured management information) and MIB (management information base). In particular, MIB I, MIB II, RMON, and specific MIBs are gaining support as SNMP penetrates the LAN fault management area. For successful LAN configuration management, three information areas are relevant:

- Attributes of each managed object
- Up-to-date connectivity data
- Status of managed objects

In the following sections, the main functional areas of LAN configuration management are outlined in some depth.

Inventory control and topology service.   Inventory and topology service are concerned with maintaining an accurate inventory of hardware,

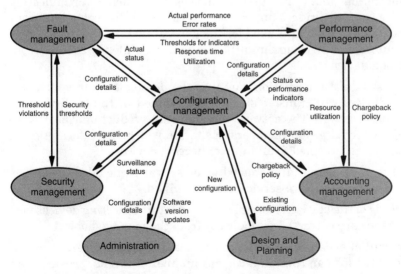

Figure 3.1   Central role of configuration management.

software, and circuits as well as with the ability to change that inventory in a smooth and reliable manner in response to changing service requirements. Configuration management affects LAN designs, performance issues, and even LAN security.

At present, inventory information is segmented, stored usually in flat files, and not organized by WANs, MANs, or LANs. Furthermore, there's no real separation between network management and systems management of LANs. In most cases, the guidelines from standards organizations in terms of managed objects and their attributes could not be taken into consideration.

One of the most basic issues for the LAN administrator is maintaining system configuration maps. *System configuration* is the list of system parameters showing who has access to given network software and given databases. While most LAN operating system software gives the administrator the ability to add, delete, and modify system configuration parameters, it typically provides little functionality in monitoring system configuration. The usual content of the inventory database may include:

- Details of addressable devices of any type on the network. A name is assigned to each device address, and the record includes the type and location of the device, a contact and phone number at the device location, and a history of device service, problems, and repair.

- Details of the configuration of all interconnection devices. The records in the database are automatically updated whenever the configuration is updated. Updates could be done centrally or locally.

- Information about the filtering database in each interconnecting device, such as bridges and routers. If the centrally located network management system is used for the general update, the results may be automatically copied into the configuration files of the interconnecting devices.

- Access control information, defining the destinations to which certain devices can transfer data, is maintained in the configuration database, as well. The network management product may be used to update access group memberships, after which the information is automatically copied to all interconnecting devices.

- Status of all essential managed objects. Status includes in-service, out-of-service, back-to-service, and undefined.

- Records of the statistics for network and interconnecting devices performance are extracted periodically from the managed objects.

- A record of events is reported to the network management product. The event log can contain a certain number of events, providing an audit trail in case of network problems.

- All trouble tickets, including their subjects, symptoms, originator, and contents.

The relationships within managed objects that are maintained by this function are extremely complex. Very often, inventory is included as well. Figure 3.2 displays these relationships (Linnel 1994) using various dimensions such as

- Suppliers
- Products
- Maintenance
- Sites
- Divisions
- Purchase
- Users
- Configurations

The recommendations from various standards bodies detail three areas:

1. Attributes of objects with static information, including names, addresses, parameters settings, location, electric parameters, and so

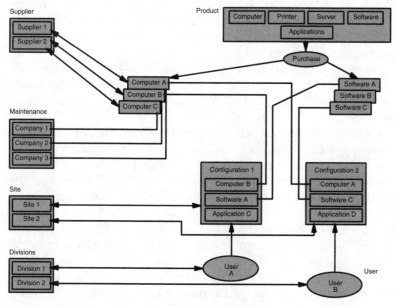

Figure 3.2   Complex relationships in inventory control.

on. Table 3.2 shows an example as recommended by the Network Management Forum.

At the most detailed level, protocol alternatives are addressed by the OSI layers, individually. Network-layer protocol options may include the following characteristics: complete source routing, partial source routing, record of route, quality of service, padding, segmentation, lifetime, aging, PDU size, and congestion notification.

2. Connectivity data indicating the topology; sometimes alternate routes are included as well. These data are extremely important for internetworked LANs using either spanning-tree or source-routing algorithms. Connection parameters are most frequently maintained at the network layer. These connection parameters may include inactivity timer, retransmission timer, persistence timer, window timer, bound-on-reference timer, time to reassign after failure, time to wait for reassignment, supervisory timer for connection establishment, supervisory timer for connection release, window size, maximum number of retransmission, checksum option setting, etc. The items to be included depend on the specifics of the installation.

3. Dynamic indicators that represent the status and help identify problems; these indicators are the bridges to fault management. Usually, status, service-level, use, and throughput indicators are included.

The management information base (MIB) of SNMP has received a lot of attention recently. MIB conforms to SMI for TCP/IP-based internets. While the SMI is equivalent for both SNMP and OSI environments, the actual objects defined in the MIB are different. In fact, the internet SMI and the MIB are completely independent of any specific network management protocol, including SNMP.

The current SNMP MIB is divided into four areas: system attributes (MIB I and II), private attributes (proprietary vendor extensions), experimental attributes (tested objects), and directory attributes (future use).

MIB I includes eight functional groups for approximately 160 managed objects: system, interfaces, address translation, Internet protocol, Internet control-message protocol, transmission-control protocol, user-diagram protocol, and exterior-gateway protocol. MIB II adds two more functional groups of transmission media and SNMP statistics.

The MIB is a virtual store of information contained within a managed device—also known as the SNMP agent. This information base is made up of objects consisting of name, syntax, and encoding information. The name is called the *object identifier* and is unique for each object. Syntax is the means by which a value, such as the number of packets sent, is displayed. Syntax types include counter, gauge, object string, network address, and integer. MIB II specifies a new type of

TABLE 3.2 Attributes of Objects

Class name: Equipment

Class definition: A physical unit. Equipment may be nested within equipment, thereby creating a parent/child relationship. A facility is supported by equipment at each end. Equipment may also connect or terminate circuits.

Equipment includes telecommunication systems that provide a service to an end user, the management systems that are used to manage such systems, and the end-user hosts and terminals. Equipment also includes physical units of functionality within these systems (e.g., CPU).

Data elements:
Equipment type
Equipment ID
Equipment alias
Equipment status
Equipment release
Parent equipment ID
Child equipment IDs
Location ID
Network IDs
Customer IDs
Provider IDs
Service IDs
Vendor IDs
EMS IDs (= equipment IDs)
Contact IDs
Effective time

Class name: Facility

Class definition: A physical connection between equipment in two different equipments without any intervening equipment. A facility is geographically distributed functionality and excludes the equipment within the associated equipments. The function of a facility is to support the transport of circuits (0 or more).

Data elements:
Facility type
Facility ID
Facility alias
Facility status
Endpoints (= 1 or if known, 2 equipment IDs)
Network IDs
Vendor ID
Effective time
EMS IDs
Contact IDs

Class name: Circuit

Class definition: A logical point-to-point connection between two end equipments that traverses one or more facilities and possibly one or more intermediate pieces of equipment. Circuits may be simple or complex. A simple circuit is supported by two end pieces of equipment and an interconnecting facility. A complex circuit is supported as well by intermediate equipments and additional facilities. In general, a complex circuit consists of an ordered sequence of (1) less complex circuits of the same bandwidth and (2) associated cross-connects within any intermediate equipments.

A parent/child relationship may also exist between circuits in that a circuit may share the bandwidth of another circuit.

TABLE 3.2   Attributes of Objects (Continued)

Data elements:
Circuit type
Circuit ID
Circuit status
Circuit alias
Circuit bandwidth
Endpoints (= 2 equipment IDs)
Facility IDs (1 or more)
Parent circuit ID
Child circuit IDs
Component circuit IDs (for complex circuits)
Cross-connect IDs (for complex circuits)
Circuit group ID
Network ID
Customer ID
Provider ID
Service IDs
Effective time
EMS IDs
Contact IDs

object string called a *display string,* which allows a string of information to be displayed to an operator without requiring the management system to execute the string. The encoding mechanism converts machine code into English, allowing a programmer or network administrator to interpret information that the network management station is collecting. The MIB adheres to the American National Standards Institute's ASN.1 Basic Encoding Rules. The encoding specifies whether an object is designated read only, read write, write only, or not accessible. In addition, status information specifies whether an object is mandatory, optional, obsolete, or decremented.

The SNMP group of MIB II contains new object identifiers that provide statistical information about network performance to the network administrator. The objects allow the NMS (network management station) to track the amount of management traffic being responded to by a device. Parameters such as the number of SNMP packets into and out of a device, the number of packets with bad community names, number of packets that didn't conform to ASN.1 encoding specification, and the total number of requests for information are provided by the SNMP group. Having this type of information on hand is becoming increasingly important as the size and complexity of networks increase exponentially. SNMPv2 includes a further MIB (called M2M) to facilitate manager-to-manager communication.

MIB II helps find the common denominator between SNMP agents of different companies. At least the "system" branch of MIB has to be the same. Vendors augment their MIBs with specific attributes. In this case, there are two important comments: the SNMP manager has to take advantage of these extensions, and vendors have to talk to each other and try to agree on additional standards for the "private" areas. In any case, the configuration data builds the basis for documentation systems.

SNMP-oriented platforms offer configuration and topology services in two different ways: the discovery function identifies all managed objects with valid IP addresses on the LAN; the mapping function goes one step further and displays the actual topology of the LAN. Figure 3.3 shows both alternatives.

Continuous monitoring in remote LAN segments requires a large number of indicators that are not included in the MIB I and II recommendations. RMON MIB provides the missing gap for this support by enabling monitored and analyzer data to be sent to the SNMP management station.

RMON MIB defines the next generation of network monitoring with more comprehensive network fault diagnosis, planning, and performance tuning features than any current monitoring solution. The RMON MIB for Ethernet and Token Ring is organized into nine groups, including segment statistics, history, alarms, hosts, hosts top N, traffic matrix, filters, packet capture, and events. Each agent need only implement any one group to conform with the standard. Thus, customers of

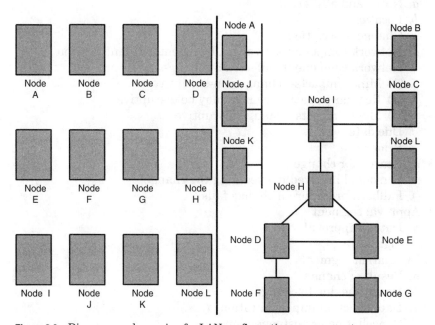

Figure 3.3 Discovery and mapping for LAN configuration management.

RMON MIB agents need to carefully determine the features they desire and seek to verify the existence of those features in actual products. Leading manufacturers of LAN monitors, analyzers, and test equipment are expected to support the new standard. Additional RMON MIBs are under development (also for ATM switches and WANs).

More examples of documentation alternatives will be given in the section on cable management.

Change management.   Changes can't be avoided in present local area networks. Well-organized change management procedures guarantee knowledge of the actual status of the configuration database. Thus, long procedures within fault management processes may be completely avoided.

It's recommended that you use a very formal procedure. Part of this procedure is meeting the change coordinator's demand for information. For scheduling and evaluating changes, the following information is needed by network configuration management:

1. Change coordinator segment
   a. Identification of the change
   b. Change number
   c. Date of request
2. Requester segment
   a. Name and affiliation
   b. Location
   c. Change description
   d. Network components involved, by inventory identification
   e. Network components affected by change
      (1) Minor impacts—change nondisruptive
      (2) Regular impacts—change may be disruptive
      (3) Major impacts—change disruptive
   f. Due date
   g. Priority
   h. Reason for change
   i. Personnel involved in executing the change
   j. Fallback procedure if change fails
3. Approval segment
   a. Date of approval
   b. Signature
4. Evaluation segment
   a. Result of change
   b. Downtime due to change
   c. Date of actual implementation
   d. Cancellation or postponement

Usually, this information is provided and updated by using inventory control products. After evaluating the information provided, approval is issued, unless objections are stated. The approval contains the accurate schedule and responsibilities (e.g., installation or software group). More frequently, single changes may invoke a chain of additional change requests for related LAN components. After execution, the documentation should still be completed, including updates in the inventory and vendor files, or in the configuration database.

Change management requires very complex relationships between functions, platforms, and human resources. The most important are as follows:

- *Prechange planning.* It assesses a change request and evaluates the impacts on other components.

- *Availability.* It schedules change-related outages and analyzes impacts on service-level agreements.

- *Preparing all the necessary documentation for executing the changes.*

- *Documentation of changes for production.* Includes scheduling, approvals, and meeting-related reports.

- *Updates of all databases and data files after successful changes.*

- *Historical analysis.* It determines who has made the changes, analyzes failure rates, execution times, and impacts on other components.

Figure 3.4 characterizes this complexity.

Change management products must meet the following criteria:

- Support electronic exchange of change request documents.
- Provide an audit trail and assist in backout.
- Significantly reduce paper flow, such as program listings, approvals, and recovery instructions.
- Support multiple users on multiple platforms, such as MVS, Unix, OS/400, OS/2, Windows, and VM.

Version control is related to change management and software distribution. Version control tracks the evolutionary history of changes to components of a software system (Linnel 1994). It may be considered as a subset to change management that applies specifically to the development environment. Archives contain the current copy of a file along with information tracing back to the original copy of the archived file. Archives contain the following:

- Changes made to a file

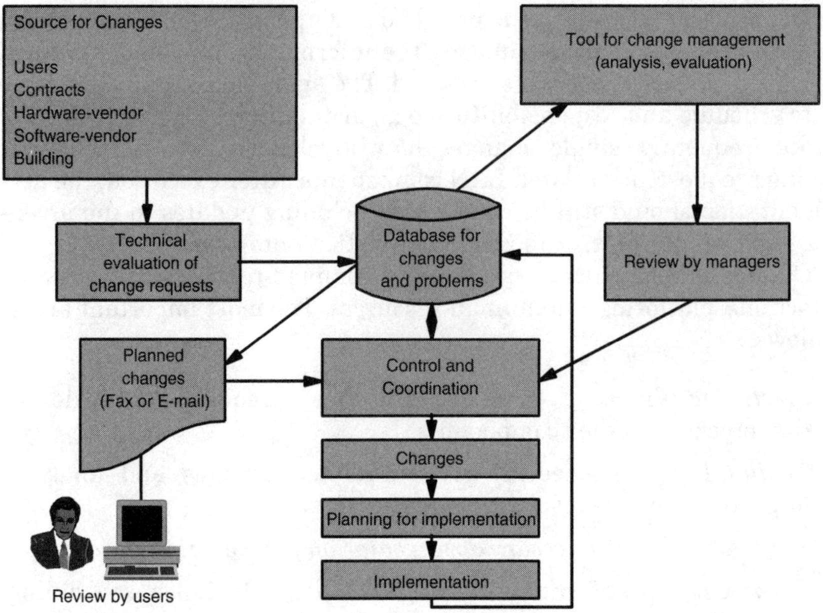

Figure 3.4   Process of change management.

- Description of the changes
- Date, time, and other related change information

  The life cycle of software usually includes four phases:

- Development of software
- Quality assurance
- Acceptance tests
- Production

In terms of selecting the right instrument to support version control, it is very important to have rapid access to all information related to current and history versions. Information is significant during backup and disaster recovery.

Naming and addressing.   Naming and addressing are not always considered part of configuration management. Most frequently, they're considered granted by the services of a LAN's operating systems. This is actually true, because LAN operating systems vendors provide utilities for users and administrators. Users usually identify their service needs by names that are translated by the NOS into addresses. This translation is becoming increasingly complex and complicated for interconnected LANs. Vendors are expected to "hide" the internal processes from LAN users. Leading vendors, such as Novell, Banyan, Microsoft, IBM, Artisoft, and 3COM, are currently addressing the need for improvement.

The principal features of advanced name services are as follows:

- Location transparency.

- No need to know the server's name to log in.

- Centralized log-in helps access.

- No need for separate log-ins to multiple servers.

- Message exchanges at the symbolic level.

- No need to update servers separately to add a user to the network.

- Utilities provide reports on network configuration across server boundaries.

- No need to know which server a resource is on to access it.

From a LAN management point of view, it's important to do the following:

- Offer transparency.

- Provide asset management capabilities.

- Access the database where names and addresses are uniformly identified.

- Help network administrators in giving unique names and addresses to components.

- Integrate conversion capabilities into LAN-internetworking devices.

- Learn about the abilities of bridges, brouters, routers, and gateways to interpret names and addresses.

TCP/IP is emerging as the protocol stack of choice for interconnecting LANs. In such internetworks, the following parameters are used for supporting configuration management.

1. IP address that can be hard coded or obtained via one of the three protocols (Huntington-Lee 1991):
   a. BOOTP
   b. Reverse Address Resolution Protocol (RARP)
   c. Dynamic RARP (DRARP)
2. Entry gateway addresses that are usually hard-coded
3. Name server location that's usually hard coded

4. Host or processor name that's hard-coded or obtained by using a boot procedure; configuration data can be downloaded via BOOTP

Some of the SNMP-based products can graphically depict the actual LAN configuration. This feature is very helpful for improving integrity between configuration and fault management. In most cases, however, the SNMP manager station can't provide the desired support for inventory and change management.

Asset and cable management.   During the last few years, a number of computerized cable management (CMS) products have become available to better manage equipment. Because of overcrowded conduits, lack of standard cabling for data processing equipment, and excessive changes, customers have started to request the routine installation of standard media. Standard media are expected to support both voice and data communications. The use of standard media has to be combined with a powerful documentation and reporting system. Basically, there are three choices for improving the quality of cable management: (1) use a product that fits into the environment without any customization needs; (2) abandon the company's own strategy and outsource cable management to vendors; or (3) design, develop, and implement a system.

When evaluating CMS systems, there are several features that are essential. The ability to track cables and cable pairs end-to-end is the most basic capability of a good CMS. The system should be able to display cable records from their originating PBX or computer ports through several levels of patching, cross-connect hardware, and finally to the end-user's desk. The system should explicitly display information, including individual cable numbers, the location of cable terminations on main and intermediate distribution frames, and cross-connect between lateral and riser cables. The system should also be able to relate this information to user and department names or room and telephone extension numbers.

This capability enables a system administrator to quickly identify available riser pairs, spare station cables, and available equipment ports. Moves, changes, and troubleshooting can be accomplished faster if this information is accurate.

It's also important that a CMS system have the capability to automatically generate information, such as on-screen cable trace, bill of quantity, cableway analysis, cable route, cable usage, cableway accommodation, cable numbers, terminations, and cross-connects. This feature is overlooked in most CMSs, which require the user to manually enter these data for each individual cable run. In a small installation, this is not a major data entry problem. But it's not practical for large organizations with a lot of move-and-change activity, or when purchasing a CMS in anticipation of managing a new installation.

If the CMS can generate detailed cable information automatically, it can be used to guide installers during the placement of new cables. With this feature, the user can actually begin to manage the cable plant as it's being built.

If purchasing a system to automate an existing plant, however, this feature will be of little use initially. The user will still probably have to go through the exercise of data entry. In the long run, however, it will save time and aggravation when installing new cables.

Scanning existing drawings would accelerate this process. During this process, paper-based documentation is converted into electronic form. Rather than manually digitalizing or re-creating an entire drawing, scanners read the raster images into the system. The scanned drawing can be used as is, or parts can be changed and new information added. Scanned images can be referenced in the nongraphic relational database, since attributes can be assigned to those images. Thus, scanned raster images can be converted into intelligent objects with database attributes. Using CAD capabilities, scanned raster images can be combined with vector images. In order to save storage, use standard output formats, including run-length code (RLC), Tagged Image File Format (TIFF), or CCITT recommendations for maximum compression. CADSCAN is a widely used solution for scanning cabling (Isicad 1991).

It's important that the format is compatible with other existing formats in the cable management area. Typically, these systems tie the user into a particular numbering or termination scheme, generally the way the telephone company did it in the past (Nuciforo 1989).

The chosen system should also be able to manage the attached equipment as well as the cable plant itself. The system should enable the user to have telecom equipment (both in-use and spare), including active and available equipment ports, location and status of end-user equipment such as telephones, terminals, and modems, as well as pending equipment orders.

A CMS system should be able to generate customized management reports. Hard-copy reports should be available from the CMS, detailing particular aspects of the telecom system. These include cable placement schedules showing the location of individual cables; riser cross-connect reports showing pair availability; work orders for adds, moves, and changes; and other management reports. Most CMSs have some report-generating capability, since it's inherent in all database management packages.

Your CMS system should have the ability to manage a wide variety of media. This important CMS feature is too often overlooked during product evaluation. The user should be able to manage different types of media, including associated equipment, termination, and cross-connect hardware.

Almost all users have, and will continue to have, multiple types of media installed in their facilities. It would be counterproductive to buy one CMS for managing unshielded twisted pair and a separate system to manage the other media. The CMS chosen today must be flexible enough to support media that the user may install in the future.

The ability to manage the facility as well as the cable is an essential CMS system feature. The need for this capability is directly attributable to the market movement toward decentralized systems. The distance limitations of LANs and other distributed systems require up-to-date records of telecommunication closet sizes and locations; the sizes, lengths, and quantity of conduits and cable ties between equipment rooms; and the available riser space.

Most computerized cable management systems don't adequately provide this information, and some vendors have ignored the requirement altogether. There are several vendors who have tried to address this issue by integrating computer-aided design packages with the CMS.

Cable management software systems can manage a variety of wiring resources, including data, voice, LAN, and, in some cases, HVAC and control cables. Ideally, the software should perform the following functions (Rothberg 1991):

- Cable and path identification
- Cable route presentation
- Assignment of cable facilities and routes
- Tracking conduit "fill" and usage
- Identification of unused cable facilities
- Equipment inventory for attached components
- Feasibility check during planning
- Proactive troubleshooting
- Tracking service order activity
- Maintenance of trouble report database
- Mechanisms for management reporting and operation reporting

Cable management systems use a variety of database resources. These relational database systems provide superior flexibility because they can use structured queries to construct different views of the information. In the case of a server-resident database in a multiuser environment, the system should also facilitate remote procedure calls (RPCs), minimizing the amount of data to be transmitted and the client workstation's processing requirements.

The database software is expected to work with the CAD portion. The LAN designer uses the CAD half to locate equipment and to establish cable routes. The facilities designer responsible for planning office space and infrastructure can use the graphics part to locate walls and furniture. Once the physical design is complete, the designer can work with the LAN administrator to locate workstations and servers, patch panels in racks, put file servers in closets, and map the cable paths between equipment. The LAN designer then uses the database half to connect the equipment in the design. After the design satisfies both parties, work orders are printed by the CMS.

The documentation of the principal layout helps both troubleshooters and LAN designers. (Figure 3.5 shows the physical layout of LANs in various buildings. Table 3.3 documents a design cable schedule. Figure 3.6 details the wiring sequence of interconnected token rings.)

The physical layout and port allocation of wires help to centralize the status updates via software techniques that are part of LAN management applications. There's a growing trend towards alliances between manufacturers of wiring hubs and other LAN components, such as NICs, bridges, and routers. Figure 3.7 shows an example, with a wiring hub in the middle of managed objects.

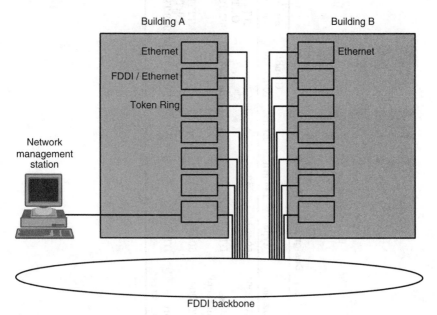

Figure 3.5   Physical layout of LANs.

TABLE 3.3 Design Cable Schedule

Cable no.	Cable type	Length	End	Gland/ connector	Equipment number	Equipment description	Location drawing no.
OGTX0001	50core	43	A	N	TYTMDF	Telephone—main distribution frame	North section layout M
			Z	N	OGTIDF	Telephone—intermediate distribution frame	North section layout M
Status markers	DTR				Route T910 T902 T901 0902 0901		
ORTX0001	50core	42	A	N	TYTMDF	Telephone—main distribution frame	North section layout M
			Z	N	ORTIDF	Telephone—intermediate distribution frame	North section layout M
Status markers	DTR				Route T910 T903 T904 0904 0903		

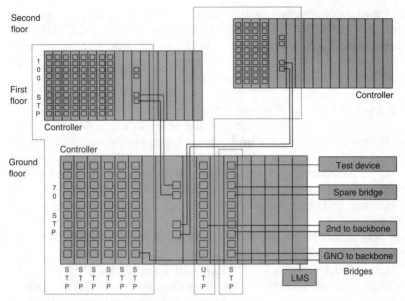

Figure 3.6 Wiring of an interconnected token ring.

In order to facilitate easy and fast access to cabling documentation, it's recommended to convert textual and graphical data into hypertext and to use powerful storage devices (e.g., jukeboxes) for storing hypertext. It's expected that hypermedia will become an essential part of help-desk instrumentation.

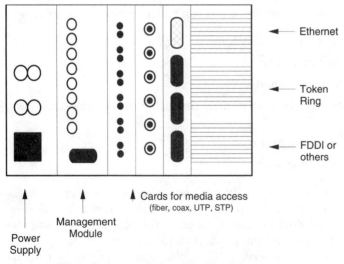

Figure 3.7 Wiring hub example from Bay Networks.

Asset and cable management systems play an even more important role in LAN management. Due to the fact of combining CAD/CAM, database, and LAN management platform capabilities, they may become the core of integrated LAN management solutions. Leading applications will be addressed in Chap. 5.

Backup and archive.   LAN components are becoming increasingly reliable, but outages cannot be ignored. In order not to lose productive work, different solutions are under consideration. The use of warm or cold redundancy in the form of built-in spare parts has been popular for a long time. Examples for this case will be shown in the fault management segment. In order to avoid more serious consequences of outages, certain components of LANs, such as principal servers, are backed up.

It is very difficult for the LAN manager of an enterprise network composed of multiple LANs that use different network operating systems and support various workstations with disparate file formats to find a single product that backs up everything. Instead, LAN managers are forced to bring multiple LAN backup software products into their environment, and then act as their own integrators to make sure all that software works with a common set of storage devices.

In cases of disasters, complete LANs had to be backed up by completely different systems: usually different sites of the enterprise or different companies are taking over the production. Backup copies of principal LAN components are also in this case key to rapid recovery from disasters. Disaster recovery will be addressed in the fault management segment.

Backup status of present solutions can be characterized as follows:

- Defective, irregular, or no backup
- No backup administrators
- Backup strategy obsoleted
- Different backup systems and methods for mainframes, servers, and PCs
- No safekeeping of backup media
- Infrastructure duplication

LAN backup software typically runs on either a server or workstation, although there are a few packages that still run on a mainframe. The backup storage devices are attached to the platform running the software. In this respect, a tight connection to hierarchical storage management (HSM) can be observed. HSM is a solution to the continuous maintenance of the enterprise storage. Data files have three statuses:

- *Online.*   Files are likely to be used.

- *Active.*   Files are likely to be requested within a short period of time.

- *Inactive.*   Files have not been requested for a longer time interval.

Criteria are set by the LAN administrator using file reference tables.

Each backup approach has its pros and cons. Determining whether server-, workstation-, or mainframe-based backup will fit depends on the overall backup strategy of the enterprise. The server-based method means backup hardware is attached to the server's bus. The software then runs as a process on the server, sometimes being just one of the many processes the server is running. Alternatively, an entire server can be dedicated to running LAN backup software only. The server-based backup approach also requires the use of a LAN backup console, typically a workstation that is attached to the server. The console is used to control the backup process. The key advantage of server-based backup is security, since the physical access to a server is generally more restricted than access to a workstation. A secondary advantage is speed. But the speed advantage is limited when the server is used to pull files off other servers and workstations across the network. The disadvantage of server backup is the possibility of crashing the server during the backup process. This disadvantage is somehow alleviated if a server is dedicated to the backup process.

Workstation-based LAN backup systems have speed limitations, because all the files come across the network from local servers, remote servers, and from other workstations. The workstation in charge of backup logs into the network as a user with high-security clearance. The advantage is much less process overhead on a server than running it directly on the server. Thus, if necessary, restoration and backup can be scheduled for productive hours without degrading the overall performance. Increased network traffic can, however, slow the response time for LAN users.

The third alternative is the use of a mainframe to run LAN backup. In this case, the mainframe becomes a superserver that offers access to mass-storage devices. This is a good option for companies who want to redefine the role of mainframes in a client/server environment.

In order to find the right product, a series a questions have to be evaluated first. The most important ones are as follows:

- Support of manual or unattended backup?
- How many different LANs must be backed up?
- What needs to be backed up—servers only, workstations only, or both servers and workstations?

- Do sensitive and nonsensitive data need to be separated during backup?
- Backup of open files?
- Support of scripting?
- Support of data compression?
- How much time is there to perform the backup?
- Where in the network the information will be stored?
- What kind of backup media should be used?
- Does someone need to monitor the backup process? Is SNMP applicable for this purpose?
- Is concurrent device support required?
- Support of housekeeping of the backed up files?
- Site of the backup system—can multiple sites be supported?
- What is the bandwidth requirement of the backup solution?
- What priority schemes can be supported?
- Is automated repetition of the backup process supported when the first backup attempt has failed?
- Do connections to industry robots exist?

Backup requires very strong administration. Reporting features belong to this requirement. The following reports may play a key role in administering backup files:

- *Backup overview.* All databases and files with a backup version are listed. The same report can identify databases and files without backup. This second list should be periodically reviewed to determine whether the lack of backups would cause security risks to the enterprise.
- *Media report.* It offers an overview about all the media that store backups. Also the location of backup copies is included.
- *History report.* This report outlines the history of backups. Information on time stamps, validity, and expiration dates are included.
- *Interval report.* It offers an overview about all backup processes for selected sites, media, servers, workstations, and applications for a definite period of time.
- *Exceptional report.* It concentrates on errors causing the backup process to break down.

There are two basic backup and restore solutions. (1) The *centralized approach* leverages

- Personnel, operations staff
- Peripherals, high quality and well maintained
- Procedures, data management and recovery

(2) The *user-controlled software backup options* offer

- Flexible scheduling
- Free choice of backup intervals
- Free choice of full, incremental, and selective backups
- Free choice of implementing backup functions, such as utilities, graphical interfaces, and directories

Directory services. It's very unlikely that integrated configuration databases will be supported soon. But users still must administer their local area networks. As mentioned earlier, vendors are working on links between existing data files and databases using X.500 as standardized service.

This function is intended to provide a more or less temporary solution for accessing and updating LAN-configuration, management-related information stored in various systems, databases, and files. These systems could be network elements or network element management systems that maintain data about specific objects they control and manage, or applications that run on a variety of processors and operating systems. Although applications don't control or manage network elements directly, they play an integral part in managing information about these elements.

The directory service is needed to maintain a centralized, logical view of the data stored in the attached network management systems. The data would actually physically reside in many of these different systems. Applications could then be written without regard to a specific database management system. Database calls would simply be made to the directory in a standard format. The directory would then forward the data request to the appropriate system for processing. Each remote system participating in the directory would have to translate the data request into the correct database call for its particular database management system and its schema.

Another illustration of a need for this type of architecture is with interfaces to other customer applications, such as inventory and change management. Many large customers have inventory systems that support the administration of the network elements comprising their corporate networks. There are more than 100 different inventory systems on the market that store data in a multitude of relational and proprietary database management systems. These inventory systems are usually mainframe-based, since they must support upward of 100 simultaneous users. The integrated network management system can't support this type of application, nor can customers be expected to recoup their investments in those systems if it did. They would, however, like the integrated network management system to have the ability to pass configuration information obtained from other network element management systems directly to their inventory systems in realtime. This way, configuration changes would have to be made to only one system accessing the directory, and the update could be propagated to all other systems requiring the data.

The directory service should manage updates to multiple systems. If an update requires records stored in several systems to be updated, some type of integrity locking must be performed on those records in each system. These locks should not be released until confirmation of a successful update has been returned from each system or some time limit threshold has been exceeded. If a successful acknowledgment is received from each system participating in the update, the locks should be released. Otherwise, the update should be aborted and backed out from each of the systems participating in the update.

The directory service is expected to incorporate a security scheme. It should be able to let customers define which terminals, user IDs, and applications can have access to different types of data. It should further define what type of access they can have. The directory service is probably going to implement the emerging OSI standards for directory services (X.500). Although these standards are not yet agreed upon, users should be aware of the progress in this area. OSI is currently working to see how the directory services attributes can be used to support distributed database access.

Role of hubs in configuration management

Hubs are taking the central role in configuring local area networks. Built-in functions of leading manufacturers offer a number of services, including database links and remote configuring LAN components. Examples follow.

Database support. The database is expected to be used locally in the hub. It is not a very extended database with many attributes. Only the most important configuration and fault-management-related data are maintained. Typical attributes include the following:

- Redundancy definitions for alternative configurations
- Inventory of hub components
- Communication data for each hub (name, IP address, MAC address)
- Hub status
- Filter parameter
- Bridge parameter
- Alarm definition
- Thresholds
- Textual comments on ports, cards, power supply

Usually, flat files with proprietary attributes are in use.

Configuring local area networks using the hub. Many vendors support the downline loading of software to support configuration changes. To download firmware, all MAC addresses and all the IP addresses in the various types of networks the hubs are supporting must be unique. The following example uses SmartLink from ADX Fibermux to configure Token Rings. The Status Window offers the following fields for configuration:

- *Max stations in ring.* A read-only field that indicates the number of stations on the ring.
- *Split ring on beacon.* Clicking on this field enables the SmartLink in the selected hub to split the ring when beaconing occurs. A check mark means the ring will be split.
- *Auto beacon isolation.* Clicking on this field enables the Token Ring SmartLink in the selected hub to automatically isolate a beacon condition. A check mark means automatic beacon isolation will occur, as long as the split ring on beacon is also enabled.

Status information is also provided by the following:

- Rings are joined (the ring is whole) or isolated (a beaconing area of the ring is split off).
- Beacon isolation is active (the auto beacon isolation feature is actively isolating a beacon condition) or inactive (beacon isolation is not in use).

Network media modules can automatically identify and correct data paths if there is a failure on media modules or links. Usually, any port to any location can be assigned in the hub. This method provides for more flexibility in setting up redundant data paths. ODS provides redundant devices using transceivers. Modules that are not inherently identified as having redundant pairs can be configured and controlled to provide redundancy. Two ports can be attached to the same location. One port is enabled, the other disabled. Hardware sensors monitor the heartbeat signal of the link. The port enabled and providing the active LAN connection is deemed the *primary port*. The other is called the *secondary redundant port*. If the link fails on the primary port, the secondary port is automatically enabled to reinstate the LAN connection. If the original primary port regains its link integrity signal, the port remains disabled to avoid an oscillating effect between the two ports. Redundant ports can also be configured using SNMP. Network management stations can poll individual Ethernet ports for the MIB variable-receive link. Intelligent decisions can then be taken to enable ports or to reassign them to other backplane segments, without human intervention.

Many vendors go even further and use the hub to control and configure not only Ethernet, Token Ring, FDDI, but also bridges, routers, terminal servers, SNA gateways and ATM switches. There is little doubt that hubs play a very important role in centrally managing complex structures.

Use of MIB PDUs to support configuration management

SNMP MIBs offer a wide choice of raw information that may be processed to support selected configuration management function. The following list (Leinwand 1993) concentrates on selected protocol data units of MIB II that may be processed into meaningful indicators of the configuration management process.

System-group	Information content
sysDescr	Description of system
sysLocation	Physical location of system
sysContact	Person responsible for system
sysName	Name of system

Interface group	Information content
ifDescr	Name of interface
ifType	Type of interface
ifMtu	Maximum datagram through interface
ifSpeed	Bandwidth of interface
ifAdminStatus	Status of interface

IP group	Information content
ipForwarding	If device is set up to forward IP
ipAddrTable	IP adress on device
ipRouteTable	IP routing table

TCP group	Information content
tcpRtoAlgorithm	TCP retransmission algorithm
tcpRtoMin	Smallest TCP retransmission timeout
tcpRtoMax	Longest TCP retransmission timeout
tcpMaxConn	Total TCP connections allowed
tcpCurrEstab	Number of current TCP connections

UDP group	Information content
udpTable	Current UDP ports accepting datagrams

Typical instruments for supporting LAN configuration management

In order to facilitate the work of LAN administrators, several products may be considered for use. Generic groups of products include databases, document managers, document/file organizers, configuration trailing tools, real-time user tracking products, front ends or platforms, audit trail utilities, and disk usage utilities.

Databases. These are used for relational or object-oriented storage of LAN configuration data. Usually, these products are well known and widely used for other purposes. Population of the database is the responsibility of the customer and/or of the vendor. These types of databases are more frequently associated with LAN managers than with LAN agents. Such databases will probably be increasingly considered, as MIB implementations proliferate. At the moment, most MIBs use flat files. Databases are expected to work with CAD software in order to provide powerful cable management capabilities.

Document managers. These help end users locate files and documents by the use of symbolic names. With document managers, users need to know only basic information to locate a file; users can call up a file by author, subject, project name, or creation date. Users can search any field to find a file anywhere in the network.

Several document managers also load the software that created the file, allowing the recipient user to work on the document. Other document managers can work with E-mail systems. Frequently, they're combined with drawing products by allowing mutual information exchange.

Document/file organizers are very useful when many people need to access a document. These systems also act as front ends, since they insulate users from the complexities of the directory structure.

Configuration trailing tools. These instruments are inserted into a server or workstation, and automatically read the configuration of that unit, printing out an inventory of disk drives, I/O ports, graphics adapter boards, and software, including operating systems and applications.

The first step in collecting network information is to determine who is using the network and when. In instances when all users must log off or be logged off before initiating a backup, a real-time user tracking tool is useful.

Real-time user tracking tools. These tools provide value-added functions that go beyond the listing of active users generally available from the LAN network operating system. Some of these value-added features include graphical floor plans, identification beyond bridges and routers, and sorting capabilities.

Front ends. These are menu-creation programs that make the network easier to use by isolating the user from operating system commands. Essentially, front ends allow users to initiate programs and manage files by selecting items from a menu. Some products enhance security management by adding greater password protection.

The best front-end products let the manager design menus from a centralized point and distribute them, rather than having to create menus at each workstation. These products may also include other features such as a screen-blanking utility, software meter, and selected user statistics.

Audit trail systems. These are a key component of security management, although the function can be considered part of accounting management. Audit trail systems provide information on user activity on the LAN. Additionally, these systems can assist in billing management by providing the data needed to charge back usage.

An audit trail system must provide streamlined, useful information. LAN managers may wish to audit only certain users, operations on files with certain extensions or in certain subdirectories, certain types of operations, or certain servers. All file and directory creations, deletions, and renames may need to be reported. A system error log report, listing all system error messages, may be advantageous in order to alert the LAN manager of potential problems.

Disk usage utilities. These are unsophisticated instruments that help to analyze the use profiles of the configuration database server. Such an analysis may help to decide whether to share or dedicate the server. In addition to use indicators, service-related metrics such as queuing time in front of resources may be reported.

Cable and asset management products. These provide the basis to maintain data about the physical infrastructure. They may be extended to include data on software, logical topology, databases, and applications.

Backup tools. These instruments help with continuous, incremental, or full backup, and with the management of backups. Also, archives can be managed with the same tools.

MIB tools. These assist LAN management with populating MIBs and getting the necessary information out of MIBs in the form of standard or ad hoc reports.

Table 3.4 summarizes the typical instruments for configuration management.

Staffing LAN configuration management

LAN administration is a clerical-type activity that requires people who have a combination of clerical and project control skills. The principal responsibilities of LAN administration include the following:

- Administer LAN configuration, including logical, electrical, and physical attributes.
- Maintain LAN database.
- Maintain vendor data.
- Coordinate planning and executing changes.
- Administer names and addresses.
- Define and supervise authorizations.
- Maintain trouble tickets and trouble files.
- Coordinate complex problem solving.
- Help to establish powerful security policy.
- Organize data export and import with central database.

LAN administrators interface with all other groups within LAN management. Outside contacts include users and vendors. Besides a general knowledge of LANs, specific knowledge of databases, file management, and data maintenance is required. Continuing education is also required. A person with a business administration degree may be appropriate for the job.

TABLE 3.4   Typical Instruments of Configuration Management

Databases
Document managers
Document and file organizers
Configuration trailing tools
Realtime user tracking products
Front ends or platforms
Audit trail utilities
Cable and asset management tools
Backup tools
MIB tools

Fault Management of Local Area Networks

Basically, four steps form the prerequisites of successful fault management:

1. Understand the particular LANs used. The following information has to be gathered:

   - Topology
   - Protocols
   - Media
   - Bandwidth
   - Applications
   - Servers
   - Workstations
   - Interconnecting devices

   Figure 3.8 shows how problem data can be collected and processed.

2. Establish a logical procedure for sectionalizing a problem. Problems can usually be determined by moving, replacing, and testing the cables, servers, and workstations or by using a meaningful correlation of events and alarms. These capabilities are provided by the majority of platform products. Empirical techniques such as moving and replacing cables, workstations, and servers are losing importance.

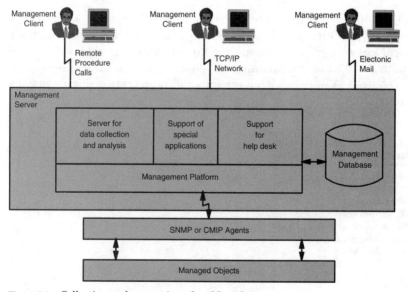

Figure 3.8   Collection and processing of problem data.

3. Apply the proper tools for diagnosing problems that are not immediately obvious after using standard features of the management platform.

4. Educate users and troubleshooters on how to use procedures and instruments.

This chapter addresses only steps 2 through 4. It's assumed that users understand the particular LANs used.

Figure 3.9 shows the fault management process in flowchart form. As a result of trouble calls or monitored messages, events, and alarms, problems in network elements and facilities may be detected, recorded, and tagged. The dynamic trouble-ticketing process, using different agents for ticket opening, status review, consolidation, and ticket closing, is in charge of directing the steps of problem determination. Besides trivial responses on behalf of the help desk, temporary fixes are offered in the form of workarounds and switchovers to spare elements. Problem determination on the second and third level may involve more sophisticated techniques and tools for identifying the nature of the problem and solving it by repair and/or replacement. Prior to restoration of a normal condition, end-to-end tests are recommended. The same or similar tests may be used for proactive fault management of LANs. In the following section, each main functional area of LAN activity is addressed.

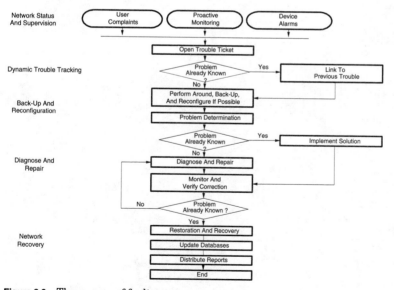

Figure 3.9   The process of fault management.

Status supervision

On the electronics level, monitored status can appear in various forms (Fig. 3.10). Monitors and LAN analyzers are able to convert these signals into meaningful metrics. After conversion, status information may be forwarded to a central LAN management entity. This procedure can be illustrated by the dialogue between SNMP managers and agents. The manager polls the agent MIB and reads the status information that's transmitted to the manager's status database. Network status consists of the vector of the element status, as shown in Fig. 3.11. Such vectors may construct the agent MIB of managed objects. The information in the vector is periodically polled by the management station. The network status may be actually shown using various display devices. Figure 3.12 shows an example using windowing.

Fault detection and alarms

Solicited and unsolicited events help in detecting abnormal operations. Usually, the problem is that there are too many messages generated in an unsolicited manner. If these are not filtered, LAN operating personnel become hopelessly overloaded. The first step is the elimination of irrelevant messages. The second step is to put together related messages to define events. Finally, events will be assigned priorities and/or thresholds. Threshold violations and events of certain priorities will

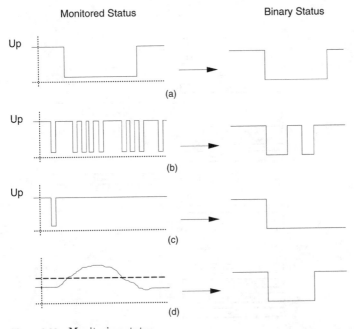

Figure 3.10   Monitoring status.

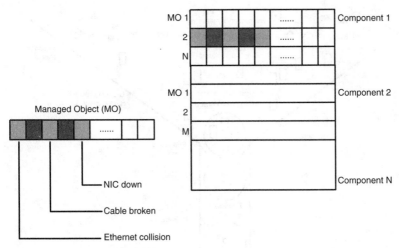

Figure 3.11   Representing LAN status.

trigger alarms. Figure 3.13 illustrates this filtering process. Depending on the protocols used, filtering may be implemented at the agent level (CMIP) or at the manager level (SNMP). The consequences for memory and bandwidth requirements are then completely different. A compromise is on the way using smart agents in a dual role. The preprocess

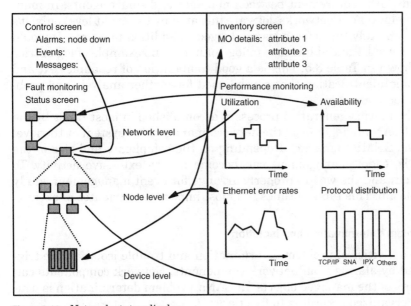

Figure 3.12   Network status display.

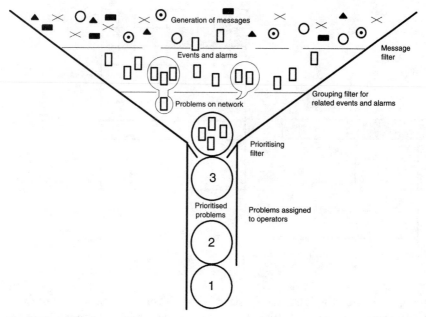

Figure 3.13 Filtering procedure.

data from local SNMP agents is then sent to the central manager. Thus, the implementation cost of agent software is still low, as is the bandwidth requirement between manager and smart agents. In managing local area networks, logs are initiated by the event level only; it's very unlikely that messages are logged in addition to events. It would mean a substantial increase in log volumes. One example of log entries is shown in Table 3.5. This is a good combination of readable text and trouble identification that can be used for further analysis and problem correlation.

The alarms-generation process is accomplished in most LANs by the local LAN manager (e.g., the network management system at the level of the SNMP manager). Depending on the complexity and size of the LANs, event management can become a very extensive activity. To understand the way to properly arrange for event management, study Table 3.6. This table outlines the most important attributes of events.

Problem determination and isolation

The activities of problem determination and trouble isolation are triggered by alarms from network components. Network components can be any of the managed objects. In LANs, problem determination is usually organized according to five tiers.

TABLE 3.5   Event-Log Entry

				Events
12:25:1989	15:37	27	08004e016a81	Local configuration update
12:25:1989	15:23	26	08004e1123f2	Filtering database full
12:25:1989	15:06	25	08004e016d13	Network manager console restarted
12:25:1989	14:43	24	08004e137f04	New root bridge
12:25:1989	14:41	23	08004e4585cb	Bridge port state change
12:25:1989	12:39	22	08004ea46d9e	Device restarted

Tier 1 problems are handled by the LAN help desk. Usually, these are of a nontechnical nature and can be resolved by troubleshooting over the phone. If it's simply a matter of educating end users, 80 to 85 percent of problems can be solved this way. The on-line trouble ticket database can be queried to determine whether the problem has been reported by any other location among the LAN segments and whether there's a known fix. Problem diagnosis is rarely necessary.

Tier 2 problems are handled in part by LAN help desk operators and in part by LAN analysts. These problems comprise about 5 to 10 percent of all problems reported to the LAN help desk and are of too technical a nature to be resolved by the help desk. An example of such a problem is when some unknown problem causes the server to malfunction. The problem diagnosis effort can be considerable.

Tier 3 problems are handled by LAN analysts supporting LAN hardware and software. Problems administered by this group are generally of a critical and complex nature and may require the involvement of

TABLE 3.6   Event Management Overview

Determination of event detection	Event priority
Status change detection	Event effects
Event report generation	Event-type dependent information
Global filtering	■ Alert time
Distribution filtering	■ Received time
Event processor filtering	■ Severity
	■ Alarm type
■ Logging	■ Object class
■ Sampling	■ Object name
■ Status posting	■ Facility type
	■ Equipment type
Event distribution	■ Source
Event types	■ Location
	■ Problem type
■ Configuration events	■ Problem identification
■ Fault events	■ Text message
■ Performance events	■ Alarm identification
■ Security events	■ Correlation
■ Accounting events	■ Owner of alarm

vendor specialists. Problems of this nature comprise only about 3 to 5 percent of all problems and are usually recognized immediately by users or are referred to by LAN help desk. Problem diagnosis requires a considerable human-resource effort and complex instrumentation.

Tier 4 problems are handled by LAN application specialists. If the symptoms indicate that application-related problems are the probable source, trouble tickets are dispatched to these persons. Such problems account for 1 to 3 percent of all problems recorded. Problem diagnosis usually requires a considerable human-resource effort and a lot of time.

Certain tier 5 problems can be handled only by vendors. When the diagnosis points in this direction, trouble records are dispatched to vendors. Electronic data exchange is a viable technique for this purpose. The problem diagnosis effort is considerable, but there's generally a lesser need for human resources. This tier accounts for between 3 and 5 percent of all problems.

In particular, tiers 3 and 4 require very sophisticated troubleshooting and problem-isolation procedures. Table 3.7 shows the logical troubleshooting sequence for CSMA/CD networks. Development of the logical sequence is based on the principle of the progressive search, starting with the most likely error causes (Fig. 3.14).

Advanced help desk tools could be very helpful in this area. Apriori from Answer Systems is using the "bubble up" technology, which suggests the most likely problem causes based on parameters that are unique to the origin of the problem (such as location, hardware or software configuration, and applications) be kept in easily accessible areas of memory. Also case-based reasoning techniques gain in popularity.

Table 3.7 includes isolation checklists for network, node, software, hardware, and hidden-component failures. Also, individual checklists may be of great help in isolating problems. Table 3.8 shows a generic checklist for Token Ring LANs.

In both cases (Tables 3.7 and 3.8), a basic level of fault management instrumentation is assumed. It's extremely important to isolate the problem as quickly as possible and, as soon as possible, get beyond the symptoms to the diagnosis and repair stages. Decision tables and flowcharts may contribute to rapid problem isolation. Following analysis of initial symptoms, specific flowcharts may be involved, as shown in Fig. 3.15 with an entry menu. Even this high-level entry requires the skills and experience of tiers 1 and 2 problem-determination staff. More specific flowcharts address the following:

- Operational problems (Fig. 3.16)
- Backbone problems (Fig. 3.17)
- Interconnecting device problems (Fig. 3.18)
- Workstation problems (Fig. 3.19)

TABLE 3.7   Problem Isolation for CSMA/CD Networks

Network hardware problems
If network hardware has failed, check that:

1. The network software is correct.
2. The network print and file servers are online.
3. The network is not overloaded with traffic.
4. Terminators are in place.
5. End connectors are correctly installed.
6. Barrel connectors are tightly connecting.
7. No coaxial sections are broken.
8. There are no cable breaks, cuts, abrasions.
9. The "state" of Ethernet is not jammed.
10. The gateways and repeaters are functioning.
11. Fan-out units are not jammed.
12. Individual network segments function.
13. Repeated segments are functioning.
14. Gateway segments are functioning.
15. Individual network cable sections are operational.
16. Transceiver tap components are functioning.
17. Transceivers are not jabbering/chattering.
18. Transceiver electronics are operational.
19. There are no software node incompatibilities.
20. Ethernet versions/variations match.
21. There is no outside electrical or radio frequency interference.

If all checks succeed, then you have a hidden component failure.

Network software problems
If network software has failed, check that:

1. The network software is correct.
2. The network is not overloaded with traffic.
3. The "state" of Ethernet is not jammed.
4. Each software node is compatible.
5. Ethernet versions/variations match.
6. The network software is performing tasks.
7. The operating network software is not corrupted.
8. The software is compatible with physical devices.

If all checks succeed, then, you have a network hardware failure or
  a hidden component failure.

Hardware or software problems
First, isolate the location:

1. Apply binary search method or apply sequential search method.
2. Check for failed node/nonoperation.
3. Check the software indicators.
4. Apply the multimeter.
5. Apply the transceiver tester.
6. Attach the time domain reflectometer.
7. Gather statistics and diagnose with the protocol analyzer.

On location:

1. Check to confirm that components are plugged in.
2. Jiggle components in case of short circuit.
3. Check for electrical shorts/breaks.
4. Replace failed components or interchange suspect components.

TABLE 3.7   Problem Isolation for CSMA/CD Networks
(Continued)

Software problems
First, isolate the location:

1. Gather statistics and diagnose with the protocol analyzer.
2. Analyze the network software.
3. Locate failed node/nonoperation.
4. Check the software indicators.
5. Root out nonfunctioning nodes.

On location:

1. Reboot system.
2. Restart software.
3. Replace software.
4. Debug/fix software.
5. Power cycle individual hardware components.

Node problems
If a node has failed, check that:

1. The workstation or node unit is plugged in.
2. The workstation has electrical power.
3. The workstation is functioning.
4. The workstation sees Ethernet and TCP/IP.
5. The transceiver drop cable connections are secure.
6. The transceiver drop cable is correct.
7. The transceiver electronics function.
8. The transceiver tap installation is to specification.
9. The Ethernet controller functions.
10. The Ethernet address is correct.
11. The Internet address is correct.
12. All other nodes are working.
13. Some other nodes are working.
14. The Ethernet versions/variations match.

If all checks succeed, then you have a network software failure,
    a network hardware failure, or a hidden component failure.

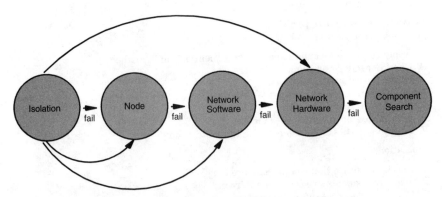

Figure 3.14   The logical LAN troubleshooting sequence.

TABLE 3.8   Problem Isolation Checklist for Token Ring

1. Perform network interface card board diagnostics by using the diagnostics disk.
2. Assess impacts and conflicts with other boards. The easiest way is to insert the cards one by one, starting with the network interface card.
3. Inspect the network interface cards for mechanical failures.
4. Check whether the power supply follows power and fuse standards.
5. Check the wiring hubs by following the procedures recommended by the manufacturers.
6. If both the network interface card and cable pass the test, but the trouble still exists, use other wiring hub ports and retest.
7. Verify that the station inserts in the ring properly by observing indicators provided by the wiring hub manufacturers.
8. Replace cables if necessary.
9. Change media if necessary.
10. Verify that no shorts are between pins of wiring hubs and connectors.
11. Validate the names and addresses using diagnostic programs, network management software, or LAN analyzers.
12. Try to control most of the above from the network management service station—LAN network manager from IBM—or by other products.

Diagnostics, backup, repair, and recovery

As a result of efforts made during the previous phase, LAN troubleshooters at least know where to go to gather more detailed information on the nature of the problem. Statistics show that many problems are encountered with cabling. In particular, cards and wiring must be checked with care.

Cards.   Network interface cards, cables, and other low-level hardware all have an impact on the LAN's operation, performance, speed, and throughput. If interface cards and cables are working properly, you can't expect speeds greater than the rated throughput. If an interface

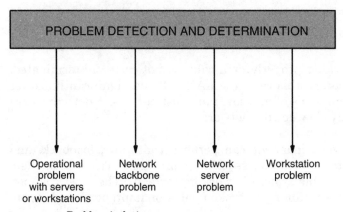

Figure 3.15   Problem isolation entry menu.

Entry point: Operational difficulty with servers or workstations

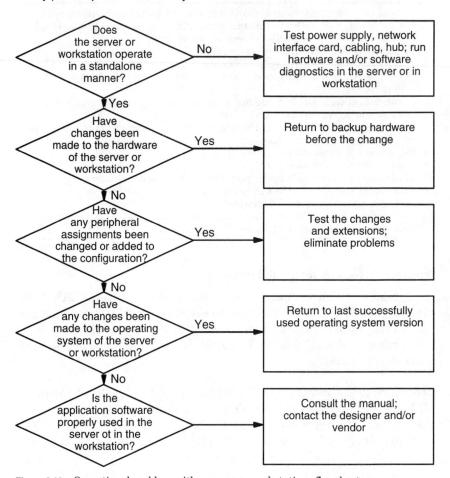

Figure 3.16   Operational problem with servers or workstations flowchart.

card is not working properly or a cable is not correctly terminated, errors may occur. In this case, the LAN will run significantly slower due to retransmissions of mutilated and lost packets. A defective card can significantly slow down a network.

Wiring.   A network manager can perform continuity, loopback, and reflectometry tests to diagnose cabling problems. These tests help ensure that the cable system is working correctly. The most common problem with LAN cabling is broken cable or improper termination.

Entry point: Backbone problem

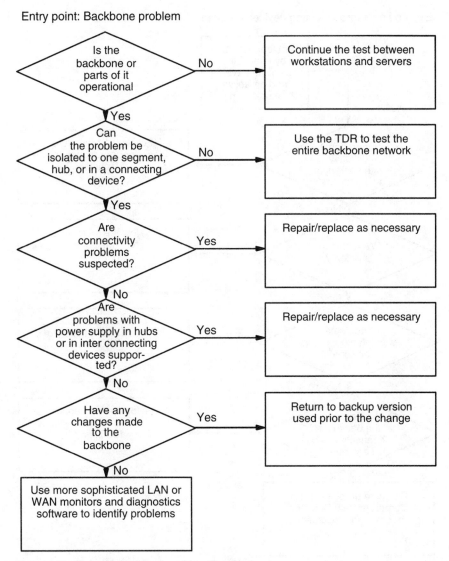

Figure 3.17 Network backbone problem flowchart.

Entry point: Interconnecting devices problem

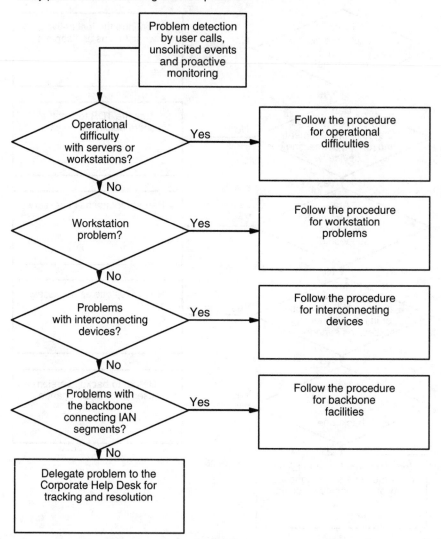

Figure 3.18   Interconnecting device problem flowchart.

Entry point: Workstation problem

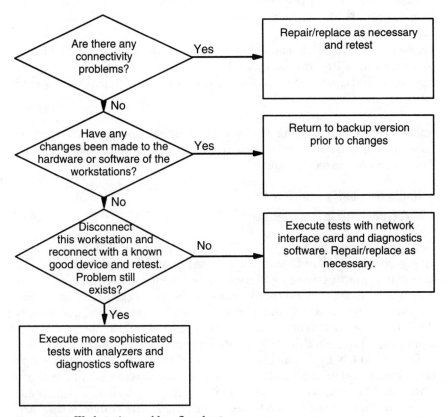

Figure 3.19 Workstation problem flowchart.

Most connectors don't handle movement well and, if left lying on the floor, they may be stepped on and broken. A regular inspection of the cable ends and connectors will help identify defective termination. There's a wide range of tools available for diagnosing cable problems.

For identifying problems, the following instruments may be considered for use:

- Ohmmeters
- Outlet testers for power supply
- Coax connectors, T-connectors, and terminators

- Oscilloscope

- TDR (time domain reflectometer)

Special transmission problems, such as crosstalk and noise, must not be ignored, either.

Crosstalk. Crosstalk is caused by the inductive or magnetic field coupling from one line into another line. It's most pronounced in cables having bidirectional transmission in the same sheath, such as twisted pair.

Noise. Noise is defined as any unwanted signal that enters the transmission line from another source and impairs communication signals. There are two classes of noise:

- Radio frequency interference

- Electromagnetic interference

Fiber-optic-based LANs require different equipment. While they provide significant advantages over conventional LANs, the fiber LAN's design necessitates more sophisticated test equipment. Fiber LAN diagnostic tools must provide comprehensive design verification, including the capability to precisely determine bandwidth, sensitivity, and linearity. These measurements can be performed only with fiber-optic test equipment that includes sophisticated parametric capabilities.

The market is experiencing an influx of test equipment that helps technicians diagnose and maintain a fiber-optic-based wiring system. These instruments vary in complexity from pocket-sized power measuring units to console-type testers. Only those instruments that are optical in nature can make performance measurements on the optical parts of any electro-optical system. Fortunately for electronics test engineers, the few optical instruments used outside research laboratories are relatively simple in design.

Special techniques may be applied in the diagnosis of server outages. In client-server environments, server failures may impact a significantly large number of clients, and this must be avoided. The techniques frequently used include detection of bad disks, mirrored disks, data protection, and transaction logging.

The techniques mentioned may fall under the auspices of fault or security management. Reliable software designs that ensure against data loss in the event of hardware failure are becoming more prevalent on the LAN market. Several server fault recovery methods are currently available (Datapro NM50 1989c):

- *Disk bad-track handling.* Very few disks have no flaws; thus, it's important to provide software that can detect flaws and deal with them transparently.

- *Mirrored disks.* This involves writing data to two separate disk drives so that both drives will contain the same data. In the event that one drive has an error, the alternate drive will continue operating without interruption to the LAN system. But this increases hardware cost.

- *Transaction commit, concurrency, and recovery.* This feature gives an application the capability to protect data files from application failure. By grouping several I/O requests into a single transaction, the operating system will not write the transaction to disk until the application has terminated or issues a commit command.

- *Transaction logging.* This technique is essentially real-time backup, and is a powerful fault management feature. After data is written to disk, the information is echoed to the server's local tape unit. As each I/O is performed on files, the data is written to the tape drive. If there's a system failure, the file state may be recovered by repeating the I/O requests for that file from data written to the tape.

When selecting a means for distributing LAN connections, LAN wiring hubs are becoming the predominant choice of LAN users. As users realize the advantages of the integrated star topology associated with hubs (central access, network management, and space concentration), they're driving vendors to provide more and more devices that are integrated into such hubs. Devices include Ethernet stars, token ring stars, Appletalk stars, FDDI stars, bridges, routers, terminal servers, gateways, and some connectivity devices.

This high level of integration introduces the serious danger of the hub becoming a critical point of possible failure, which could result in bringing down full enterprise networks. Fault management solutions should concentrate on surviving cable plant failures and surviving hub failures.

Surviving cable plant failures. Without sufficient redundancy, a cable that's connecting hubs can disable the entire enterprise network. Prevention of cable failures includes manual or automatic switchover to a redundant link, correlative loop, and continuous idle.

Surviving hub failures. Since active electronics are involved, hubs are more likely to experience failures. Two types of solutions should be implemented to survive hub failures: (1) engineering hubs (power supplies, modular construction, automatic switchover, and decentralization of functions) and (2) network design and implementation methods to plan hub topology with fault tolerance (see Chap. 6 for more details).

In order to increase data integrity, there are several techniques in use. In particular, the Novell environment offers various solutions. The outages of file servers impact LAN operations severely. Novell offers various levels of integrity improvements:

System Fault Tolerant (SFT) I.   In this case, two File Allocation Tables are provided. The tables are implemented on different disk areas. In case of a failure of one directory partition, the second can take over immediately. Figure 3.20 shows this solution. Additional functions include directory checkup, read control, and hot fix of nonreadable disk area.

System Fault Tolerant (SFT) II.   This alternative offers a full duplicate of all data using mirrored disks but still one controller. Writes are executed simultaneously to both disks. In case of disk errors, switchover is automatic; no data are lost. Figure 3.21 shows this solution.

System Fault Tolerant (SFT) III.   This alternative unifies the first two and mirrors the servers. Using this solution, a fully redundant system is available for critical servers. The operating systems are mirrored and functional all the time. The servers are using high-performance Microchannel Architecture (MCA) or Extended ISA (EISA). UPS is part of this configuration enabling the server to continue even in case of power failures. Figure 3.22 shows this configuration of mirrored servers.

In combination with the methods just mentioned, *continuous backup systems* should be considered as well. A continuous backup system is a utility that replicates all changes that are written to a disk as they're made. These systems don't necessarily replace the traditional tape-

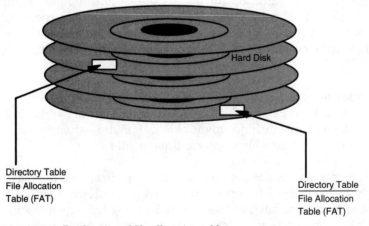

Directory Table
File Allocation
Table (FAT)

Directory Table
File Allocation
Table (FAT)

Figure 3.20   Duplication of file allocation tables.

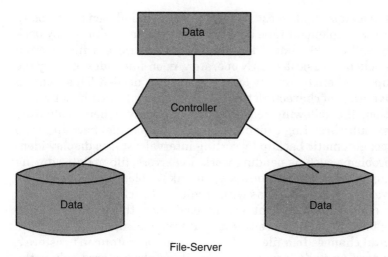

Figure 3.21   Mirroring hard disks.

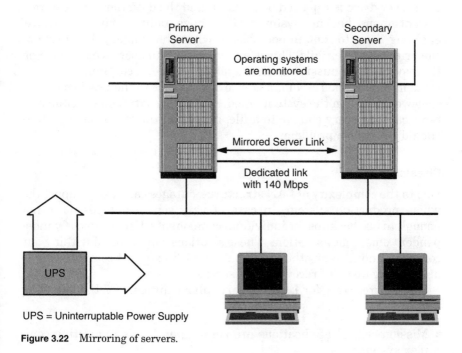

UPS = Uninterruptable Power Supply

Figure 3.22   Mirroring of servers.

oriented backups that most network managers depend on today. Rather, they supplement tape backup. Most off-line products may back up easily and quickly, but if it's necessary to retrieve a file, it often requires help from a skilled LAN operator. An on-line index of every file backed up may help to quickly locate a file when needed. This solution takes advantage of characteristics that are inherent in Unix networks. In addition, the following features are important when evaluating products: multithreading capability supporting parallel backup to the same tape; automatic backup by setting intervals; status display identifying problems such as pending work, I/O errors, file updates during the backup process; and communication link problems.

However, there are problems with traditional backup methods. Such backups often skip files that are in use when the backup routine attempts to copy them. Since traditional tape backup doesn't capture incremental changes to a file as they occur, an operator can't restore a file to its most up-to-date condition. The file can be restored only to the condition it was in at the time of the backup.

In addition, traditional tape backup doesn't provide system fault tolerance. If the server drive fails, the system fails and can't be used until the server drive is repaired or replaced and the data files are restored.

Continuous backup systems often have built-in fault tolerance, enabling them to remain operational when the primary disk drive or the primary server fails. This is a great benefit to users who depend on their systems for mission-critical applications. Also, continuous backup systems enable the LAN manager to restore files to the exact condition they were in when the system failed. And since continuous backup systems capture every change to a file, retrieving the status of open files should never be a problem.

Disaster recovery

Due to the complexity of LAN structures, outages can easily impact the whole production system. In case of very severe outages, it is not enough to use backups for individual components. Use completely independent emergency solutions. These solutions can be found within your company and also at other locations or with external companies who are offering disaster recovery as a service.

Disaster/recovery for LANs is particularly difficult for the following reasons:

- Mission-critical applications are running on LANs requesting complex systems.

- Applications are implemented and executed at decentralized locations.

- Multivendor, heterogeneous systems are used.

- The responsibility is moving from central IS departments to users.

Prior to deciding on a disaster/recovery strategy, the following questions should be answered:

- What is supposed to be covered under "recovery"?
  Which applications are in this category?
  Which databases and files are used by these applications?
  Where are these applications?
  Which processing resources are necessary to run these applications?
  How long does it take to get the backup databases and files?
  Where are the backup databases and files?
  Are recovery procedures available?
  Which networking resources are necessary for recovery?
  What are the data dependencies?
- Which applications could be recovered independently from each other?
- What are the priorities of the recovery sequence?
- What is the estimated duration of the recovery process?
- How can the recovery process be continuously supervised?

There is a very tight connection between disaster/recovery and backup. Figure 3.23 shows a rapid disaster/recovery solution, assuming powerful backup processes are in use. This figure assumes the following:

- Stable files are using the baseline backup.
- One copy identical to the online version can be found in the optical library.

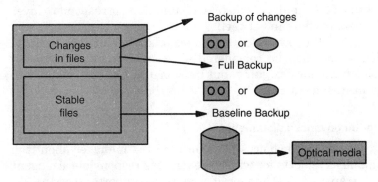

Figure 3.23 Rapid disaster recovery.

- In case of a disaster, the baseline copy will be retrieved first, followed by the changes that can be retrieved from other storage media.

- Backup administration is absolutely necessary in order to find the right backup copies rapidly.

The success of disaster/recovery depends on the following factors:

- Availability of a disaster/recovery plan detailing systems, applications, databases, files, and human resources

- Identification of sites that are responsible for executing disaster/recovery; these could be internal or external

- Very clear description of information flows for critical situations, including human responsibilities

- Identification of sources for system and network maps that should be implemented during recovery by internal or external resources

- Justification of costs of disaster/recovery in light of business risks due to disasters

The cost analysis of disaster/recovery is very important to build. The losses due to disaster must be quantified first. The magnitude depends on the business applications that are not running during fatal outages. The quantification takes time, and complete accuracy can probably not be accomplished. But the range of losses should guide the decision for the right disaster/recovery alternative.

The needs for disaster/recovery are known to suppliers; the problem is, however, that there are not many suppliers who offer this service for local area networks.

In certain cases, LAN analyzers have to be used to identify problems of the higher protocol layers. These instruments actually collect everything that flows through the interface. Depending on the required presentation level, LAN analyzers display results that correspond to layer 4, layer 7, or somewhere in between.

Finally, Table 3.9 shows a few examples of symptoms that indicate failure. This table may be considered—in combination with trouble tickets—as a basis for designing and implementing expert systems to support fault management.

NerveCenter for advanced diagnostics

SNMP agents have two choices for informing the manager about the status of managed objects for which the agent is responsible. An agent can send a trap to the manager if something important occurs. In SNMP implementations this is the exception rather than the rule.

TABLE 3.9   Possible Causes of Failure, According to Symptoms

Symptoms	Probable cause
Performance management	
Slow response	Overloaded segment or network
	Too many taps on a coax segment
	Improper grounding
Collisions	Overloaded segments or network
	Improper grounding
	Too many taps on a coax segment
	Improper shielding from noise
	Drop cable not properly connected
	Bad transceivers
	Mismatched hardware
	Bad tap
	Defective drop cable
Retransmissions	Overloaded segments and network
	Tap probe is not in contact with coax
	No transceiver heartbeat
	Improper shielding from noise
Fault management	
No network service	Overloaded segments or network
	Open break on network
	Open short on network
	Bad tap
	Tap probe not in contact with coax
	File server has broken down
	File server is overloaded
	Systems software fault
Workstation jammed	Overloaded segments or networks
	Drop cable not properly connected
	Defective drop cable
	No transceiver heartbeat
	Bad transceiver
	Systems software fault
	Mismatched hardware
Bad packets	Overloaded segments or network
	Improper shielding from noise
	Bad transceiver
	Transceiver edge connector broken
	Transceiver tap probes broken
	Drop cable not properly connected
	Drop cable has defect
	Bad tap
	Malfunctioning interconnecting device
	Mismatched hardware
File problems	Improper shielding from noise
	Bad transceiver
	Drop cable not properly connected
	Drop cable has defect
	Bad tap
	Systems software fault
	Mismatched hardware

TABLE 3.9   Possible Causes of Failure, According to Symptoms (Continued)

Symptoms	Probable cause
Fault management	
Nodes not responding	Open break on segments
	Open short on segments
	Malfunctioning repeater or other interconnecting device
	Transceiver edge connector broken
	Transceiver tap probes broken
	Mismatched hardware
	Improper shielding from noise

More often, the manager sends a request to the agent to obtain information. Normally, the SNMP manager polls agents for information, relegating agents to a passive role.

In diagnostics, both information alternatives are important. Traps can trigger the initialization of the diagnosis process; polling agents helps to progress with diagnosis. The challenge in using SNMP is to minimize the communication overhead and still obtain all of the information necessary to identify and resolve problems.

NerveCenter from Seagate is an advanced rules-based alarm service that enables the operator to diagnose problems, including faults and unusual traffic conditions. When NerveCenter is fully integrated into management platforms, third-party applications will also be able to take advantage of it. NerveCenter is using a combination of trap messages and polling based on user-defined conditions. The user can configure alarms to filter traps or the results of polls, and then implement corrective actions automatically when predefined conditions occur. Conditions can be set using a graphical user interface. Both simple conditions (such as thresholds) and complex conditions (such as increasing or decreasing values over a specified time interval) can be defined.

Figure 3.24 shows the NerveCenter model.

Automated actions help to circumvent problems. In the case of diagnostics, multiple iterative steps are necessary between NerveCenter and the agents. Sometimes, multiple operators are linked to handle specific situations. NerveCenter offers options to increase the efficiency of diagnostics in the following ways:

- Dynamic selection of monitored and polled elements helps to concentrate on just the managed objects that may be the cause of the problems.

- Property groups allow creation of different classes, such as router, bridge, and hubs. These classes can be used to define the scope of polls and alarms.

NetLabs/NerveCenter

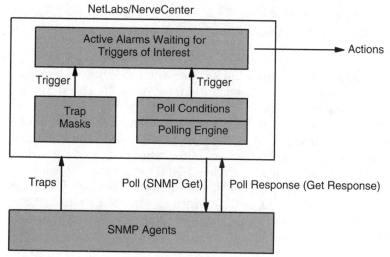

Figure 3.24   NerveCenter model.

NerveCenter can deal with all types of traps, not only those that have been standardized with SNMP. Each vendor has the option of defining traps for their specific needs. These traps send information about a specific device (e.g., hub) from that vendor. Decoding the information sent is the responsibility of NerveCenter.

During diagnostics, the operators define which MIB information should be collected via polling. Any single poll collects information about only one object, except when using smart agents. When a poll is set up (e.g., for hubs), the operator defines its polling rate, trigger names for invoking actions, and poll conditions. Poll conditions consist of one or more relational expressions. To create a relational expression while conducting diagnostics, attributes are selected from the attributes list of the object under consideration. Conditions may be modified during the diagnostics process. Conditions may be chained by multiple expressions into a fewer number of polls. In this way, poll conditions can be created that can automatically evaluate the MIB data in practically any combination. Setting and modifying polling conditions may be driven by the results of previous polls.

NerveCenter can also recognize results originating in RMON probes. In this case, which device is housing the RMON probe is irrelevant.

The actions taken (e.g., audible beeps, displaying information, logging data, invoking applications, sending mail, invoking Unix scripts, turning off polls, issuing SNMP sets, opening/closing trouble tickets, issuing traps) can be specified by the Action Router feature of Nerve-Center. There are two components to the Action Router:

- Rules with the associated actions to take
- Engine that evaluates the status of specific alarms to see if the rules apply

These features are extremely important when diagnostics are conducted in an automated or semiautomated way. In this function, NerveCenter approaches the level of an expert system.

NerveCenter Pro uses behavior models to correlate network conditions and to identify problems. The application can then filter out superfluous events, enabling an administrator to take appropriate action. The application can correlate SNMP events and OpenView OperationsCenter messages from Unix systems and Seagate LANAlert messages from Windows NT and NetWare servers. Notification of correlated events can be sent to any OpenView Network Node manager or OperationsCenter console.

Use of hubs for advanced LAN diagnostics

Hub manufacturers try to integrate fault management applications into their hubs. There is a wide range of examples starting with maps and ending with expert systems such as sophisticated diagnostics.

Network maps. Graphical representation is usually supported for a logical view, physical view, and for hub details. LANVision hub tool is ODS' comprehensive management solution. Its graphical user interface is based on OSF/Motif to provide system-level configuration and resource allocation and for simple point-and-click management of ODS intelligent hubs and other networking components. It assigns users and devices to logical network segments via GUI interfaces dynamically, thus allowing the network manager to focus on configuration, planning, and proactive network management.

Device topology views permit evaluation of the actual port-to-port connections for actual packet paths using Cabletron hubs. In each view, a variety of hub labels such as name, address, and special comments on location may be included and displayed.

An application view helps to dynamically display applications supported by the hub (e.g., routing, bridging, monitoring). The Unified Management View from ODS makes it possible from a single instance of a hub view to configure and to collect status or statistics from Ethernet, Token Ring, and FDDI management cards present in the Infinity hub chassis. It is a new way to view information from multiple MIB lookup tables for different agents. From the same hub view, network administrators are able to set up specialized RMON tables to gather specific network traffic information. In addition, third-party products, such as Cisco routers and Fore ATM switches, may be supported the same way.

Controlling cards, ports, and power supply. The hub detail windows display a graphic representation of the cards, ports, and power supplies in a selected chassis or in selected hubs. With such a detail window, a number of control tasks can be performed and port indicators viewed.

The card information window displays information about selected cards and their ports or about an extended hub. The operator can enable and disable ports. Different versions of card information exist, depending on the nature of the segment the cards are representing. Usually, the following fields are offered in this window:

- Card ID
- List of ports
- Enabling/disabling icon
- Port status
- Link status
- Open alarms
- Remarks

All ODS Infinity hubs support rear-mounted, redundant, load-sharing, hot, swappable power supplies. Power supply conditions are displayed on the front panel of the management card and are alarmed via SNMP traps to the management software. When a second power supply is installed, each shares 50 percent of the total load. Each power supply has separate power connections and will immediately provide 100 percent of the power load without delay or data interruption if another fails. In a redundant configuration, a power supply can be inserted or removed while another is running. Each power supply is also protected by a special fuse to prevent a card short or lightning strike from a user port or backplane.

Port indicators are the same as those introduced for Ethernet and Token Ring segments. The same types of reports can be generated, but at a much more detailed level.

Threshold alarms. The right setting of thresholds against all of the hub and port indicators helps to proactively recognize performance bottlenecks and deteriorating hub conditions. Most vendors differentiate between threshold alarms and trouble alarms. *Threshold alarms* include all the indicators supported for ports and hubs. *Trouble alarms* may include the following:

- Primary communication lost
- Secondary communication lost
- Power failure
- Port not functional
- Card not functional
- Beaconing
- No token available
- Temperature over threshold
- Humidity over threshold
- Fan failure

With SNMP, alarms may be implemented in the form of traps. Writing and implementing traps is a real differentiator between vendors. The customization time and expenses must not be underestimated. Most alarms can be set for the hub, for cards, or for individual ports.

Figure 3.25 shows a broadcast storm. In such a case, the network administrator uses a RMON application to identify the MAC address of the offending node. The administrator must then use a hub application to find the port to which the MAC address is connected and then manually disable the port. Because the two applications are unable to interact, the network administrator must intervene to solve the problem. As the figure illustrates, seven steps are required to disable the offending port.

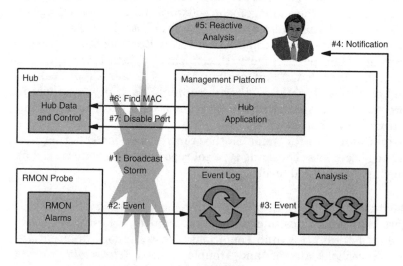

Figure 3.25 Multiple problem-solving steps using today's reactive network management.

Ungermann-Bass with Access/EMPower moves beyond intelligent SNMP agent technology by empowering the hub not only to collect and reduce data, but also to analyze, correlate, and respond to the data in real time based on preset policies without intervention from the management platform. This represents a far more distributed approach to management automation than can be achieved using traditional network management platforms. Ungermann-Bass implements key platformlike features in the agent:

- An event management system with which applications may integrate via APIs in order to act on events within the hub.

- An application API that allows applications to both interact and access common data stored in the extensible SNMP agent.

- A structured, systemlike environment that supports the deployment of applications in a real-time environment. This includes standardized software installations, a version-tracking system, and a mechanism for dynamically linking and loading applications during run time.

Distributing self-management responsibility to the hub frees the network management platform to serve a more crucial role as an application platform for historical analysis, planning, accounting, problem management, systems management inventory control, and policy creation. Policy-based management is based on the concept that policies can be written to represent a predefined approach on how to deal with a network event or condition such as a broadcast storm or bandwidth contention. These policies allow network managers to capture the knowledge that is used to solve a problem so that it can be automatically applied again whenever the same problem occurs. Figure 3.26 shows an example of how the NetStorm Terminator application running under Access/EMPower can change the reactive response to a proactive response. In this case, the network administrator can define a broadcast storm policy that makes use of both RMON events and hub data so that an informed decision can be written. It also uses the embedded port-to-MAC address-mapping database that is maintained by Access/EMPower. A RMON rising threshold of approximately 1000 broadcasts/second results in an event logged by RMON in the internal event management system. NetStorm receives the event from the event management system and proceeds to set on RMON HostTopN study to gather additional critical data about the broadcast storm. NetStorm Terminator evaluates this data based on user-defined policies, such as the degree of broadcast traffic that may be generated by a single host. If the offending host exceeds this limit, NetStorm logs an event to the event management system that contains the MAC address of the offending host. This event will be forwarded as an SNMP trap to

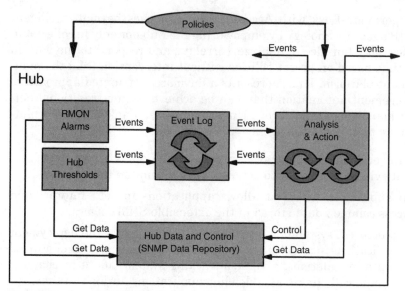

Figure 3.26   Access/EMPower allows the hub to respond proactively to network events.

the network management station. However, NetStorm continues its work by consulting the embedded MAC address-to-port mapping database; it identifies the hub slot and the individual port to which the offending host is attached. After determining that the port does not exceed a "number of devices per port" policy, it disables the port and reports the corrective action to the event management system. After the time period specified in the policy, NetStorm reenables the port.

Dynamic trouble ticketing

In order to control the processes of problem determination, isolation, diagnostics, backup, repair, and recovery, trouble tickets are very useful. Figure 3.27 shows the typical cycle of trouble tickets: opening it, processing it, tracking trouble resolution, and finally closing it. Usually, trouble tickets are tightly coupled with help desk instruments that are covered under administration in this chapter. The trouble ticket database will likely be relational for ensuring flexible information retrieval. This database may be linked to the configuration database.

The trouble ticketing process drives problem resolution by maintaining communication connections to a variety of functions within and outside fault management. In the event the network is unavailable, parts of it are down, or performance is impaired anywhere on the net-

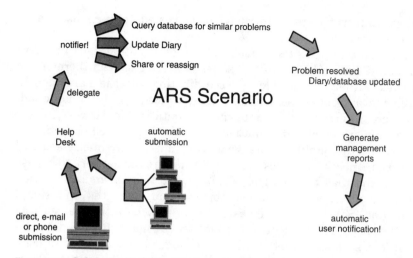

Figure 3.27   Life cycle of trouble tickets (Action Request System from Remedy).

work, trouble ticket activity would be invoked. The word *problem* means an incident or event that causes a LAN not to function as expected. Problems may be categorized as follows:

- Handling errors that result from users, due to lack of education or training

- Device or equipment faults detected automatically or semiautomatically

- Facility faults detected automatically or semiautomatically

- Intermittent faults of equipment and/or facilities, with discontinuous or fluctuating characteristics

- Chronic faults whose trend is to cause increasingly severe faults

Trouble tickets may be very successfully utilized as the basis of expert systems. They contain all the necessary information about symptoms, resources, diagnostics, and resolution. Starting with this data is definitely less expensive than interviews with experts. Interviews should be conducted in the follow-up phase of fine-tuning and implementing expert systems.

Testing

Tests are initiated on demand. The goals are twofold: to get more detailed information on faults, and to ensure that repair and recovery have successfully been accomplished. Tests can basically be categorized as nonintrusive tests, intrusive tests, remedial functions, or analog measurements.

Nonintrusive tests, as the name implies, are tests that don't interfere with main-channel data traffic. A series of these tests can therefore be performed without the need for any coordination with the main application or the associated personnel. *Intrusive tests,* on the other hand, cause some interruption in main-channel data traffic. However, these tests offer more precise information about the high-speed operation of modems and the quality of the whole transmission channel. *Remedial functions* are necessary to restore and reconfigure the network to bypass any fault that has been diagnosed. *Analog measurements* can provide further quantitative information about signal strengths and signal degradation. Some of these measurements may be intrusive, such as those that need to substitute a test tone for the main-channel data signal. Others, such as those that identify changes in phase jitter and signal level, are nonintrusive. These analog measurements are not precise and may only be used to indicate problems on a particular analog circuit. Further intrusive tests are then generally required to pinpoint the source of the problem—the failing modem or the telephone line.

Use of MIB PDUs to support fault management

SNMP MIBs offer a wide choice of raw information that may be processed to support selected fault management function. The following list (Leinwand 1993) concentrates on selected protocol data units of MIB II that may be processed into meaningful indicators of the fault management process.

System group	Information content
sysObjectID	The system manufacturer
sysServices	Which protocol layer the device services
sysUptime	How long the system has been operational
Interface group	Information content
ifAdminStatus	Whether the interface is administratively up/down/test
ifOperStatus	Whether the interface operational state is up/down/test
ifLastChange	Time when the interface changed operational state
IP group	Information content
ipRouteTable	IP routing table
ipNetToMediaTable	IP address translation table
EGP group	Information content
egpNeighState	State of each EGP neighbor
egpNeighStateUps	When an EGP neighbor enters an UP state
egpNeighStateDowns	When an EGP neighbor enters a DOWN state

**Typical instruments for supporting LAN
fault management**

In order to facilitate the LAN troubleshooter's work, several products
may be considered for use. Generic groups of products include ohmmeters, outlet testers, coax connectors, T-connectors, terminators, oscilloscopes, time domain reflectometers (TDRs), LAN analyzers, LAN
monitors, NOS monitors, trouble ticketing systems, and continuous
backup systems.

Ohmmeter. This instrument is a simple tool that measures impedance. You can use an ohmmeter to locate open or shorted cable. If the
impedance reading matches the rated impedance of the cable, the cable
is fine. If the reading doesn't match the rated impedance, then the LAN
has a short, a crushed cable, or a cable break somewhere along the cable
run. Ohmmeters cannot be used in fiber-optic-based LANs.

Sometimes the problem is not the cable, but rather the electrical outlet, and then you would need an outlet tester. For example, if an outlet is
not grounded properly, noise or current may be introduced through the
power supply into the workstation, and then through the network interface card onto the copper-based (twisted-pair or coaxial) LAN cable.

Coax connectors, T-connectors, and Terminators. These are also important
products for a LAN troubleshooter. Extra terminators are a basic
requirement, particularly on a bus network. Extra terminators can be
used to isolate sections of the cable for testing.

Oscilloscope. This allows the network manager to examine the
cable's waveform. An oscilloscope helps detect the existence of noise or
other disturbances on the wire, such as continuous voltage spikes.
Again, this applies only to LANs that use copper-based wiring.

Time domain reflectometer. This instrument operates by sending an
electrical pulse over the LAN cable, monitoring for signal reflections.
On a good cable there will be no reflections, indicating that the cable is
clean, with no breaks or shorts. If there's a break or short in the cable,
however, the time it takes for the pulse reflection to return gives the
TDR a very accurate idea of where the fault is located. Many TDRs can
locate cable breaks to within a few feet. TDRs have traditionally been
relatively expensive instruments. A new, less expensive generation of
TDR equipment is now available. These new instruments are more
compact than their predecessors, often measuring about the size of a
paperback book or smaller. The newer TDRs are also easier to use and
still accurate to within a few feet.

Fiber-optic instruments can be divided into three general categories:
power meters, optical time domain reflectometers (OTDRs), and optical
bandwidth test sets.

Power meters (optical loss test sets). These measure the optical power from a length of fiber in much the same way that conventional power meters measure electrical power. These tools are used to perform a one-way loss measurement. The loss may occur in the fiber, connectors, splices, jumper cables, and other system areas. Some power meters also have a built-in transmit source. Two sets, both with transmit and receive capability, are used together to make measurements in both directions without having to relocate personnel or equipment. The individual power meter is a single unit consisting of an optical receiver and an analog or digital readout. A light source, typically at the point of origination, supplies the power that's detected at the end of the fiber link or test access point. The meter displays the power detected in decibels. The wavelength range often given indicates the various wavelengths that the meter can detect. The resolution parameter indicates the smallest step that the meter will display.

Optical time domain reflectometers (OTDRs). Network managers can use these to characterize a fiber wherein an optical pulse is transmitted through the fiber, and the resulting light that's scattered and reflected back to the input is measured as a function of time. OTDRs are useful in estimating the attenuation coefficient as a function of distance and in identifying defects and other losses. These devices operate on basically the same principles as copper-based TDRs. The difference is one of cost.

Optical bandwidth test sets. These instruments consist of two separate parts: (1) the source, whose output data rate varies according to the frequency of input current applied to the source (specified by frequency range parameter) and (2) the detector, which reads the changing signal, determines the frequency response, and then displays a bandwidth instrument. The instrumentation is calibrated using a test fiber; the actual measurement results are compared to the calibrated value to display the bandwidth value.

LAN analyzers. These are products for in-depth measurement for diagnosing problems. They passively listen to traffic and may time-stamp events and register dialogues between users and servers. In certain cases, the same instruments may be used as load generators.

LAN monitors. These are products for supervising the principal status and use indicators on a continuous basis. They're inexpensive and don't introduce too much overhead.

NOS monitors. These are products that may be seen as extensions of LAN operating systems. They can usually be easily activated or deactivated. The overhead doesn't seem to be critical.

Trouble ticketing systems. These are vendor-independent products that are usually offered together with configuration management instruments; they run on dedicated servers.

Continuous backup system. This is a utility that replicates all changes that are written to a disk as they're made. These systems don't necessarily replace the traditional tape-oriented backups that most network managers depend on today. Rather, they supplement tape backup. (Table 3.10 summarizes the typical instruments for fault management.)

Staffing LAN fault management

LAN fault management is a combination of help desk and analysis activities. The help desk tasks are more human oriented, and analysis is more technology oriented. The principal responsibilities of the help desk include the following:

1. Supervising LAN operations

2. Registering troubles identified by monitors and users

3. Opening trouble tickets

4. Implementing procedures for tier 1 problem determination

5. Invoking corrections

6. Escalating problems, depending on priorities, to central network management center or to peer help desks

7. Communicating with users

8. Communicating with vendors

9. Activating and deactivating local area networks

10. Generating reports on network problems

TABLE 3.10   Typical Instruments of Fault Management

Ohmmeters
Outlet testers
Terminator testers
Oscilloscopes
Time domain reflectometers
Power meters
Optical time domain reflectometers
Optical bandwidth testers
LAN analyzers
LAN monitors
NOS monitors
Trouble ticketing systems
Continuous backup systems

11. Closing trouble tickets

12. Reviewing documentation of change management

13. Setting priorities for problem diagnosis

14. Registering security management problems

The principal responsibilities of LAN analysis activities are as follows:

1. Conducting LAN tuning studies

2. Executing specific LAN measurements

3. Designing and executing performance and functionality tests

4. Defining performance indicators

5. Selecting LAN management instruments

6. Surveying performance needs of LAN users

7. Maintaining the LAN performance database

8. Generating reports

9. Maintaining the LAN baseline models

10. Sizing LAN resources

11. Customizing LAN instruments

12. Analyzing workload and use trends

13. Preparing checklists and fault management procedures for the LAN help desk

14. Helping to install LAN management instruments

15. Specifying and documenting LAN configurations

Help desk personnel and analysts interface with all other groups within LAN management. Outside contacts include users and vendors. Besides communication skills, basic knowledge of LANs is required for the LAN help desk functions. Analysts require in-depth knowledge of all managed LAN objects. Continuing education is required for both positions; communication-oriented courses should be required of LAN help desk personnel, and a B.S. in Engineering is recommended for LAN analysts.

Performance Management of Local Area Networks

LAN performance management functions are not yet fully implemented; in most cases, only sporadic measurements are conducted when performance bottlenecks are suspected in LAN segments. RMON implementations will change this situation dramatically by continuously offering supervising-standard measurement indicators for Ethernet and Token Ring with affordable measurement-probe prices. In this following section, the main functional areas of LAN performance management are outlined in some depth.

LAN performance indicators may be grouped into fixed, variable, and performance measurement metrics (Lo 1990).

Defining performance indicators

Fixed metrics

Transmission capacity. The transmission capacity is normally expressed in terms of bits per second. Although the bite rate is fixed, the total capacity can be divided into multiple smaller capacities to support different types of signals. One of the common myths regarding LAN transmission capacity is that Ethernet is saturated at an offered load (the actual data carried on the channel, excluding overhead and retransmitting bits) of 37 percent. Many studies have shown that Ethernet can offer a 10-Mbps data rate under a distance of 1 kilometer with the CSMA/CD protocol. With switching technology, the full bandwidth can be made available to servers and workstations.

Signal propagation delay. Signals are limited by the speed of light, and the longer they propagate, the longer they delay. *Signal propagation time* is the time required to transmit a signal to its destination and generally is 5 microseconds per kilometer. Therefore, cabling distance is a factor that affects signal propagation delay. In the case of satellite communication, signal propagation delay plays an influential role, as the distance between an earth station and the satellite is about 22,500 miles. Within LANs, the internodal signal propagation delay is negligible. However, the signaling technique used (i.e., baseband or broadband—see details in Chap. 2) can produce different levels of delays.

Topology. As described in Chap. 2, a LAN can be either a star, tree, ring, bus, or combination of star and ring. The type of LAN topology will affect performance. For example, a bus LAN (e.g., Ethernet) and a token ring LAN (e.g., IBM's Token Ring) have a different built-in slot time—the time of acquiring network access. The topology also limits the number of workstations or hosts that can be attached to it. Ethernet limits the number of nodes per cable segment to 100, and the total number of nodes in a multiple-segment Ethernet is limited to 1024. A single IBM Token Ring supports 260 nodes. The higher the number, the greater the performance impact, since all network traffic is generated from these nodes. Virtual LANs will redefine topology by offering topological flexibility at the logical level. The physical level is still the same; a powerful hub supports start-type wiring to LAN stations.

Frame/packet size. Most LANs are designed to support only a specific, fixed-size frame or packet. If the message is larger than the frame size, it must be broken into smaller sizes occupying multiple frames. The greater the number of frames per message, the longer delay a message can experience. Like every other LAN, Ethernet, for example, has a minimum packet size requirement: it must not be shorter than the slot time (51.2 microseconds) in order to be able to detect a collision. This limit is equivalent to a minimum length of 64 bytes, including headers and other control bytes. Similarly, Ethernet has a maximum of 1518 bytes as the upper boundary in order to minimize access time.

Variable metrics

Access protocol. The type of access protocol used by a LAN is probably the most influential metric that affects performance. IBM's Token Ring uses a proprietary token access control scheme, in which a circulating token is passed sequentially from node to node to grant transmissions. A node must release a token after each transmission and is not allowed to transmit continuously on a single ring architecture. Ethernet, on the other hand, employs the I-persistent CSMA/CD access control, in which a node that waits for a free channel can transmit as soon as the channel is free with a probability of I (i.e., 100 percent chance to transmit).

User traffic profile. A computer system and network is lifeless without users. There are many factors constituting a user's traffic profile: message/data arrival rate (how many key entries a user makes per minute); message-size distribution (how many small, medium, and large messages are generated by a user; type of messages (to a single user, multiple users, or all receivers); and the number of simultaneous users (all active, 50 percent active, or 10 percent active).

Buffer size. A buffer is a piece of memory used to receive, store, process, and forward messages. If the number of buffers is too small, data may suffer delays or even be discarded. Some LANs have a fixed number of buffers, and some use a dynamic expansion scheme based on the volume of the messages and the rate of processing. In particular, LAN internetworking devices are likely sources of buffer problems.

Data collision and retransmitting. Data collision is inevitable, especially in a bus LAN, unless the transmission is controlled in an orderly manner. Two factors need to be considered: (1) how long it takes nodes to detect a data collision and (2) how long it takes to actually transmit the collided messages. Various detection schemes are used by different topologies. For example, Ethernet employs a *jam* time, which is the time allowed for transmitting 32 to 48 more bits after a collision is detected by a transmitting station, so that other stations can reliably detect the collision. The more influential factor is the time it takes to actually transmit the data after collision. Many LANs use a binary exponential back-off scheme to avoid a situation in which the same two colliding nodes collide again at the next interval. Both collision detection and retransmitting contribute delays to the overall processing delay. Generally, waiting time is dependent on network load and may become unacceptably long in some extreme cases.

Performance measurement metrics. The performance of a LAN can't be quantified with a single dimension. It's very hard to interpret measured metrics without knowing which applications and which users are involved. The following measurement metrics are generally obtainable. In this respect, the data units offered by RMON will change and extend this set of metrics. Vendors are offering numerous management applications that address these indicators, but in much more detail.

Resource usage. Processor, memory, transmission medium, and in some cases, peripheral devices all contribute to the processing of a user request (e.g., open a file, send a message, or compile a program). How much of their respective capacities are used and how much reserved capacities are left need to be evaluated in conjunction with processing delay information (in some cases, the user's service-level goals).

Processing delays. A user's request is likely to suffer delays at each processing point. Both host and network can cause processing delays. Host delays can be divided into system processing delays and application processing delays. Network delays can be viewed as a combination of delays due to hardware and software. However, at the end-user level, a total processing delay (or response time) is the only meaningful performance metric.

Throughput. Transmission capacity can be measured in terms of throughput, the number of messages or bytes transmitted per unit of time. In LAN measurement, throughput is an indication of the fraction of the nominal network capacity that's actually used for carrying data. In general, packet headers are considered useful in estimating throughput if no other measurement facilities are available, since the header contains the number of bytes in a frame. A metric related to throughput is channel capacity. Each transmission medium has a given maximum capacity (e.g., bits per second), which is a function of message volume and message size.

Availability. From an end user's point of view, service availability is determined by both availability and consistency. A network can be in operation, but if a user suffers long delays, as far as the user is concerned, the network is virtually unavailable since its availability is unreliable. Therefore, reliability measurement is a permanent measurement metric. However, most LAN measurement tools are able to measure only availability (up and down times), since timing measurement may add several orders of magnitude of complexity to measurement tools.

Fairness of measured data. Since network traffic tends to be sporadic, the measured period and the internal data recording rate are quite important. An hourly averaged measured data rate may not be able to reveal any performance bottlenecks; a 1-second recording rate can generate an enormous amount of data that requires both processor time and storage. As a general practice, a peak-to-average ratio is used in which data in short intervals with known high activity are collected. The ratio between the high-activity periods and the average periods can be established for studying network capacity requirements.

Communigram. In order to quantify the traffic between communication partners, the volume is quite important. The measured and reported intervals are very important. An hourly averaged rate may not be able to reveal any performance bottleneck; a 1-second recording rate can generate an enormous amount of data that requires both processor time and storage. As a general practice, a peak-to-average ratio is used in which data in short intervals with known high activity are collected. The ratio between the high-activity periods and the average periods can be used for sizing resources supporting the communication between partners. (Table 3.11 shows all of the metrics in a table format.)

TABLE 3.11   LAN Performance Indicators

Fixed metrics
- Transmission capacity
- Signal propagation delay
- Topology
- Frame/packet size

Variable metrics
- Access protocol
- User traffic profile
- Buffer size
- Data collision and retransmission

Performance metrics
- Resource usage
- Processing delays
- Throughput
- Availability
- Fairness of measured data
- Communigram

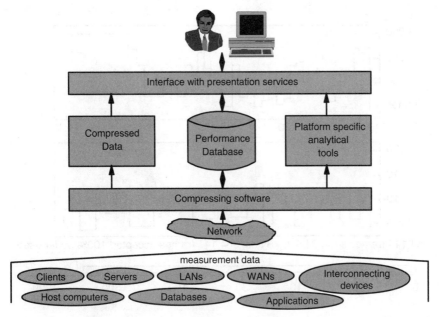

Figure 3.28   Collecting and processing performance data.

Performance monitoring

In order to early recognize performance bottlenecks, measurements must be continuously (e.g., using RMON) or periodically (e.g., using LAN monitors) performed. Raw data are expected to be maintained in performance files or databases. Figure 3.28 shows a structure of performance data collection and consolidation.

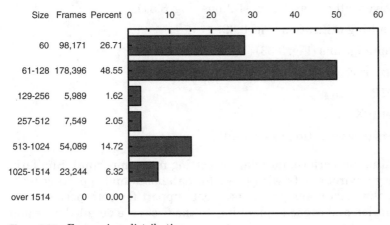

Figure 3.29   Frame sizes distribution.

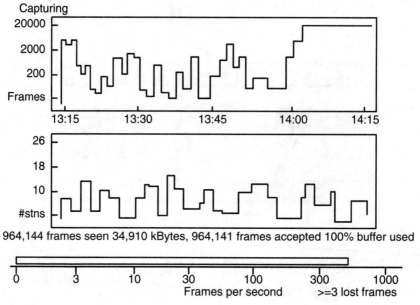

Figure 3.30   Ethernet performance measurements.

There are many examples of performance measurement results with Ethernet and Token Ring:

- Ethernet bandwidth utilization
- Frame sizes distribution (Fig. 3.29)
- Number of active stations combined with utilization limits (Fig. 3.30)
- Relative traffic to and from stations (Fig. 3.31)
- Token Ring utilization (Fig. 3.32)
- Communigrams (Fig. 3.33)
- Bridge or router profile
- TCP/IP traces
- Novel IPX traces
- Others (see reporting examples)

Maintaining performance data is getting more important. Similarly to legacy environments with powerful databases and reporting techniques, the LAN manager wants to get support for both performance optimization and capacity planning. In the first case detailed data and in the second case compressed data are required.

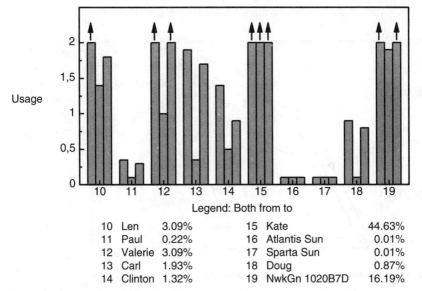

Figure 3.31 Relative traffic statistics to and from stations.

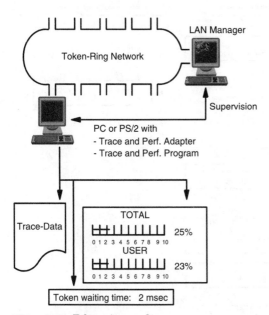

Figure 3.32 Token ring performance measurement results.

Average traffic throughout the period, by hour, in bits per second

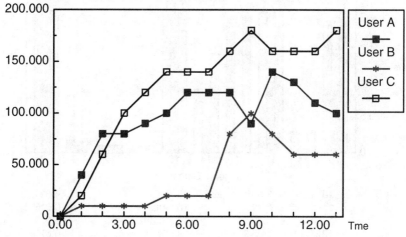

Figure 3.33 Top transmitters in interconnected LANs.

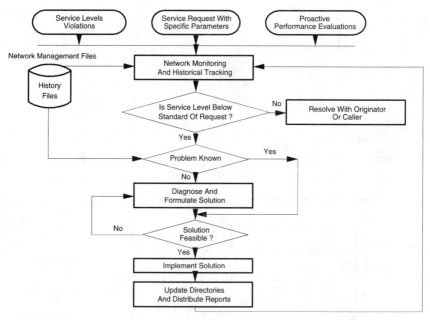

Figure 3.34 Performance tuning procedure.

Tuning of local area networks

Figure 3.34 shows the principal steps and functions needed for analyzing and tuning local area networks. Requests for analysis and performance improvement occur when the service-level expectation can't be met, or performance studies are required when proactive performance evaluations are initiated. The process starts with defining performance metrics, and continues with monitoring in the LAN segment by extracting data from the performance database. In most cases, however, the level of detail doesn't satisfy the information need. The database is considered the basis of thresholding and performance reporting. On rare occasions, the experience file of historic tuning data may help to quickly recognize similarities with past problems. Once the hypothesis has been formulated, cost efficiency and technical feasibility should be tested step-by-step in order to exclude uneconomical and nonfeasible alternatives. Frequently, technical and economic performance evaluations are supported by modeling techniques. After implementation, measurements should check and prove performance improvement. In the case of nonfeasibility or insufficient improvement, an additional hypothesis should be worked out. If the results are still unsatisfactory, capacity planning actions are required.

Regarding tuning, all LAN components may be performance bottlenecks; priorities and weights have to be set after performance measurements have been conducted and evaluated. LANs are most widely used for supporting client/server systems. In such environments, the primary tuning targets are as follows:

- LAN servers, in particular their CPUs and I/O devices
- LAN drivers
- LAN interface cards
- LAN operating systems
- Workstations
- Peripherials

LAN servers.   LAN servers have a major impact on the performance of the network. Almost independently, whether the servers are high-end or low-end, they are equipped with systems management software, automatic server recovery, remote maintenance, and predictive diagnostics. They use complex instruction-set computing (CISC) or reduced instruction-set computing (RISC) chips and support industry-standard PC-I/O buses, such as Extended Industry Standard Architecture (EISA), Micro Channel architecture (MCA), and Peripheral Component Interconnect (PCI). Despite technological advances, bottlenecks may occur at the CPU and at I/O devices.

Increasing the speed or number of CPUs improves performance, but provides only a partial solution. Without sufficient work, the CPU is in a waiting state. This is why high-performance servers use special cache designs, bus designs, memory management, and other architectural features to keep the CPU busy. These enhancements apply to servers that run in asymmetric multiprocessing (ASMP) mode, which dedicates individual CPUs to independent tasks; SMP mode, which enables multiple CPUs to share processing tasks and memory; and clustering mode, which enables CPUs on multiple servers to work in ASMP mode. To prevent the CPU from accessing main memory too often, high-speed cache memory is placed between the CPU and main memory. Cache memory is actually placed within the CPU and also outside the CPU. Measurement results confirm efficiency improvements of the CPU in the range of 10 to 20 percent.

There is another technique, called *pipelining*, that prevents the CPU from waiting unnecessarily while data is being transported from memory. The transport process requires a cycle of time on the CPU-to-memory bus. In a nonpipelined architecture, a second cycle is not started until the first one completes, and there is a time delay before the second cycle starts. In a pipelined bus architecture, the second cycle begins before the first cycle completes. This way, the data from the second cycle is available immediately after the completion of the first cycle.

The size of the cache is usually determined by the vendor; the LAN analyst is expected to set the systems parameters accordingly.

Cache systems are designed to keep the CPU supplied with instructions and data by managing access to main memory. However, bus-controlled I/O devices also contend for access to main memory, and they run at a much slower speed then the CPU. Therefore, CPU-to-memory operations should take priority over I/O-to-memory operations, but not at the expense of interrupting these I/O operations. This is why most high-performance servers are engineered to let the CPU and I/O devices simultaneously access main memory by maximizing concurrency and minimizing contention. Maximizing concurrency is supported by placing buffers between high-speed system buses and the I/O-to-memory bus. These buffers capture data reads and writes between buses to prevent one device, such as a CPU or I/O-card, from waiting for another to finish. Vendors use these buffers in segmented bus architectures that can segregate different devices on various buses. This technique is expected to be enhanced continuously.

Disk I/O bottlenecks are identified by such applications as high-volume transaction processing that moves many small transactions between the CPU and disks, and decision support systems with many record moves. In these and similar cases, performance is affected by disk speed, the number of disk drives, and the intelligence and speed of drive array controllers. The number of disk drives in the system has a greater effect on server performance than the speed of individual drives. This is because of reduced latency in the positioning of drive heads and because more than one set of read/write heads may be active at a given time. The greater the number of drives, the greater the performance of drive array. There are still other ways to improve disk I/O performance. Intelligent array controllers support more than one disk channel per bus interface and implement support for multiple Redundant Array of Inexpensive Disks (RAID) levels of hardware.

LAN drivers.   Another important set of elements affecting local area network performance are the software routines called *drivers*. Drivers accept requests from the network and provide the interface between the physical devices (disk drives, printers, network interface cards) and the operating system. The drivers also control the movement of data throughout the network and verify that the data have been received at the appropriate address.

The critical role that drivers play, however, means that driver problems can have a large impact on the performance of the overall network. Drivers have traditionally been supplied by the LAN vendors and have been tailored to their operating systems and varied according to size. Today, it's more likely third-party software developers will provide customized drivers for networks.

These customized drivers, however, can be rather detailed and lengthy. If a driver takes up too much RAM, other applications will have insufficient room in which to operate, causing them to alter their normal operating procedures in order to reduce memory requirements. Also, the larger a driver is, the more code it has to execute, causing the network to delay when responding to additional requests, such as requests for printer services or requests from other users for processing jobs.

Interface cards can also affect performance. Memory management is crucial to speed and performance. Factors such as DMA versus shared memory, and onboard processors and buffers can mean large differences in two cards' actual throughput on the network. The performance difference, for example, between Ethernet cards can be as high as 50 percent.

LAN interface cards.   When data from the CPU is being sent to a network port of a disk, it can cause a different bottleneck and limit the number of users that can simultaneously make server requests. The network is expected to become the bottleneck with file and print services, video servers, and imaging systems. In other cases, high-performance, low-utilization network interface cards are used. The performance of a server-to-LAN channel is affected by NIC driver optimization, the bus mastering capabilities of the controller, concurrent access to server memory, and the number of LAN channels per bus interface.

But in cases where CPU utilization is an issue, there is a critical limit at which placing additional NICs in the server will not improve the performance, due to the overhead associated with routing and servicing the NIC. The practical threshold is around three NICs per server. Vendors will address how to connect servers to high-speed technologies such as ATM, FDDI, frame relay, and 100-Mbps Ethernet. They will also address the concept of placing servers on dedicated, high-speed LANs and of using switching to keep the server and end users from waiting for the network.

LAN operating systems.   Usually, the LAN operating system is the most prominent factor affecting the performance of a local area network. The function of the operating system is manyfold and includes the communication with operating systems of servers and clients, the support of interprocess communication, the maintenance of networkwide addressing, the moving of data within the network to manage the files and to control the input and output requirements from interconnected LANs. The more efficiently the LAN operating system is able to perform these tasks, the more efficiently the LAN will operate.

High performance combined with low purchase costs and low operating expenses cannot be met by many vendors. The LAN operating systems' market concentrates gradually around a very few powerful products, such as NetWare, Windows NT, LAN Manager, Vines, and LANtastic.

Workstations.   Another element affecting performance is the network workstation, often called the *client*. The performance of a workstation has more impact on both the perceived and the actual system performance than any other component. The operating systems are frequently the same as with servers. In this case, coordination between the two is easier over the LAN. In other cases, with a powerful file server on a 10-Mbps LAN, an older PC with DOS and with limited RAM may become the bottleneck, since it cannot accept or display data as fast as the file server and the network hardware can supply it. At times, it is cheaper and more practical to upgrade the workstation rather than the LAN itself. Adding more RAM or a coprocessor could improve the overall performance substantially. The protocol software can also affect the workstation performance. A full seven-layer OSI stack requires considerable resources to run. Even with more user-friendly protocols we may have major effects on performance depending on how they select packet sizes, transfer buffers, and translate addresses.

The network workstation is just as important to the overall performance of the LAN as the server and operating system. The workstation executes the network's protocols through its driver software; a faster workstation will add to the performance of the LAN. One factor to consider is whether the workstation should contain a disk drive of its own or not. Obviously, a diskless workstation will ease the budget and improve security somewhat.

But diskless workstations have their own set of costs. For one, these workstations are dependent on shared resources. If the work being performed at the station doesn't involve sharing resources, a workstation with its own disk may be more appropriate. Moreover, diskless workstations add to the traffic load on the LAN. This could be significant, especially if the workstations are for programmers who typically don't need to share files but who often work on files that are extremely large. The bandwidth on the LAN may become a performance bottleneck of the future.

Peripherals. Printing requirements also affect LAN performance in a variety of ways. Modern printers provide much more advanced printing capabilities than were available just a few years ago. Complete pages are transmitted all at once with improved fonts and high-end graphics.

These printing capabilities, however, if not handled properly, can degrade network performance. If you run into such performance problems, and if enough printers are available, redirecting the printing job to a local printer can help. You can also add another server dedicated to handling printer functions.

Another way to avoid bottlenecks caused by heavy printing requirements is to use a network operating system that incorporates a spooler to control these requirements. Spoolers are designed to accept a printing request from the network, logically and in order, and they complete print requests without additional help from workstations.

Effective filtering across bridges ensures that traffic volume is not too high throughout the network and keeps performance constantly high. If high volumes indicate the need for partitioning, it's recommended to place bridges between departments. The first part of Fig. 3.35 indicates that most information arriving at the bridge is addressed to a file server on the other port and must be forwarded by the bridge. After partitioning, most information arriving at the bridge is addressed to a file server on the same port and may be discarded by the bridge. The two segments thus work in much greater harmony and with improved efficiency.

These examples represent a certain type of client/server-oriented network. Other rules apply in a peer-to-peer LAN and in interconnected LANs. In the latter, routers take over a lot of responsibilities by directing traffic to the targeted destinations. But routers have limited

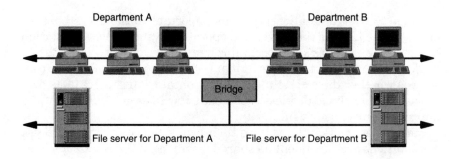

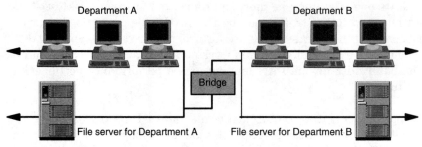

Figure 3.35 Reconfiguration of LAN bridges.

performance in terms of receiving, interpreting, and forwarding packets, frames, and messages.

Figure 3.36 shows the typical three operating areas of routers:

- Below A: normal performance
- B: stress point
- Beyond B in the area of C: degraded performance

Other types of performance bottlenecks may include the following:

- Too many collisions due to too many stations and/or messages
- Bandwidth of the LAN too narrow
- Retransmissions required by high error rates
- Message storms
- An uncontrolled chain of confirmations and reconfirmations in the LAN

Modeling and performance optimization

In order to optimize performance, you first need to analyze throughput capabilities and limits. Figures 3.37 and 3.38 show the dependence of

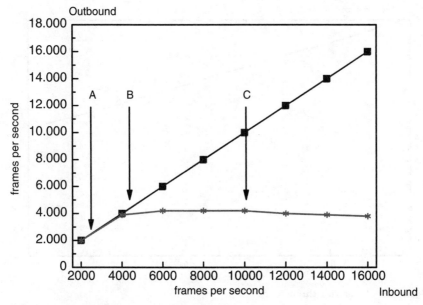

Figure 3.36   Evaluating router performance.

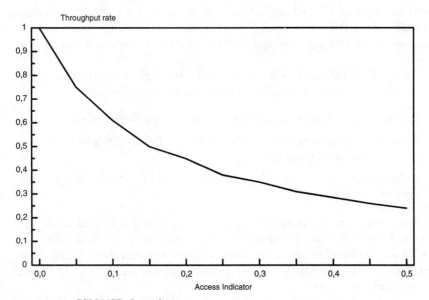

Figure 3.37   CSMA/CD throughput.

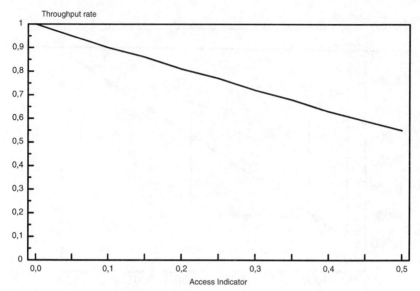

Figure 3.38   Token ring throughput.

throughput rate as a function of an access indicator. The access indicator computes the average access time as a function of LAN parameters such as number of stations, token size, estimated number of simultaneously active stations, speed of propagation, bandwidth, average message size, bit latency, average collision distance, repeater delay, and so on.

Figure 3.39 (Infotel 1990) compares the throughput performance for both principal access methods. The results are as follows:

1. Relatively constant throughput by the 4-Mbps Token Ring

2. Reasonable performance of the 16-Mbps Token Ring over a long range of the access indicator A

3. A throughput drop on the 10-Mbps Ethernet to a stable 35 to 40 percent use ceiling

These curves are the result of stress testing using artificial load. The idea behind it is that the planner and analyst may evaluate how the LANs are performing under overload or close to saturation. Once these performance limits are known, operating areas can be easily determined and supervised.

Using the same LAN parameters, analytical modeling techniques may be used to answer what-if questions regarding LAN parameters, LAN configurations, and load indicators. For both stress testing and analytical modeling, LAN monitors may be utilized. In the modeling

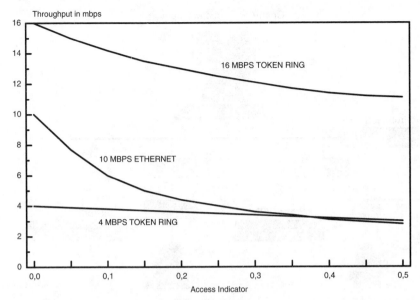

Figure 3.39   Comparison of CSMA/CD and token ring.

mode, LAN monitors are used as load generators. They may use real workload or artificial workload to drive the LANs.

Based on the applicability of RMON, a new term is frequently used: *baselining*. Baselining is the process of sampling network activity at a certain rate for an extended period of time. The purpose is to produce a statistically valid characterization of normal network behaviors over an extended period of time rather than a specific interval, taking into account varying levels at different weeks, days, and hours. By identifying network performance through a series of statistical calculations and averages, it is possible to establish a profile, called *baseline of the LAN,* to be used for capacity planning and in-depth performance analysis.

Figure 3.40 shows a simple structure with RMON probes that are collecting and compressing performance data. Selecting representative time intervals, every organization can determine the individual load limits when performance starts to deteriorate.

Reporting of performance

All users' expectations can't be met by the reporting capabilities of LAN analyzers. Most frequently, measurement data are ported from the analyzer to other databases or to spreadsheets for further processing. In the early days of reporting, only spreadsheets were used. Even in such cases, good-quality information could be provided. Protocol dis-

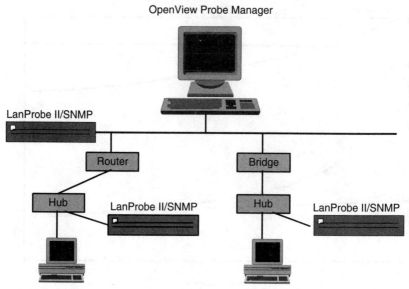

Figure 3.40   LAN performance management using RMON probes.

tribution, packet size distribution, and interarrival times are shown in
Fig. 3.41. Today, more powerful solutions are provided by vendors or by
third parties, such as SAS, BGS, and Computer Associates, who concentrate on performance evaluation and reporting.

LAN managers are interested in the following types of reports for
bandwidth utilization (actual and trends): circuit status; user's inventory
(status, adds, drops); overview of LAN addresses; communigrams; key
changes over time interval; LAN/WAN connections overview and use;
passwords in use; incident reports by category; inventory of instruments;
applications used by whom over time interval; equipment inventory; and
downtime by circuit, by equipment, by application, and by users.

Role of hubs in performance management

Hubs play a very important role in managing local area networks. The
role can even be expanded by using hubs to collect and preprocess
performance-related information. This section shows a few examples
for Ethernet and Token Ring segments.

Ethernet indicators.   Hub-level indicators provide information about
the data transmission results on a logical hub. These statistics actually
consist of multiple physical-level port statistics. Typical statistics
required for diagnostics and performance analysis are as follows:

■ Peak traffic in the segment within a specified time window

1	Frames in DB:	106		
2				
3	Protocol	Number of packets		
4	TCP	37		
5	PRINTER	2		
6	SMTP	27		
7	RWHO	4		
8	DNS	35		
9	Telnet	1		
10		106		
11				
12	Packet size	Packets by size		
13	0-59	0	0.00%	0
14	60-127	86	81.13%	1
15	128-255	6	5.66%	2
16	256-383	0	0.00%	3
17	384-511	0	0.00%	4
18	512-1023	14	13.21%	5
19	1024-2047	0	0.00%	6
20	2048-4095	0	0.00%	7
21	4096 and over	0	0.00%	8
22		0		
23	Interarrival time	Packets by interval		
24	0-0.000009	1	0.94%	0
25	0.00001-0.09	76	71.70%	1
26	0.1-0.19	12	11.32%	2
27	0.2-0.29	4	3.77%	3
28	0.3-0.39	1	0.94%	4
29	0.4-0.49	0	0.00%	5
30	0.5-0.59	2	1.89%	6
31	0.6-0.69	0	0.00%	7
32	0.7-0.79	3	2.83%	8
33	0.8-0.89	1	0.94%	9
34	0.9-0.99	6	5.66%	10

Figure 3.41 Using spreadsheets for reporting.

- Average traffic in the segment for a specified period of time
- Current traffic at the time of the last sample
- Total packets received
- Total bytes received
- Missed packets
- Number of cyclic redundancy-check errors on the segment
- Frame alignment errors on the segment
- Collision rate in the segment for a specific period of time

Token Ring indicators.   Token Ring indicators consist of hard- and soft-error indicators and of general-performance statistics. The hub vendors usually support most of the indicators referenced as follows:

Hard-error indicators

- Ring purges by the active monitor
- Number of times input signal is lost
- Beacons in the ring for a specified period of time

Soft-error indicators

- Number of line errors
- Number of burst errors
- Number of AC errors
- Number of abort sequences
- Number of lost frames
- Number of receive-data congestion errors
- Number of frame-copied errors
- Number of token errors due to token loss or frame circulation
- Number of frequency errors

General indicators

- Cumulative number of bytes on the ring for a specified period of time
- Frame count
- Average and peak utilization level
- Average and peak frame rate
- Bytes per second on average or peak
- Average frame size for a specified period of time
- Current and peak number of stations on the ring
- Current operating speed of the ring

SNMP and RMON support.   SNMP and RMON are considered by all vendors as the basis of generating, collecting, processing, and transferring management data. The support of SNMPv1 is a must. RMON is built in by cooperating with RMON-probe vendors, and SNMPv2 may be supported very soon. Basically, these standards are very helpful, but they are not without problems.

LanVision RMON MIB from ODS is an advanced LAN analyzer product that is capable of gathering statistical information on traffic activity and has the ability to perform multilevel protocol decode for a wide variety of commonly used protocols. With LanVision, RMON, SNMP, and protocol analyzer capabilities are centralized on one powerful management platform. The functions include the following:

- Centralized LAN analyzer, which provides full RMON statistics monitoring displayed in a tabular or graphical format
- Color-coded, seven-layer protocol decode for virtually all standard and de facto protocols
- Audible and visual alarms to identify fault conditions
- Real-time graphical display at network activity
- Data display in summary, detail, and in hex format
- Zoom-in capabilities at any protocol level for detailed analysis
- Support for both Ethernet and Token Ring RMON groups

SNMP management station in its central role has a number of shortcomings. The most important are as follows:

- Single point of failure due to the central platform
- Dependence on the network for exchanging commands and responses
- Overhead on communication channels
- Inability to respond in real time due to limited intelligence of the agents
- Lack of true integration between platform and applications

Use of MIB PDUs to support performance management

SNMP MIBs offer a wide choice of raw information that may be processed to support selected performance management functions. The following list (Leinwand 1993) concentrates on selected protocol data units of MIB II that may be processed into meaningful indicators of the performance management process.

Interface group	Information content
ifInDiscards	Rate of input discards
ifOutDiscards	Rate of output discards
ifInErrors	Rate of input errors
ifOutErrors	Rate of output errors
ifInOctets	Rate of bytes received
ifOutOctets	Rate of bytes sent
ifInUcastPkts	Rate of input unicast packets
ifOutUcastPkts	Rate of output unicast packets
ifInNUcastPkts	Rate of input nonunicast packets
ifOutNUcastPkts	Rate of output nonunicast packets
ifInUnknownProtos	Rate of input unknown protocol packets
ifOutQLen	Total packets in the output queue

Computing the following indicators is recommended

1. % input error rate = $\dfrac{\text{ifInError}}{(\text{ifInUcastPkts} + \text{ifInNUcastPkts})}$

2. % output error rate = $\dfrac{\text{ifOutErrors}}{(\text{ifOutUcastPkts} + \text{ifOutNUcastPkts})}$

3. Total number of bytes within one polling interval =

   (ifInOctets\<y\> – ifInOctets\>x\>) + (ifOutOctets\<y\> – ifOutOctets\<x\>)

4. Total number of bytes per second = $\dfrac{\text{total number of bytes}}{\text{y} - \text{x}}$

5. Line utilization = $\dfrac{(\text{total number of bytes per second} \times 8)}{\text{ifSpeed}}$

where polling time stamps are identified by y and x.

IP group	Information content
ipInReceives	Rate of input datagrams
ipInHdrErrors	Rate of input header errors
ipInAddrErrors	Rate of input address errors
ipForwDatagrams	Rate of forwarded datagrams
ipUnknownProtos	Rate of input datagrams for an unknown protocol
ipInDiscards	Rate of input datagrams discarded
ipInDelivers	Rate of input datagrams
ipOutRequests	Rate of output datagrams
ipOutDiscards	Rate of output datagrams discarded
ipOutNoRoutes	Rate of discards due to lack of routing information
ipRoutingDiscards	Rate of routing entries discarded
ipReasmReqds	Rate of datagrams needing reassembly
ipReasmOKs	Rate of datagrams successfully reassembled
ipFragCreates	Rate of fragmention reassembly failures
ipFragFails	Rate of unsuccessful fragmentations
ipFragCreates	Rate of fragments generated

For detailed analysis the following indicators may be computed:

1. % IP input errors

   $= \dfrac{(\text{ipInDiscards} + \text{ipInHdrErrors} + \text{ipInAddrErrors})}{\text{ipInReceives}}$

2. % IP output errors

   $= \dfrac{(\text{ipOutDiscards} + \text{ipOutHdrErrors} + \text{ipOutAddrErrors})}{\text{ipOutRequests}}$

3. IP packet forwarding rate

$$= \frac{(ipForwDatagrams<y> - ipForwDatagrams<x>)}{y - x}$$

4. IP packet receipt rate

$$= \frac{(ipInReceives<y> - ipInReceives<x>)}{y - x}$$

where polling time stamps are identified by y and x.

TCP group	Information content
tcpAttempFails	Number of failed attempts to make a connection
tcpEstabResets	Number of resets from established connection
tcpRetransSegs	Number of segments retransmitted
tcpInErrs	Number of packets received in error
tcpOutRsts	Number of times TCP tried to reset a connection
tcpInSegs	Rate of input TCP segments
tcpOutSegs	Rate of output TCP segments
UDP group	Information content
udpInDatagrams	Rate of input datagrams
udpOutDatagrams	Rate of output datagrams
udpNoPorts	Rate of datagrams that were not sent to a valid port
udpInErrors	Rate of UDP datagrams received in error
EGP group	Information content
egpInMsgs	Rate of messages received
egpInErrorsw	Rate of errors received
egpOutMsgs	Rate of messages sent
egpOutErrors	Rate of messages not sent because of error
egpNeighInMsgs	Rate of messages received from this EGP neighbor
egpNeighInErrs	Rate of errors received from this EGP neighbor
egpNeighOutMsgs	Rate of messages sent to this EGP neighbor
egpNeighOutErrs	Rate of messages not sent to this EGP neighbor because of error
egpNeighInErrMsgs	Rate of EGP error messages received from this EGP neighbor
egpNeighOutErrMsgs	Rate of EGP error messages sent to this EGP neighbor

Typical instruments for supporting LAN performance management

In order to facilitate the work of the LAN performance analyst, several products may be considered for implementation. Generic groups of products include the following:

LAN analyzers. Products for in-depth measurement for diagnosing problems. They passively listen to traffic and may time-stamp events and register dialogs between users and servers. In certain cases, the same instruments may be used as load generators.

LAN monitors. Products for supervising the principal status and use indicators on a continuous basis. They're inexpensive and don't introduce too much overhead.

NOS monitors. Products that may be seen as extensions of LAN operating systems. They can usually be easily activated or deactivated. The overhead doesn't seem to be critical.

Disk-usage monitoring. Utilities are needed to monitor disk usage for those operating systems not providing detailed information (such as NetWare). This helps the LAN manager assess whether a user is monopolizing the server and facilities configuration management in terms of sizing out file server needs. Additionally, the manager will be able to forecast the need for new facilities at future times. Disk-usage statistics include the number of files that are in a given directory or volume, the owner of the file, the size of the file, and access chronology. Exception reporting for users colonizing more than a specified threshold of space is available with some products. Also, some products allow the end user to check disk usage. Other products provide partial NetWare security reports by listing users, access privileges, and group membership.

Traffic-monitoring tools. To undertake performance management, a network manager needs a complete matrix of LAN traffic patterns. With this information the manager can subsequently look at the LAN configuration to determine, for example, if a server is being used too heavily, or if the network should be partitioned using bridge technology. A protocol analyzer provides detailed information about packets and related protocol data unit (PDU) headers that populate the LAN transmission medium, and the analyzer can compile traffic matrices.

Software-based traffic monitors will collect some of the needed traffic statistics. In addition to traffic collection, some of these systems can send probes to diagnose nodal problems. Some systems log errors and issue an alarm when a user-selected threshold is exceeded. A typical performance tool monitors traffic and records how much data is sent to and received from every network node, documenting the packet size, frequency, and type (data or system packet). For system packets, these monitors typically distinguish between commands and internal operating messages. The data should be collected into sequential ASCII files or a spreadsheet file.

Modeling devices. These consist of products that help in running experiments without the actual network. As a result, the impact of parameter changes and load increases can be evaluated very rapidly.

RMON probes. These probes may be hardware- or software-based. They continuously collect and preprocess performance data for a definite number of RMON groups. Depending on the product, they can monitor both Ethernet and Token Ring. Usually, they store data for up to 24 hours, and after being polled by the SNMP manager, they forward it to him or her.

Reporting software.   This consists of independent software packages in charge of processing and reporting data collected by various monitors in LANs. They can usually be combined to process and report data monitored in WANs and also in systems.

Database.   In order to maintain performance data, data files, but more frequently databases, are used. Their use can be shared between configuration and performance management.

Table 3.12 presents a summary of typical instruments of performance management.

Staffing LAN performance management

LAN performance management consists of technically oriented analysis activities. Principal responsibilities include conducting LAN tuning studies, executing specific LAN measurements, designing and executing performance and functionality tests, defining performance indicators, selecting LAN management instruments, surveying performance needs of LAN users, maintaining the LAN performance database, generating reports, maintaining the LAN baseline models, sizing LAN resources, customizing LAN instruments, analyzing workload and use trends, preparing checklists and processes for the LAN help desk, helping install LAN management instruments, and specifying and documenting LAN configurations.

LAN analysts interface within LAN management and with all other groups. Outside contacts include users and vendors. In-depth knowledge of all managed LAN objects is necessary. Continuing education is required. A B.S. in engineering is a prerequisite or target for LAN analysts.

TABLE 3.12   Typical Instruments of Performance Management

LAN analyzers
LAN monitors
NOS monitors
Disk usage monitors
Traffic monitoring tools
Modeling devices
RMON probes
Reporting software
Database

Security Management of Local Area Networks

Security management functions are not yet fully implemented in LANs.

Security on LANs must be discussed separately because such networks are used more publicly than wide area networks. LAN security risks involve tapping, radiation leakage, file and program protection, and physical security. Authentication, audit trails, and encryption may be handled similarly to WANs and other networking resources. The reasons for different security measures and instrumentation are the following:

- PC LAN users are more sophisticated than terminal users. With more knowledge about the LAN and operating systems, they generally have an increased understanding of internal security structures.

- In the LAN environment, more devices store and maintain data. Protecting these data becomes increasingly difficult.

- There are far too many utilities available to bypass copy protection, expose disk structures, and perform sophisticated file/disk copying. For all practical purposes, data are exposed to security risks.

- Cables are one of the primary and easiest places for security violations to occur. Both copper-based and fiber-optic cables can be tapped, each using different technologies at different costs. Tapping, in combination with monitoring devices, allows the violator to read passwords, analyze traffic patterns, and actually capture sensitive information. In addition, electromagnetic signal leakage causes additional vulnerability for LAN security.

- Usually, low-security LANs are less expensive and allow the choice of a wider selection of software and hardware, while high-security requirements may reduce the selection list to only a few options. Additional hardware and more expensive software are generally required for the more secure LAN installations. Implementation of a very secure LAN is considerably more costly than a single workgroup LAN. In the following section, the main functional areas of LAN security management are outlined in some depth.

- The number of people in the mobile workforce has increased.

- There are access needs from multiple entry points into LANs, including Internet, mainframes, midrange systems and PCs.

Identifying the sensitive information to be protected

Sensitive information is any data an organization wants to secure, such as that pertaining to customer accounts, price lists, research and development, payroll, addresses, bill of material processors, acquisition and marketing plans, product announcement schedules—the possibilities are almost limitless.

The identification is positively a team effort where practically all departments or business units are participating. After agreeing on the sensitive information, the team is expected to determine the most likely location where this information is kept. It could become a relatively long list due to the distributed nature of LANs. Most likely, locations are the mainframe that may play the role of a big server or the database engine and all the servers in the interconnected LANs. Occasionally, even workstations maintain important information that should be protected.

Analyzing threats and defining security indicators

One of LAN management's functions is to decide which indicators need to be supervised. Access authorization, user authentication, and password administration are the most important indicators. In order to find and implement the most efficient ones, it's useful to construct the LAN threat matrix (Table 3.13).

The construction of this matrix occurs in multiple steps: (1) classification of threats, such as natural disasters, hackers, sabotage by hostile employees, user mistakes, viruses, and industrial espionage;

TABLE 3.13   LAN Threat Matrix

Threats	Passive threats	Active threats	Unintentional operational threats
Principal network segments			
End user	H	H	L
Workstation	H	H	L
LAN: Cable	M	M	M
Fiber	L	L	M
MAN: Cable	L	L	L
Fiber	L	L	L
WAN: Cable	H	H	M
Fiber	L	L	L
Microwave	H	H	M
Satellite	M	M	M
Servers (HW, SW)	L	M	M
Databases	L	M	L
Applications	M	H	L

H = High threat
M = Medium threat
L = Low threat

(2) identification of principal network elements that may be vulnerable to threats; (3) evaluation of the risks as high, medium, or low.

Results may help to better distribute investments in the LAN security area. There's no absolute security, not even with unlimited financial resources. Depending on the industry, the enterprise has to find the right balance between security risk and investment. At least, a strategy for detecting LAN's penetration must be established. Key items for the detection of security violations are: looking for changes in the average number of active users, looking for unusual references to sensitive data stored on servers, monitoring more frequently during periods of hardware and software configuration changes, looking for nonscheduled changes in access control parameters, and looking for unexplained system crashes. This function finds the weak points where threats are real and of high priority. Threats may also be classified as passive, active, or unintentional operational threats.

Reviewing and analyzing the framework for security services

The framework for security consists of the following functions as defined by the Network Management Forum.

Authentication check on communicating partners. This function includes the following goals: defining the basic concepts of authentication, identification of the possible classes of authentication mechanisms; definition of the services for these classes of authentication mechanisms; identification of functional requirements; and identification of general management requirements for authentication. The framework enables verification of the identity of individuals. The basic function is the unique identification of users and programs. Verification of these identities assures individual accountability. Authentication includes mutual authentication as well as single user-to-system authentication.

Access control. The prevention of unauthorized use of a resource, including the prevention of use of a resource in an unauthorized manner. Access control allows the installation to protect critical resources by limiting access to only authorized and authenticated users. Depending on the environment, access may be controlled by the resource owner, or it may be done automatically by the system by using security labels. The resource owner can specify who can access the information, how it can be accessed, when it can be accessed, and under what conditions it can be accessed (e.g., when executing specific applications, programs, or transactions). The functional goal is to ensure that security is maintained for resources, whether they are in a central system, distributed, or mobile.

Nonrepudiation. Nondenial by one of the entities involved in communication of having participated in all or part of the communication. Nonrepudiation may be viewed as an extension to the identification and authentication services. The nonrepudiation service can protect a recipient against the false denial by a recipient that the data has been received. In general, nonrepudiation applies to the transmission of electronic data, such as an order to a stockbroker, a doctor's order to medicate a patient, or approval to pay an invoice. The overall goal is to be able to verify, with virtually 100 percent certainty, that a particular message is associated with a particular individual, just as a handwritten signature on a bank check is tied to the account owner.

Ensuring data privacy. This service protects data from being read by unauthorized parties. Privacy may relate to the connection, to special files, or even to selected fields of files.

Avoidance of traffic flow analysis. This special service helps prevent unauthorized users from making conclusions based on analysis of the pattern of communication traffic between different kinds of users. Traffic analysis protection must be considered for end-to-end encryption (Cooper 1990). The intent of traffic analysis protection is to mask the frequency, length, and origin destination patterns of the message traffic. If encryption were performed in the presentation layer, an analyst could determine which presentation, session, and transport entities could be associated with a particular traffic pattern. Performing encryption at the transport layer would limit the information association by not identifying higher-level entities. Additional protection can be provided by continually or randomly flooding the communication channel with dummy traffic. The price paid is lost channel efficiency.

Data integrity. This is the property that data has not been altered in any way. Data integrity provides detection of the unauthorized modification of data. Organizations must allow the usage of data by authorized users and applications as well as the transmission of data for remote processing. Data integrity facilities can indicate whether information has been altered. Data may be altered for two reasons: (1) because of hardware or transmission errors or (2) because of an attack. For years, many products have used a checksum mechanism in disk and tape storage systems and in network protocols to protect against transmission and hardware errors. Active attacks on data integrity require a different mechanism, which uses cryptography and allows for the verification of data integrity.

Confidentiality. The property that information is not made available or disclosed to unauthorized individuals, entities, or processes. Confidentiality protects sensitive information from disclosure. When it is stored locally, sensitive data can be protected by access controls or encryption mechanisms. For network communication security, sensitive data should be encrypted as it is transmitted from system to system.

Security audit and alarming. Data is collected and potentially used to facilitate a security audit.

Key management. This refers to the generation, storage, secure distribution, and application of keys in accordance with a security policy.

Sender and/or receiver acknowledgment. The sender/receiver receives a confirmation or acknowledgment that a certain amount of information has been sent/received. This service helps to avoid occasional debates about information exchanges not properly protocoled by either sender or receiver.

LAN security issues fall into the following three major areas: physical access, logical access, and administrative control.

Physical access. Security in any data processing environment starts with controlling access to the equipment. Although intrinsically distributed in topology, LAN security requires installing the file servers and printers in secured access rooms. Access to the LAN's cabling system is also a concern because of the potential to "tap" into the network, insert new nodes, or monitor network data traffic. Access control to the PC workstation itself must be considered. Even without the network or server available, the local hard disk of the workstation can pose a security risk for loss of data.

Logical access. Physical access techniques are designed to keep unauthorized users off the network. Logical access techniques are designed to keep unauthorized network users away from authorized files. Access to the data is the responsibility of the network operating system. It's via the NOS (network operating system) that the logical control for information access is carried out. Password access to servers and I/O rights to directory or file structures represent typical support features provided by a network operating system. The level of security required by any site will dictate the LAN manager's final choice of LAN software.

Administrative control. An important but often neglected aspect of LAN security is the role of the LAN manager. It's this individual who is responsible for physical and logical access control, in addition to undertaking fault recovery procedures, performing backups, and monitoring for potential security infractions.

Analyzing and selecting investment directions

Investment can be directed toward improving server security, connection security, station security, or a combination of all these types of security. The techniques used are a combination of those addressed in the previous section. In summary, the following components-managed objects can be protected:

1. Server security
   a. File servers
   b. Print servers
   c. Applications
   d. Files
   e. Network operating systems
   f. Passwords and authentication
2. Connection security
   a. Shielded twisted pair
   b. Unshielded twisted pair
   c. Coax
   d. Fiber
   e. Microwave
   f. Encryption devices
   g. Radiation
3. Station security
   a. Chip key or chip card
   b. Public and private keys in connection with servers
   c. Biometrics that are using physiological (retina of the eye, palm, fingerprint) or behavioral (voice, signature dynamics, keystroke dynamics) attributes of the user

Implementing security management services

In order to provide powerful services as addressed in the previous section, adequate solutions—a combination of tools and techniques—are required. The following services may be implemented:

Entity authentication.   This mechanism provides verification of the identity by comparing identification information provided by the entity to the content of a known and trusted information repository. This information may take the form of something the user knows, something the user has, or something the user is. For stronger verification, more than one of these characteristics may be required.

Access control lists and security labels.   Access control lists are a form of information repository that contains data relative to the rights and permissions of access granted to each authenticated identity known to the system. Security labeling provides a mechanism to enhance or refine the levels of control imposed on a resource or entity. This is done by defining specific controls on the label tag itself.

Encipherment/decipherment. Cryptography is the mechanism used to provide for confidentiality service. It is also used quite frequently to complement some other mechanisms in providing total security solutions. Encipherment and decipherment essentially deal with the transformation of data and/or information from an intelligible format to an unintelligible format and back to an intelligible format. This is basically a mathematical process employing the use of keys and algorithms that apply the key values against the data in a predetermined fashion.

Modification detection codes and message authentication codes. Data integrity is supported by the use of some sort of checking code. Three methods of calculating the checking code are in common use: cyclic redundancy check (CRC), modification detection codes (MDC), and message authentication codes (MAC). A CRC is relatively easy to compute and has typically been used to recognize hardware failures. It is a weak check for detecting attacks. An MDC is computed using cryptography, but no secret key is used. As a result, MDC is a much stronger check than CRC, because it is very difficult to find a second message with the same MDC as the legitimate one. However, an MDC has the same delivery requirements as a CRC in that a CRC or MDC may be delivered with data by encrypting it using a secret key shared by the sender and recipient. The MAC is cryptographically delivered using a secret key shared by the sender and recipient, so it may be delivered with the data being protected without further trouble.

Digital signature. In addition to data integrity, nonrepudiation services such as digital signature are becoming more important to many customers. Digital signatures provide proof of data origin and/or proof of delivery. The first provides the recipient with proof of the data sender's identity. The second provides the sender with a receipt for the delivery of data to the intended party.

Automatic dial-back. Upon password receipt, the receiver disconnects and after table lookup dials back using a prestored number. In this case, only the sender is authenticated. The advantage is that the availability of specialized audit trails and real-time monitoring may deceive the intruder by playing along with him or her in order to trace the physical location and escalate alarm actions. The disadvantages are the need for an additional network element (hardware or software), the restriction to a specific device location, readability of the called number—if not encrypted—and, probably, higher costs.

User passwords are vulnerable. There are some safeguards against this. The NOS can insist on changing passwords regularly or at random. Minimum and maximum lengths of use may be required as well. Certain third-party products help in this respect by not allowing escaping (Sabre menu), disabling devices (Sitelock), or offering virus-checking facility (Sitelock) in addition.

Authentication by special equipment. Recently, new solutions have been introduced for identifying the user to his or her workstation or terminal. The use of chip cards is based on a personalized set of information hard-coded into the chip. Loss of the card or key may still lead, however, to unauthorized use (Brigth 1990).

Authentication by personal attributes. In very sensitive areas, personal attributes, such as keystroke dynamics, signature dynamics, voice, color of eyes, hand scans, fingerprints, and the like, may be used as the basis for identification. The cost of this technique, however, can very rarely be justified.

Improving data integrity. Similar to data protection, this technique deals with solutions based on a checksum computation. The results are used to expand the message that will be sent to the destination address. The techniques are expected to be sophisticated enough not to be broken easily. The original message and the checksum are encrypted together. Also, time stamps and message identification have to be added to help reconstruct the message. Those additional flags may be encrypted as well.

Prevention of traffic flow analysis using fillers. Fillers may be used to fill time gaps between real data transmissions. If both communications can be encrypted together, the penetrater can't recognize any rationale or trend, or any random, periodic, or other pattern by listening to the traffic. On the other hand, the use of fillers is not unlimited. It may become very expensive, and communication facilities may be temporarily overloaded, resulting in serious performance bottlenecks.

Routing control by dynamic bandwidth management. State-of-the-art networking services enable users or the security officer to dynamically change or adapt the bandwidth assignment. This reassignment ensures higher security, when, for example, communication forms, applications, or users are temporarily separated in order to avoid security risks due to resource sharing.

Use of an arbiter (judge) function. For ensuring the reconstruction of all transactions and messages sent and received, a central administration function may be required. The function is similar to the control entity in a message-switching system. The function may be implemented as one of the responsibilities of the security officer.

In order to improve the overall security of LANs, security servers are under consideration. Figure 3.42 shows such an arrangement. This figure shows the cooperation of three different servers:

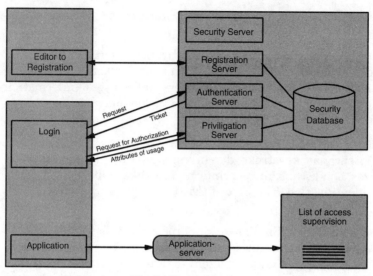

Figure 3.42 Architecture of the LAN security servers.

- Registration server to edit users and user's rights
- Authentication server to check personal attributes
- Privileges server to check the authorization for certain functions and applications

All servers are tightly coupled with the security database. In cases where security is even tougher than this arrangement, time limits can be set for the validity of tickets, or challenges can be issued in addition to the tickets.

LAN virus safeguards. A *virus* is a program that destroys data files or application programs or both. They have existed in one form or another since data processing started. With the widespread use of bulletin boards in interconnected LANs, virus programs are finding their way onto many LAN servers. Recommended preventive actions are as follows:

- Prohibit downloading of free software to use on LANs or PCs.
- Require tests of all new programs on a test server not connected to LANs and WANs. The tests should check for accuracy of output and potential destructive tendencies. The programs must be pushed to their input and output maximum values to test their accuracy under extreme conditions.
- Through audit trails, identify the person who has uploaded the program to the LAN.

- Limit the upload authorization and privileges.
- Routinely scan for viruses on servers and workstation.

In judging products, both detection and removal capabilities must be evaluated. They have to be rated based on their ability to handle a number of virus infection scenarios, including boot-sector virus infections and file infections by common and exotic viruses.

In order to evaluate feasible solutions against potential threats, Table 3.14 summarizes the threats and their remedies (Patterson 1991).

LAN security in a broader sense includes power supply, reliability of servers, and the choice of backup media (Theakston 1991). For the highest level of security, on-line resiliency services are recommended. The size of batteries in the UPS determines the load that can typically be supported. The support times range between 15 and 60 minutes, with power ranging from 500 Va up to 5 kVa.

The resiliency of the file servers is very critical in most environments. Two techniques are widely used, particularly in PC LANs: disk mirroring and disk duplexing. With disk mirroring, data is simultaneously written to two disks. If one disk fails, processing carries on using the second unit. Disk duplexing works like disk mirroring, but security is further enhanced by duplexing the disk controller.

The choice of a backup medium depends in most cases on the cost. Device classes, such as Exabyte (based on video recording products), digital audio tape (from audio recording), and erasable optical storage devices (based on compact disk technology) help to provide sufficient storage at various prices. Besides investment cost, the most significant factor is time to write and read the data. During the write, data has to be locked to other users. The shorter the time, the less impact is on LAN performance. Restoration time depends on searching efficiency and on reading the data. The first is more significant than the second. The expected performance in this respect depends on the technology chosen.

Figure 3.43 shows an example for implementing LAN security management services. The figure indicates both active and passive actions on behalf of the LAN security officer.

Securing the LAN management system

A protocol analyzer in the hands of the wrong person can be a security threat. If an infiltrator can get access to a LAN port or is able to tap the cable, the analyzer can reveal useful penetration information. An analyzer can capture the entire dialog taking place over the LAN and can display passwords in an easily readable form. Appropriating passwords is easy with analyzers, but passwords may still be useful in a properly designed LAN. It's possible, for example, to restrict the sta-

TABLE 3.14 Security Threats and Their Remedies

Threats				Remedies				
	Cryptography	Authentication	Checksum	Traffic management	Audit trails	Authorization	Virus safeguard	Disaster recovery
Natural disaster								x
Hackers	x	x	x		x	x	x	
Hostile employees	x	x	x		x	x	x	
User mistakes		x	x		x	x	x	
Viruses							x	x
Industrial espionage				x				

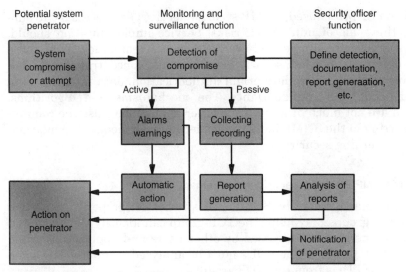

Potential system   Monitoring and   Security officer
penetrator   surveillance function   function

Figure 3.43 Implementing LAN security services.

tion(s) a user can log in from; thus, although the infiltrator may have
the manager's password, he or she can't log in as the supervisor without using the actual manager's terminal. In addition, audit trail utilities can report log-ins and log-outs, with special attention paid to the
manager's ID. This is why reliable security measures that go beyond
basic password protection are needed.

While protocol analyzers can present problems for LAN security,
they can in turn be used to monitor the network for infractions. One
simple technique involves looking for stations that are not supposed to
be on the network. The manager can set the display to depict unknown
stations. This is done by declaring an easily readable name for each
LAN station. If a program claims to lock certain files, for example, the
analyzer can be used to test that claim. With some analyzers, the network manager can write programs in C for specialized functions, such
as monitoring compliance with security procedures. For example, such
a program might look through the data to find stations that are logged
on to a file server but show no activity for long periods of time. This
may indicate a station where the user has walked away without logging off, which is a violation of security policies in most institutions.

Many LAN management systems will use SNMP. Currently, SNMP
shows many voids in terms of security. The goals of improving SNMP
security derive from the special threats against SNMP. Principal
threats are (Galvin 1991): unauthorized access; modification of information (e.g., parameters for the SET command); changed sequence of
messages; information disclosure; service denial; and traffic analysis.

When SNMP is used, SNMP security services are necessary to support the goals of minimizing risks. Service implementation should, however, remain simple, and overhead should remain low. With these two objectives in mind, security services must concentrate on the following (Galvin 1991): data origin authentication, data integrity, data sequencing, and confidentiality. The mechanisms and algorithms, which are not much different from other applications, use the community string in the SNMP message header to accommodate the information concerning security.

Use of SNMP PDUs for security management

Security management by SNMP PDUs is not yet properly supported. Only two groups may help. The TCP group can identify the users and applications that are accessed by other users and applications using the TCP/IP protocol. The PDUs must be analyzed manually. The same applies for PDUs from the UDP group.

Typical instruments for supporting LAN security management

In order to facilitate the work of LAN security officers, several products may be considered for use. Frequently, products from the fault and performance management areas may be used. Generic groups of products include LAN analyzers, LAN monitors, NOS monitors, continuous backup systems, audit trail utilities, and access surveillance tools.

LAN analyzers. Products for in-depth measurement for diagnosing problems. They passively listen to traffic and may time-stamp events and register dialogs between users and servers. In certain cases, the same instruments may be used as load generators.

LAN monitors. Products for supervising the principal status and use indicators on a continuous basis. They're inexpensive and don't introduce too much overhead.

NOS monitors. Products that may be seen as extensions of LAN operating systems. They can usually be easily activated or deactivated. The overhead doesn't seem to be critical.

Continuous backup systems. A continuous backup system is a utility that replicates all changes that are written to a disk as they're made. These systems don't necessarily replace the traditional tape-oriented backups that most network managers depend on today. Rather, they supplement tape backup.

Audit trail utilities. Audit trail systems are a key component of security management, although the function can be considered part of accounting management. Audit trail systems provide information on user activity on the LAN. Additionally, these systems can assist in billing management by providing the data needed to charge back usage.

An audit trail system must provide streamlined and useful information. LAN managers may wish to audit only certain users, operations on files with certain extensions or in certain subdirectories, certain types of operations, or certain servers. All file and directory creations, deletions, and renames may need to be reported. A system error log report, listing all system error messages to alert the LAN manager of potential problems, may be advantageous.

Access surveillance tools. These are logging instruments for analyzing access by authorization. Also, access denials, including reasons, are included. A postprocessor is one tool that provides statistics on security violations by LAN workstation and/or LAN user. The result of using such tools may be to tune security services and other instruments.

Virus safeguard tools. Usually, software programs to detect and remove viruses that are infecting the boot sector or files. Table 3.15 summarizes the typical security management instruments.

Staffing LAN security management

Security management of LANs is not yet always considered a separate functional area. This may very likely change as more and more mission-critical applications are moved to LANs and interconnected LANs.

In smaller organizations, the LAN administrator is expected to be responsible for principal security management functions, including the definition and supervision of access authorization, security risk analysis, and determination of feasible security services. In this function, the LAN administrator interfaces to the LAN manager and to vendors of LAN security management products.

In larger organizations, security must have dedicated human resources whose principal responsibilities include the following:

**TABLE 3.15 Typical Instruments
of Security Management**

LAN analyzers
LAN monitors
Continuous backup systems
Audit trail utilities
Access surveillance tools
Virus safeguard tools

- Evaluation of security risks in LANs
- Identification of potential threats
- Supervision of security rules
- Evaluation of security violations
- Making decisions against violators
- Assisting in elaborating security plans
- Protection of the LAN management systems
- Managing passwords
- Selection of security management–related instruments

Accounting Management of Local Area Networks

Accounting management functions in LANs have not yet been consistently implemented. Many users consider LANs a part of a company's infrastructure and are more willing to invest in software meters than in accounting procedures. There are two situations to consider: (1) accounting for LAN segments and (2) accounting for interconnected LANs.

In the first case, simple techniques, such as software meters and audit trails, may be used. In the second case, there are similarities with WANs; LAN segments are considered a traffic source for a wide area network. In such a case, traffic volumes have to be identified by their source. Interconnecting devices are expected to provide for raw accounting data. In the following section, the main LAN accounting management functions are briefly addressed.

LAN accounting management functions

Cost control is a must. LAN management needs to be fully aware of expenses. Cost components for LANs usually include:

- *Hardware.* Servers, peripherals, LAN interconnecting devices, wiring concentrators, workstations, network interface cards, modems, CDU/CSUs, extenders, repeaters, bridges, routers, brouters, gateways, memory.
- *Cables.* Purchase price and maintenance fee for cables and their connecting devices.
- *Software.* LAN OS, software in all of the hardware components, and management software.
- *LAN management systems.* Management systems, monitors, databases, test instruments.

- *Facilities.*   Leased lines, packet switching, circuit switching, microwave, satellites, frame relay, cell relay, SMDS, packet over cellular links or radio to connect LAN segments to each other.

- *People.*   LAN Manager, LAN Administrator, LAN Analyst, LAN Troubleshooter, LAN Designer and Planner, LAN Installer.

- *Other fixed costs.*   Building, preventive maintenance, etc.

- *Other fixed operating costs.*   Energy, heating and cooling, LAN management services (when outsourcing agreements are in place).

As a result of cost quantification, the "price" of LAN ownership may be determined, too.

Bill verification

Correctly processing vendor bills is principally a question of establishing well-defined procedures that are then carried out by trained accounting personnel. No significant problems exist in this area, as they may with costing and billing.

What's most important, however, is the procedure to verify the accuracy of vendor bills before these bills are paid. Significant overcharges can often be found through precise written procedures that analyze and verify vendor bills. Additionally, to prevent duplicate charges and/or penalties, clearly defined procedures for tracking and recording all bills are necessary.

Usually, bill processing is part of more complex billing systems. Network billing systems can capture call data directly from voice-switch SMDR ports. Calls can then be grouped for reconciliation and user billing. A central database also permits call-pattern studies and exception monitoring of network abuse. Some systems can even help the manager estimate and prepay call charges and avoid carriers' late payment penalties. Attention needs to be paid to correctly linking the billing system to configuration management—in particular, with inventory control and order processing.

Interconnected LANs may use various transport capabilities; in each case the supplier will bill for the facilities. Additional bills are expected from vendors of LAN hardware and LAN software components.

Determining resource use

Using measurement tools, resource use can be pinpointed for LAN management. Not every resource, but certainly the most important ones, need to be measured. Depending on available instrumentation, resources, such as servers and channels, may be measured continuously or periodically. As basis indicators for accounting, the following ones may be considered: number of transmitted bytes or frames or packets, number of server accesses, and resource use on servers.

Sampling (periodic monitoring) applies when continuous monitoring of each segment can't be cost-justified. It's extremely important to collect information on traffic as it leaves the LAN segment. Unfortunately, bridges, routers, brouters, and gateways are usually not equipped with internal traffic-monitoring features. RMON may be helpful in this respect by continuously recording the information exchange. Communigrams can clearly determine the initiators of communication dialogs.

Billing

A *charge-back system* can be defined as the assignment of communication costs to users. In some organizations, real dollars change hands; in others, bookkeeping entries are made, or statements are issued, but money transfers don't take place.

To be successful, a charge-back system must:

- Be understandable to the user.
- Be predictable so managers can plan effectively.
- Reflect economic reality.

The benefits of a charge-back system are as follows:

- It's a proven way of allocating expensive resources.
- It encourages users to make economical use of services.
- It promotes efficient service by controlling demand.
- It decentralizes control to enable users to make choices.

Potential drawbacks of a charge-back system are as follows:

- It entails overhead costs that reduce profits.
- It makes life difficult for LAN management centers.
- It usually results in complex rates and rules.
- It may result in underused resources.
- It encourages large groups to seek special benefits.
- It may remove an essential source for some users.

LAN management has to decide on the LAN usage indicators that will be used as the basis of the charge-back system. Depending on this decision, usage information has to be collected and processed. Corporate policies differ, and the following three alternatives may be distinguished.

Zero charge-back. Some corporations don't charge users with any LAN-related costs. These are simply considered corporate overhead, similar to the company cafeteria or company newspaper. Other corporations use a variation of this in "show-back accounting," whereby user groups are provided with "average cost" information, but no actual charge-back.

Partial charge-back. Most corporations levy partial charge-backs against users. In these situations, some LAN costs are absorbed by the corporation, some by certain groups such as corporate IS, and the remaining costs are charged directly to the user, based on specific rates and usage factors.

Full charge-back. A few companies attempt to charge all LAN costs to the user based on services provided. Very often these charges involve negotiated costs and prices. Profit centers may use this approach.

Supervising the use of applications: software licensing

A relatively new area with strong product support may help to improve the quality of billing. Software license management is closely related to software distribution and maintenance. Businesses have a legal responsibility for their licensed software. Network and system administrators are at risk if they do not control the application packages loaded on and available from the network. License management improves quantification in two respects:

- Accounting and charge-back within the company based on actual use of applications and resources
- Controlling the licensing agreement with the vendor

In most organizations today, license management is made difficult because of many factors. First, pricing structures offered by software vendors are obsolete and no longer accepted by users. Often, organizations exercise practically no control over who is using what types of software. Typically, internal charge-back is based upon resource categories rather than actual use of applications and systems resources.

As with electronic software distribution, practically no standards and no recommendations exist for license management application programming interfaces. The only exception is the guideline from the Open Software Foundation (OSF) with Network License (NetLS) Server from Gradient Technologies. NetLS consists of the license server software, which issues permission to run applications over the network. At the same time, the usage counter is increased for the user who has requested the permission. NetLS may also be utilized as the basis of the inventory software and track program versions, user identification, and usage. This would allow businesses to eliminate applications that are not being used or to buy additional licenses for high-demand applications. In addition to NetLS, there is another de facto standard, called Licensing Service API (LSAPI), that defines how applications talk to the licensing server. The two de facto standards do not conflict because they address different areas (Fig. 3.44).

The Network License Server may be extended by a software application depot. In such cases, licensing means that users may use the whole library, but they will be charged for the actual use—as controlled by the Network License Server. Such a library will typically be sent to the user on a CD-ROM disk, which is the preferred delivery solution for suppliers with a large number of software products and a large installed base.

Suppliers are expected to incorporate license calls into their applications using LSAPI. Each call will generate a request to a license manager, who will distribute a license key giving information about the license. Additional control opportunities may be incorporated in the license server. In order to control the usage of certain applications and to optimize systems and network load, permissions may be granted only for certain periods of time. If permitted, the server returns a key and the application is allowed to run, provided the user has the valid

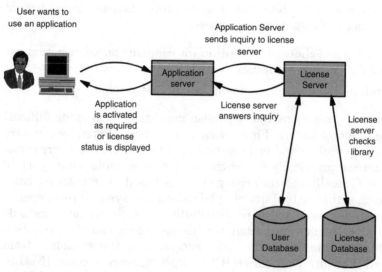

Figure 3.44 Software licensing.

security clearance. If the system is overloaded, user requests may be put into a temporary queue.

In many cases, these tools are combined with software distribution tools. Tools will be introduced in Chap. 5.

Use of MIB PDUs for accounting management

SNMP MIBs offer a wide choice of raw information that may be processed to support selected accounting management functions. The following list (Leinwand 1993) concentrates on selected protocol data units of MIB II that may be processed into meaningful indicators of the accounting management process.

Interface group	Information content
ifInOctets	Total bytes received
ifOutOctets	Total bytes sent
ifInUcastPkts	Total unicast packets received
ifOutUcastPkts	Total unicast packets sent
ifInNUcastPkts	Total nonunicast packets received
ifOutNUcastPkts	Total nonunicast packets sent
IP group	**Information content**
ipOutRequest	Number of IP packets sent
ipInDelivers	Number of IP packets received
TCP group	**Information content**
tcpActiveOpens	Number of times this system has opened a connection
tcpPassiveOpens	Number of times this system has received a request to open a connection
tcpInSegs	Total number of TCP segments received
tcpOutSegs	Total number of TCP segments sent
tcpConnTable	Current TCP connections
UDP group	**Information content**
udpInDatagrams	Total number of UDP datagrams received
udpOutDatagrams	Total number of UDP datagrams sent
udpTable	Current UDP ports accepting datagrams

Typical instruments for supporting LAN accounting management

In order to support LAN accounting management functions, several products may be considered for use. Resource use may be determined by LAN analyzers or monitors. For supporting bill-back and bill verification, new applications need to be designed and implemented. Costing remains for a period of time a manual process. Generic groups of products include the following.

LAN analyzers. Products for in-depth measurement for diagnosing problems. They passively listen to traffic and may time-stamp events and register dialogs between users and servers. In certain cases, the same instruments may be used as load generators.

LAN monitors. Products for supervising the principal status and use indicators on a continuous basis. They're inexpensive and don't introduce too much overhead.

NOS monitors. Products that may be seen as extensions of LAN operating systems. They can usually be easily activated or deactivated. The overhead doesn't seem to be critical.

Audit trail utilities. Audit trail systems are a key component of security management, although the function can be considered part of accounting management. Audit trail systems provide information on user activity on the LAN. Additionally, these systems can assist in billing management by providing the data needed to charge back usage.

Software meters. Products that help to control software product licensing and deter illegal copying. The frequency of use is recorded for costing and charging. The information collected also helps bill verification. But the security risk of viruses must not be ignored. Often, vendors bring in dormant modules that may destroy (deactivate, disable) the product unless bills have been paid properly. (Table 3.16 summarizes the typical accounting management instruments.)

Staffing LAN accounting management

Accounting management is not yet a dedicated organizational entity. In most corporations, the LAN administrator is expected to be responsible for LAN accounting–related functions. This situation will most likely change, as a significant amount of money is going to be spent on transmission facilities for interconnecting LANs. After the change, LAN administrators are expected to be responsible for the following tasks:

- Determination of the necessary details for accounting records
- Assisting in developing accounting equations

TABLE 3.16   Typical Instruments of Accounting Management

LAN analyzers
LAN monitors
NOS monitors
Software meters
Audit trail utilities

- Selection of accounting instruments
- Definition of accounting indicators for LANs and WANs
- Administration of accounting logs
- Administration of software licenses
- Negotiation with vendors on software licenses

Administration of Local Area Networks

Functions not addressed in the previous sections are summarized under the generic term *administration*. The functional area concentrates on LAN documentation, software distribution, user administration, and LAN maintenance.

LAN documentation.   This function is tightly coupled with asset management, topology services, and configuration management. Satisfactory solutions are very rare due to the large number of components in LANs. The majority of products offer solutions for a definite size of LANs without scalability. Migration to more powerful documentation tools is very difficult because LAN managers do not want to replace something that is functioning. Today, there are documentation solutions for the following:

- Servers
- Clients (workstations)
- WANs
- MANs
- LANs

Formats and syntax are different, and information export and import is practically impossible. The first attempt of integration could be the LAN management platform responsible for at least a subset of information relevant to all components in LANs. The ultimate solution is expected to come from asset or cable management instruments outlined and addressed in the configuration management section of this chapter. They represent the high-end solution with relational databases, CAD/CAM technology, and a network management platform. They offer a large number of templates representing the most widely used LAN components. Otherwise, present solutions show are as follows:

- *Documentation tools on PCs with standard products.*   Here we actually see a spreadsheet with graphics (e.g., Excell with PowerPoint).

- *Documentation tools on PCs with special products.* Here we see products from individual software vendors (e.g., GrafBase and NetWiz).

- *Asset and cable management products.* These use the power of Unix-based management platforms (e.g., Commend 5000 from Isicad or Mountain View from Accugraph).

- *Data repositories.* Here large data amounts can be stored and maintained. Included are graphical visualization solutions (e.g., data repository and Graphic Monitor Facility from IBM).

The area of LAN documentation is very dynamic, and more powerful solutions are expected soon. Product examples are covered in Chap. 5.

User administration. LAN management and software cover a wide range of applications and functions. In broad terms, this LAN management function can be divided into two classes: user support and system support.

User support capabilities insulate users from the complexities of the LAN and reduce the amount of training and interaction that must be undertaken by the LAN manager. These tools include front-end, document-organizer, and remote-user support.

System support capabilities give the network manager information about the LAN itself. System support utilities provide data on user activity, disk usage, network traffic, system configuration, and so on. These tools complement local area network operating systems. Some available tools address shortcomings of LAN operating systems.

User administration functions. User administration functions have two major goals: to enhance the end user's working environment and to help detect, diagnose, and correct problems caused by users, applications, or managed objects.

Front ends are menu-driven interfaces that insulate users from the native environment. The menus will convert from the user-friendly commands to the necessary Unix, OS/2, or Windows NT operating system commands. End users should not be expected to know the LAN software protocol stack and other details such as software version numbers.

Many front-end systems provide a template that the network manager can customize for different LAN user groups; these menus can typically be produced at the manager's terminal and distributed over the network. A front end may perform additional functions as well. Some front ends provide basic usage tracking. While these reports are not as detailed as those produced by sophisticated audit trail tools, front-end systems can report how much time a user spends on a particular application. Others may blank out the screen after a period of inactivity or even log off the user. Other front ends have a software meter, which monitors application usage to support adherence to the license restrictions.

Maintenance of user data. Remote user support tools allow the network manager to gain access to the remote workstation or PC; access to the keyboard and screen can be acquired remotely so that the manager can determine the possible problem source. In some systems, the manager is automatically informed regarding what hardware the user has. In addition, some of these systems maintain statistics on who was helped, the nature of the assistance, and the duration of the session. This data can be used to bill back support costs and/or to design training programs.

Detecting, diagnosing, and correcting problems. This function is implemented with a combination of local and remote help desks. A local help desk may be useful for a large site serving multiple local area networks. The help desk is expected to be equipped with various analyzer instruments, automated call distributors, and with troubleshooting guidelines.

Local help desks are expected to work with the central help desk in troubleshooting serious problems. Trouble tickets are electronically communicated to central help desk.

A centralized help desk may be useful in situations where there are many distributed local area networks that are geographically far from each other, but which may be internetworked using bridges, routers, brouters, or gateways.

The central help desk is equipped with various stand-alone instruments, LAN management products or platforms, automated call distributors, and troubleshooting guidelines. A central help desk may be shared between WANs and LANs. Management of MANs will most likely be integrated in the future.

The help desk has a special combination of instruments and a varying degree of administration experience. In order to support administration functions, implementation may be borrowed from WAN help desks.

Automated operations are very helpful in accelerating problem recognition and elimination. The problem is that there's always some event that they're not prepared to handle because it has not come up before or it's not considered part of the system's work (Weissmann 1991). In such situations, an automated or semiautomated problem management system must take over. A good system must be rule-based and have a base of knowledge that it applies to the LAN problem. The content of this knowledge includes the following: who should be contacted, when they should be contacted, how they should be contacted, what to do if they can't be contacted, what to do if they don't fix the problem, and how long to wait for a fix before further escalation.

Such a system is basically a real-time update of the available human resources that may be dispatched to solve LAN problems. Many extensions may be considered, which include voice output, use of various priorities of escalation, and use of artificial intelligence for the rule base.

Many problems that end users attribute to LANs are, in fact, problems that stem from the user's lack of familiarity with the various LAN applications he or she wants to employ. Network managers can resolve such problems by using remote access tools to determine the causes of application problems.

Many of the tools available today provide extensive features that let help desk staff resolve common problems within a short period of time. Most of the tools speed up problem resolution or preventively avert trouble. Examples include links to electronic mail systems and to management platforms. Better tools will help in effectively dealing with a breadth of new technology spreading across LANs. Without such new tools, the spread of LAN technology would overwhelm the staff's ability to keep pace. New and better tools help to centralize help desk services, which may lead to significant cost reductions. Product examples will be referenced in Chap. 5.

Software distribution

Electronic software distribution allows network administrators to distribute, install, and maintain software throughout an internetwork, using either a distributed or centralized method. It supports both the push and pull models of software distribution. The push model requires the server to load the software to the workstation; the pull model requires the workstation to request the software from the server (Fig. 3.45).

Software distribution and updating is one of the major reasons for high operating costs of managing client/server systems. Manufacturers that offer distribution services estimate that approximately 20 percent of the real cost of software lies in distribution and installation. Basically, desktops with software are much more difficult to manage than legacy-type terminals.

Electronic software distribution can reduce labor costs substantially by eliminating site visits, reducing the cost and length of time for a software change, enforcing version control, synchronizing software changes, helping vendors prevent unauthorized copying, and simplifying software installation by automation. It is also helpful in managing vendor license agreements.

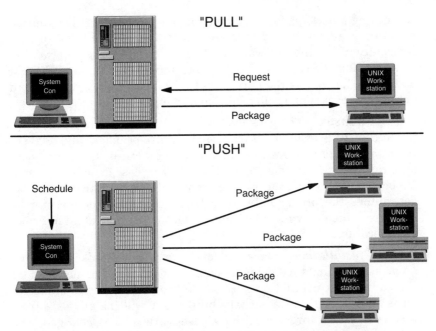

Figure 3.45 Pull and push techniques to support electronic software distribution.

There are, however, still many unresolved issues regarding electronic software distribution. Some vendors resist changing their distribution mechanisms; some products are still immature. The majority of users must control versions of software running on multiple servers and clients. Consequently, distribution services must be able to communicate with different servers and clients installed by different vendors running under various operating systems, such as Unix versions, OS/2, DOS, and Windows NT. Finally, distribution over WANs may be expensive due to high bandwidth requirements.

The distribution process is broken down into basic functions that are treated as individual modules. These modules include package creation, distribution scheduling, package transfer, and package installation.

- *Package creation.*   The first step in distributing software is to create a software package. Each software package is a set of programs and data files with installation and back-out methods that are assembled for distribution into one file called a *package*. The package moves around the network as one unit and is not unpacked until it reaches its destination (the target machine). Packages are the smallest unit of distribution.

- *Distribution scheduling.*   Distributing a package involves moving it from its source location to one or more target machines. Similar to scheduling a package for delivery using a parcel carrier, distribution scheduling allows the system administrator to specify "shipping" information for the software package. The shipping information includes the source and target machines (e.g., TO and FROM addresses) as well as the dates and times (i.e., when to pick up and deliver the package) for distribution and installation.

- *Package transfer.* The package transfer object functions as the shipper in the above example. It picks up software packages and delivers them to their proper destination. Some electronic distribution packages can specify multiple destinations. In this case, a package transfer object handles duplication to minimize network traffic. It also determines the proper network path to take when delivering the software, which may include dropping off the package at an intermediate location.

- *Package installation.* Once the package is delivered, it must be unpacked and installed using its embedded installation methods. By embedding the installation methods in the package, an administrator is guaranteed that a package built today will install years from now, even if the target machine's base software has changed. The package installation object unpacks the package after its installation time is reached. It verifies the contents of the package, installs, and notifies one or more administration machines of its progress.

These processes do not occur in isolation. Rather, they are usually seamlessly coupled to other management functions, such as inventory management, managing the installed software, and license management.

Prior to distributing software, maintaining an accurate software configuration inventory is very important. The control software is expected to locate all targeted servers and clients on LANs, MANs, and WANs. It configures them so they will report their inventory each time a distribution is intended. Agents will report any changes in memory, disk space, versions, applications supported, and other system conditions. In the future, desktop management standards will incorporate distribution guidelines as well.

During the distribution process, back-outs may be required if the distribution does not go as planned. If the administrators distribute a package and it cannot be received and installed on the target machine due to turned-off power or insufficient disk space, distribution will be automatically backed out. An alarm, which may be customized, notifies the control software of the back-out. Not only does the control software automatically back out distribution, but the administrator also has the option to manually back out the distribution.

After successful distribution, systems management functions are executed continuously. These functions are supported by other protocols.

Figure 3.46 shows a simplified structure for the distribution process. The management system may be a stand-alone system, but the preferred alternative is to implement the distribution control software on the same platform used for other management applications. The software depots are implemented by relational or object-oriented databases. In complex networks, additional depots can be installed serving various LANs. The workstation of the manager is equipped with standard systems and GUIs such as Motif, OpenLook, and Xwindows. Finally, Fig. 3.47 shows a combination of distribution alternatives.

Product examples for electronic software distribution will be referenced in Chap. 5.

LAN maintenance

In order to guarantee high service quality, LAN components must be maintained. Also included are maintenance and control functions with service suppliers and vendors. Status of existing solutions may be summarized as follows:

- Service-level agreements with suppliers and vendors are on the way, but not yet completely implemented.

- Functional and performance tests of spare parts are not yet fully understood and implemented.

- Proactive tests and measurements are considered overhead and rarely conducted.

- Administrative items with supplier and vendor contracts are taken by various departments without the necessary synchronization.

- Performance statistics of suppliers and vendors are not being consistently evaluated.

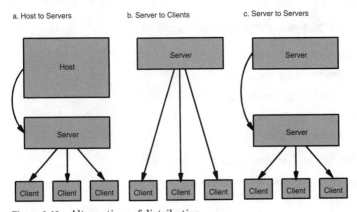

Figure 3.46   Alternatives of distribution.

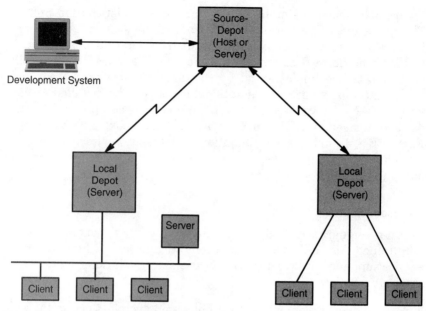

Figure 3.47   Combined distribution alternative.

- Inspection-type activities, such as support of administrative security, are usually neglected.

Actually, there are two principal processes that may be differentiated here. The first deals with establishing and maintaining a database or database segment with all the necessary data on contracts, suppliers, and vendors. The second process is responsible for the use of this database to conduct various maintenance functions.

Doing this, occasional links to other databases or database segments may be required. Figure 3.48 displays these processes in a graphical form.

The following types of information are necessary:

- Data on suppliers and vendors
- Data on service level agreements
- Actual status on inventory items
- Inventory of spare parts
- Maintenance schedules
- Test plans for proactive tests and measurements
- Performance parameters of components
- Inspection schedules

These data can be borrowed from other databases or collected from devices and vendors individually.

Functions to be supported by LAN maintenance concentrate on the following items:

- *Establishing company internal standards.* In order to ensure long-term interoperability between networking components, standards must be set for both physical and logical components. Examples for the physical layers are cabling types and categories, low-, medium-, and high-speed interfaces, network interface cards, transceivers, analog-digital and digital-analog converters, and other hardware

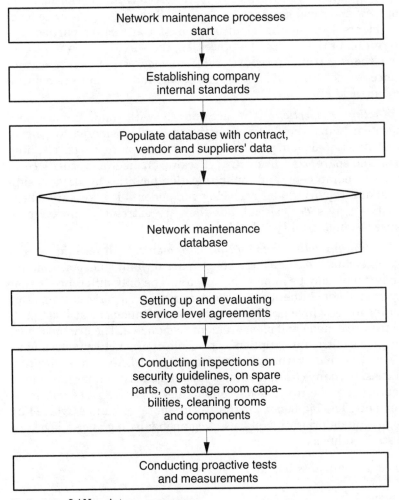

Figure 3.48   LAN maintenance process.

specified by the LANs. Examples for the logical layers are operating systems, access methods, compaction and compressing techniques, presentation services, LAN operating systems, network protocols and architectures.

- *Population of the database.* It is assumed that a commercially available database is used to maintain data of suppliers, vendors, and contracts. Population may use different techniques, including typing, electronically transferring, or scanning. Basically, this database may be identical with asset or configuration database. If it is shared, this function is using various segments of the same database, partitioned by accessing and security rules.

- *Setting up and evaluating service-level agreements.* Performance of suppliers and vendors must be quantified in writing. Service-level agreements include the identification of contracting parties, the description of the work to be processed, the service levels to be provided, the reporting procedure and frequency, penalties for noncompliance, ways for modifying the agreement, and the expiration day of the contract.

- *Conducting inspections.* In accordance with maintenance and inspection plans, the following activities are considered to be executed: functional and performance tests on spare parts; cleaning rooms and spare parts from dust; checking on meeting security rules for rooms, equipment, and communication facilities by services suppliers; and repairing and replacing components if necessary. These activities may seem clerical, but they are extremely important to ensure the high quality of LAN operations.

- *Conducting proactive tests and measurements.* All techniques and tools introduced earlier for tests as part of fault and performance management may be applied here again. The only difference is that they are part of neither troubleshooting nor performance tuning. But in order to recognize problems early on, continuous or at least periodic tests are made and measurements conducted. The principal goal is to have as little interruption as possible of productive tasks and as little as possible overhead on equipment and LAN communication facilities. In many cases, priorities must be clearly set for how many resources may be utilized for conducting proactive tests and measurements. The big benefit is that future outages can be avoided by recognizing deteriorating status of components (e.g., noise levels or crosstalk on lines).

Typical instruments include:

- Databases
- Asset management tools

- Test devices for LANs, MANs, and WANs
- Monitors for WANs, MANs, and LANs
- Administration software to generate reports
- Modeling devices for predicting performance impacts
- Scheduling and project management tools for inspection and maintenance tasks

Typical instruments for supporting LAN user administration

In order to support administration functions, a variety of instruments may be used. Basically, there are two groups of instruments: user support tools and system support tools. User support tools insulate users from the complexities of the LAN and reduce the amount of training and interaction that must be undertaken by the LAN manager. Systems support and documentation tools give LAN managers information about the LAN configuration. These utilities provide data on user activity, disk usage, network traffic, system configuration, and so on. Many tools that were described earlier may also be used for supporting LAN user administration.

Besides monitoring devices referenced before, special user administration tools include the following:

Documentation instruments. This category includes simple products in most cases based on PCs. The product price is relatively low, but populating the tools and maintaining the data is very labor-intensive.

Front ends. These instruments offer better user interfaces through menus and application customization techniques. They're installed as add-ons to the operating system in servers or as support programs in the workstations.

Remote user support tools. These instruments relieve end users from diagnosing problems at their own workstations or servers. The central or local help desk may gain access and troubleshoot the problem.

Console emulation tools. Products to consolidate operations by physically linking LAN management instruments to a management workstation. Dedicated windows may be opened for each individual management system. Alarm correlation, however, is accomplished by the LAN operator.

Help desk instruments. New techniques and instruments include:

Automated call distributors.

Interactive voice response. Also, integrated interactive voice response (IIVR) may be used to support the help desk of local area networks. IIVR is a dynamic voice mailbox for exchanging experience data on certain troubles. The IVR approach allows receiving the data from the trouble database; the voice mail option allows help desk personnel to expand or even change the information stored.

Voice mail.

Jukebox storage for diagnostics and trouble tickets.

Hypertext for user education, trouble tickets, diagnostics, and tutorials.

Expert systems for easy problem determination rules.

Software distribution tools. This category includes instruments that support electronic distribution using the push or pull technique or a combination of both.

Staffing LAN administration

LAN administration is a dedicated organizational entity. The LAN administrator has a number of responsibilities, including the following:

- Maintaining the documentation of LANs
- Control of hardware and software inventory, including versions
- Distribution of software to servers and clients
- Administration of software licenses
- Administration and training of users
- Selecting and maintaining the instrumentation of LAN administration

Table 3.17 summarizes the instruments for user administration.

Summary

After discussing individual LAN management functions and generic instruments, it's useful to summarize the general applicability of instruments to functions. Table 3.18 shows the applicability matrix;

TABLE 3.17   Typical Instruments of User Administration

Front ends
Remote user support tools
Console emulation tools
Help-desk instruments
Documentation instruments
Software distribution tools

TABLE 3.18   Allocation of LAN Management Instruments to LAN Management Functions

Management functions	Management functions*						
	CM	FM	PM	SM	AM	LA	PL
Management platforms	x	x	x	x	x	x	x
Databases	x		x			x	x
Backup utilities		x		x			
Diagnostic tools		x	x				
Analyzors		x	x				
Monitors		x	x	x			
RMON probes		x	x				
Emulators							x
Modeling tools							x
Simulators							x
Metering tools					x		
Software distribution						x	
Asset management	x					x	
Trouble ticketing		x	x				
Security auditing				x			
Document managers	x	x			x	x	
Reporting software		x	x				x
MIB tools	x	x	x	x	x	x	x

* CM = configuration management; FM = fault management; PM = performance management; SM = security management; AM = accounting management; LA = LAN administration; PL = LAN design and planning.

"X" indicates the most likely use of instruments by a particular LAN management function. The two major conclusions are:

- Most instruments are universal enough to be used by multiple functions.
- Each function requires a combination of instruments.

Instruments will be addressed in greater depth in Chap. 5.

Standardizing LAN Management

LAN management product solutions are greatly affected by emerging standards, which are the topic of this chapter. Standards include de facto solutions, such as TCP/IP-based techniques and open solutions based on OSI recommendations. After summarizing the driving forces for standards, the five emerging trends will be briefly introduced. The competing and complementary standards, OSI-CMIP and TCP/IP-SNMP, will be addressed in greater depth, including principles of work, implementation examples, and comparison of functionality. The final part of this chapter will deal with leading manufacturers' strategies. These strategies include architectures and platform examples. The distributed management environment (DME) decision on how to integrate leading solutions will also be addressed. The final part of this chapter will deal with the following LAN management platforms:

- Unix-based solutions (OpenView, NetView for AIX, OneVision, Sun-Net Manager, Spectrum, DiMONS, and ISM)

- Windows-based solutions (OpenView, NMC Vision, ManageWise, MSM)

- Systems management solutions (Tivoli Management Environment, CA-Unicenter, OperationsCenter, SMS NetView for OS/2, and NetView for Windows)

Integration of leading platform solutions and management applications will also be addressed.

The Need for Standardization

Enterprisewide networking requires that each client and server be able to communicate with all others. That's not an easy requirement to meet in a multivendor environment with many different products and networking architectures. The origin of the incompatibility problem lies in the fact that manufacturers developed their own solutions to providing interoperability among their own devices. This level of interoperability may involve a tremendous amount of investment by leading manufacturers, such as IBM, DEC, Novell, Microsoft, Tandem, Unisys, Siemens, Xerox, Hitachi, and so on. These companies will not likely be willing to give up their architectures and investments just to support standards. But communication standards can improve the efficiency and reduce the cost of linking clients and servers.

Both ISO and IEEE were working on defining standards for the communications industry, but neither could be responsible for devising one single standard. What finally emerged from the efforts of these and other standards-creating bodies was not a single standard, but the Open System Interconnection (OSI) Reference Model, a framework that could accommodate many standard protocols and combinations of protocols. At the top of the OSI model are the application, presentation, and session layers. Together, they're responsible for turning conditioned, formatted data into a stream that can travel on a generic network, defined by the bottom layers. These bottom layers—transport, network, data link, and physical—transfer traffic effectively and efficiently to the destinations. The same seven layers operate at the receiving end, in the opposite order, to condition and format the arriving information stream. Network management applications are implemented in layer 7 using CMISEs (common management information service elements). The underlying layers are used as service providers.

In order to serve users' connectivity and standardization needs faster, TCP/IP (Transmission Control Protocol/Internet Protocol) has been introduced. TCP/IP differentiates between three groups of layers: namely, application, logical, and physical (Fig. 4.1). Needless to say, TCP/IP will play a significant role as a common denominator in interconnecting devices and networks. The majority of management solutions are based on TCP/IP as an information source and information carrier.

The network access layer contains the protocols that provide access to a communication network, such as local or wide area networks. Protocols at this layer are between a communication node and an attached host. The TCP/IP suite does not include any unique protocols at this layer. Rather, the protocol appropriate for a particular network is used. The internet layer consists of the procedures required to allow data to traverse multiple networks between hosts. Thus, it must provide a routing function. This protocol is implemented within hosts and routers. A router relays data between networks using an internetwork protocol. The protocol at the layer is the internet protocol. A typical use

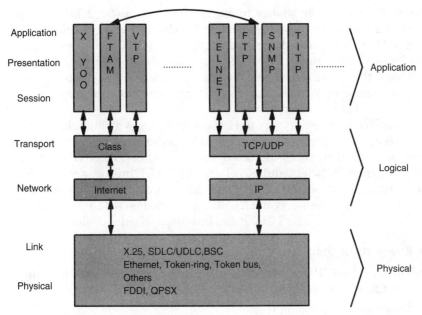

Figure 4.1 Layers of OSI and TCP/IP standards.

of IP is to connect multiple LANs within the same building or to connect LANs at different sites through a wide area network. The host-to-host layer provides the logic for ensuring that data exchanged between hosts are reliably delivered. It is also responsible for directing incoming data to the intended application. The protocol at this layer is the transmission control protocol. Finally, the process layer contains protocols for specific user applications. For each different type of application, such as file transfer, a protocol is needed that supports that application. Three such protocols are included into the TCP/IP protocol suite: SMTP, FTP, and TELNET.

The Simple Mail Transfer Protocol (SMTP) provides a basic electronic mail facility. It offers a way of transferring messages among separate hosts. Features of SMTP include mailing lists, return receipts, and forwarding. But it does not specify how messages are to be created. Some local editing or native electronic mail facility is required. Once messages are created, SMTP accepts the message and makes use of TCP to send it to an SMTP module on another host. The target SMTP module will make use of a local electronic mail package to store the incoming message in a user's mailbox.

The File Transfer Protocol (FTP) is used to send files from one system to another under user command. Both text and binary files are accommodated, and the protocol provides features for controlling user access. When a user wishes to engage in file transfer, FTP sets up a TCP connection to the target system for the exchange of control messages. Once a file transfer is approved, a second TCP connection is set up for the data transfer. The file is transferred over the data connection without the overhead of any headers or control information at the application level. When the transfer is complete, the control connection is used to signal the completion.

TELNET provides a remote log-on capability, which enables a user at a terminal or personal computer to log on to a remote computer and function as if directly connected to that computer. TELNET is actually implemented in two modules: (1) *user* TELNET interacts with a local terminal, and (2) *server* TELNET interacts with the application. Traffic between user and server TELNET is carried on a TCP connection.

The benefits of using TCP/IP can be summarized as follows:

- Every major computer vendor supports TCP/IP.
- The TCP and IP specifications, along with many source-code implementations are publicly available.
- There are no licensing fees.
- TCP/IP implementations require relatively little system memory and in most cases require far fewer processor resources than do most proprietary protocol alternatives.
- This protocol has been analyzed, refined, and debugged for more than two decades.
- Many of today's most popular applications can run TCP/IP, because many platforms, operating systems, and network operating systems are integrating TCP/IP support.

On the other hand, there are some risks to using TCP/IP as a strategic choice for users seeking broad, multivendor connectivity and a single network transport:

- IP addresses are in short supply. This mainly affects organizations planning widespread, direct connectivity to many users.
- Limited security may prohibit the use for sensitive applications, unless firewalls are implemented between the Internet and user nodes.
- TCP/IP represents an old technology that may not be efficient with state-of-the-art networking technologies.

SNMP is residing at the process layer. It takes advantage of transport services by TCP/IP or UDP/IP with version 1 or in addition of transport services, such as OSI, AppleTalk, or Novell-IPX with version 2. Migration to OSI is not very likely. The most pressing concern with TCP/IP was to manage network layer gateways in the Internet. An interim solution called Simple Network Management Protocol (SNMP) was provided, with the long-term solution of using the OSI management framework and protocols. This approach is referred to as CMIP over TCP (CMOT). Both protocols work with the same core management information base (MIB) defined for the TCP/IP Internet.

MAP/TOP envisions local area networks with heterogeneous nodes, some of which have implemented the entire seven layers of OSI protocol stacks, and some of which have implemented the lower layers only.

Thus, MAP/TOP had to find unique ways to manage its objects. In managing full stack nodes, OSI network management solutions are called for; in other cases, with a thin protocol stack, very basic management capabilities are in place.

The standardization process altogether shows satisfactory progress at lower layers. Besides working standards at the physical, data link, and network layers of WANs, lower layers have been successfully standardized for MANs and LANs. Figure 4.2 shows the results, including the reference to coexistence with OSI standards. Table 4.1 gives short definitions of the standards shown in Fig. 4.2.

In summary, there are five emerging network management standards:

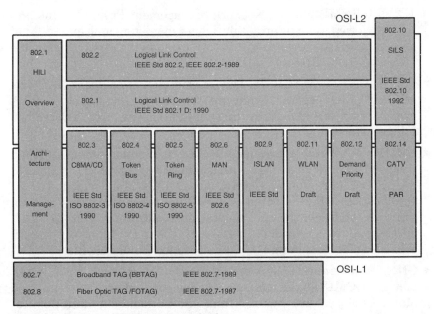

Figure 4.2   Devices of IEEE 802.X standards.

TABLE 4.1   Definition of 802.X Standards

802.1—an overview on LAN architecture, LAN and higher layer (i.e., metropolitan area networks) interface, internetworking, and network management. It is still in the draft stage.

802.2—defines logical link control and was recommended as standards in 1985 and adopted by ISO and OSI standard 8802/2 in 1987.

802.3—defines CSMA/CD access and physical layer specifications and was recommended as a standard in 1985 and adopted by ISO as an OSI standard 8802/3 in 1987.

802.4—defines token-bus access and physical layer specifications and was recommended as a standard in 1985 and adopted by ISO as an OSI standard 8802/4 in 1987.

802.5—defines token-ring access and physical layer specifications and was recommended as a standard in 1985 and adopted by ISO as an OSI standard 8802/5 in 1987.

802.6—defines metropolitan area network (MAN) access and physical layer specifications. It is still in the draft stage.

- Open System Interconnection (OSI) Management, which employs the Common Management Information Protocol (CMIP). The OSI, ISO/IEC Joint Technical Committee 1 (JTCI) has defined five sets of management facilities within the scope of OSI Management: configuration, performance, fault, accounting, and security. While current ISO standards-development activities may seem to have little impact on LAN management, future LAN management systems will undoubtedly be OSI compliant, to facilitate exchange of management data with other LAN systems and with wide area network (WAN) and integrated network management systems.

- TCP/IP's SNMP (Simple Network Management Protocol). This protocol is viewed as an interim solution for managing multiple Internet networks linked via gateways. SNMP exploits the capabilities of the User Datagram Protocol (UDP).

- CMOT (CMIP over TCP/IP). The Internet Activities Board (IAB) has adopted CMOT as the long-term solution for managing TCP/IP-based networks and for providing a migration path from TCP/IP to a full OSI stack.

- LMMP (LAN MAN Management Protocol). In order to manage Token Ring and Ethernet networks with a homogeneous protocol stack, IBM and 3COM are offering Heterogeneous LAN Management (HLM) specifications. HLM is based on CMIP, but will address low protocol layers. In addition, the LLC (logical link control) layer of the IEEE 802.2 standard is considered the target. The combination of both will give a lot of implementation help to practical environments.

- GNMP (Government Network Management Profile). The GNMP mandates CMIP as the management information exchange protocol. Managed objects are included from international standard publications. Five systems management functions are outlined: object man-

agement, state management, attributes for representing relationships, alarm reporting management, and event reporting. GNMP is
the management information specification of the networks defined
by GOSIP.

Figure 4.3 shows the basic relationship between manager and agent.
Depending on the protocol, the initiation of the dialog is different.

Open Network Management Architectures

Based on the seven-layer model, network management-related applications are also supported. Applications are implemented in layer 7.
Layers 1 through 6 contribute to network management by offering the
standard services to carry network management-related information.
Systems management application entities (SMAE) have three key
components—so-called application service elements—that are vital to
network management:

- ACSE (association control service elements) is responsible for an
  association establishment and a release establishment for an application association.

- ROSE (remote operation service elements) is responsible for connection establishment and release.

- CMISE (common management information service elements) is
  responsible for the logical part of communicating network management information.

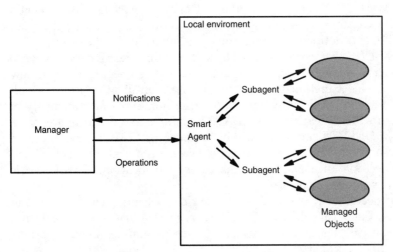

Figure 4.3 Communication paths between manager, agents, subagents, and
managed objects.

The M-INITIALISE service is used by a CMISE service user, such as a managing process, to establish an association with a peer CMISE service user, such as a managed process. The M-INITIALISE service forms the first phase of an instance of management information service activity. It's only used to create an association and may not be issued on an established association. M-INITIALISE is defined as a confirmed service (e.g., meaning that the target CMISE acknowledges to the initiating CMISE that the service has been provided). It's routed to ACSE to establish an association with a peer CMISE service user.

The M-TERMINATE service is used by a CMISE service user to cause a normal release of an association with a peer CMISE user. M-TERMINATE is defined as a confirmed service. It's routed to ACSE to cause a normal release of an association with a peer CMISE service user.

The M-ABORT service is used by a CMISE service user to cause an abrupt release of association with a peer CMISE service user. The M-ABORT is defined as a nonconfirmed service. It's routed to ACSE to cause an abort release of an association with a peer CMISE service user.

The M-EVENT-REPORT service is used by a CMISE service user to report an event associated with management information to a peer CMISE service user. M-EVENT-REPORT is defined as either a confirmed or nonconfirmed service.

The service is used by a CMISE service user to retrieve management information values from a peer CMISE service user. M-GET is defined as a confirmed service.

The service is used by invoking CMISE service user to request the modification of management information values by a peer CMISE service user. M-SET is defined as a confirmed and a nonconfirmed service.

The M-ACTION service is used by a CMISE service user to request a peer CMISE service user to perform an action on a managed object. M-ACTION is defined as a confirmed and nonconfirmed service.

The M-CREATE service is used by an invoking CMISE service user to request a peer CMISE service user to create a representation of a new managed object instance, complete with its identification and the values of its associated management information, and simultaneously to register its identification. M-CREATE is defined as a confirmed service.

The M-DELETE service is used by an invoking CMISE service user to request a peer CMISE service user to delete a representation of a managed object instance, and to deregister its identification. M-DELETE is defined as a confirmed service.

It's expected that two additional services become part of this set of services. These are M-CANCELGET and M-ADD/REMOVE. Using these service elements, a variety of system management functions (SMF) can be supported:

- Object management
- State management
- Workload monitoring
- Resource utilization
- Alarm management
- Test management
- Measurement summarization
- Relationship management
- Billing
- Event report management
- Log control
- Security alarming
- Security reporting
- Bill verification

SMFs carry out the management processes, or activities, specified by the various specific management functional areas (SMFA). It's clearly specified which of the SMFs are used by which SMFAs. For example, a state management SMF is used by the fault management and configuration management SMFAs. SMFs are defined in the SMF document. System management functions are detailed in the following section.

Object management

Object management uses OSI services, such as those specified in the Common Management Information Services (CMIS) standard, to perform actions on managed objects. For example, object management may invoke the CMISE service M-DELETE to delete a managed object from an open system.

Within object management definitions, services are specified that allow reports about object management activities to be communicated to other open systems. For example, an attribute change event report service can be used to send an event report to another open system if an object's attributes change.

In terms of modeling MIBs, there are two alternatives (Bapat 1991):

- *Object-oriented (OO) modeling.* The benefits of this technique are the well-structured class hierarchy, and the inheritance relationship from the superclass to the subclass.

- *Entity-relationship (ER) modeling.*   This technique is well suited for defining generalized relations between MIB objects. Parts of the OO model can be subsumed within the ER model.

Both alternatives are well understood. Current OSI-based standardization efforts concentrate on OO modeling, with supplementary information from ER diagrams.

State management

State management describes services that allow the OSI Management user to monitor the past state of managed objects and receive notices, or alarms, in response to changes in the state of managed objects.

The State Reading service uses the M-GET service of CMIS to retrieve information from managed objects. For example, M-GET may be used to retrieve an indication of whether a managed object is accessible by the management system.

The State Change Reporting service calls on the attribute change event report service of Object Management to notify users of changes in either the administrative or operational state of managed objects.

Relationship management

Relationship management describes services that create, delete, change, and report relationships among managed objects. Relationships among managed objects is a complicated issue. In general, a *relationship* is a set of rules that describes how the operation of one managed object affects the operation of another managed object within an open system. For example, two managed objects in an open system may have a relationship in which one is activated in the event that the other fails as a result of a fault management diagnostic.

Error reporting and information retrieval

Error reporting and information retrieval allow various types of information to be reported and retrieved through the open system. Descriptions of error types, probable causes, and measures of severity are specified. This type of functionality will be essential in integrated network management scenarios where users have more than one network in place. For example, a single network-management system's ability to access information about errors occurring in two open systems could be important in situations where a relationship exists between the two open systems.

Types of errors defined by this SMF are communication failure, quality of service failure, processing failure, environment failure, and equipment failure. Error reporting services for each type of error are defined in this SMF.

Probable-cause information provided by this SMF would indicate the problem source that results in an error. For example, in the case of a communication failure, a probable cause might be a call establishment error.

Five severity parameters are defined: indeterminate, critical, major, minor, and warning. In a network management application of this SMF, the ability to categorize alarms by severity helps the network manager quickly decide which alarms must be responded to immediately and which ones can wait. This SMF uses the CMIS service M-GET to perform information retrieval.

Management service control

This describes services that allow the management system user to determine which event reports are to be sent where. For example, this SMF could play a key role in network management systems scenarios by allowing the network manager to specify which information can be exchanged between manager processes and agent processes. Consider a scenario in which a user has one manager process that centralizes management of multiple, separate agent processes.

The management service control function allows the user to choose which types of event reports will be exchanged between the manager process and the individual agent process.

Confidence and diagnostic testing

Confidence and diagnostic testing allows tests to be performed on managed objects. The purpose of such tests is to allow the management system to determine the quality of services and to assist in the diagnosis of faults within the open system. For example, this SMF might be used to initiate bit error rate tests on remote modems.

Log control

This service allows users to choose which event reports the system will log. The log control function also enables an external managing system user to change the criteria used for logging event reports.

The application of the log control function in a network management scenario is very important. The network manager wants the ability to specify which events should be logged, but the ability to add or delete event reports to be logged is also very important. For example, the user may want to log only critical event reports, but at a later date, perhaps the need to track all reports on a historical basis will become important.

The implementation targets are SMFAs (specific management function areas), which represent the principal network management applications, including configuration, fault, performance, security, and accounting management.

OSI includes the concept of managed objects. It specifies their attributes, operations that may be performed upon them, and the notification that may result. The set of managed objects in a system, together with their attributes, constitute that system's management information base (MIB). In addition to MIB, the structure of management information (SMI) defines the logical structure of OSI management information. Both MIB and SMI are subject to special customization by manufacturers and users.

The strengths of CMIP include the following:

- General and extensible object-oriented approach
- Support from the telecommunication industry
- Support for manager-to-manager communications
- Support for a framework for automation

The weaknesses of CMIP are as follows:

- It is complex and multilayered.
- High overload is the price of many confirmations.
- Few CMIP-based management systems are shipping.
- Few CMIP-based agents are in use.

CMIP assumes the use of the OSI stack for exchanging CMIP protocol data units. In layer 7, there are also other applications which may be combined with CMIP.

Simple Network Management Protocol (SNMP)

Simple Network Management Protocol (SNMP) originated in the Internet community as a means for managing TCP/IP networks and Ethernet networks. During 1990 and 1991, SNMP's appeal broadened rapidly beyond Internet, attracting waves of users searching for a proven, available method of monitoring multivendor networks. SNMP's monitoring and control transactions are actually completely independent of TCP/IP. SNMP requires only that the datagram transport mechanism operate. It can, therefore, be implemented over any network media or protocol suite, including OSI.

SNMP operates on three basic concepts: manager, agent, and the management information base (MIB). (See Fig. 4.4.) (Datapro NM40 1990). Imagine Fig. 4.3 with different protocol data units and commands, and it's similar to SNMP.

An *agent* is a software program housed within a managed network device (such as a host, gateway, bridge, router, brouter, hub, or server). An agent stores management data and responds to the manager's request for this data.

A *manager* is a software program housed within a network management station. The manager has the ability to query agents using various SNMP commands.

The management information base (MIB) is a virtual database of managed objects, accessible to an agent and manipulated via SNMP to achieve network management.

Agent responsibilities

Each agent possesses its own MIB view, which includes the Internet standard MIB and, typically, other extensions. However, the agent's MIB doesn't have to implement every group of defined variables in MIB specification. This means, for example, that gateways need not support objects applicable only to hosts, and vice versa. This eliminates unnecessary overhead, facilitating SNMP implementation in smaller

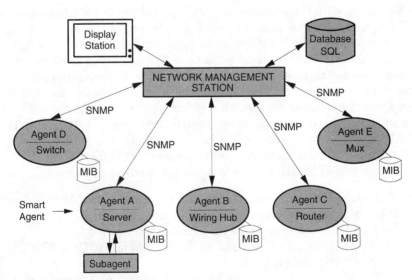

MIB   = Management Information Base
SNMP = Simple Network Management Protocol

Figure 4.4 Structure of SNMP-based management solutions.

LAN components that have little excess capacity for bearing overhead. An agent performs two basic functions:

- Inspects variables in its MIB
- Alters variables in its MIB

Inspecting variables usually means examining the values of counters, thresholds, states, and other parameters. Altering variables may mean resetting these counters, thresholds, and so on. It's possible to actually reboot a node, for example, by setting a variable.

An MIB implementation can be hosted on several types of platforms (Bapat 1991):

- Object-oriented databases
- Relational databases
- Flat-file databases
- Proprietary-format databases
- Firmware

Basically, MIB information is distributed in agents. A typical configuration may include at the agent level a disk-based relational database, or a combination of PROM with static object attributes, and a RAM with dynamically changing information.

An agent with full functionality will typically require 50 or more KB of program code and memory. About 50 percent of the manufacturers have implemented SNMP agents in software, which means the agents are loaded into memory from an outside storage device or downloaded from a server after startup. Other manufacturers have implemented their agents in read-only memory chips, or programmable ROM. These implementations can be upgraded, usually by the user in the field. The most advanced implementations, electrically erasable PROM and flash PROM, can be reprogrammed without physically changing the module. Thus, they offer excellent flexibility at minimum interruption.

The trends of SNMP agents may be summarized as follows:

1. The quality of agents is getting better because the SNMP technology is becoming better understood by implementors.
2. Performance and speed depend on the agent's platform.
3. Memory requirements depend on the functionality (Case 1992).
   a. 32 KB without an MIB
   b. Support of timers, drivers, operating system and protocol stacks, approximately 48 KB
   c. Approximately 0.25 KB for each MIB variable that's supported by the agent

4. Penetration of new managed objects, such as traditional networking devices, packet switching nodes, FDDI nodes, frame relay nodes, networking infrastructures, voice components, and applications.
5. Ability to run multiple agents from the same or different manufacturers on the same platform.
6. More education for properly using the "SET" and "TRAP" commands to reduce unnecessary overhead due to polling and due to an increase in the control capabilities of the management station.

The MIB (management information base)

The MIB conforms to the structure of management information (SMI) for TCP/IP-based internets. This SMI, in turn, is modeled after OSI's SMI. While the SMI is equivalent for both SNMP and OSI environments, the actual objects defined in the MIB are different. SMI conformance is important, since it means that the MIB is capable of functioning in both current and future SNMP environments. In fact, the Internet SMI and the MIB are completely independent of any specific network management protocol, including SNMP.

MIB is documented as a chain of numbers in hierarchical order. Internet is in the middle of this hierarchy, as shown in Fig. 4.5.

The SNMP-MIB repository is divided into four areas:

- Management attributes
- Private attributes

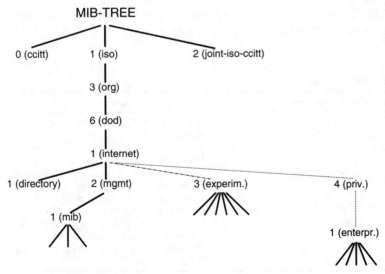

Figure 4.5 Hierarchy of MIB components.

- Experimental attributes
- Directory attributes

All documentation is written in ASN.1 (Abstract Syntax Notation One). ASN.1 is no replacement for other programming languages, but it offers many benefits, such as flexibility, definition of new structures, and writing of new macros. The clear structure and ease of specification helped ASN.1 become the common denominator of SNMP documentation.

MIB I includes a limited list of objects only. These objects deal with IP internetworking routing variables. MIB II extends the capabilities to a variety of media types, network devices, and SNMP statistics, not limited to the territory of TCP/IP. There have been many attempts to improve the performance of MIB accesses. A query language interface seems to offer a number of new capabilities, such as a relational mask and fast access.

In terms of MIBs, there are a lot of changes. In addition to standard MIBs, such as MIB I and MIB II (Table 4.2), the IETF has defined a number of adjunct MIBs covering hosts, bridges, hubs, repeaters, FDDI networks, AppleTalk networks, and frame relay networks. Some indicators are shown in Table 4.3.

Application problems are getting more complicated than hardware outages, and there is a definite lack of standards-based management tools. In order to support monitoring and analyzing applications, vendors need to agree on a management information base. The basic application MIB would need to contain three types of information: definition variables that identify key characteristics of the application, state variables that indicate whether the application is up or down or running at an appropriate performance level, and relationship variables that con-

TABLE 4.2   MIB II Structure

11 categories of management (2) subtree	Information in the category
system (1)	Network device operating system
interfaces (2)	Network interface–specific
address translation (3)	Address mappings
ip (4)	Internet protocol–specific
icmp (5)	Internet control message protocol specific
tcp (6)	Transmission protocol specific
udp (7)	User datagram protocol specific
egp (8)	Exterior gateway protocol specific
cmot (9)	Common management information services on TCP specific
transmission (10)	Transmission protocol specific
snmp (11)	SNMP specific

TABLE 4.3 A Comparison of MIB Coverage

MIBs statistics	MIB II	Host MIB	Bridge MIB	Hub MIB	RMON MIB
Interface statistics	x				
IP, TCP, UDP statistics	x				
SNMP statistics	x				
Host job counts		x			
Host file system information		x			
Spanning-tree performance			x		
Wide area link performance			x		
Link testing			x	x	
Network traffic statistics			x	x	x
Host table of all addresses				x	x
Host statistics				x	x
Historical data					x
Alarm thresholds					x
Configurable statistics					x
Traffic matrix with all nodes					x
HostTopN tables					x
Packet capture/protocol analysis					x
Distributed logging of events					x

tain information on how the application and other resources on the network depend on each other (Sturm 1995).

This MIB defines SNMP tables that capture variables according to the three-stage life cycle of a distributed application. This information pertains to software that has been distributed, configured, and is running. The first implementation examples define a number of useful and important tables, such as the following:

- Installed unit includes manufacturer's name, file names, and release number.

- Installed process includes the resource requirements of the application processes.

- Distributed application contains a collection of distributed software tools that could be used to solve an application problem.

- Configured unit represents a configured package of software.

- Realizable process represents a discrete application process, which can be invoked, monitored, or controlled by other applications.

- Business function is a table including definition and relationship variables that define an aggregation of various distributed applications for a specific administrative function.

- Process is a table containing definition, relationship, and state variables concerning a running application program.

- Files and mailboxes include configuration, relationship, and state variables that describe files and interprocess communications mechanisms that an application process uses while executing.

There are examples today that applications are managed by known management platforms.

The management attributes are expected to be the same for all agents supporting SNMP. Thus, SNMP managers may work with agents from various manufacturers. In order to offer more functionality, vendors populate the private attributes as well. Figure 4.6 shows an example of how the private variables are structured by Cisco. It's similar to other vendors' structures, but may be completely different in the context of the indicators. As a result, the portability of solutions is somewhat limited.

Using MIBs, the partitioning will play a very important role in the future. The following discussion assumes that a minimal configuration for a network management product consists of a management station with some storage capability and that this station is connected to managed objects equipped with agent capabilities.

Frequently, network resources are capable of being downloaded for certain management attributes (e.g., configuration, fault, and performance attributes). Further, they're capable of being polled and queried for current status. In such cases—the general idea of SNMP—it's not necessary to store this information in the central database of the net-

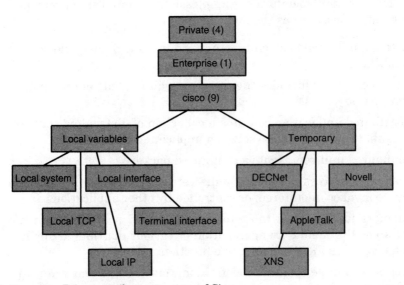

Figure 4.6   Private attributes structure of Cisco.

work management station. Certain other network objects may be capable of storing MIB information, not only about themselves, but also about other managed objects as well. Good examples are multiplexer, PBXs, routers, and bridges. They maintain information about connected or owned components. This type of information doesn't need to be duplicated in the central database.

On the other hand, there are information groups that are optimally stored in a central database, including the central directory of managed objects, and LAN-wide topology information. The following architectural principles may be applied toward distributing MIB information (Bapat 1991).

The internal information storage capabilities of every managed object must be determined. If the resource can store nonvolatile information, and is capable of being queried for that, those attributes don't need to be stored centrally. If the managed object can store only volatile information that needs to be supplied to it, then copies of this information must be stored in a central database. Systemwide information, such as directory, connectivity, high-level security management functions, maintenance of historical data and accounting information, is optimally stored in the central database.

In the hierarchy of management entities, where the intermediate entity also has storing capabilities, some of the data should be maintained in the intermediate entity. However, query requirement on behalf of the management station must not exceed a reasonable limit. Reliability and fault-tolerance requirements may result in maintaining two copies of relevant information. LAN objects using wireless connection technologies are expected to use SNMP for management. Accessibility of objects by SNMP managers may be supported by both wireless and wire-based techniques.

The first SNMP-based products use a combination by maintaining information in both databases. In order to keep the price of a managed object low, just the necessary amount of information is stored in the objects. In terms of how much information should be stored in objects, OSI and SNMP guidelines strongly disagree.

Real MIB implementations may require extensions, incorporating other types of information to be stored for supporting operations. Such extensions may include the following (Bapat 1991):

- Improving security management by including security information about access to various managed objects, access to the network management system itself, and access to manipulating the MIB.

- Extended user data may help to manage users and groups of users. Users and user groups can themselves be managed objects that must be created, maintained, and eventually deleted in the MIB.

- Configuration histories and profiles support for retrieving past information, for reporting, or for supporting backup, and alternate routing as part of LAN fault and performance management.

- Trouble tracking helps to resolve networking problems more rapidly. The augmented MIB would provide the ability to translate event reports into trouble tickets, assign work codes to staff, recognize and categorize types of problems, relate problems, escalate problems by severity, and close trouble tickets after eliminating the problem and its causes.

- Extended set of performance indicators that supports more advanced performance management by reporting on resource use, on threshold violations, on trends, and on the quality of managing bandwidth between interconnected LANs. A concrete extension example is RMON.

Performance of MIBs and their counterpart at the network management station must be observed very carefully. Observation includes the registration of the actual frequency of command, number of traps, frequency of information retrievals by GetNextRequest, and the relation of positive to negative poll responses. MIBs are performing optimally only when tuned to special environments.

The Remote MONitoring (RMON) MIB will help to bridge the gap between the limited services provided by management platforms and the rich sets of data and statistics provided by traffic monitors and analyzers. RMON defines the next generation of network monitoring with more comprehensive network fault diagnosis, planning, and performance-tuning features than any current monitoring solution. The design goals for RMON are as follows (Stallings 1993):

- *Off-line operation.*   In order to reduce overhead over communication links, it may be necessary to limit or halt polling of a monitor by the manager. In general, the monitor should collect fault, performance, and configuration information continuously, even if it is not being polled by a manager. The monitor simply continues to accumulate statistics that may be retrieved by the manager at a later time. The monitor may also attempt to notify the manager if an exceptional event occurs.

- *Preemptive monitoring.*   If the monitor has sufficient resources, and the process is not disruptive, the monitor can continuously run diagnostics and log performance. In the event of a failure somewhere in the network, the monitor may be able to notify the manager and provide useful information for diagnosing the failure.

- *Problem detection and reporting.*   Preemptive monitoring involves an active probing of the network and the consumption of network resources to check for error and exception conditions. Alternatively, the monitor can passively—without polling—recognize certain error conditions and other conditions, such as congestions and collisions, on the basis of the traffic that it observes. The monitor can be configured to continuously check for such conditions. When one of these conditions occurs, the monitor can log the condition and notify the manager.

- *Value-added data.* The network monitor can perform analyses specific to the data collected on its subnetworks, thus off-loading the manager of this responsibility. The monitor can, for instance, observe which station generates the most traffic or errors in network segments. This type of information is not otherwise accessible to the manager that is not directly attached to the segment.

- *Multiple managers.* An internetworking configuration may have more than one manager in order to achieve reliability, perform different functions, and provide management capability to different units within an organization. The monitor can be configured to deal with more than one manager concurrently.

Table 4.4 summarizes the RMON MIB groups for Ethernet segments. Table 4.5 defines the RMON MIB groups for Token Ring segments. At the present time, there are just a few monitors that can measure both types of segments using the same probe.

RMON is very rich in features and there is the very real risk of overloading the monitor, the communication links, and the manager when all the details are recorded, processed, and reported. The preferred solution is to do as much of the analysis as possible locally, at the monitor, and send just the aggregated data to the manager. This assumes powerful monitors. In other applications, monitors may be reprogrammed by the managers during operations. This is very useful when diagnosing problems. Even if the manager can define specific RMON requests, it is still necessary to be aware of the trade-offs involved. A complex filter will allow the monitor to capture and report a limited amount of data, thus avoiding overhead on the network. However, complex filters consume processing power at the monitor; if too many filters are implemented, the monitor will become overloaded. This is particularly true if the network segments are busy, which is probably the time when measurements are most valuable.

The existing and widely used RMON version is basically a MAC standard. It does not give LAN managers visibility into conversations across the network or connectivity between various network segments. The extended standard RMON2 is targeting the network layer and higher. It will give visibility across the enterprise. With remote access

TABLE 4.4   RMON MIB Groups for Ethernet

Statistics group	Features a table that tracks about 20 different characteristics of traffic on the Ethernet LAN segment, including total octets and packets, oversized packets, and errors.
History group	Allows a manager to establish the frequency and duration of traffic-observation intervals, called *buckets*. The agent can then record the characteristics of traffic according to these bucket intervals.
Alarm group	Permits the user to establish the criteria and thresholds that will prompt the agent to issue alarms.
Host group	Organizes traffic statistics by each LAN node, based on time intervals set by the manager.
HostTopN group	Allows the user to set up ordered lists and reports based on the highest statistics generated via the host group.
Matrix group	Maintains two tables of traffic statistics based on pairs of communicating nodes; one is organized by sending node addresses, the other by receiving node addresses.
Filter group	Allows a manager to define, by channel, particular characteristics of packets. A filter might instruct the agent, for example, to record packets with a value that indicates they contain DECnet messages.
Packet capture group	This group works with the filter group and lets the manager specify the memory resources to be used for recording packets that meet the filter criteria.
Event group	Allows the manager to specify a set of parameters or conditions to be observed by the agent. Whenever these parameters or conditions occur, the agent will record an event into a log.

and distributed work groups, there is substantial intersegment traffic. The following functionalities are included.

Protocol distribution and protocol directory table. The issue here was how to provide a mechanism that will support the large number of protocols running on any one network. Current implementations of RMON employ a protocol filter that analyzes only the essential protocols. RMON2, however, will employ a protocol directory system that allows an RMON2 application to define which protocols an agent will employ. The Protocol Directory Table will specify the various protocols an RMON2 probe can interpret.

Address mapping. This feature matches each network address with a specific port to which the hosts are attached. Also identifies traffic-generating nodes/hosts by MAC, token ring, or Ethernet address. It helps identify specific patterns of network traffic. Useful in node dis-

TABLE 4.5   RMON MIB Groups for Token Ring

Statistics group	This group includes packets, octets, broadcasts, dropped packets, soft errors, and packet distribution statistics. Statistics are at two levels: MAC for the protocol level and LLC statistics to measure traffic flow.
History group	Long-term historical data for segment trend analysis. Histories include both MAC and LLC statistics.
Host group	Collects information on each host discovered on the segment.
HostTopN group	Provides sorted statistics that allow reduction of network overhead by looking only at the most active hosts on each segment.
Matrix group	Reports on traffic errors between any host pair for correlating conversations on the most active nodes.
Ring station group	Collects general ring information and specific information for each station. General information includes: ring state (normal, beacon, claim token, purge); active monitor; number of active stations. Ring Station information includes a variety of error counters, station status, insertion time, and last enter/exit time.
Ring station order	Maps station MAC addresses to their order in the ring.
Source routing statistics	In source-routing bridges, information is provided on the number frames and octets transmitted to and from the local ring. Other data includes broadcasts per route and frame counter per hop.
Alarm group	Reports changes in network characteristics based on thresholds for any or all MIBs. This allows RMON to be used as a proactive tool.
Event group	Logging of events on the basis of thresholds. Events may be used to initiate functions such as data capture or instance counts to isolate specific segments of the network.
Filter group	Definitions of packet matches for selective information capture. These include logical operations (AND, OR, NOT) so network events can be specified for data capture, alarms, and statistics.
Packet capture group	Stores packets that match filtering specifications.

covery and network topology configurations. In addition, the address translation feature adds duplicate IP address detection resolving a common trouble spot with network routers and virtual LANs.

Network-layer host table.   Tracks packets, errors, and bytes for each host according to a network-layer protocol. It permits decoding of packets based on their network-layer address, in essence permitting network managers to look beyond the router at each of the hosts configured on the network.

Network-layer matrix table.   Tracks the number of packets sent between a pair of hosts by network-layer protocol. The network manager can identify network problems quicker using the matrix table, which shows the protocol-specific traffic between communicating pairs of systems.

Application-layer host table.   Tracks packets, errors, and bytes on an application-specific basis (e.g., Lotus Notes, E-mail, Web, etc.) Both the application-layer host table and matrix table trace packet activity of a particular application. This feature can be used by network managers to charge users on the basis of how much network bandwidth was used by their applications.

Application-layer matrix table.   Tracks packet activity between pairs of hosts by application (e.g., pairs of hosts exchanging Internet information).

Probe configuration.   Currently, vendors offer a variety of proprietary means for configuring and controlling their respective probes. This complicates interoperability. The Probe Configuration Specification, based on the Aspen MIB, defines standard parameters for remotely configuring probes—parameters such as network address, SNMP error trap destinations, modern communications with probes, serial line information, and downloading of data to probes. It provides enhanced interoperability between probes by specifying standard parameters for operations, permitting one vendor's RMON application to remotely configure another vendor's RMON probe.

History group.   The RMON2 history group polls, filters, and stores statistics based on user-defined variables, creating a log of the data for use as a historical tracking tool. This is in contrast to RMON1, where historical data is gathered on a predefined set of statistics.

After implementation, more and more complete information will be available for performance analysis and capacity planning.

Manager responsibilities

Managers execute network manager station (NMS) applications and often provide a graphical user interface that depicts a network map of agents. Typically, the manager also archives MIB data for trend analysis. The archivation may be implemented in two different ways (Fig. 4.7).

Each agent's MIB entries are copied into the dedicated MIB segment, or MIB entries are copied into a common area for immediate correlation and analysis.

At the manager level, presentation services and database services are offered. Presentation services are most frequently implemented on SUN;

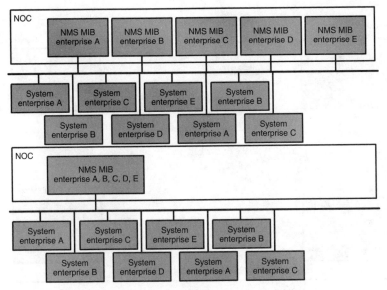

Figure 4.7   MIB templates at the SNMP Manager.

databases are usually relational or object-oriented. Figure 4.8 depicts a typical arrangement, indicating the wide opportunities of managing agents residing in file servers, bridges, routers, and X.25 gateways.

It's very important to choose the right database at the manager level. Some issues involved are the use of object-oriented databases, the use of relational databases, and the use of other databases.

Object-oriented databases have several advantages (Bapat 1991). They're naturally suited to an MIB because the MIB itself is formally described as a set of abstract data types in an object-oriented hierarchy. Object-oriented databases have the ability to model interface behavior through the ability to store methods.

Object-oriented databases also have several disadvantages. The technique is not yet mature for product implementations; there are no standards yet for query and manipulation languages; the MIB object class hierarchy is broad and shallow in an inheritance tree, and performance characteristics are not yet well documented.

The use of relational databases also has several advantages. The relational techniques are mature, stable, and have many supporters; there's a standard access language (SQL); there are quality translators for translating ER models into relational schema, and there are many choices of applications.

The disadvantages of relational databases are: they're not well suited to store OO models; performance depends on tuning the database; and relational databases are highly application dependent.

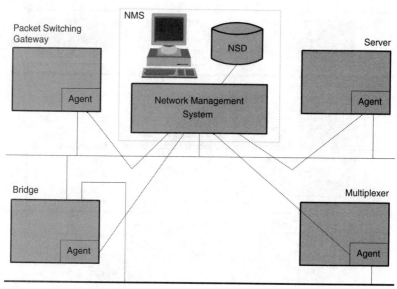

NMS   Network Management Station
NSD   Network Statistical Database

Figure 4.8   Network management system structure.

Other types of databases can also be used. Flat-file databases and other proprietary formats can be tailored very specifically to MIBs and can be optimized for performance. But, the design and implementation of network management applications may become more complex and time consuming to develop and maintain.

The trends of SNMP managers may be summarized as follows:

- Many users and manufacturers have recognized that managers and agents from different suppliers could interoperate and have found it unnecessary to supply separate management stations for each family of agents.

- Many management stations are expensive and are hard to install, coordinate, and maintain.

- Low-end, but still friendly, management systems are expected to be offered and implemented soon.

- More applications are needed in order to interpret and correlate data from MIBs; in particular, applications are needed to collect data, process it to produce information to answer questions, solve problems, and generate reports.

- Management stations are expected to augment control capabilities by properly using the "SET" command.

To carry out these duties, SNMP specifies five types of commands or verbs, called *protocol data units* (PDUs): GetRequest, GetNextRequest, SetRequest, GetResponse, and Trap.

GetRequest, GetNextRequest, and GetResponse. An agent will inspect the value of MIB variables after receiving either a GetRequest or GetNextRequest command (PDU) from a manager. Then, with a GetResponse verb, the agent then sends back the data it gathers.

The agent will alter MIB variables after receiving a SetRequest command. Using SetRequest, an NMS could, for example, instruct an agent to modify an IP route. **SetRequest** is a powerful command and, if used improperly, could corrupt configuration parameters and seriously impair network service. Due to SNMP's lack of inherent security measures, some component vendors have not implemented or enabled SetRequest within their SNMP agent implementation. Many vendors are working to enhance security features within their products.

Traps. Trap is a special unsolicited command type that agents send to a manager after sensing a prespecified condition such as ColdStart, WarmStart, LinkDown, LinkUp, AuthenticationFailure, EGPneighborLoss, or other enterprise-specific events. Traps are used to guide the timing and focus of polling, which SNMP employs to monitor the network's state.

Transport mechanisms

As mentioned previously, managers and agents exchange commands in the form of messages. There are currently two standard SNMP transport mechanisms: Unreliable Datagram Protocol (UDP) and Ethernet frames.

Other transport alternatives (e.g., OSI mechanisms) could also be implemented to carry the SNMP message. The message itself is constructed from data (type, request ID, error status, index, variables), the community string, and the version number. (See Fig. 4.9.)

SNMP is usually used in TCP/IP networks. SNMP operates over the transport and network layers of any protocol stack. Presently, UDP (User Data Protocol) is the most popular version of the transport protocol used. For the network layer, IP is the usual choice. But users with multiple protocols are facing the question of the applicability of other protocols. Early implementation examples include Apple Talk instead of IP, IPX, or DECnet. In these cases, a replacement in layers 3 and 4 may be observed. In other cases, SNMP is transported directly over the logical link control layer (LLC). Using this alternative, memory requirement savings are minimal.

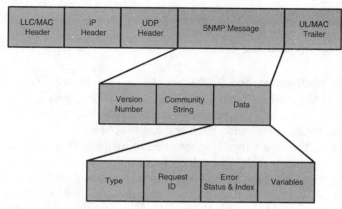

Figure 4.9   SNMP message format.

SNMP proxy agents

Proxy agent software permits an SNMP manager to monitor and control network elements that are otherwise not addressable using SNMP. For example, a vendor wishes to migrate its network management scheme to SNMP, but has devices on the network that use a proprietary network management scheme. An SNMP proxy can manage those devices in their native mode. The SNMP proxy acts as a protocol converter to translate the SNMP manager's commands into the proprietary scheme. This strategy facilitates migration from the current proprietary environment, which is prevalent today, to the open SNMP equipment (see Fig. 4.10).

Proxy agents are well suited for vendors with an existing base of non-SNMP devices communicating efficiently under a proprietary scheme. By using a proxy agent, the vendor can reduce the investment risk of putting SNMP equipment in the field.

SNMP is being continuously improved and extended. SNMPv2 addresses many of the shortcomings of version 1. SNMPv2 can support

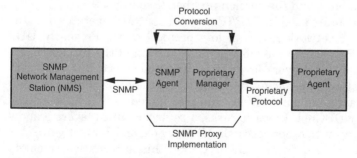

Figure 4.10   SNMP proxy implementation.

either a highly centralized management strategy or a distributed one. In the latter case, some systems operate in the role of both manager and agent. In its agent role, such a system will accept commands from a superior manager; these commands may deal with access of information stored locally at the intermediate manager or may require the intermediate manager to provide summary information about subagents. The principal enhancements to SNMPv1 provided by version 2 fall into the following categories (Stallings 1993):

- Structure of management information is being expanded in several ways. The macro used to define object types has been expended to include several new data types and to enhance the documentation associated with an object. Noticeable is the change that a new convention has been provided for creating and deleting conceptual rows in a table. The origin of this capability is from RMON.

- Transport mappings help to use different protocol stacks to transport the SNMP information, including user datagram protocol, OSI connectionless-mode protocol, Novell internetwork (IPX) protocol, and Appletalk.

- The most noticeable change of protocol operations includes two new PDUs. The GetBulkRequest PDU enables the manager to efficiently retrieve large blocks of data. In particular, it is powerful in retrieving multiple rows in a table. The InformRequest PDU enables one manager to send trap-type information to another.

- MIB extentions contain basic traffic information about the operation of the SNMPv2 protocol; this is identical to SNMP MIB II. The SNMPv2 MIB also contains other information related to the configuration of SNMPv2 manager to agent.

- Manager-to-manager capability is specified in a special MIB, called M2M. It provides functionality similar to the RMON MIB. In this case, the M2M MIB may be used to allow an intermediate manager to function as a remote monitor of network media traffic. Also, reporting is supported. Two major groups—Alarm and Event groups—are supported.

- SNMPv2 security does include a wrapper containing authentication and privacy information as a header to PDUs.

The SNMPv2 framework is derived from the SNMP framework. It is intended that the evolution from SNMP to SNMP2 be seamless. The easiest way to accomplish this is to upgrade the manager to support SNMPv2 in a way that allows the coexistence of SNMPv2 managers, SNMPv2 agents, and SNMP agents. Figure 4.11 shows this coexistence by using a proxy agent (Stallings 1993).

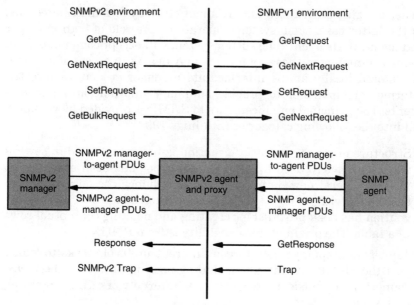

Figure 4.11   Coexistence between SNMPv1 and v2.

This figure also shows the mapping of protocol elements. The actual implementation of the proxy agent depends on the vendor; it could be implemented into the agent or into the manager.

In summary, SNMP's major advantages are as follows:

- Its simplicity eases vendor implementation effort.
- It requires less memory and fewer CPU cycles than CMIP.
- It has been used and tested on the Internet.
- SNMP products are available now, and are affordable.
- Development kits are available free of charge.
- It offers the best direct manager-agent interface.
- It is robust and extensible.
- The polling approach is good for LAN-based managed objects.

SNMP has several disadvantages, including the following:

- Weak security features
- Lack of global vision
- Problems with the Trap command
- No object-oriented data view

- Integration with other approaches difficult due to unique semantics
- High polling overhead
- Too many private MIB extensions

A lot of progress is expected in the area of security features. SNMP security specifications under development define a security architecture, protocols, and a new MIB variable that can be managed by SNMP. The security technology uses the MIT (Massachusetts Institute of Technology) algorithm for authentication, and can control who is authorized to access and change information. SNMP messages are divided into two basic components for safety purposes. The first component is constructed by the SNMP protocol data units, which transport management information. The second component is the authentication segment, which provides the authentication, authorization, and access control information. Changes to the second segment don't have any impact on the first. In particular, this new feature is very valuable when the "set" command is widely used.

Comparing CMIP and SNMP

For managing heterogeneous local area networks, two competing standards are under consideration: CMIP (Common Management Information Protocol) and SNMP (Simple Network Management Protocol). Despite contradictory opinions and expectations, the coexistence of both protocols is in sight (Fisher 1991).

Since quite recently, more time has been spent on identifying the best-suited application areas for both alternatives. In order to promote availability of both, this section concentrates on similarities and differences of CMIP and SNMP.

Similarities

Goals. Both protocols have the same ultimate goal of moving network management-related information from one place to another in order to execute network management functions, such as fault, configuration, performance, and accounting management.

Managed objects. Both protocols work with managed objects. OSI objects are defined with attributes, with generated events and performance options. Furthermore, objects are scoped by numerous hierarchies (e.g., for the purpose of inheritance or containment). ASN.1 is used as an object-oriented specification language to define this characteristic (Rose 1991).

In contrast, SNMP views managed objects as little more than simple variables in a virtual store. The SMI (structure of management information) is used as the schema for this database and provides a naming relationship between managed objects. ASN.1 is used as a description language.

Management information base (MIB). Both alternatives use the concept of a MIB, and allow for vendor-specific extensions to the MIB. These extensions could allow users to control devices more specifically and implement more detailed performance metrication. It's likely that both products will borrow modules from each other. However, some differences will remain (Rose 1991).

- SNMP-based MIBs have no optional objects. Instead, related objects are grouped, and these groups form the basic unit of conformance.
- SNMP defines a core MIB first, containing only essential objects in the public area; later, other objects may be added from the private area.
- OSI-CMIP is using eventing for transporting MIB variables; SNMP is using traps very infrequently.

Commands. Although command sets are different, the targets of information retrieval, updates, reporting on events, and triggering actions are the same. Table 4.6 compares both command sets; this table doesn't include the confirmed version of OSI commands.

Differences

Data access and retrieval. SNMP is oriented toward retrieving individual items of information; CMIP is more oriented to retrieving aggregate information. With SNMP, the manager has to be specific with the inquiry, issued as a "GET." With CMIP, more information can be transmitted easier for in-depth analysis at the manager level; most of this information is not needed. SNMP tries to chain information retrieval units by "GET-NEXT." CMIP may require more resources; SNMP may fail in transmitting files at a reasonable performance level.

TABLE 4.6   Comparison of OSI-CMIP
and SNMP Command Sets

Commands	CMIP	SNMP
Get	X	X
Set	X	X
Event	X	
Create	X	
Delete	X	
Action	X	
Trap		X

Polling versus eventing. SNMP works by polling or regularly inquiring on the status of objects, while CMIP uses eventing or has the objects inform the manager of their status when it changes. Eventing may require some intelligence built into the managed objects, which may not be the case with simple products. On the other hand, frequent polling may exceed reasonable overhead limits when many objects have to be polled for their status.

Number of managed objects to be supervised. Accurate calculations may help in both cases to determine the number of devices that may be continuously supervised by the manager. The number of managed objects depends on the SNMP polling interval T and the average duration D of each poll:

$$N < \frac{T}{D}$$

D can be calculated by adding up the delays caused in the management system, in the network, and in the managed objects. The delay component differs in LANs (around 1 ms) and WANs (around 500 ms). Assuming a polling interval of 15 minutes, a processing time in the manager and in the managed objects of 50 ms, 4500 objects in a LAN, then just 750 objects in an interconnected LAN environment may be continuously supervised.

With eventing (CMIP) or traps (SNMP), events are sent to the manager in an unsolicited manner. Assuming the same processing demand of 50 and 500 ms, respectively, and that each fifth polling is answered by a change in status, five times more objects may be continuously supervised.

From another perspective, the bandwidth requirements may be calculated as follows (Leinwand 1993): Assume that each SNMP query and response is 100 bytes long, including data and header information. For a network of 30 devices, the management station would send and receive 100 bytes for each device. This would give a total of (100 bytes + 100 bytes) × 30 devices = 6000 bytes (= 48,000 bits) of bandwidth requirement for each polling cycle. Polling every 60 s would average 48,000 bits divided by 60 s = 800 bits/s of bandwidth requirement. Considering the total bandwidth requirement for an hour, 48,000 bits × 60 polls = 2,880,000 bits should be transmitted in the wide and local area networks, depending on the polling hierarchy.

Storage requirements. Considering the protocol stack and protocol encode/decode requirements (Datapro NM40 1991), SNMP needs considerably less storage; estimates indicate approximately 70 to 80 KB for SNMP, and over 300 KB for CMIP.

Functionality.   Basically, CMIP offers more capability for network management functions support. In certain cases, in order to be comparable, SNMP implementations need more elaborate implementation work. But most CMIP functions can be implemented by SNMP as well.

Size and performance.   There's less SNMP support code, and it's faster and less expensive than a CMIP implementation. Most of this is because of the polling-versus-eventing issue; eventing requires more intelligence in the managed objects: SNMP puts the intelligence into the manager; CMIP requests more functionality at the managed object level.

Transport services.   For its underlying transport mechanisms, SNMP requires connectionless (CL) datagrams. This means that it can be used with Ethernet, IPX, UDP, XNS, and other simple communication protocols. CMIP requires a reliable transport layer, such as OSI's connection-oriented (CO) TP-4 transport protocol. CL techniques are more useful in fault cases; CO techniques are better suited for retrieving large amounts of data.

   In both cases, however, other architectures may be used at lower layers. Even proprietary solutions may call for an interesting combination, such as CMOL, where IBM and 3Com try to reduce the need for the full OSI stack in managed objects. Another solution would be the use of a proxy that would accomplish the work outside the managed object.

Standards and testing.   CMIP is controlled by international standard bodies such as the ISO. Vendors can test their implementations against a conformance test suite from the COS (Corporation for Open Systems). Vendors are offering to demonstrate the interoperability of their products at trade shows. SNMP is controlled by the Internet Activities Board. Vendors check their implementation with interoperability testing.

Availability of products.   SNMP has in this respect an undeniable advantage. Most LAN interworking products support SNMP, either at the agent or the manager level. Many vendors support both. CMIP implementations are fewer, but it's only a matter of time before its use is more widespread.

   Table 4.7 summarizes the strengths of both alternatives. It's likely that in the future they will be used in combination; CMIP will solve the problems of intercommunication between management systems, and SNMP will most likely concentrate on the manager and managed-objects area. SNMP support for the leading de facto and open standards will become a high-priority item.

TABLE 4.7   Strengths and Weaknesses of OSI-CMIP and SNMP

Comparison Criteria	CMIP	SNMP
1. Functional		
Configuration management	+	+
Fault management	++	++
Performance management	++	+
Security management	+	
Accounting management		
Planning		
2. Operational		
Number of objects being supervised	++	+
Efficiency	+	++
Personnel required	+	++
Simplicity		++
User friendliness	+	+
3. Implementation		
Memory cost		+++
Processing cost	+	++
Application cost	+	++
4. Support by manufacturers of		
Processors	+	++
LAN software		+
Internet products		++
LAN hardware		+
Number of products		+++
5. Maintenance expenses	+	
6. Centralization		++
7. Decentralization	++	
8. Future trends		
Extensions	++	+
Scaleability	++	+
Inheritance of attributes	++	
Protocol dependability	++	

+++ very strong
++ strong
+ fair
weak

As SNMP applications are more widely used, vendors and users are interested in improving the performance and extending the functionality. The first customization examples include the extensive use of traps, use of dialogs, multilevel polling, compression of GETs, improved security functions, use of dynamic polling, and support of trouble tickets. Implementation examples may be seen with NCE (Network Control Engine) from Bay Networks and MultiMan from Lannet.

LAN Management Concepts

LAN management concepts are expected to support an enterprise's strategic network management implementation decisions, such as integration, automation, centralization, and database support. From the perspective of instrumentation, integration is usually addressed first.

Most managed-objects-level vendors provide products that engender useful individual functionality, but they're limited in that they can't easily be integrated into a system vendor's network management offering. Future integrated solutions are expected to solve this problem by offering horizontal integration across (Terplan 1991b): communication forms (data, voice, image, video); WANs, MANs, and LANs; private, public, and virtual networks; multivendor architectures; processing and communication systems.

Figure 4.12 shows an example of horizontal integration. System vendors have developed single network management protocols (e.g., NMVT from IBM) to facilitate data collection and integration about both physical and logical components, as long as data may be collected from the components supported by the protocol. But this type of vertical integration is not easy, in particular owing to the proprietary nature of applications and logical session management. Future integrated solutions are expected to solve this problem by offering verti-

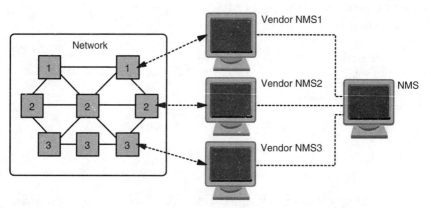

Horizontal integration of equipment from multiple vendors doing similar functions
Degree of Integration
  displays
  controls
Intelligence
  display
  controls

NMS = Network Management System

Figure 4.12   Horizontal integration.

cally integrated applications across logical and physical network components, and across applications and network components.

Figure 4.13 shows an example of vertical integration. In addition, users and suppliers are expected to work more closely together by comanaging their instruments (e.g., by using electronic data interchange techniques).

Integration will require multiple steps in terms of depth of integration. One will start at the physical terminal level by emulating multiple consoles' images in various windows of an intelligent workstation. In this case, the native protocols, messages, and commands of the emulated vendors are in use. But concentrating the screens in one area on a few workstations helps to substantially improve efficiency. Next, the emulated third party or the integrator, or both, will convert to a unique protocol or format, such as NMP from AT&T or NMVT from IBM. In this case, messages and commands are unique up to the third parties' demarcation line. Ultimately, real integration is achieved with two approaches (Fig. 4.14), both offering either horizontal or vertical integration, or both (Herman 1991a). In this case, information from various sources is integrated.

The first approach is the manager of managers, a hierarchical approach in which an integrated manager interfaces to a lower-level element management system. The premier examples of such systems are all SNMP managers for simple and small networks, NetView for MVS from IBM, NetExpert from Objective Systems Integrators, and

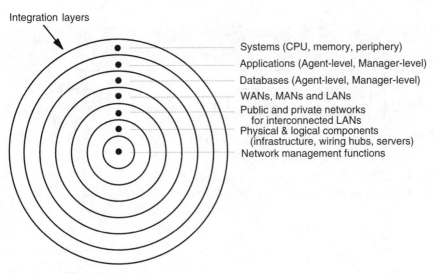

Integration layers

Systems (CPU, memory, periphery)
Applications (Agent-level, Manager-level)
Databases (Agent-level, Manager-level)
WANs, MANs and LANs
Public and private networks
  for interconnected LANs
Physical & logical components
  (infrastructure, wiring hubs, servers)
Network management functions

Figure 4.13   Vertical integration.

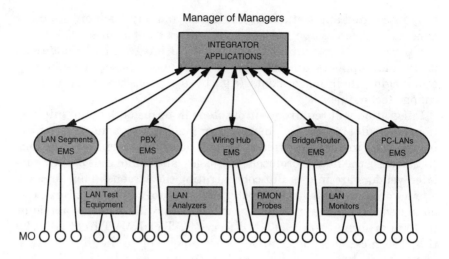

EMS   Element Management System
MO   Managed Object

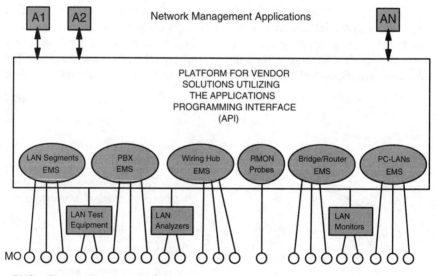

EMS   Element Management System
MO   Managed Object

Figure 4.14 Hierarchical versus platform LAN management integration.

MAXM/Enterprise from MAXM. The last three are capable of managing very complex networks. The second general approach is the platform approach, in which multiple vendors write network management applications to a standard set of application programming interfaces (APIs). The premier examples of this approach are OpenView for Unix and for Windows from Hewlett-Packard, SunNet Manager from Sun-Soft, OneVision from AT&T, NetView for AIX from IBM, Spectrum from Cabletron, DiMONS from Netlabs, NetView for OS/2 and for Windows from IBM, and ManageWise from Novell.

The platform approach to integrated management offers the possibility of a greater degree of multivendor integration than the manager of managers scheme. In the manager of managers architecture, interactions among management systems from different vendors are accomplished through a standardized protocol interface and a standardized set of management data definitions. This hierarchical way of aggregating management information requires that a single vendor—the provider of the integrator—develop all the multivendor network management application software. Other vendors merely provide raw data to the integrated manager through open interfaces and accept commands through open interfaces.

In practice today, only a few applications of the integrated manager exist, so most functionality is obtained through windowed access to device manager applications, called *cut-through* or *terminal emulation*. Moreover, this approach multiplies management systems at a time when operations centers are looking to reduce the number of management systems they use. It may also result in multiple network management databases.

In the platform strategy, the eventual goal is to develop a single management system that can handle a diverse, multivendor network. Rather than do it alone, the platform vendor creates an open development environment in which multiple vendors can write software that shares common user views and a common data repository. If the platform offers a rich set of services and advanced capabilities, such as an object-oriented user interface or relational database, many vendors may find it attractive to implement their management software on such platforms rather than developing their own base at considerable cost and risk.

The advantage of the manager of managers approach is that it builds on existing management systems. Using this approach, IBM shows how to integrate WAN and LAN management. Token Ring has a stand-alone management capability using the LAN Network Manager. Fault, performance, and configuration management are also supported without NetView. But a more complete solution is using NetView as the focal point. In this structure, bidirectional information exchange is supported. The platform strategy in its pure form requires writing all new management software. In practice, the two approaches can be combined if necessary. But the platform strategy aims at reducing the number of management systems, which is highly appealing to network owners. The manager of managers approach, on the other hand, is necessary in order to reserve an installed base of management systems. The platform concept is most appealing when new software has to be written anyway.

Another argument against proprietary or OSI-based manager of managers solutions to multivendor network management is that no one vendor can meet all the management application needs of a large enterprise. With the platform approach, many vendors can simultaneously work on management software that will play together. If a particular platform achieves a critical mass of important applications, then there's a good chance that users will choose it, since applications are what the user really wants. If users start buying a particular platform, then more application software developers will want to write for that platform, since the market for their creations will be large.

Independently, whether the manager of managers or the platform approach is selected, the ultimate goal is multivendor management. Vendors may support proprietary, de facto, or open standards at the managed-objects or management-application level. Figures 4.15 and 4.16 (Datapro NM40 1990) show examples with SNMP and CMIP, indicating also that proprietary solutions—in the form of proprietary MIBs—are supported. Cross connection via gateways (proxy agents) is expected to be supported, as illustrated in Fig. 4.17.

Other Unix-based platforms are offered under other norms, such as AIX (IBM) and SINIX (Siemens). In particular, the AIX platform on RISC/6000 from IBM is a source of contradiction. Which is IBM's strategic platform: AIX or OS/2? The company populates both with network management-related solutions. In any case, either one of IBM's platform solutions will help to build hierarchical or peer-to-peer network management architectures, and to off-load the usually centrally located NetView. MS-DOS-based solutions still exist with LAN element management systems, but their importance is decreasing.

In order to increase flexibility, distributed architectures may help. They're still immature, but they improve the reliability of the network management system by distributing functions to multiple servers. The vulnerable point of distributed architectures is the process manager, which is responsible for coordinating between various agents and managers. This coordination task includes the following:

- Unwrapping protocol headers and trailers in order to interpret the "useful" information of protocol data units

- Forwarding this information to managers, which are responsible for processing and forwarding the results to applications

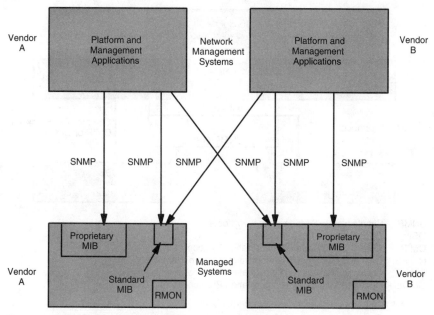

Figure 4.15 Emerging SNMP network management systems.

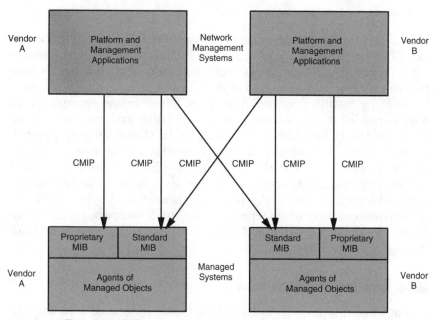

Figure 4.16 Emerging CMIP network management systems.

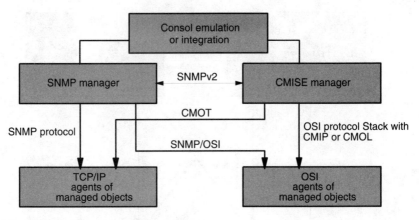

SNMP   Simple Network Management Protocol
OSI   Open Systems Interconnected
CMIP   Common Management Information Protocol
CMISE   Common Management Information Service Element
CMOT   Common Management Information Protocol over TCP/IP
CMOL   Common Management Information Protocol over LLC

Figure 4.17   Management of heterogeneous LANs.

- Ensuring that final results have reached the user using presentation services

This coordinator function has been implemented by the manufacturers differently. Hewlett-Packard is using CMIP as a common denominator between communicating modules. DEC and Sun use remote procedure calls (RPCs) to export and import messages between communicating modules. WizardWare from Tivoli is an example of an object-oriented message-passing approach. Other systems use a combination of the three techniques discussed. In almost all cases, proprietary features are added. RPC implementations seem to lead the market now; object orientation will increase, but its penetration speed is hard to predict. This speed will be largely influenced by how inventory and configuration databases are implemented. Despite databases, a coexistence of relational techniques (e.g., fault and performance management), and object-oriented techniques (e.g., configuration and fault management) is likely.

Management Platform Services

Management platform services include basic services, such as autodiscovery, SNMP supports database support, graphical user interface, some alarming features, and some application programming interfaces. Advanced services are targeting automapping, advanced event and alarm processing, LAN modeling, distributed management, management-to-management communication, development toolkits, and the support of more management protocols.

The management platforms can be grouped as follows:

1. *Unix-based management platforms*

   OpenView from Hewlett-Packard

   NetView for AIX from IBM

   OneVision from AT&T

   Sunnet Manager (Soltrice) from Sunsoft

   Spectrum from Cabletron

   DiMONS from netlabs

   Integrated Systems Manager from Bull

2. *Windows-based management platforms*

   OpenView from Hewlett-Packard

   NMC Vision from Network Managers

   ManageWise from Novell

   SNMPc from Castle Rock

   NMS/100 from Network Applied Technology

3. *Special platforms for systems management.* LAN management may not strictly be restricted to manage LAN segments and inter-networking components. In many cases, additional components of client/server systems, such as servers and clients, must be managed as well. There are other platforms serving the special needs of systems management. The most interesting products are

   ■ Tivoli Management Environment from Tivoli

   ■ Unicenter from Computer Associates

   ■ OperationsCenter from Hewlett Packard

   ■ NetView for OS/2 and for Windows from IBM.

   But these platforms will not be described in detail.

A *platform* is a set of generic capabilities implemented in software, which enable and facilitate the creation and operation of applications. A general-purpose platform does not make specific assumptions about the nature of applications that it supports.

A *management framework* goes further and offers a set of generic capabilities for managers and agents, and for the communications mechanisms between them, which enables and facilitates the management of networks and systems.

An *application* is software that is developed for a specific purpose, using the generic capabilities provided by the platform. Platforms, frameworks, and applications make sense only in relation to each other.

This section concentrates on platforms only. If appropriate, references will be given to frameworks. Applications are addressed in Chap. 5.

Products will be characterized by platform attributes. Priorities for attributes should be set by the users. References will be made in text to the very basic attributes that must be supported in order to be recognized as a platform.

Platform attributes

The basic attributes follow.

Hardware platform of the product.   One observes here a wide variety of hardware, including Intel 386/486, Pentium, HP 9000, RS/6000, Sun Sparc, Tandem, Alpha, Syste/88, and eventually others. Backup support should be addressed here as well.

Operating systems.   The industry expects a certain streamlining or, in other words, a shakeout with respect to operating systems supporting the management platform. At the present, the operating systems to be considered include AIX, DOS/Windows, OS/2, SunOS, Ultrix, Sinix, Unix, Windows, Windows NT, and eventually others. Future solutions will concentrate around a Unix version and/or Windows NT.

Network architectures.   The targeted networks to be managed are very different. Many products are expected to manage legacy networks and more open networks at the same time. The most widely used protocols supporting network architectures include DECnet, IPX/SPX, OSI, SNA, DSA, APPN, TCP/IP, Guardian, and eventually others. Capabilities of managing SNA and TCP/IP are the highest priority.

Network management protocols.   The products are expected to support at least SNMP. It is an additional advantage when they can do more. SNMP support may include the capabilities of working with proxy agents capable of connecting non-SNMP into SNMP. Protocols to be supported include CMIP, CMOT, LNMP, NMVT, RMON, SNMPv1, SNMPv2, and eventually DMI to manage desktops.

All leading management platforms today support SNMP. Seagate's/DiMONS and HP OpenView Distributed Manager (DM) Platform also support CMIP. Currently, most end users are familiar only with SNMP support.

The management platform provides SNMP support in several ways. First and foremost is the ability to poll SNMP devices and receive

SNMP TRAPS, as described previously. However, in order to configure polls on MIB variables of various devices, one must first know what those variables are. Management platforms provide MIB browsers for this purpose. A MIB browser queries a user-selected SNMP network device and displays its MIB values. In addition, most platforms can display line or bar graphs of those MIB values, provided they are in numeric form (counters, etc.).

MIB browsers are crude tools at best, displaying raw and often cryptic, low-level-device information. For this reason, platforms also provide MIB application builders that allow users to quickly create applications for displaying information on MIB objects in a more meaningful way. MIB applications may include graphing real-time information on selected network nodes. However, even MIB applications builders are limited in supporting high-level analysis that is more open provided by third-party applications.

MIB compilers allow users to bring in third-party, device-specific MIBs (also called *private,* or *extended,* MIBs) and register them with the management platform. While most platforms ship with a number of third-party MIBs, they do not include all possible MIBs from all vendors. A MIB compiler is necessary for adding support for third-parties whose MIBs are not shipped as part of the standard platform.

Some MIB compilers are more robust than others. Some MIB compilers will fail or abort processing if there is an error in the MIB being compiled. Unfortunately, errors in third-party MIBs are not rare. Therefore, it is desirable to have a MIB compiler that can flag errors and recover, rather than stop dead.

Graphical user interface. GUI's basic job is to provide color-coded display of management information, multiple windows into different core or management applications, and an iconic or menu-driven user interface. By providing a standardized interface between the user and the underlying tools, the GUI simplifies what a user needs to learn and provides a standard tool for application developers.

Most management operations are available from a menu bar; others from context menus. Point-and-click operations are standard features, as is context-sensitive help. Most platforms allow some degree of customization of maps and icons.

While most platform GUIs are the same, there can be a few subtle differences. Some GUIs have larger icons than others. While this makes it easier to read information on the icon and distinguish status changes more quickly, a screen can quickly become cluttered with just a few large icons. Icon size is strictly a matter of user preference. The most widely used GUIs are Motif, OpenLook, OS/2 Presentation Manager, and Windows.

Database support.   The database is the focal point for key data created and used by the management applications. They include MIB data, inventories, trouble tickets, configuration files, and performance data.

Most platforms maintain event logs in flat-file ASCII format for performance reasons. However, this format limits the network manager's ability to search for information and manipulate the data. Therefore, links to relational database management systems (RDBMSs) are now important aspects of platform architecture. Example databases supported include Ingres, Sybase, Informix, and Oracle.

An RDBMS is essential for manipulating raw data and turning it into useful information. Users can obtain information from an RDBMS by writing requests, or queries, in Structured Query Language (SQL), a universal standard language for relational database communication.

Integral RDBMSs are also appearing in high-end applications, such as Cisco's CiscoWorks and Isicad Command.

While most management platforms also supply report-writer facilities, these tools are generally not top-notch. However, most higher-quality third-party reporting applications can extract data from an RDBMS using SQL.

Core management applications.   The management platform is expected to offer core services and interfaces to other applications. The basic management applications to be provided are discovery/mapping, alarm management, and platform protection.

Discovery and mapping.   Device discovery/network mapping discovery refers to the network management system's ability to automatically learn the identity and type of devices currently active on the network. At minimum, a management platform should be capable of discovering active IP devices by retrieving data from a router's IP tables and address resolution protocol (ARP) tables.

However, even this capability does not guarantee that all IP devices on a given network will be detected. For example, relying solely on routing tables is inadequate in purely bridged networks where there are no routers. Thus, a more comprehensive discovery facility should also include other mechanisms such as broadcast messages (PING and others) that can reach out to any IP device and retrieve its address and other identifying information.

On the other hand, discovery mechanisms that rely completely on broadcasting (e.g., PING) will incur a tremendous amount of overhead in finding devices out on the network. Ideally, a management platform should support a combination of ARP data retrieval and broadcasting.

Furthermore, a complete network discovery facility should be capable of detecting legacy system nodes, such as DECnet and SNA. Currently, most platforms rely on third-party applications or traffic monitoring applications to supply discovery data on non-TCP/IP devices.

Another desirable feature is the ability to run automatic or scheduled "dynamic discovery" processes after the initial discovery, to discern any changes made to the network after the initial discovery took place. In large networks especially, overhead and consumed bandwidth for running a dynamic discovery process continually in background mode may be too great; therefore, the ability to schedule discovery at off-peak hours is important.

It is also important for the user to have the ability to set limits on the initial network discovery. Many corporate networks are now linked to the Internet, and without predefined limits, a discovery application may cross corporate boundaries and begin discovering everything on the global Internet. Some management platforms allow users to run discovery on a segment-by-segment basis. This can help the discovery process from quickly getting out of hand.

Many management platforms are capable of automatically producing a topological map from the data collected during device discovery. However, these automatically generated maps rarely result in a graphical representation that is useful for humans. In particular, when there are hundreds of devices the resulting map can look cluttered enough to be of little use.

Even when the discovery process operates on a limited or segment-by-segment basis, there is eventually going to come a time when the operator must edit the automatically generated network map to create a visual picture that is easier for human beings to relate to. Therefore, the ability to group objects on the map and move them around in groups or perform other types of collective actions can be a real time-saving feature.

Alarm capabilities. Management platforms act as a clearinghouse for critical status messages obtained from various devices and applications across the network. Messages arrive in the form of SNMP traps, alerts, or event reports when polling results indicate that thresholds have been exceeded.

The management platform supports setting of thresholds on any SNMP MIB variable. Typically, management platforms poll for device status by sending SNMP requests to devices with SNMP agents, or Internet Control Message Protocol (ICMP) echo requests (*pings*) to any TCP/IP device.

The process of setting thresholds may be supported by third-party applications or by the management platform. Some platforms allow operators to configure polls on classes of devices; most require operators to configure a poll for each device individually.

Most platforms support some degree of alarm filtering. Rudimentary filtering allows operators to assign classifications to individual alarms triggered when thresholds are exceeded, such as "informational," "warning," or "critical." Once classifications are assigned, the user can specify, for example, that only critical alarms are displayed on the screen, while all other alarms are logged.

More sophisticated alarm facilities support conditional alarms. An example of a conditional threshold may be "errors on incoming packets from device B > 800 for more than 5 times in 25 minutes." Conditional alarms can account for periodic spikes in traffic or daily busy periods, for example.

Finally, the platform should support the ability to automatically trigger scripts when specific alarms are received.

Platform protection. The platform is expected to offer security features that go beyond the attribute of the operating system. Feasible choices include password, standard and user-definable privileges, encryption, and access control.

Application programming interfaces (APIs) and development toolkits.

APIs and Developer's Toolkits platform vendors encourage third-party applications by providing published application programming interfaces (APIs), toolkits that include libraries of software routines, and documentation to assist applications developers. Another aspect to this effort is the "partners programs"—the marketing angle of encouraging third-party applications development.

An API shields applications developers from the details of the management platform's underlying data implementation and functional architecture. Management platform vendors generally include in their developer's kits several coded examples of how APIs can be used, along with the APIs themselves.

In most cases, when an application takes advantage of platform APIs, it must be recompiled with the platform code—resulting in a tightly integrated end product. Many independent software vendors (ISVs) and other third-party developers lack resources necessary to pursue this level of integration. Or perhaps a more accurate way of stating this is that ISVs aren't convinced that putting out the extra effort to fully integrate their applications with all leading management platforms will result in a proportionally larger revenue stream. ISVs and other third-party developers face a choice: tightly integrate their products with one management platform vendor or loosely integrate them with all leading platform providers. Most third parties have chosen the latter route, as they are unwilling to turn off prospective customers who may have chosen a different platform vendor as their strategic management provider.

As a result, at least 80 percent of the third-party applications available today are only loosely integrated with the underlying management platform—at the menu bar—and completely ignore APIs and other environment libraries. This is expected to change as the market matures and as platform vendors begin to offer high-level APIs that make porting applications from one management platform to another into an almost trivial exercise.

In summary, published APIs and libraries make it possible for independent software vendors (ISVs) and other third parties to write applications that take advantage of other basic services provided by the management platform. To date, few third parties have taken full advantage of platform APIs, although this is expected to change over the next two years.

More advanced platform attributes include the following.

Distribution capabilities. Depending on the geographical locations of LANs, some companies prefer to control entire networks from a centralized workstation. Others want to distribute some function. And still others want individual departments or business units to manage their departmental resources independently. Management platforms can be configured in different ways, including client/server, peer-to-peer, or management domain. If multiple managers are in use, manager-to-manager communication is essential. SNMPv2 supports this communication. This item is a real differentiator between platform products.

LAN modeling. LAN modeling is an artificial intelligence capability that can assist in automated fault isolation and diagnosis as well as performance and configuration management. Modeling allows a management system to infer status of one object from the status of other objects.

Network modeling is facilitated by object-oriented programming techniques and languages such as C++. The goal of modeling is to simplify the representation of complex systems (such as networks), creating a layer of abstraction that shields management applications from underlying details.

The building block of this technology is the "model" that describes a network element, such as a router. A model consists of data (attributes) describing the element as well as its relationships with other elements. Abstract elements such as organizations and protocols can also be modeled, as can nonintelligent devices such as cables. A model may use information from other models to determine its own state; modeling can reduce the complexity of management data and highlight the most important information. In this way, fault isolation and diagnosis can be automated. In addition, models can be used to depict traffic patterns,

trends, topologies, or distributions to assist in performance and configuration management.

Support of frameworks. Standardization committees have been trying
to streamline integration efforts. They offer recommendations for platforms, including the communication between managers and agents,
more core applications, and for the depth of application integration.
Known frameworks are OMNIPoint and Spirit from the Network Management Forum, and DME/DCE from the Open Systems Foundation.

Object orientation. Object-oriented and object-based technologies are
helpful in relation to user interfaces, protocols, and databases. The use
of object request brokers (ORB) provides the glue needed to accomplish
interoperability between heterogeneous systems.

Leading LAN Management Platforms

Unix-based management platforms

OpenView from Hewlett-Packard. Hewlett-Packard OpenView is actually the name of a product service family, and not a particular product.
The OpenView family includes both DOS and Unix products. The Unix-
based OpenView products include Network Node Manager, the HP
OpenView SNMP Management Platform, and the Distributed Manager (DM) Platform. The API services differ among these offerings. The
core offering is the HP OpenView SNMP Platform, which provides
basic platform services and developer's environment. However, "HP
OpenView" is most commonly used to refer to HP's Network Node Manager. This product includes the HP OpenView SNMP Platform and, in
addition, multiple third-party MIBs, a MIB application builder, and
other application-level functions for end users. HP OpenView Distributed Management (DM) Platform is actually a different product;
while it includes the SNMP Platform, it also has added functions and
APIs for supporting OSI CMIP. HP OpenView DM is targeted for
telecommunications and OSI environments, and it is not intended to be
purchased by end users for managing TCP/IP internetworks. Also,
HP offers a DOS-based product called HP OpenView for Windows.
Hewlett-Packard has been extending and enhancing its platform constantly. Under the umbrella, different applications suites for commercial networks, telecommunication networks, and for systems take
advantage of the basic and enhanced services of the platform.

Strengths. HP OpenView Network Node Manager has a fast-
growing installed base of approximately 18,000 Systems as of mid-
1995. HP OpenView also provides a very friendly development environment, and many third parties are enthusiastic about creating
applications for the platform, even though the developer's kit is priced

much higher than competing vendors' offerings. There are approximately 70 third-party applications running on HP OpenView for Unix as of mid-1995. Also, in recent versions of Network Node Manager, event types can be customized on a node-by-node basis. This helps operators distinguish between the critical crash of a mission-critical server and the less critical system crash of a one-user PC. Due to cooperation with solution partners, OpenView has been promoted into the role of the principal management integrators.

Limitations. HP OpenView Network Node Manager lacks alarm correlation, multiuser, manager-to-manager communications and sophisticated polling features necessary for managing complex networks comprising thousands of nodes. But this weakness can be eliminated by fully integrating licensed code from Seagate-Netlabs.

OpenView Network Node Manager (NNM) from Hewlett-Packard

1. Hardware platform of the product	HP9000, Sun SPARC.
2. Operating systems	HP-UX, Solaris.
3. Network architectures	TCP/IP, IPX/SPX (by third parties only), DECnet OSI is supported by OpenView DM—a separate platform.
4. Network management protocols	SNMPv1, SNMPv2, CMIP, RMON.
5. Graphical user interface	Motif.
6. Database support	Ingres and flat-file database.
7. Core management applications Discovery and mapping	Yes, both are supported, but no automatic grouping of node types is supported. Continual auto-discovery supports a backoff mechanism that polls nodes on less and less frequent intervals to detect network changes.
Alarm capabilities	Yes, it is supported, next releases will deploy NerveCenter; includes a Data Collector feature that can be set up to poll on individual object's MIB variables.
Platform protection	Yes for password access and encryption.
8. Application programming interfaces (APIs) and development toolkits	It provides the following APIs: OpenView Windows API and SNMP API. The OpenView kit provides OpenView Windows API and XMP API.

9. Distribution capabilities	Yes, with the Distribution Manager. But, there are still limitations with consolidating displays.
10. LAN modeling	Not supported.
11. Support of frameworks	OMNIPoint, DME, and DMTF.
12. Object orientation	Yes, with the embedded Netlabs-technology.

NetView for AIX from IBM. This product is an SNMP-based element management system for TCP/IP networks; the system can also act as a service point for an enterprisewide NetView management system. NetView for AIX uses HP OpenView Network Node Manager core technology with IBM-provided enhancements. Digital Equipment Corporation has licensed NetView for AIX and is using it as the basis for its Polycenter Manager on NetView product.

Strengths. IBM is adding alarm filtering and event management features that are lacking in the HP OpenView core. NetView for AIX is becoming an increasingly important part of IBM's network management strategy, and its importance may one day eclipse mainframe NetView, as customers move toward distributed systems computing. In response to customer demand, IBM is developing SNA management applications for NetView for AIX. IBM is putting a lot of muscle behind its support program, both for end users and third-party vendors who join the NetView Association. This platform is just one of many under the SystemView umbrella. In connection with the others, practically all types of enterprise networks can be managed.

Limitations. It is the author's opinion that to maximize the sales potential of this product, IBM will have to increase its focus on sales and support of its AIX/UNIX products and reduce emphasis on proprietary solutions and on mainframe NetView in particular. The number of third-party applications shipping for NetView for AIX still trails the tallies for HP OpenView and SunNet Manager, but this gap is expected to narrow substantially during the next couple of years. A further weakness is that cross-communication between platforms is supported via NetView for MVS only. The common denominator is still the mainframe NetView; but not everybody wants to continue with this expensive product.

NetView for AIX from IBM

| 1. Hardware platform of the product | RS/6000, SunSPARC, Intel 386/486. |
| 2. Operating systems | AIX, SunOS, Windows (OEM'd), OS/2—also with a separate IBM product. |

3. Network architectures	TCP/IP, DECnet (by third parties), SNA, IPX/SPX (by third parties).
4. Network management protocols	SNMPv1, SNMPv2, NMVT, RMON, CMOT, CMIP.
5. Graphical user interface	OS/2 (separation is taking place), Motif.
6. Database support	Oracle, DB2, Sybase, Ingres, Informix, and flat files.
7. Core management applications	
Discovery and mapping	Both are supported. Discovery can be limited to geographic areas to reduce the overhead and time.
Alarm capabilities	Filtering rules are supported, and they can span multiple objects. Also thresholds can be defined by users. Selected SNMP events can be displayed.
Platform protection	Yes for application and system level; password and user-definable security.
8. Application programming interfaces (APIs) and development toolkits	Service Point API, SNMP API, and OpenView Windows API. Support for OSF/DME Consolidated Management API is also provided.
9. Distribution capabilities	Supported, also manager-to-manager dialogs. Client/server architecture allows many GUIs clients per server.
10. LAN modeling	Not supported.
11. Support of frameworks	OMNIPoint, DME, and DMFT.
12. Object orientation	RODM under MVS for object-oriented repository.

OneVision from AT&T. This platform is a unique combination of Base-WorX and OpenView. BaseWorX is targeted toward the telecommunications industry, offering a sophisticated, object-oriented basis to develop and deploy operations support systems. OpenView is considered more for the commercial user.

Strengths. This platform unifies over the middle range two completely different directions, strongly addressing the needs of practically any enterprise. Also, separate modules can be tailored and implemented. AT&T has been pursuing network management for decades; GIS (formerly NCR) has been developing and deploying management products for many years; the key is to port existing applications to the new platform and integrate them with applications running under OpenView and OpenView/DM.

Limitations.   The real integration is yet to come. The technologies of the two contributing platforms are different; users do not yet know how deep integration will be. In terms of available third-party management applications, OneVision is tracing other platforms.

SunNet Manager (Solstice) from Sunsoft. SunNet Manager was first introduced in 1989. The product was the first open management platform on the market to gain a critical mass of third-party support. SunNet Manager is based on a protocol-independent architecture that uses Sun's Open Network Computing Remote Procedure Call (ONC RPC) messaging services. The product supports SNMP via proxy agents. SunNet Manager can also communicate to any proprietary management protocol through a proxy written to its agent services API.

Strengths.   SunNet Manager has one of the largest installed bases of any Unix-based management platform, with over 15,000 copies installed as of mid-1995. Its popularity is due to its very affordable price, Sun's vast installed base of Unix workstations, and its early entrance into the market. More than 80 third-party applications were shipping for SunNet Manager as of mid-1995. This positions SunNet Manager in the number one spot for third-party support, although Hewlett-Packard and IBM are expected to at least equal that position during the next couple of years. In order to support more advanced SNMP applications, SunSoft has been licensing modules of Seagates' DiMONs. One of the modules is NerveCenter, which is a very intelligent SNMP manager. Using DiMONS code, distribution capabilities are greatly improved.

Limitations.   SunNet Manager is a very basic platform. It provides support for integrating SNMP devices, including third-party private MIBs; however, it is very weak in alarm filtering, configuration, and accounting management. SunNet Manager uses an SNMP proxy implementation rather than native SNMP support. This means that all communications use Sun's Remote Procedure Call/Open Network Computing (RPC/ONC) protocols, and communications with non-Sun devices must go through a proxy agent (protocol converter). In some cases, this proxy-based architecture is a drawback, because it can slow down performance. For this reason, some third-party applications developers, including Cisco and Bay Networks, support their own SNMP stack to improve performance when running with SunNet Manager. On the other hand, SunNet Manager's ONC/RPC-based architecture does provide a measure of flexibility. For example, proxy agents in Sun workstations can perform a limited amount of polling and processing and forward alarms to the SunNet Manager console. Also the proxy architecture simplifies development of support for legacy devices, such as switches, front ends, and controllers. In upcoming releases, SunSoft plans to add "smart request" polling for enhanced ease of use, which would support configuring polls on groups of devices, rather than just on individual devices.

SunNet Manager from Sunsoft

1. Hardware platform of the product — SunSPARC and RS/6000.

2. Operating systems — SunOS, Solaris.

3. Network architectures — DECnet, OSI, SNA, TCP/IP, ONC/RPC.

4. Network management protocols — NMVT via proxy agents, SNMPv1, SNMPv2.

5. Graphical user interface — OpenLook.

6. Database support — Indexed sequential files.

7. Core management applications
   Discovery and mapping — Both are supported.

   Alarm capabilities — Basic alarming capabilities are supported on the basis of SNMP.

   Platform protection — Yes for password access and encryption.

8. Application programming interfaces (APIs) and development toolkits — Three types are supported. Manager Services API is supporting ONC/RPC-based communication services; Agent Services API allows users to write proxy agents for managing other devices and objects; Database/topology MAP API lets developers modify the database and customize the topology display.

9. Distribution capabilities — Yes, with Solstice Enterprise Manager (EM).

10. LAN modeling — Not supported.

11. Support of frameworks — OMNIPoint with Solstice Enterprise Manager.

12. Object orientation — Yes, with Solstice Enterprise Manager.

Spectrum from Cabletron. Cabletron is a leading provider of intelligent concentrators (smart hubs) and networking solutions. Because network management is a key differentiator in the smart hub market, Cabletron has invested heavily in developing leading-edge network management technology to help maintain its leading position as a hub provider. Cabletron's Spectrum is the most advanced open management platform in its class on the market today. The product's installed base still lags behind SunNet Manager and HP OpenView. Cabletron has had difficulty garnering third-party support for Spectrum, although it appears that the vendor started to achieve greater success in that area with the release of Spectrum 3.0. They are behind other platforms, but in special areas such as systems management, the number of management applications supporting Spectrum is growing.

Strengths. Cabletron Spectrum is capable of managing large, heterogeneous internetworks; it operates at a higher level than other platforms due to its artificial intelligence capabilities. Spectrum uses inductive modeling technology and an object-oriented database; this supports modeling the entire network, forming a relationship between devices. This allows Spectrum to provide useful information and perform proactive functions without human intervention. Spectrum supports a client/server architecture supporting multiuser access—in contrast with most other management platforms, which are single-user systems relying on X-Terminal windows for remote access. The company is penetrating the market with application suites that have been tailored to Spectrum, with the result of eliminating the need for application integration. Overall performance is better, and integration expenses are lower.

Limitations. Spectrum's primary weakness has been its lack of third-party support. As of mid-1995, third-party applications available for Spectrum included Remedy Action Request System, Isicad Command 5000, Atrium for Spectrum from Calypso), NetTech BlueVision, and an SAS Gateway. However, third-party support is expected to increase substantially during the next couple of years, with the addition of important ISV applications such as HP NetMetrix and CA-Legent Paradigm. While a comprehensive Spectrum package can be fairly expensive, modular packaging allows users to start small and scale up in order to manage the largest interconnected LAN networks.

In order to compete for enterprise client/server management, Cabletron integrates a number of third-party applications for systems management. Key among the offerings is an application called Atrium EMS from Calypso Software that performs policy-based management for desktop workstations, servers, and applications. Other applications include LANAlert from Seagate for managing NetWare and Windows NT systems, and an application called Best/1 from BGS Systems for managing applications. The Cabletron products for workstation hardware management are called Workstation Management Modules. They collect data on system resources and performance, as well as user administration from Unix workstations, and import into the knowledge base of Spectrum. In addition, an Oracle management module is provided to model and manage Oracle databases.

Cabletron is using the Internet for the distribution of performance reports. The Spectrum SNMP console is equipped with a report generator that posts management statistics into a stand-alone Web server. Authorized users may browse this server and import information.

Spectrum from Cabletron

1. Hardware platform of the product	RS/6000, Sun SPARC, Silicon Graphics, AppleMac, DEC 2100/3100, Windows NT, Hewlett-Packard.
2. Operating systems	AIX, SunOS, Ultrix, SG-IRIX, HP-UX.
3. Network architectures	DECnet, SNA, TCP/IP.
4. Network management protocols	NMVT, RMON, SNMPv1, SNMPv2, ATM.
5. Graphical user interface	Motif.
6. Database support	Object-oriented databases and ISAm files; connections to SAS.
7. Core management applications	
Discovery and mapping	Strong support for both with many additional features.
Alarm capabilities	Strong support using an inference engine with expert capabilities.
Platform protection	Password for access protection.
8. Application programming interfaces (APIs) and development toolkits	Eight APIs have been published: X 11/Motif API, SpectroServer API (it does include SNMP services), Inference Handler API, Basic Extentions API, Extensive Integration API, Generic Information Block Editor API, Icon Information Block API, Model Type Editor API.
9. Distribution capabilities	Strongly supported; multiple clients can communicate with multiple SpectroServers.
10. LAN modeling	It is indirectly supported by the inference engine.
11. Support of frameworks	No one supported.
12. Object orientation	Yes.

DiMONS from Seagate. Seagate with the products of NetLabs is a very influential player in the SNMP-based management market, even though the installed base of the NetLabs/DiMONS product lags far behind HP OpenView and SunNet Manager. Under the terms of a licensing agreement, AT&T GIS has been using NetLabs/DiMONs as the basis for its AT&T OneVision product for several years. Indeed, most of NetLabs' revenue has come from OEM agreements with AT&T and several other vendors. Hewlett-Packard is licensing NetLabs' NerveCenter technology and plans to incorporate it into future versions of HP OpenView. NetLabs, then, will evolve into a purveyor of network management technology and applications rather than a provider of end-user, open management platforms.

Strengths. The product's chief strength is its configurable polling and NerveCenter alarm capability that supports recognition of conditional-state alarms. NetLabs/DiMONS can manage networks of up to 10,000 devices; its architecture supports multiuser/multidomain configurations. NetLabs/DiMONS flexible conditional-state alarm model and polling features can also be very useful in large networks. Upward scaling is achieved by interconnecting the NetLabs/100 entry-level model at remote sites, linking them to a central NetLabs' DiMONS.

Limitations. NetLabs is a small company whose profitability depends solely on network management. There are few third-party applications shipping, for DiMONS NetLabs does not have the name recognition of the other leading vendors. The acquisition by Seagate may change this situation.

DiMONS 3G from Seagate-NetLabs

1. Hardware platform of the product	Sun SPARC, RS/6000, Intel 386/486, Intergraph InterPro 2000, Siemens MX 500.
2. Operating systems	SunOS, Unix, Windows, Sinix.
3. Network architectures	TCP/IP, DECnet, Transdata, SNA, OSI.
4. Network management protocols	SNMP MIB I and II, SMUX, RMON, CMIP.
5. Graphical user interface	OSF/motif.
6. Database support	Informix, Informix Wingz.
7. Core management applications	
Discovery and mapping	Yes, with complete discovery and also with fast discovery.
Alarm capabilities	Very strong with NerveCenter including powerful alarm correlation.
Platform protection	Yes for password access and security services API.

8. Application programming interfaces (APIs) and development toolkits	Multiple APIs are published. The NetLabs Application eXchange program provides third-party developers with a mechanism for marketing and distributing their applications to a variety of vertical markets.
9. Distribution capabilities	Supported via CMIP, distributed message-passing capabilities, and distributed data model are available. Applications can be installed remotely from the platform. Distributed message passing between consoles allows multiple copies of DiMONS 3G to be kept up to date without redundant polling; ensures data integrity when multiple users write to the network map simultaneously.
10. LAN modeling	Not supported.
11. Support of frameworks	GDMO and OSF.
12. Object orientation	Yes.

Release 1.2 will be the last. This will ship with tools to help customers convert their data to OpenView format.

Integrated Systems Manager from Bull.   ISM is the management component of Bull's Distributed Computing Model (DCM). ISM supports both systems and network management in Unix and in heterogeneous environments. ISM supports modules for managing Novell NetWare LANs, Microsoft LAN Manager, and Bull's Open Team LANs, as well as for Unix systems. Bull's Consolidated Management API (CM-API) was adopted by both X-Open and the OSF, and it was renamed XMP.

Strengths.   ISM provides comprehensive support for both systems and network management. The product includes integrated modules for Unix file system monitoring, Unix operating system monitoring, backup/restore capabilities, software distribution, and user administration as well as a network alarm facility and SNMP support.

Limitations.   The product is not yet well known in the United States. To date, there are only a handful of third-party applications supporting ISM.

Integrated Management System from Bull

1. Hardware platform of the product	Bull 090 to 490.

2. Operating systems   GCOS, Unix.

3. Network architectures   DSA, SNA, TCP/IP, OSI.

4. Network management protocols   SNMPv1, SNMPv2, CMIP, DSAC
                                              NAD.

5. Graphical user interface   OSF/Motif.

6. Database support   Oracle, DPX/2, DPX/20, GCOS 7.

7. Core management applications
   Discovery and mapping   Automatic discovery and drawings
                                              of IP and IPX routers, gateways,
                                              and other SNMP nodes.

   Alarm capabilities   It supports incoming alarms as
                                              well filtering and alarm logging.

   Platform protection   Password protection.

8. Application programming   ISM's Consolidated Management
   interfaces (APIs) and   API Library supports access to the
   development toolkits   CM-API (also known as XMP).
                                              Third-party developers can build
                                              extentions to the management
                                              system without impacting the
                                              product.

9. Distribution capabilities   Yes with CMIP.

10. LAN modeling   Not supported.

11. Support of frameworks   OSF.

12. Object orientation   Yes.

Windows-based management platforms

OpenView from Hewlett-Packard. HP OpenView for Windows is designed to manage PC LAN networks from 50 to 1000 nodes. The product currently supports a MIB compiler for monitoring any SNMP-based device. Tighter integration with HP OpenView for Unix is expected in the future. Until 1994, Hewlett-Packard marketed HP OpenView for Windows strictly on an OEM basis; vendors such as Cabletron used HP OpenView for Windows as a basis for their own entry-level management products. Hewlett-Packard is now retooling HP OpenView for Windows as a general-purpose management platform capable of supporting multiple third-party applications.

Strengths. HP OpenView for Windows is an extremely affordable, low-end platform. Its support for Visual Basic should encourage a flood of third-party applications in the future.

Limitations. HP OpenView for Windows provides only the basic management "shell" functions (alarm management, device discovery, and SNMP interface). Functionality is supplemented by Hewlett-Packard's Workgroup Node Manager application and third-party applications.

OpenView for Windows from Hewlett Packard

1. Hardware platform of the product	Intel 386/486.
2. Operating systems	Windows.
3. Network architectures	TCP/IP, IPX/SPX.
4. Network management protocols	SNMPv1.
5. Graphical user interface	Windows.
6. Database support	Paradox.
7. Core management applications	
Discovery and mapping	Autodiscovery only.
Alarm capabilities	Event forwarding, but no correlation; some filtering. Traps can be forwarded to OpenView Network Node Manager.
Platform protection	Password protection.
8. Application programming interfaces (APIs) and development toolkits	Visual Basic.
9. Distribution capabilities	Not supported.
10. LAN modeling	Not supported.
11. Support of frameworks	OSF.
12. Object orientation	Not supported.

NMC Vision from Network Managers.   Network Managers' product strategy is to market third-party applications (called *product-specific modules* or PSMs) rather than to rely solely on outside vendors. These PSMs are tightly integrated into the NMC platform. Network Managers, Limited, is pouring significant money into enhancing and expanding product functionality.

Network Managers provides some unique technology, including a lightweight object request broker and "adapter" layers that shield third-party applications developers from the differences between various management platforms. For this reason, Network Managers recently entered into several significant strategic partnerships with major vendors, including IBM, Microsoft, and AT&T. NMC's Vision line of products includes NMC Vision 1000 for Windows, NMC Vision 3000 for Unix systems, and NMC Vision 4000 for Windows NT.

Strengths.   The tightly integrated product-specific modules offered by Network Managers provide third-party device management and one-stop shopping at the same time. Network Managers is also very active in the Network Management Forum, and its Open Management Edge implementation provides a practical and affordable migration path to Forum interoperability and eventual compliance with Forum specifications. This is particularly important in Europe and Asia. The cooperation with Microsoft opens many doors in the combined systems and networks management area. The company is penetrating the market with application suites that have been tailored to Spectrum with the result of eliminating the need for application integration. Overall performance is better, and integration expenses are lower.

Limitations. While the vendor has several large PTTs as customers, as a recent startup, Network Managers is not well known outside of Europe.

NMC Vision from Network Managers

1. Hardware platform of the product	SunSPARC, RS/6000, Windows NT.
2. Operating systems	SunOS, OS/2, Unix, Windows.
3. Network architectures	IPX/SPX, TCP/IP.
4. Network management protocols	SNMP with MIB I, II, FDDI MIB, Hub MIB, Router MIB, NMVT, XNS, CMIP.
5. Graphical user interface	Motif and Windows.
6. Database support	Ingres and Informix.
7. Core management applications	
Discovery and mapping	The products support automatic tracking of connections between maps, and ensure network connection continuity. Both autodiscovery and mapping are supported.
Alarm capabilities	Polling is used to detect status; supports user-defined alarm thresholds on multiple severity levels. Trouble ticketing and tracking are also included.
Platform protection	Password protections for access.
8. Application programming interfaces (APIs) and development toolkits	Class libraries are included that provide the basis for developing new applications. APIs define the interface to class libraries and show how objects can be used.
9. Distribution capabilities	Not supported.
10. LAN modeling	Not supported.
11. Support of frameworks	OSF, OMNIPoint, Edge.
12. Object orientation	Yes.

ManageWise from Novell. Novell NetWare Management System (NMS) is a DOS-PC based system that runs under Microsoft Windows. While it supports Novell and third-party applications for managing routers and hubs, it is primarily used in the local LAN environment for managing NetWare servers. ManageWise supports monitoring of NetWare servers and management through access to NetWare's RCONSOLE and FCONSOLE utilities, but requires additional applications for full management of PC workstations. Given an adequate hardware base with additional hard drives and lots of memory, NMS can scale upward to manage larger LANs and at least a dozen routers. This suite incorporates the software distribution package and LANDesk Manager for systems' administration.

In particular, the following modules are controlled by the ManageWise console:

- NetWare Management Agent provides configuration and real-time performance data.

- NetExplorer builds logical maps of the network topology.

- LANAnalyzer monitors network traffic from the segments directly attached to this server.

- LANDesk Virus Protect scans the server volumes for known virus patterns.

- LANDesk Inventory Manager collects hardware and software information about each client workstation.

Strengths.   ManageWise is affordably priced. The product is excellent for managing distributed NetWare servers—including monitoring status and performing administrative tasks such as software distribution and backups. The product is well suited for Windows environments. Due to integration with many applications and loadable modules from third parties, it offers a strong suite of platforms for primarily Novell networks.

Limitations.   Lack of multiuser support, limited alarm filtering, and inflexible polling-map editing make ManageWise a better choice for smaller networks.

The integration with applications does not function at full efficiency due to the nonfeasibility of certain releases. This platform is suited primarily for Novell networks, and less for enterprise management.

ManageWise from Novell

1. Hardware platform of the product	Novell servers on Intel 386/486.
2. Operating systems	NetWare, Windows.
3. Network architectures	TCP/IP, IPX/SPX.
4. Network management protocols	SNMPv1, SNMPv2, RMON, NMVT.

5. Graphical user interface

Windows.

6. Database support

Btrieve.

7. Core management applications
   Discovery and mapping

Both are supported on the basis of SNMP.

Alarm capabilities

Yes, but with third-party applications.

Platform protection

Password for access protection.

8. Application programming interfaces (APIs) and development toolkits

Provides published APIs and a software developer's kit. NetWare Loadable Modules can be provided by third parties.

9. Distribution capabilities

Intelligent agents in distributed NetWare can off-load some processing.

10. LAN modeling

Not supported.

11. Support of frameworks

No one supported.

12. Object orientation

Not supported.

Special platforms for systems management

LAN management may not strictly be restricted to manage LAN segments and internetworking components. In many cases, additional components of client/server systems, such as servers and clients, must be managed as well. There are other platforms serving the special needs of systems management. The most interesting products follow.

Tivoli Management Environment from Tivoli. The Tivoli Management Environment (TME) is a suite of products designed for managing distributed Unix computers. Tivoli differs from its competitors in that it employs strictly an object-oriented approach and supports a distributed object database. TME consists of Deployment Management Products and Operations Management Products residing on the object-oriented Tivoli Management Platform. The Deployment Management Products include the following:

- Tivoli/Admin, supporting system administration, user/group management, configuration management
- Tivoli/Courier, supporting software distribution management
- Tivoli/Print supporting distributed printer management
- Tivoli/Partners, supporting database administration

The Operations Management Products include the following:

- Tivoli/Enterprise Console
- Tivoli/Workload
- Tivoli/EpochBackup
- Tivoli/Sentry

Strengths. This platform offers a very broad functionality for both administration and deployment. The Enterprise Console has been licensed by IBM to unify the view across various SystemView products. It offers a very strong object-oriented approach combined with an object-oriented database.

Limitations. Due to the systems orientation, network management–related functions are not yet fully supported; in this respect, Tivoli needs partners. There is no support for resource accounting and charge-back. The acquisition by IBM will eliminate these shortcomings.

Tivoli Enterprise Environment from Tivoli

1. Hardware platform of the product	HP 9000 series 700 or 800, RS 6000.
2. Operating systems	HP-UX, Solaris 2.3, SunOS, AIX 3.2.5.
3. Network architectures	RPC.
4. Network management protocols	It can process SNMP traps.
5. Graphical user interface	Motif.
6. Database support	Sybase.
7. Core management applications	
Discovery and mapping	No real support.
Alarm capabilities	Rules-based, filtering at central server; threshold monitoring and automated actions by distributed agents (intelligent agents on distributed nodes). The Event Server performs the following functions: logging events, applying rules, correlating events, responding automatically to events, updating event consoles, processing input from event consoles, delaying responses to events, and escalating events. Events can be received from logfiles, SNMP traps, Windows NTs, HP-NNM, AIX, SunNet Manager, TME notifications, Tivoli/Sentry events, and Tivoli/Workload events.

Platform protection	Supports of security features of the operating systems.
8. Application programming interfaces (APIs) and development toolkits	Three toolkits are available enabling users or software developers to extend Tivoli applications or develop completely new applications: Tivoli/Application Extention Facility, Tivoli/ Enterprise Integration Facility, and Tivoli/Advanced Development Environment. In addition, Application Management Specification is supported which is actually the Desktop Management Interface.
9. Distribution capabilities	Servers can communicate events with each other.
10. LAN modeling	Not supported.
11. Support of frameworks	CORBA, DME and DMTF.
12. Object orientation	Yes, very strongly supported.

Unicenter from Computer Associates. CA-Unicenter for Unix is a systems management product for HP 9000 processors running HP-UX; an optional package called CA-Unicenter/Star can also gather information from MVS hosts. Support for Sun workstations is forthcoming. CA-Unicenter's architecture centers around a relational database structure. Support for "wildcards" to select data based on user-defined criteria assists systems administrators in obtaining information based on demands of specific users, groups, or departments without having to reorganize stored data into separate files. CA-Unicenter also supports a central calendar system for scheduling all operations.

Strengths. Computer Associates owns a large number of products that offer a great potential for integration. Concentrating management applications outside the mainframes meets the expectations of practically all users. The company addresses practically all resources and all management areas.

Limitations. Network management, software distribution, and accounting are not yet sufficiently supported. This void can be filled by the cooperation with Sun and Ungermann Bass.

CA-Unicenter from Computer Associates

1. Hardware platform of the product	Hewlett-Packard servers, Windows NT Tandem, Digital, AT&T SVR4, ICL, Intel.

2. Operating systems	AIX, HP-UX, DG-UX, Solaris, OS/2, Unix OSF/1, OS/400, Sinix.
3. Network architectures	TCP/IP, proprietary CA90 messaging middleware.
4. Network management protocols	SNMP trap processing for HP-UX only.
5. Graphical user interface	Motif.
6. Database support	CA-Ingres, CA-DB.
7. Core management applications	
Discovery and mapping	Not supported today; forthcoming product will provide some representation.
Alarm capabilities	Messages, captured from Unix "syslog" daemon can be highlighted, forwarded, suppressed, or automated actions can be triggered via scipts.
Platform protection	Functions of the operating systems are implemented.
8. Application programming interfaces (APIs) and development toolkits	Applications may be developed under any of the operating systems mentioned above. AgentWorks technology and SystemsAlert offer additional interfaces for alarms processing.
9. Distribution capabilities	Via sockets based message redirection, only. The current architecture is not yet scalable.
10. LAN modeling	Not supported.
11. Support of frameworks	None of them are supported.
12. Object orientation	Proprietary middleware objects only.

OperationsCenter from Hewlett-Packard. HP OperationsCenter is primarily a fault management tool for centralizing the operations and problem management of distributed Unix systems, including HP 3000, HP 9000, IBM RS/6000, and Sun SPARCstations. OperationsCenter runs on top of the HP OpenView SNMP platform. OperationsCenter is a distributed, client/server program that operates from a central management station and interacts with intelligent software agents installed on the managed systems.

HP PerfView and the new PerfRX applications can run under OperationsCenter. HP PerfView tracks recent performance data for HP-UX and SunOS systems. PerfRX is a performance analysis tool for evaluating historical trends, load balancing, and problem diagnosis. HP PerfView includes two components: (1) central analysis software (incorporating HP Network Node Manager) and (2) intelligent agents that reside on the managed systems.

Strengths. There is strong correlation between the contributing products under the OpenView umbrella. AdminCenter will join this group to complete network, systems, and performance management.

Limitations. The distribution capabilities could be improved. It is necessary for enterprise networks to establish local centers with well-defined functionality. In order to support multiple systems from multiple users, Hewlett-Packard needs Solution Partners.

Systems Management Server from Microsoft. SMS is turning into a serious management platform upon which many users depend and for which third-party independent software vendors are developing applications. The platform is equipped with six main functional areas, such as inventory control, remote control of PCs, troubleshooting of PCs, software distribution, application monitoring, and low-level network traffic monitoring. Technology acquired from Network Managers, called NMC 4000, is extending the scope of SMS into areas of management—in addition to just administration.

SMS functions are used within a three-tiered structure that is similar in design to the domain concept being used by other management platforms. In this structure, the central site is used for enterprise data collection, license management, and control of the subsites via Microsoft's central database repository, called the SQL Server. Under the control of the central site, there are primary and secondary sites. The primary site provides local administration and database storage. The secondary site is a group of clients or servers grouped together because of their function or location. It does not contain its own SQL Server. Microsoft also uses a fourth category, called *domain,* to refer to clients and servers grouped according to technical or organizational functionality.

Strengths. This product offers a platform for administering a high volume of systems with emphasis on Microsoft products. The partner, NMC 4000 provides real-time SNMP-based monitoring of network devices as well as topology mapping of LANs and internetworks with a variety of protocols, including Netbeui, AppleTalk, IP, IPX, and others. Interesting third-party products concentrate on more advanced inventory management (NetCensus) and software metering (Centameter and Express Meter).

Limitations. This platform does not yet offer application suites for more accurate device configuration, backup management, hierarchical storage management, unattended monitoring of remote sites, secured

Internet connectivity, usage-based metering, and advanced inventory management. Users report that the Microsoft Test Program, MS Test, is difficult to handle; most users try to bypass it by using Stuffit Installer Maker version (Aladin Systems), Wise Installation (Great Lakes Business Solutions), or WinInstall (OnDemand Software). Further limitation is that the MIF Structure varies slightly from the DMTF MIF specifications.

Systems Management Server from Microsoft

1. Hardware platform of the product	Intel 386/486.
2. Operating systems	Windows, Windows NT.
3. Network architectures	TCP/IP, AppleTalk, NCP, IPX/SPX, NetBIOS.
4. Network management protocols	SNMPv1, SNMPv2.
5. Graphical user interface	Windows.
6. Database support	Microsof SQL Server.
7. Core management applications	
Discovery and mapping	Yes for both with NMC Vision.
Alarm capabilities	Yes, with NMC Vision.
Platform protection	Password protection for access.
8. Application programming interfaces (APIs) and development toolkits	SNMP for management applications; the SMS database can be accessed from any ODBC application, enabling reports of inventory information to be quickly generated. DMI is also supported.
9. Distribution capabilities	Multiple domains can be supported.
10. LAN modeling	Not supported.
11. Support of frameworks	DMTF.
12. Object orientation	Not supported.

Summary

Standardization of local area networks management has recently been significantly accelerated by available SNMP solutions. At the moment, over 85 percent of router vendors, over 70 percent of bridge vendors, over 70 percent of hub vendors, and over 50 percent of server vendors are supporting SNMP with their products, at least at the agent level. Many of them are supporting users by offering applications such as alert logs, filtering, reporting, diagnostics, autotopology, electronic mail, and trouble ticketing at the manager level. SNMP is, however, not the ultimate goal, due to obvious shortcomings such as performance, excess overhead, and limited functionality. Open standards will slowly spread throughout the market, introducing more functionality and interoperability. Implementation speed is affected by overhead, volume of changes needed, performance, and user acceptance. Proprietary solutions that are not supporting de facto or open standards will have significantly limited usage and life cycles.

In many cases, the strategy and architecture of leading manufacturers will not differentiate between LANs and WANs, but will embed both. MAN management will follow almost automatically.

Two principal enhancements will significantly increase the life expectations of SNMP: Emanate and SNMPv2. A new API called Enhanced Management Agent (Emanate) defines how one master SNMP agent can communicate with multiple subagents on the same managed object. It consists of interface specifications, master agent source code and subagent source code. This new arrangement will simplify SNMP structures and reduce the overhead of polling to single subagents. SNMP version 2 offers a broader view of managing networks and systems. The improvements include security features, a bulk data retrieval capability to support performance management, manager-to-manager interaction supporting flexible hierarchies of management structures, better error handling by including meaningful error messages, exception reporting, better definition of managed objects, and expanded network protocol support. Both manufacturers and users are very satisfied with these extensions.

Local Area Network Management Products

A brief look at the applicability of LAN management products shows the following:

- LAN management functions are well understood and categorized.
- There are a number of instruments that are able to support single LAN management functions or even a group of functions.
- The allocation of tools to functions is not yet well understood; experiences stemming from WANs are expected to help.
- There are high-end LAN management integrators, such as OpenView, NetView for AIX, OneVision, Sunnet Manager, and Spectrum.
- There are also low-end LAN management integrators, such as OpenView for Windows, NMC Vision, NetView for OS/2, NetView for Windows, PC SystemView, ManageWise, and SMS from Microsoft in combination with other products.

Instrumentation of local area network segments and interconnected LANs starts with fragmented products that address individual functions providing monitoring, testing, and analyzing services, or providing databases or front ends to user administration. LAN instrumentation trends may be summarized as follows:

- SNMP (Simple Network Management Protocol) is continuing to make inroads into network management systems. Support by virtually all vendors for LANs and for internetworked LANs can be assumed.

- Hundreds of products will incorporate SNMP agent capabilities. Fewer companies will provide generic or specific SNMP management capabilities.

- Unix seems to be the delivery platform for many network management products. The most popular combination is with Sun. Also, an integrated relational database with SQL is offered.

- SNMP will support LAN management with both of its versions, but version 2 will not be implemented in the near future due to disputes in the security area.

- Management integrators will follow two principal directions: the powerful products will concentrate on Unix and Windows NT as platforms; the less powerful ones will be implemented on Windows and OS/2.

- A GUI (graphical user interface) provides color-coded alarms, click-and-zoom capability, and manipulatable icons.

- IBM is becoming very active in this area. Besides solutions for their offerings, the company has teamed up with 3Com to offer CMOL—a de facto protocol for layer 2 below LLC. IBM implements CMIP between LAN Network Manager and its agents.

- OSF (Open Systems Foundation) is a consortium of users and vendors cooperating to achieve a standard implementation of Unix. Distributed management environment (DME) has received a lot of attention from leading vendors. DME may influence future network management standards.

- With time, dual interfaces will be supported. In other words, not only SNMP agents, but also CMIP and CMOT agents will be supported by generic network management solutions. The very same management station may also support proprietary agents using simple or complex protocol converters, called *proxy agents*.

This chapter addresses the following subjects: categorization of LAN management products, LAN management platforms and platform-independent applications, stand-alone products, PC LAN management capabilities, LAN element management systems, integrated LAN management solutions, and LAN management services.

Categorization of Products

There's a variety of products available to manage LAN segments and interconnected LANs. For the sake of simplicity, this chapter discusses the following groups:

- Stand-alone products addressing special tests, monitoring, LAN analysis, LAN documentation, LAN topology visualization, MIBs, and reporting

- LAN segment monitors, supporting fault and performance management for Ethernets, Token Rings, and FDDI; PC LANs are also included in this category

- Device-dependent LAN management applications addressing internetworking components such as routers and bridges

- LAN performance management applications using RMONs in LAN segments

- Device-independent applications, including asset management, trouble ticketing, surveillance of power supply, LAN security, and managing LAN legacy components

- Systems management applications focusing on Unix management, Unix security, backup, software distribution, software metering, database, and application management

- LAN measurement, monitoring, and reporting services

Integration Between LAN Management Platforms and Management Applications

Platforms are powerless without management applications. Platform vendors, device vendors, and independent software vendors are busy developing and implementing management applications. The number of applications for networks and systems management is doubling every six months. Currently, there are approximately 150 management applications available that are applicable for one or more SNMP platforms. However, there is still a void in applications for critical areas, such as PC-LAN monitoring and management, non-SNMP device monitoring, and management for accounting and charge-back.

While the number of applications is steadily increasing, the degree of integration between applications and underlying platforms is still inadequate. A tremendous opportunity exists to automate, simplify, and enhance management of distributed systems and networks by forging integrated links between various third-party applications. Several system integrators are now working on this problem.

Most applications today are very loosely integrated with the platform; a few are moderately integrated; and even fewer are tightly integrated. While in general, tighter integration supports a higher level of automation, a moderate level of integration is perfectly adequate for supporting process automation in many cases. The primary integration methods are listed below (Terplan 1995):

- *Menu-bar integration.*   The application is launched from the platform menu, and no contextual information is passed from the platform to the application or vice versa.

- *Map integration.*   An application is launched from the platform menu with limited context of network and systems' state, such as the meaning of an icon on a map, and their principal attributes.

- *Command-line integration.*   An application obtains limited context of network or systems' state from parameters passed via the platform's command line interface rather than from the GUI.

- *SQL interface.*   The application can access the platform's event database and modify the data if necessary.

- *Protocol integration.*   In addition to making a device's MIB data available to the platform, the application can access SNMP services of the platform.

- *Event filtering integration.*   It supports the correlation of event filtering across multiple applications.

- *Broad product support.*   It coordinates file usage, placement, tracing and logging functions, and process management between different third-party applications.

- *High-level API.*   Applications can access the platform using protocol-independent, object-oriented interfaces that shield the application from details of the platform.

The availability of integrated applications lags behind customer demand. This is because there are still technological and economic barriers to meeting market demand. The largest technological barrier is the multiplicity of APIs supported by various management platforms. Each platform has at least several APIs, affording varying levels of integration. Furthermore, each platform supports a completely different set of APIs with different coding conventions and libraries than the next. Third-party developers have neither the economic resources nor the expertise to create software that takes advantage of all available APIs, and few vendors are willing to choose one platform vendor over another to begin the effort, for fear of alienating other platform vendors and their customers.

Figure 5.1 shows how platform and LAN management applications are supposed to work together.

Stand-alone LAN Management Products

Stand-alone products serve special functional areas without aiming at the general applicability of LAN management integration. Stand-alone

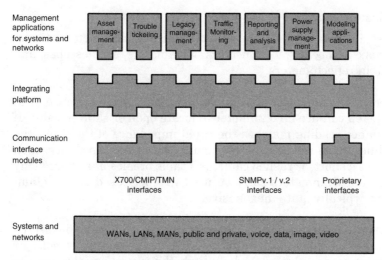

Management applications for systems and networks

Asset management · Trouble ticketing · Legacy management · Traffic Monitoring · Reporting and analysis · Power supply management · Modeling applications

Integrating platform

Communication interface modules

X700/CMIP/TMN interfaces   SNMPv.1 / v.2 interfaces   Proprietary interfaces

Systems and networks

WANs, LANs, MANs, public and private, voice, data, image, video

Figure 5.1   Integrated management product.

products are characterized and evaluated according to a number of criteria, as listed in Table 5.1.

Differences in methods of implementation and degree of functionality, for both hardware and software, distinguish one product from another. These differences vary in importance with users and their networks. Practically no product is equipped with all features, making it difficult to decide which product is best for a given environment. Stand-alone products may be further subdivided into test instruments, analyzers, monitors, and special instruments.

TABLE 5.1   Common Features of Stand-Alone LAN Products

User interface
Which networking segments can be analyzed
Which protocols can be decoded and analyzed
Capture buffers
Filtering
Triggers
Search capabilities
Time-stamping
Traffic generation
Use of symbolic station names
Self-test diagnostics
Hardcopy printing
Password protection

LAN test instruments

The most important test instruments include ohmmeters, outlet testers, coax connectors, T-connectors, terminators, oscilloscopes, and time domain reflectometers.

Ohmmeters. An ohmmeter is a simple tool that gives impedance measurement. You can use an ohmmeter to locate open or shorted cable. If the impedance reading matches the rated impedance of the cable, the cable is fine. If the reading doesn't match the rated impedance, then the LAN has a short, a crashed cable, or a cable break somewhere along the cable run. Ohmmeters can't be used in fiber-based LANs. Ohmmeters are typically quite inexpensive.

Outlet testers. Sometimes the problem is not the cable, but the electrical outlet. For example, if an outlet is not grounded properly, noise or even current may be introduced through the power supply into the workstation, and then through the network interface card onto the copper-based (twisted-pair or coaxial) LAN cable. An outlet tester, which is very inexpensive, can help detect this type of problem.

Coax connectors, T-connectors, and terminators. Extra terminators are a basic requirement, particularly on the bus network. Extra terminators can be used to isolate sections of the cable for testing.

Oscilloscope. An oscilloscope allows the network manager to examine the cable's waveform. An oscilloscope helps detect the existence of noise or other disturbances on the wire, such as continuous voltage spikes. Again, this applies only to copper-based LANs.

Time domain reflectometers (TDRs). A time domain reflectometer operates by sending an electrical pulse over the LAN cable, monitoring for signal reflections. On a good cable there will be no reflections, indicating that the cable is clean, with no breaks or shorts. If there's a break or short in the cable, however, the time it takes for the pulse reflection to return gives the TDR a very accurate idea of where the fault is located. Many TDRs can locate cable breaks to within a few feet. TDRs have traditionally been relatively expensive instruments.

A new, less expensive generation of TDR equipment is now available. These new instruments are more compact than their predecessors, often measuring about the size of a paperback book or smaller. The newer TDRs are also easier to use and still accurate to within a few feet. A time domain reflectometer (TDR) is built as a combination of a pulse generator, a voltage sampler, and an output amplifier, supplying either a display or an oscilloscope.

Because of their distributed-star topologies, ARCNET, token ring, StarLAN, and IEEE 10BASE-T networks are easiest to test when a specific cable segment is isolated and inactive. A TDR can be used on a live Ethernet, however, if a very short pulse (of less than 10 nanoseconds duration) is used and if that pulse is of a negative polarity. Positive-pulse TDRs have to be avoided, since they can affect transceiver operation.

The TDR's operation is similar to radar. An electrical pulse of known amplitude and duration is transmitted from one end of the cable. Any changes in the cable's characteristic impedance will cause reflections of the transmitted pulse. If no cable faults exist, and the cable is terminated at the far end in its characteristic impedance, no pulse reflection will occur.

A variety of cable problems, such as shorts, opens, faults, or improper terminations, kinks, bends, crimps, shorted taps, or impedance mismatches (from mixing different types of coaxial cable), produce a unique signal reflection known as a *TDR fault signature.* Typical results include the display of shorted, open, crimped, and frayed cables. Troubleshooting LANs requires a tool set including various types of instruments.

Category-5 UTP cable testing with Fluke instruments.   In order to support higher-speed information transmission, the physical plant, cables, and connecting hardware will have to provide better performance at higher signal frequencies and support higher bandwidths. This has led to the widespread installation of Category-5 LAN cabling, an unshielded twisted-pair (UTP) copper medium that has been certified by the Telecommunications Industry Association/Electronics Association (TIA/EIA), International Electrotechnical Commission (IEC), and International Organization for Standardization (ISO) to perform at frequencies as high as 100 MHz.

There is one problem, though. After a customer invests a considerable amount in the installation of a new cabling plant, there has been no way to verify the performance of this high-performance cabling for a number of reasons. And since the fast network protocols have yet to receive widespread acceptance, much of this installed cabling has yet to really be put to the test.

Problems in two areas can be identified with the existing field test equipment that has been introduced to test and verify the performance of category-5 UTP cable installations:

1. Which standard defines the performance level for installed cabling, including connecting hardware and workmanship?

2. What is the proper measurement technique, and can users trust the results of the field test equipment?

Existing field portable test equipment that claims to certify category-5 cabling installations has not demonstrated the ability to provide repeatable or accurate results, especially for the critical parameter called near-end crosstalk (NEXT). The shortcoming in the accuracy of this equipment, coupled with the fact that the standards to which the equipment tests are freelance adaptations of a laboratory specification, combine to deliver test results that are very much suspect.

As more and more information on the direction of the TIA/EIA standards was made available, it became clear that there are major stumbling blocks to the attempts of today's analog testers to meet the accuracy requirements of the imminent standard, the most troublesome being connector compensation when measuring near-end crosstalk (NEXT).

Fluke decided to take a completely new approach to address issues such as accuracy and connector compensation and to be compliant with the upcoming standards. To this end, Fluke has developed a new cable test technology—based on digital signal processing—to allow the user to test, with the utmost confidence, the performance of high-speed LAN links. The new Fluke DSP-100 CableMeter uses this new digital test technology. It delivers test results with the accuracy of laboratory-level test equipment with the touch of one button in less than 20 seconds. In addition to speed and accuracy, this new digital technology delivers detailed diagnostic information about failing cables—including the location of a NEXT fault. Although a standard has not yet been approved and released, the Fluke DSP-100 meets all the Level II requirements that have been proposed and discussed by the Link Task Group to test LAN cable links. In addition, the Fluke DSP-100 provides some unique features that will be much appreciated by the market. Some examples of both requirements and new features follow.

If a cable fails the NEXT test, a patented technology called Time Domain Crosstalk allows the tester to pinpoint the location(s) along the cable where the excessive crosstalk occurs. Rather than to tell the technician that a link fails because the worst-case NEXT value exceeds the limit at, say, 85.6 MHz (as analog testers do, for example), the DSP-100, in addition to identifying the occurrence of a fault, can report that the major contribution to that crosstalk is occurring at 42 m from the tester. Figure 5.2 shows an example of such a diagnostic plot of a category 5 link in which a category-3 connector had been installed.

The technician can immediately identify this location with a cross-connect or other type of connecting point and go right ahead to perform the corrective action. This is more advanced than the general "Fail" message, which requires that the technicians perform a number of additional measurements to locate the link segment in which the defect is located, causing replacement or rework connections, which means continual retesting during this trial-and-error process.

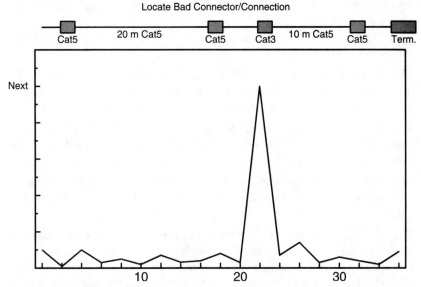

Figure 5.2   DSP-100 fault isolation using Fluke instruments.

NEXT is a critical performance parameter for installed UTP links. The NEXT of a link not only depends on the performance of the cable itself but is very much impacted by the connectors along the link (including the end connectors) as well as the workmanship of the connections (the distance over which the pairs of wires have been untwisted).

Unfortunately, the ubiquitous RJ-45 modular plugs and jacks make a very measurable contribution to the NEXT performance of a link. This is precisely one of the technical difficulties that has occupied the Telecommunications Industry/Electronics Industry Association (TIA/EIA) standards task group. How can a field cable tester accurately measure the NEXT value of a link if the connectors that the users plug into the tester contribute in a sizable way to the outcome? The existing technology that uses an analog frequency sweep to measure crosstalk at many points in the spectrum cannot undo or "separate" the effect of the instrument connector and provide answers within the specified limits of accuracy.

The digital test approach implemented in the Fluke DSP-100 can automatically compensate for the effect of these end connectors and measure the NEXT of the link with the accuracy of better than +2 dB, resulting in full compliance with the TIA's stringent Level II accuracy requirements, which specify the accuracy level of tester to be used for link certification.

The following 600-series products have been introduced by Fluke:

- The 610 CableMapper, an easy-to-use wire mapper with high-end functions at a low cost.

- The 620 CableMeter, a highly usable handheld cable tester for installer and network managers. The 620 offers the convenience of 50-hour battery life and the simplicity of one-button operation.

- The 650 CableMeter, a reliable, user-friendly cable testing device that costs about half that of its competitor, with nearly all the same features.

- The 652 CableMeter, a more powerful version of the 650 for those needing more comprehensive cable testing and certification capabilities.

- The 670 Token Ring LANMeter, a handheld network tester used to spot and solve a vast array of network problems quickly and easily. Unlike any LAN diagnostic tool currently on the market, the 670 has carved out a unique product niche by combining the best features of protocol analyzers (sophisticated, bulky and expensive tools) and cable scanners (like the 650), and adding functions not found in either of these product categories.

- The 672 Ethernet LANMeter, the power of the Token Ring LANMeter engineered specifically for Ethernet networks. The 672 has a unique set of features that enable Ethernet LAN managers to effectively troubleshoot their networks faster.

- The 675 Token Ring/Ethernet LANMeter, the all-in-one version that combines all the functionality of both the Token Ring and Ethernet versions of the LANMeter. This product is ideal for those companies that have both types of networks and need the troubleshooting power of both in a single tool.

- The DSP-100 LAN CableMeter, a 100-MHz tester for Category 5 LAN cabling, which uses digital signal processing technology to provide unprecedented accuracy.

LAN analyzers

These are sophisticated instruments whose ultimate goal is to support performance or fault management, or both. They usually offer measurement for a large number of indicators. Measurements are conducted with high accuracy. In order to avoid having unnecessarily large amounts of data to deal with, analyzers are not used continuously. Chapter 3 gave examples for compressing data and generating reports. Without differentiation, products offer indicators for the following:

- Service (delay time, transfer time, dialog time).

- Use (global use of bandwidth, specific use by applications and/or by users).

- User profiles (what applications, what activities).

- Server profiles (internal use, queuing delays in most cases). (Cooperation is required by the operating system.)

Domino Analyzers from Wandel and Goltermann. The DominoLAN and DominoWAN protocol analyzers combine affordability, portability, and capacity in a protocol analyzer that can be attached to any Windows-based workstation or notebook computer. The analyzers can also be connected to a wide range of WANs and LANs, such V.24, V.35, V.36, and V.11 for the DominoWAN and RJ-45, BNC, and AUI for the DominoLAN including both Ethernet and Token Ring technologies.

The Domino series was built to address two basic analysis problems: a lack of processing power and the prohibitive cost of distributed, portable analyzers. To meet these needs, the Domino WAN/LAN analyzers have been built as portable boxes, housing two RISC processors that capture, decode, and process network information. This system then transfers protocol data to a Windows-based computer over an IEEE P1284 bidirectional printer cable.

Figure 5.3 shows the basic configuration of the Domino series.

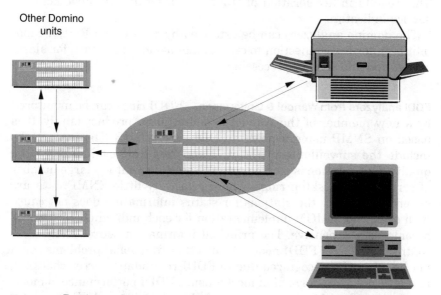

Other Domino units

Figure 5.3 Domino analyzer setup including Domino units, PCs, and peripheral devices.

The Domino series does not yet support emerging high-speed LAN technologies such as ATM and FDDI despite the fact that the units provide the same processing power as DA-30, another analyzer from the same company. Domino analyzers can be daisy-chained for simultaneous capture and analysis sessions. A connection between two Domino analyzers and a host PC, for example, will create a protocol analyzer with the same power as a single DA-30, giving users the same power as the DA-30 at much lower costs. By attaching a Domino analyzer to a tape drive, for example, users can automatically capture data to tape.

The Domino series also emphasizes remote management capabilities. Users do not have to connect the Domino unit to a workstation or notebook computer. Instead, they can attach any number of Domino units to a network, reducing the field personnel required to maintain the network.

By means of this unique combination, the user can accomplish the following:

- Analyze LANs and generate LAN statistics.

- Determine WAN bandwidth efficiency.

- Analyze LAN traffic running on the WAN for pinpointing the sources of WAN congestion or detecting unnecessary traffic on the WAN.

- Analyze in detail upper-layer LAN traffic on the WAN link to maximize LAN payload versus overhead.

This results in acceleration of troubleshooting and improvements of service indicators.

The domino analyzers can be extended by SNMP and RMON capabilities, allowing connection to central management stations for alarm correlation and further processing.

FDDI analyzers from Wandel & Goltermann.   FDDI rings can be monitored by a new member of the Wandel & Goltermann product family. It is based on SNMP using a private FDDI service MIB. The main tasks include the surveillance of the ring and real-time evaluation of the quality. This solution is particularly suitable to monitor a large number of servers and desktop rings, where relatively little SNMP data are generated. Polling the stations for status information does not cause high overhead. RMON implementation for each individual ring would become very expensive. The principal information source is the self-control function of FDDI nodes. Many other functional problems could not be otherwise recognized due to FDDI redundancy, error checking, and internal error-correction mechanisms. FDDI performance is monitored using the SMT functions that collect data into a MIB-like database. The FDDI monitor polls these data, converts them into SNMP format, and sends them to the management station for alarm management, correlation, and further processing.

This monitor can be connected to HP OpenView, NetView for AIX, and to SunNet Manager using inband or outband connections.

The OMS-200 modular, rack-mount optical measurement system reduces the time required to perform multiple tests on optical components, subsystems, and systems.

The OMS-200 is for manufacturing operations with high-speed production lines, because it integrates virtually every required optical measurement into a single, upgradeable instrument. Adding or deleting test functions does not require modification of the mainframe, since all of the configuration routines are handled by resident software. Consequently, as test needs increase, the OMS-200 can change easily to accommodate them. Only additional modules must be purchased (not complete instruments), which can result in significant long-term savings.

The OMS-200 is completely modular, consisting of a mainframe into which up to eight test modules can be installed. The mainframe is responsible for evaluating the results delivered by the test modules and communicating them to the host system. The modules contain all of the hardware and software required to perform a specific optical measurement, such as loss, power, back-reflection.

The test modules are complete measurement subsystems in themselves. Modules currently available for the OMS-200 include LED and laser sources, power meters, attenuators, back-reflection meters, and switches. Test modules can be interchanged by simply plugging them into the mainframe. The instrument's operating software recognizes the modules and automatically integrates them into the system. There are no complex programming routines to perform and no manual configuration steps.

The instrument is designed to be operated by a microcomputer or dedicated instrument controller under IEEE-488 bus or RS-232C control, and all instrument functions are available on the bus. The firmware within the OMS-200 contains application software that allows automated test sequences to be constructed with only simple programming.

The OMS-200 is available with drivers for LabWindows for DOS and LabWindows/CVI for Windows; drivers for LabView and HP VEE are available on request. All of the software required to allow the OMS-200 to be integrated into an automated measurement system is included within the instrument. The software runs under Windows.

The other instrument represents the handheld family. It combines exceptional optical performance, rugged reliability, and the ability to simultaneously measure attenuation at 1310 and 1550 nm without changing sources.

The OL series is designed to offer the best combination of accuracy and convenience when used in installation, maintenance, and repair of fiber-optic networks. The new instruments in the OL series include the OLP-15 power meter, OLS-15 laser source, and OLA-15 attenuator. Every model in the series is built into a rugged, nonslip, shockproof case that also provides protection against water.

The increased deployment of FDDI networks has also motivated other vendors to develop and implement special FDDI analyzers. Digital Technologies' LANHawk Network Analyzer functions as a passive monitor or, with an optional simulation module, as an FDDI station generating traffic. Channel-LAN 100 from Tekelec acts as an FDDI repeater and connects to the network as dual—or single—attached station. Simulation is supported with a special option. Evaluation criteria for LAN analyzers are shown in Table 5.2.

LAN monitoring systems

This family of tools supports continuous monitoring by offering a data collection unit in each LAN segment. The master monitor's capabilities are similar to a LAN analyzer's, but they're extended by control software to communicate with the remote data collection units.

Incorporating fault management functions for LANs into centralized fault management applications is not easy. Downtime and delayed service may severely impact targeted service-level agreements. There are fragmented monitoring applications supporting performance management, but continuous monitoring for supporting fault management is still very rare. A growing number of manufacturers have recognized the need and offer solutions for remote monitoring LANs. The central station or focal point may reach across via network or dial-up connections, providing the equivalent of very remote terminal and keyboard operations. They may also have additional filtering and analysis capabilities.

Distributed Sniffer System from Network General. Today's client/server networks demand a cost-effective network analysis solution. Users need to solve network problems and monitor multiple network segments across the country and around the globe from a central office. The Distributed Sniffer Systems (DSS) is Network General's answer to the challenge of managing complex, geographically dispersed networks from centralized locations.

DSS delivers remote monitoring (RMON) and Expert Analysis solutions for proactively managing network performance and solving net-

TABLE 5.2   Evaluation Criteria for LAN Analyzers

General features
Dedicated device or PC
Standards supported
   Ethernet
   Token Ring
   Token Bus
   FDDI
Scalability for WAN analysis
Dimensions
Weight

Hardware architecture
What hardware
On-board memory
On-board CPU
Memory size
What printer and plotter
Ability to analyze
   Ethernet (cabling, reflectometer, collisions, wrong packets)
   Token Ring (media test, rotating time and recovery time measurements)
   Support of remote monitoring and analysis

Software features
Number of input channels
Filtering
Time stamps
Monitoring stations
Buffering
Triggering
Presentation
List of alarms
Protocols measured
Overhead
Statistics and performance reports
Interface to spreadsheets and databases
SNMP support

Screen and handling
Size of screen
Color codes
Resolution
What graphic cards are supported
Use of function keys
Use of maps
Use of pop-up menus

References
Number of installations
Price
Conditions
Training

work problems. With DSS, the user can view network activity from a central location using one of the popular network management platforms. As a result, users can leverage their expertise across every segment, save valuable time and money, and manage the entire network from end to end without leaving the central office.

The Distributed Sniffer System offers the following benefits:

- *Proactive management.*   DSS gives LAN managers proactive control over the entire network. They can baseline the network's normal behavior to help identify incremental changes and potential problems. Because DSS notifies them of potential problems before an end user calls to complain to LAN managers, DSS can solve underlying issues before they become headaches.

- *Fast problem resolution.*   DSS targets the underlying cause of problems on Ethernet and token ring LANs as well as bridged and routed internetworks. The user can look at detailed interpretations of over 140 protocols. DSS identifies network problems and provides LAN managers with suggestions for corrective action to help expedite problem solving.

- *Maximizes performance.*   DSS reports a number of statistics from all seven OSI layers in real time. This information helps keep the network running, enabling operators to solve problems before they cause downtime. Using historical statistics, DSS helps in planning server placement and segmentation to maximize network performance.

- *Reduces network management costs.*   Users can manage remote locations without the time and expense of traveling. DSS automates software distribution and provides out-of-band serial support. This helps to centrally monitor and analyze network performance and resolve problems without delay.

Figure 5.4 shows the members of the Sniffer family of products.

DSS offers a range of scalable analysis and monitoring solutions in a variety of configurations, operating systems, and price options to match the LAN management budget and users' specific network management needs.

Analysis solutions feature expert analysis and protocol interpretation applications. Users can rely on DSS analysis solutions to keep network backbones and mission-critical segments up and running.

Monitoring solutions include standards-based remote monitoring (RMON). DSS monitoring solutions help LAN managers proactively baseline and identify changes in network behavior.

Using innovative software based on artificial intelligence technology, the expert analysis application helps find and resolve complex network

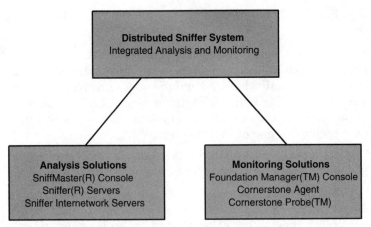

Figure 5.4 Members of the Sniffer family.

problems in real time. These problems are automatically discovered at all seven OSI layers and explained in plain English. Consequently, operators can easily understand and solve complex network problems.

Expert analysis provides three types of information—symptoms, diagnoses, and explanations to help quickly resolve performance, protocol, internetwork, and physical layer problems:

- Symptoms are clues to potential problems that might be lurking on the networks. Expert analysis symptoms provide a means to proactively manage your network.

- For serious problems expert analysis delivers automatic diagnoses to help LAN managers resolve bottlenecks and performance problems that may bring your network down.

- For every potential and existing problem, expert analysis provides supporting data and automatically recommends solutions.

With a single keystroke, expert analysis displays packets associated with the discovered problem so LAN analysts can investigate it in even greater detail. A complete record of expert analysis information can be written in CSV format and uploaded to a console for use in spreadsheet, database, reporting, and plotting applications. Use this information to analyze statistics and generate management reports.

DSS with expert analysis alerts LAN managers to many common network problems, including the following:

- *Performance bottlenecks.* The expert analysis application helps detect distributed segment inefficiencies by analyzing and interpreting network data, such as multiple retransmissions, which consume bandwidth.

- *Internetworking problems.* Expert analysis identifies problems that impact the performance of internetwork links. Duplicate network addresses are readily detected and the nodes involved are identified automatically. This helps to improve application throughput, avoid the purchase of unnecessary equipment, and boost end-user productivity on multisegment enterprise networks.

- *Protocol violations.* As part of DSS, the expert analysis application recognizes nonstandard protocol activity and suggests solutions for protocol problems.

- *Physical layer problems.* DSS with expert analysis speeds the process of identifying and solving Ethernet and Token Ring lower-layer problems, including congestion and ring beaconing.

The protocol interpretation application enables LAN operators to troubleshoot complex network problems by providing full decodes for over 140 protocols. With a detailed view of the composition of data packets, the user can see the actual communication occurring on the network and get to the cause of network communication problems. Protocol interpretation displays the contents of each frame in English-language text for each of the seven OSI layers.

Network traffic is displayed in three ways—Summary, Detail, and Hex—to provide progressively more detail about a packet and its protocols. For quick comparison, packets can be compared side by side on the same screen. A sophisticated filtering system allows users to easily manipulate and isolate only the packets they want to examine for faster problem resolution.

The DSS RMON application offers standards-based monitoring and enhanced performance analysis capabilities for distributed network segments. To protect investments in other RMON technologies, Network General's standards-based monitoring solution fully supports all the RMON MIB groups for Ethernet and Token Ring LANs. Discover how this unique RMON solution aids in the following:

- *Remote office management.* The DSS RMON application helps users to see what is happening inside remote segments. Cornerstone Agents and Cornerstone Probes have the unique ability to collect, process, and track segment activity on individual nodes, routers, and servers. This allows LAN managers to use Cornerstone Agents and probes as a remote office management system.

- *Communications management.* DSS RMON information also gives proactive control to manage the communications on distributed network segments. Using Foundation Manager, the user can view traffic between remote segments and nodes based on real-time traffic flow, continuous discovery, and automatic updates of network configurations.

- *User analysis.* The Foundation Manager and Cornerstone Agents or Probes can be utilized to determine overall usage patterns for distributed LAN segments and at the entire enterprise network. This helps tracking network usage at the workstation level to analyze end-user impact on distributed segments.

- *Change detection.* This RMON solution allows you to set customized alarm thresholds to detect abnormal network changes. The change management capabilities provided by Foundation Manager, Cornerstone Agents, and Probes allow you to spot potential problems before they become network failures.

LAN managers can proactively monitor network activity on every segment with this DSS monitoring solution. DSS also integrates trouble prevention, early detection, and problem resolution for distributed network segments. Users can quickly transition from DSS monitoring to analysis on the same console by saving RMON data in Sniffer trace file format. Then LAN performance analysts can analyze RMON data using DSS Expert Analysis and Protocol Interpretation applications.

Figures 5.5 and 5.6 position DSS components in local and remote networks.

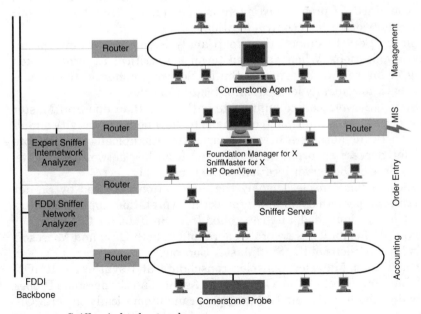

Figure 5.5 Sniffers in local networks.

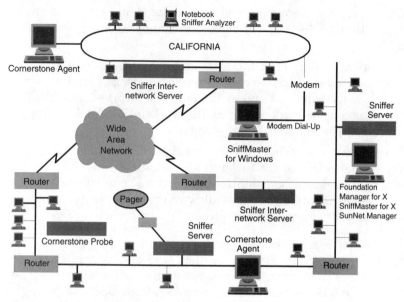

Figure 5.6   Sniffers in remote networks.

DSS analysis solutions consist of two components: Sniffer Servers and SniffMasterConsoles. DSS standards-based monitoring solutions consist of three components: Foundation Manager Consoles, Cornerstone Agents, and Cornerstone Probes. Scalable DSS components can be combined to proactively monitor and quickly troubleshoot your entire network from a central location.

Sniffer Servers support the expert analysis and protocol interpretation applications. When attached to mission-critical Ethernet, token ring, or internetwork segments, Sniffer Servers communicate information back to centrally located SniffMaster Consoles.

Sniffer Servers can communicate with more than one SniffMaster Console, allowing multiple technicians to view network activity simultaneously. Advanced features such as automatic uploads from remote Sniffer Servers ensure data is collected from key network segments, regardless of the server location or the time of day.

SniffMaster Consoles display the information gathered by Sniffer Servers. Expert analysis and protocol interpretation applications are downloaded, launched, and controlled from SniffMaster Consoles. For maximum flexibility, Network General offers both Unix and Microsoft Windows versions of the SniffMaster Console.

Foundation Manager Consoles consolidate and synthesize RMON information collected from Cornerstone Agents and Cornerstone Probes on a distributed network. LAN analysts can automatically save RMON data in Sniffer trace file format to quickly troubleshoot alarms with Network General's expert analysis and protocol interpretation applications. This provides a seamless, icon-based transition from monitoring to analysis from a centralized console.

Cornerstone Agents and Cornerstone Probes gather statistical information specific to the standard RMON management information base (MIB) groups for both Ethernet and Token Ring LANs. When attached to remote segments, Cornerstone Agents and Probes gather RMON statistics, generate alarms, and relay information back to centrally located Foundation Manager Consoles. Agents and Probes can also send SNMP alarms to SNMP management systems.

The Cornerstone Agent has a local user interface for on-site monitoring. It also communicates RMON data to centralized Foundation Manager Consoles. Cornerstone Agent software can be installed in any 486+ PC running Microsoft Windows or OS/2 to leverage the users' existing hardware investment.

Cornerstone Probe is comprised of an RMON agent preinstalled in a server. Cornerstone Probes collect and send RMON data to Foundation Manager Consoles to enable centralized monitoring and performance analysis of remote LAN segments.

DSS fully supports Ethernet, Token Ring, and internetwork segments with multitopology network analysis solution. LAN managers can track multiprotocol communications traveling over distributed multitopology networks from the comfort of a central office with DSS.

DSS integrates both analysis and monitoring solutions in a single system with centralized control. When the DSS monitoring application identifies a potential problem, the user can seamlessly transition to DSS analysis applications to resolve critical situations. By integrating RMON, expert analysis, and protocol interpretation applications, DSS gives all of its users an end-to-end view across geographically dispersed, multitopology networks.

DSS has multiple alarm notification options to meet specific needs. Alarms can be sent to popular management platforms, SniffMaster Consoles, Foundation Manager Consoles, pagers, or electronic mail. These comprehensive alarm options help pinpoint the location and severity of network problems anywhere on your client/server network.

With DSS serial support, LAN operators can access Sniffer Servers on remote network segments even if they are experiencing router problems. Using the SniffMaster for Windows out-of-band communications, they can dial into remote Sniffer Servers via modem to analyze remote segments.

DSS helps leverage investments in network management platforms. DSS offers platform integration at multiple levels—from maps and alarms to shared databases. Using existing management platforms,

DSS and other network management applications can be ported to each other with the click of an icon.

The seamless mapping and alarm integration between DSS and popular management platforms helps identify critical problems quickly. By clicking a highlighted icon on an OpenView, SunNet Manager, or NetWare Management System map, the user can launch analysis and monitoring applications to solve problems anywhere on distributed network segments.

The Network General Reporter application helps to collect and present DSS analysis and monitoring data. The Reporter offers over 20 standard report formats to document and graphically depict network usage over time, error summaries, baseline comparisons, and enterprise-level trends. LAN managers can use the Reporter in conjunction with DSS analysis and monitoring solutions to effectively solve network problems, justify support costs, and plan for the future.

Network General's family of Sniffer Network Analyzers is the de facto industry standard for analyzing multiprotocol, multitopology, multivendor networks. Today, an expanded line of Sniffer products connects to more physical topologies and interprets more protocols than any other portable analysis solution available.

Expert Sniffer Network Analyzers for Ethernet, Token Ring, internetwork, and FDDI topologies utilize a user-friendly menu and command system. Designed to run on industry standard PCs rather than expensive proprietary hardware, Expert Sniffer Network Analyzers are ready to solve network problems right out of the box.

Expert Sniffer Network Analyzers utilize Expert Analysis to help solve problems fast:

- *Automatic problem identification.* As soon as it is plugged into your network, the Expert Sniffer Network Analyzer automatically targets network problems—from the physical through the application layers. Problems are identified while traffic is moving across the network. As a result, LAN operators can find and resolve problems before end users even notice them.

- *Quick problem resolution.* The Expert Sniffer Network Analyzer automatically gives detailed, real-time explanations of network problems. Users can pinpoint and solve problems faster, resulting in reduced network downtime.

- *Real-time configuration discovery.* The Expert Sniffer Network Analyzer automatically learns a network's logical configuration and constantly updates it in real time. In addition, this powerful tool learns the names and addresses of network nodes for analysis of communications between these connections.

- *Automatic data collection.* LAN managers can also proactively schedule the collection of expert analysis information. Based on the time intervals users specify, Expert Sniffer Network Analyzers can save captured packets, reset statistics, load setup files, and save data in CSV format for reporting. Consequently, technicians do not have to be at the segment site to collect important network data.

Portable Expert Sniffer Network Analyzers deliver full decodes for over 140 protocols with detailed seven-layer interpretations in plain English. A sophisticated filtering system helps focus on trouble areas immediately. Our seven-layer analysis makes data easy to understand and lets users actually see what is happening inside their network.

Expert Sniffer Network Analyzers are practical, too. They monitor LAN segments and provide statistics, alarms, and reports. Audible and on-screen alarms notify you immediately of network problems. You can also collect historical network data and define customized statistical reports.

Notebook Sniffers Analyzers deliver Network General's analysis solutions on a variety of lightweight notebook PC platforms. Based on Personal Computer Memory Card International Association (PCMCIA) standards, the Notebook Sniffer Analyzer quickly solves problems on Ethernet and Token Ring LANs.

Portable Notebook Sniffer Analyzers are ideal for field service technicians on-the-go. Your portable notebook PC can be used as a Notebook Sniffer Analyzer as well as a workstation. Notebook Sniffer Analyzers provide access to Windows 3.1 and DOS 6.x applications. This improves mobility, minimizes costs, and expands your hardware vendor options.

Network General developed the first analysis solution designed to solve problems on router-based internetworks and manage bandwidth costs. By providing a comprehensive view of communications traveling over internetwork links, Expert Sniffer Internetwork Analyzers pinpoint internetwork bottlenecks and offer recommendations to improve bandwidth efficiency, application throughput, and response times.

Network General's portable analysis tools offer the widest range of features for analyzing data traffic across internetworks, including the following:

- Expert analysis of internetworks for automatic problem identification

- Seven-layer analysis of over 140 LAN protocols encapsulated within leased-line (HDLC), frame relay, and X.25 protocols

- Utilization statistics of internetwork bandwidth for performance analysis
- Capture of network traffic at data rates of up to 2.048 Mbps

Expert Sniffer Internetwork Analyzers also meet the needs of the traditional terminal-to-host WAN configurations. This portable tool addresses a range of traditional wide area communications modes and protocols from async, bisync, and frame relay to X.25 and SNA. Supporting speeds from 50 bps up to 2.048 Mbps, Expert Sniffer Internetwork Analyzers meet existing and future internetwork speed requirements.

Collected data with the Sniffer family can also support performance modeling and capacity planning. Optimal Performance uses expert analysis information to automatically generate a baseline model of an organization's network, including topology, LAN and WAN traffic, protocols and applications. Predefined elements in the model include bridges, routers, hubs, switches, and protocols.

Chapter 6 addresses modeling tools for LANs, including some details about Optimal Performance.

NetMetrix from Hewlett-Packard. The product offers workstation-based traffic monitoring and analysis on multiple platforms, including HP OpenView, SunNet Manager, and NetView for AIX. The integration methods used are SNMP traps, command line interface, and enhanced command line interface.

HP NetMetrix incorporates the best features of the traditional traffic monitors and analyzers—such as the ability to simulate network loads, gather statistics, perform traces, and provide seven-layer packet decode—and removes the encumbrances of proprietary hardware probes and clumsy user interfaces. The result is a workstation-based (UNIX/SPARC) segment monitor and an X-windows graphic user interface (GUI) supporting a suite of five very useful NetMetrix applications:

1. Traffic generator simulates network load, can generate user-defined packet streams, and can respond to decoded packets in real time.

2. Protocol analyzer is providing seven-layer packet decode on most major protocols.

3. Load monitor correlates traffic statistics to help users optimize bridge/router placement and answer other critical questions for fine-tuning.

4. NFS monitor measures NFS load and response time (by server, client, NFS procedure, or time interval), client/server distribution analysis, and server performance comparisons.

5. Internetwork monitor coordinates multiple agents across the network to provide a cohesive picture—such as displaying which groups as well as hosts are talking to each other.

NetMetrix provides a distributed architecture, supporting continuous monitoring and analysis of all segments in real time. While several other products provide similar capabilities, NetMetrix is less expensive than these products and more comprehensive—particularly in analyzing NFS traffic. However, Hewlett-Packard's aggressive pursuit of simple, effective methods for platform-application and application-application integration put the company ahead of its competitors in providing automated network management for its customers.

The standard features include a protocol analyzer for various protocols, such as AppleTalk, DECnet, IPX, SNMP, SNA, TCP/IP, and Vines. Figure 5.7 shows a typical NetMetrix configuration.

Other products addressing LAN monitoring include the following:

LANVista from Digilog

Remote Monitoring Option from Spider Systems

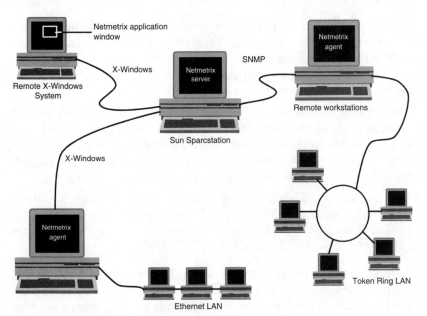

Figure 5.7 NetMetrix from Hewlett-Packard.

Trakker from Concord Communications

Network Advisor from Hewlett-Packard

LAN Analyzer from Novell

Documentation Tools

Large-scale or interconnected LANs require powerful documentation systems or, in other words, an enterprisewide library of data accessible by any user on the LAN. A user should be able to access any document without prior knowledge of where it physically resides. On the basis of basic information about a document, a user should be able to formulate a query, and the document management system is expected to search, find, retrieve, and route the document to the requester. The documents may be in image or in coded formats (Network Management, Inc., 1990). LANfolio is one example offering support for document management. LANfolio is structured around a three-tiered, client/server model. The ultimate goal of this product is to solve two common problems: the successful accommodation of large numbers of users requiring simultaneous access to an enterprisewide resource (e.g., the document database), and remote offices querying a centrally located database without performance bottlenecks.

The three tiers are as follows:

- *Workstation.* This is the front-end section of LANfolio and the part that interacts with users. The Document Profile Screen displays fields into which critical information about a document is entered. Any of the fields can be used to formulate a query. Also, a combination of fields may be used as search criteria.

- *Document request server.* This is an interface between users and the database server executing distributed control tasks and syntax conversion. Each document request server can be configured to query one or several database servers in a user-defined sequence, based on what the probability is of a given document's location.

- *Database server.* This is an SQL-based database engine. LANfolio can span multiple disk volumes and even multiple file servers. Due to SQL, other SQL-based minis and micros may be integrated into the "directory" service capabilities of LANfolio.

LANfolio first and foremost supports configuration management and user administration. LANfolio is, however, not connected to real-time network status supervision and displays that are key components of fault management. The LAN support product family focuses on three LAN management issues: software control (protection against viruses), network printing (sharing printers and pop-up access among all users), and user support (control of all PCs residing on the LAN segment from one workstation).

Graphical LAN documentation tools

Changes, ongoing maintenance, troubleshooting, as well as technical and customer support, all need accurate network documentation. These are a few easy-to-use instruments that incorporate graphical capabilities.

ClickNet from PinPoint Software Corporation. ClickNet visually represents any size of network with a few mouse clicks. Its interface allows you to create most diagrams simply by dragging and dropping an icon from the object window. This makes it much easier to use than any other product based on CAD technology. With its comprehensive, professionally drawn library of over 1300 images, networks can be constructed within a short period of time.

ClickNet includes the following modules:

- *A powerful drawing utility.* This drawing program is the backbone of ClickNet Professional. And it was optimized specifically for creating network diagrams.

- *An indispensable database.* Each network symbol comes with its own data set of information about the equipment symbolized. This gives the user an automatic way to keep track of all the elements on the network.

- *A complete set of predesigned reports.* As the user diagrams its network, the information in the database becomes automatically available in any of 25 predefined network management reports—from a simple segment/mode listing to full network load analysis.

In particular, the following features are important to the network professional:

- Smart lines move with symbols.
- Store multiple levels of information.
- Dynamic database functionality.
- 25 predefined, ready-to-run management reports.
- Extensive library of over 1300 network and computer images.
- Intuitive icon-based interface that runs under Windows.
- Easy-to-use toolbar for quick access to common functions.

- Handy palettes for instant changes in colors and styles.
- Self-correcting lines and grid background ensure total precision in length, angle, and alignment.
- On-line help, plus context-sensitive pop-up menus.
- Complete undo functionality; up to 20 steps can be undone if necessary.

In addition to all these features, ClickNet allows what-if scenarios to evaluate various configuration alternatives.

NetViz from Quyen Systems, Incorporated.   Accurately and thoroughly documenting a network is a multidimensional task including various technologies, geographical access, networking services, business applications, and users. It involves graphics (across two dimensions) and different levels and data (a variety of details about nodes and links). Effective network documentation must establish and maintain the interrelationships between these two kinds of information. Thus, traditional drawing programs and database management programs, even when used together, are inadequate for documenting networks. This product takes an innovative approach to the network documentation challenge. The unusual Windows program integrates data with graphics, broadening the users' ability to organize, manage, access, and use information about the network. It provides a broad array of capabilities:

- Drag-and-drop graphics
- Graphics are completely under users' control
- Multilevel documentation capability
- Integrated data manager
- On-screen data display
- Graphics export capability

NetViz is ideal for diagramming and documenting network, systems, and processes. The networks can be divided into manageable pieces and linked together to increase visibility. Figure 5.8 shows a "flat" organizational chart of communication nodes. A diagram with multiple dimensions with more user-friendliness is shown in Fig. 5.9. Any time the user wants to drill deep, the product is extremely helpful.

The differentiators with this product are as follows:

- Object-oriented business graphics plus integrated dynamic data management.

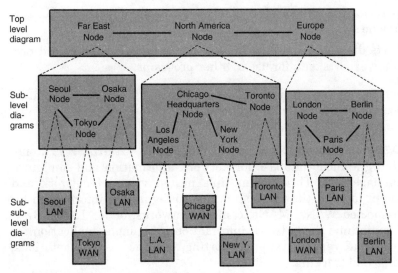

Figure 5.8 NetViz display for nodes structure.

- Drag-and-drop simplicity in the creation or change phase.
- Supports multilevel network topologies; by double-clicking on any node, subnetworks can be viewed in unlimited depth.
- Imports text files so the user can use data stored in existing databases and spreadsheets.

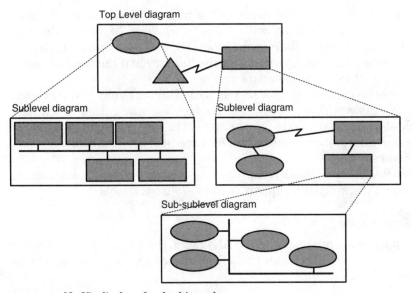

Figure 5.9 NetViz display of nodes hierarchy.

- Imports map and floor plan graphics for backgrounds; imports custom node symbols.

- Exports diagrams and data for use in presentations and word processing; exports data for use in other programs.

Considering all these features, NetViz offers an easy-to-use alternative for documenting and visualizing relatively simple networks.

GrafBASE from Network Dimensions, Incorporated. GrafBASE is a one-of-a-kind graphical database for network information and configuration management. Through multiple nested views of network and equipment layouts, the user can access configuration information for interconnected WANs, MANs, campus networks, or for LANs. Graf-BASE maintains the network information in a single application for instant visual representation, reporting, data access, presentations, planning, and tracking.

Features concentrate on network mapping, network documentation, exporting/importing graphics and data, and real-time alarm management.

GrafBASE's object-oriented graphics allows you to create your own network elements of different classes and types that uniquely define the network. These elements define the different devices, links, and LANs that comprise the network. Network elements are represented pictorially in the GrafBASE tools box. The users define these elements with icon representations of their choice and provide each element its own data attributes.

To create networks, the users pick a network device from the tools box and place it in a panel with the network view. To connect devices, just pick a network link from the tools box, and click on the devices to be connected. GrafBASE will create the links, even if the two end nodes are within different subnetwork panels.

Users can create multiple panels with different subnetwork views, and then relate these hierarchically for easy navigation. Each network element that makes up the networks can be documented with detailed information, which can be accessed from GrafBASE's formatted reports.

GrafBASE can simplify the daily tasks for network engineering, planning, tracking, and support with the following tools.

Network mapping

- Map the wide area network (WAN) hierarchically from a worldview to a specific country. Then zoom for further expansion to a county or metropolitan area.

- Map the local area network (LAN) from a campus view to a building, floor, or a single room.

- Interrelate all views, so the user can access any view simply by traversing the network configuration hierarchy.

- Includes GrafBASE's high-quality maps for geographical backgrounds and brings in externally created bit maps or CAD (DXF) backgrounds.

- Specifies a latitude/longitude coordinate, and GrafBASE will correctly locate nodes on a geographical map. Alternatively, includes GrafBASE's area code/prefix data (in the United States and Canada), for automatic placement of nodes on geographical maps.

Network documentation

- Creates the users' own classes and types of network objects for the GrafBASE tools box

- Defines the users' own attributes for each network object appearing in the GrafBASE tools box

- Specifies detailed descriptions for each network node and link

- Accesses detailed formatted reports for managing network information

Export/import graphics and data

- Enters network data from a text file easily created through current applications, a database, or word processor

- Exports graphics to word processors or other graphics drawing tools with Windows clipboard

- Imports graphics in bit-mapped (BMP) format, or from CAD programs, that creates DXF files

- Imports users' own icons for representing network objects

Real-time alarm management

- GrafBASE provides real-time network alarm management by polling data in a text file

- GrafBASE can be integrated as a front-end GUI interface for existing and planned network management applications

Particularly in regard to real-time capabilities, it differs from other offerings. As a result, it can be used to perform dynamic status surveillance of networks, where icons are connected to predefined alarms that are processed by the network management application.

With GrafBASE the user can do the following:

- Define networks visually in detail.

- Track network equipment and facilities.

- Plan and present different network layouts to management and customers.

- Quickly create and access network information for troubleshooting engineering, reporting, service, and support.

GrafBASE saves time and money by letting the users consolidate network information and access it both visually and in report format from a single, MS-Windows, PC 386/486-based application.

GrafBASE runs on low-cost IBM 386- or 486-compatible computer with up to 6 MB available on hard disk. It uses the familiar graphical interface of Microsoft Windows™, version 3.x (running standard or enhanced mode). Mouse and EGA or higher-resolution color monitor are required. Hard disk required will vary from 2 to 6 MB depending on data options installed. The minimum hard disk space required is 2 MB for program files. Print and plot to any device supported by Microsoft Windows.

Besides supporting visualization and documentation, GrafBASE can also be used as planning instrument. Users can combine GrafBASE with analytical and simulation models to quantify the results of network planning.

DeskTalk TrendAnalyzer.   The main function of this product is the common viewing and reporting for multiple applications and platforms. It captures performance and event data from various platform and application databases and puts it into a common relational database where it can be viewed by the user, because it graphically depicts common data. It runs on SunNet Manager. The integration method supports applications to communicate with DeskTalk's version of SunNet Manager's Manager Services library.

DeskTalk TrendAnalyzer (also called "Cooperative Reporting" by SunConnect) acts as a common database for platform and application data, providing the user with one access point to all information in the network management system. TrendAnalyzer goes beyond providing ASCII files and a MIB browser; the product includes graph tools and tabular display tools, providing easy-to-read default displays for each table in the TrendAnalyzer database. Each data column is named and time-stamped.

TrendAnalyzer captures data that would normally be sent by the platform or applications to the SunNet Manager Services library. TrendAnalyzer uses both SNMP traps and RPCs as the mechanisms for transferring data. TrendAnalyzer aggregates the data and converts it into time and value information.

Monies from Stonehouse. Monies Graphics is a PC-based graphical user interface for network management. Monies Graphics provides users with both a geographical and hierarchical view of their voice and data networks. This high-quality graphics product allows users to build visual displays of complex network layouts, with real-time, color-coded monitoring of their network hardware and services.

Running on inexpensive PCs under Windows or OS/2, this easy-to-use facility uses Monies Inventory parent-pointer configurations to automatically build the initial network layouts. Monies Orders module keeps them current in real time, and trouble tickets are monitored by Monies Problem Management module. Network components with open trouble tickets will be indicated in the network diagram, allowing the user to have alarm conditions visually presented for quick recognition and resolution of problems. Monies Graphics is shown in Fig. 5.10.

Key features of the graphics interface are as follows:

- Displays network layouts on high-quality, geographical map backgrounds for global, country, regional, state, or city-street views

- Designs network layouts on bit-map graphic images for campus- or equipment-level views

- Displays multilayered network and open hierarchically related views with a point-and-click interface

- Builds initial network layouts automatically with Monies Inventory

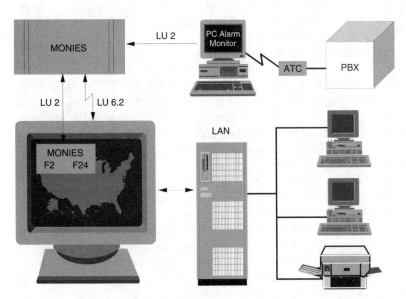

Figure 5.10 Monies Graphics.

- Accesses Monies from a window using an LU2 (3270) session
- Utilizes LU6.2 (APPC) as the communications protocol between the host and Monies Graphics workstation
- Creates and links in the users' own device icons, and visually depicts alarms and status with color changes of device icons
- Displays network alarm reports showing opened, changed, and closed trouble tickets in Monies Problem Management
- Keeps networks current using interface to Monies where new orders automatically update inventory

Besides the graphics program, Monies offers a report writer. It provides service order, trouble tickets, asset, financial, directory, and network analysis information for extraction. Reports can be created with a few English-like statements. It is not necessary to copy files to SAS or other databases. On-line report preparation, execution, and printing options are within the product.

Monies Report Writer can be considered as the central repository of all LAN-related fault and performance data.

SAS System for Computer Performance Evaluation for Open Systems from SAS Institute. The main function of this product is detailed data analysis and reporting. The applications run on SunNet Manager, Cabletron's Spectrum, HP OpenView, and IBM NetView for AIX by using menu bar integration.

SAS/CPE for Open Systems from the SAS Institute is a fully-integrated component of the SAS System for Information Delivery. This family of data analysis and reporting software packages has long been popular in the mainframe world. SAS is finding a new market for its products as an adjunct to distributed Unix computing systems and SNMP management platforms. While most leading SNMP platforms include their own report writers, these tools are notoriously limited and provide few data analysis features. Currently, SAS/CPE for Open Systems is one of the few products in the third-party applications market that targets statistical analysis and report writing.

SAS/CPE for Open Systems is designed to make it easier for network administrators to analyze large quantities of management data to accomplish performance management and capacity planning. Network administrators can use SAS/CPE to establish performance baselines and then compare ongoing measurements to detect bottlenecks, hardware problems, and other anomalies. Measurements can include utilization or error rates, for example. Those comfortable with SAS find it extremely useful in staying on top of network conditions, thereby avoiding downtime and performance degradation.

The product can help network administrators read and validate raw data. Once validated, the data is fed into a performance database (PDB) which is a collection of SAS data sets. The SAS PDB is currently proprietary technology and non-SQL, although SAS may soon support standard SQL databases in response to customer requests.

SAS/CPE continually performs data reduction by replacing multiple data values with collective values such as the mean, range, or standard deviation, summarized over larger and larger time intervals. Management data is stored in nine SAS data libraries, including DAY, WEEK, MONTH, YEAR, DETAIL, DICTLIB, and three additional work libraries. The DETAIL library contains raw performance data with only minor transformations, such as converting continuously ascending counters into rates per second. In general, network administrators find it best to store only a few days' worth of data in the DETAIL library before converting it to the more summarized and reduced formats found in DAY, WEEK, MONTH, and YEAR libraries.

SAS/CPE provides menu screens that assist network administrators in using the PDB for the following purposes:

- *Problem determination.*   For common network problems.

- *Establishing performance baselines.*   For various network topologies.

- *Service-level reporting.*   This includes using measurements such as network and system response time, application throughput, and hardware/software component availability to report on service levels.

- *Network performance analysis.*   This includes analyzing network traffic patterns, including setting thresholds for certain measurements, detecting congestion, examining utilization rates for various network topologies, and analyzing error rates.

- *Workstation performance analysis.*   This includes analyzing CPU utilization (queue lengths and percent utilization), memory utilization (paging and swapping rates), disk usage (queue lengths, I/O rates, and the file system), network interface (queue lengths and I/O rates).

SAS/CPE for Open Systems provides a number of canned reports as well as an excellent facility for defining customized reports. Predefined reports include baseline, trend, and exception analysis reports. Reports are in either tabular or graphic format. Programmers with SAS experience find SAS/CPE extremely flexible, as the product allows users to code SAS macros outside of the menu interface. Macros may be created to build, manage, and analyze the PDB in numerous ways to run batch jobs.

The user can customize the performance database (PDB) to determine how much data is kept and for how long. Data can be reduced from the detail level into day, week, month, and year reduction levels. At each of these levels, the user can choose which variables and statistics need to be kept for reporting purposes. This customization is simple and interactive. It never requires a complicated procedure to determine which data are kept. The performance data base is self-describing, so it may be moved to another system for analytical purposes.

This product helps to a great extent to combine performance evaluation for both systems and network components. Figure 5.11 shows an example for the utilization of communication lines.

MIB tools

Instruments to manipulate MIB entries can be very helpful on a network management system. These applications concentrate on the following tasks (Leinwand 1993):

- A MIB compiler, which loads MIBs into the system, can assist users in obtaining the necessary data from a large variety of devices on the LANs. This facility can also provide users with a means to relate MIB attributes to graphical elements on the network map.

- A MIB browser is an electronic means of browsing the MIB after it has been loaded in order to find specific information that is interesting to the user.

Communication lines

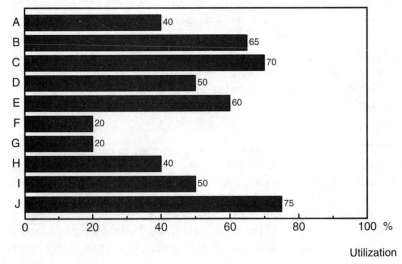

Figure 5.11   Utilization of communication lines.

- A MIB alias tool can associate potentially confusing MIB object names to references that are more familiar to the users.

- A MIB query tool can poll agents in the network devices in order to examine the values returned, which can help LAN administrators to decide if polling for an object is useful or not.

Health Profiler from Remedy Corporation. The main function can be defined as follows: data analysis and reporting of network status and performance using graphical elements. Currently included with the product are libraries for Cabletron IRM2 hubs, Chipcom ONline hubs, Sun workstations, SynOptics 3000 hubs, and Wellfleet routers. Also, Profiler includes an SNMP library, a Unix library, and an RMON MIB library.

Platforms supported are SunNet Manager, HP OpenView, and IBM NetView for AIX. The integration methods concentrate on SunNet Manager Manager Services API.

Health Profiler is a data analysis and reporting tool that can provide both real-time and historical interpretations of SNMP management information base (MIB) data. While other applications are able to provide similar capabilities on a device-specific basis, Health Profiler presents meaningful status and performance information across a range of devices. Health Profiler is tightly integrated with both the underlying SNMP-based network management platform and the various devices from which the application collects raw data.

Remedy's Health Profiler is one of the few management applications capable of graphically presenting meaningful status and performance information about a variety of network devices and systems. Other vertical applications can depict management data from a specific device; however, each application may have its own user interface. In contrast, Health Profiler is a horizontal application that processes data from multiple SNMP management information bases (MIBs), providing a common interface for all managed equipment.

SNMP-based management platforms such as SunConnect SunNet Manager typically provide a limited set of reporting capabilities. However, these tools are restricted to displaying raw data, such as the value of a single counter in a device MIB. Health Profiler uses raw data collected by the management platform and greatly improves the presentation of that data by displaying it in user-friendly "dashboard" views. Furthermore, Health Profiler lets the user combine individual MIB variables and apply algebraic expressions to come up with statistics that convey network health in a much more meaningful way. The chief advantage of Health Profiler is that it can help hide the complexity of MIBs and the hundreds of data variables therein and help the user focus more clearly on useful "health metrics."

Health Profiler has a client/server implementation in which the clients and servers communicate using remote procedure calls (RPCs). The server communicates with the management platform's application programming interfaces (APIs) to obtain raw MIB data. The client provides the user interface, obtaining the information from any Health Profiler server. A server can support multiple clients, and clients can be distributed anywhere across the network.

From the user's perspective, Health Profiler is made up of two components: the User Tool and the Administration Tool (both of which are part of the client). The User Tool allows the user to select which data to gather, which devices to monitor, and which views and reports to display. The Admin Tool allows users to customize views, reports, expressions, and history models.

Health Profiler simplifies the task of managing a network by supporting arithmetic manipulation of MIB data and by highlighting the key MIB variables in a given device library. Health Profiler's history modules can also assist with baselining and trending analysis.

Health Profiler ships with a number of predefined views and reports for several different types of third-party devices. These libraries were developed under the direction of technical representatives from these third parties; thus, they reflect the expertise of each device vendor. In effect, Remedy has sifted through the hundreds of MIB variables supported on a given device and selected the few metrics that provide the best indication of device status and overall network health. The libraries can, therefore, spare the users the time of sifting through arcane MIB variables to determine what's important. Users can, of course, customize these views as they become more experienced with SNMP-based management.

It is worth considering the combination of Health Profiler and SAS; in such a case, Health Profiler would provide the necessary raw information, and SAS would be responsible for statistical data processing and reporting.

eXpert Remote Systems Assurance (XRSA) from Elegant Communications. Unix and other open systems are changing the face of computing. The challenge is managing this new environment. Unix systems can deliver substantial business benefits because of their flexibility, expanded variety of equipment, reduced capital costs, and greater functionality. However, there are risks to be managed. The critical issues in this respect are as follows:

- Data severity
- System integrity
- System availability
- Cost-effective management

XRSA software is a set of automated tools that audit, report, and enable the successful management of distributed Unix systems. XRSA software performs the tasks that are required to maintain trustworthy systems in a systematic, comprehensive, and consistent manner. It executes a disciplined routine that only automation can achieve. The automation of processes and workload structuring will allow the LAN management staff to be proactive and more productive. Vital information is distributed throughout the enterprise to the key personnel who can best act on it. XRSA software audits Unix systems and reports on their operations. The numerous analyses automatically performed on each system ensure that integrity is maintained.

Availability of mission-critical systems is substantially increased because problems are identified and resolved before they can affect your business. Secure operations require an enforceable security policy. XRSA software fulfills the requirements for maintaining secure operations through comprehensive automated testing and reporting. XRSA reports provide the information needed for effective security and centralized control.

XRSA consists of three parts: the monitor, the expert, and the reports. Figure 5.12 shows the structure of the product. The full cycle can be characterized as follows:

- *Collection.* The monitor software is installed on all Unix systems, from large database servers to desktop workstations. These

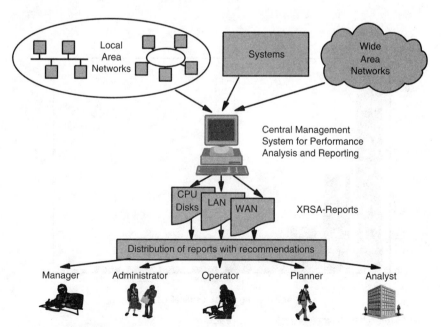

Figure 5.12 XRSA Report generation and distribution structure.

monitored systems can be located anywhere and can be from any manufacturer. The monitor's responsibility is to audit each system, automate local administrative tasks, and report daily to the expert.

- *Analysis.* The expert software is usually installed on an existing workstation or server, making it the central management system. The eXpert's responsibility is to interpret the monitor logs and to produce and distribute reports.

- *Informing.* The reports provide visible confirmation that service-level goals are being achieved and that policies are being followed. The right information is provided to the right people—from status summaries for senior management, to specific corrective actions for field support engineers.

- *Distribution.* LAN administrators can choose the appropriate delivery methods for the LAN management personnel, alert system administrators of performance bottlenecks by E-mail, inform a senior manager of policy exceptions by hardcopy, or use a custom interface to provide information to an SNMP-based network management system.

Sample reports include the following:

- Disk usage analysis indicating the heavy and light users (Fig. 5.13)

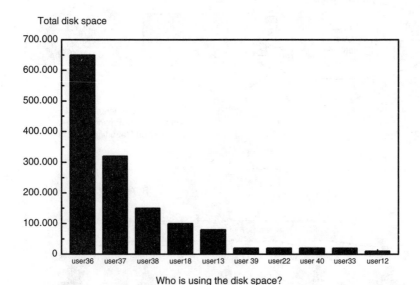

Figure 5.13 Disk usage analysis.

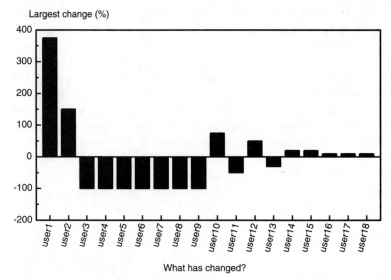

Figure 5.14   Changes in using disk space.

- Changes in using disk space indicating changes over specific time periods for each user across all file systems (Fig. 5.14)
- Trend analysis for free disk space, reporting the minimum and maximum space used for specific time periods (Fig. 5.15)

This product is very important when client/server performance analysis is targeted in addition to LAN performance reporting.

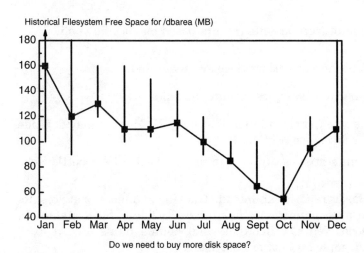

Figure 5.15   Trend analysis with free disk space.

NetTune from HawkNet, Incorporated. This product addresses network performance issues without costly hardware upgrades. With this product network administrators can take control of network performance by adjusting internal NetWare operating-system-settable parameters. A Windows client-user interface makes it easy. The NetTune NLM resides on the NetWare file server. The result is direct, real-time feedback on file server activities. The client interface puts easy control via Windows. Most NetWare parameters can be tracked and supervised. Examples for these parameters are as follows:

- Communication
- Memory
- File cache
- File system
- Lock
- Transaction tracking
- Disk
- Directory cache

    Highlights of the product are as follows:

- View real-time file server activities with colorful, 3-D displays.
- Graphically set parameters to accommodate changes in network usage.
- Schedule unattended, settable parameters, even on a time/date basis.
- Optimization of NetWare file servers based on specific applications can occur.
- Reports on file server performance are generated.

    Selected reporting examples include the following:

- NLM memory map helps to highlight large NLMs that may degrade NetWare performance (Fig. 5.16).
- LAN segment statistics can help to find and solve LAN bottlenecks (Fig. 5.17).
- NetWare Basics reports can include tracking and monitoring results for cache usage, connections, disk totals, FAT info, file system info, memory pools, NICs, utilization, and volume totals. Figure 5.18 shows an example for network statistics.

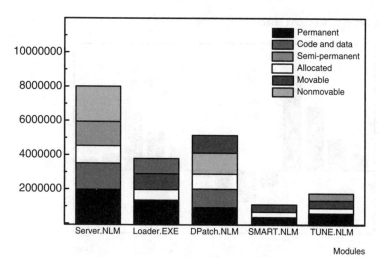

Figure 5.16 Overview of NetWare loadable modules (NLM) (NLM Memory Map).

This product in combination with specific LAN monitors helps to fine-tune the performance of client/server systems.

Best/1-Visualizer from BGS. The first step of modeling and predicting performance is the visualization of present performance. This product helps to manage the performance of business workloads running on distributed Unix systems. Built-in Activity Mapper and I/O-Diagrammer help to further detail performance indicators. User may

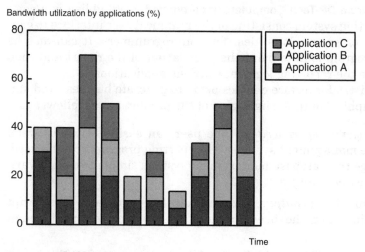

Figure 5.17 LAN segment statistics.

Number of connections related to baseline

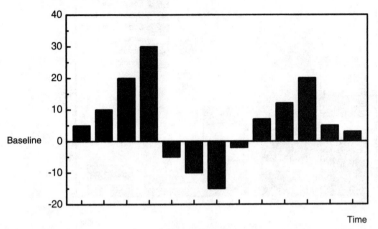

Figure 5.18   NetWare Basics—number of connections.

play back the Unix CPU and Unix I/O activity of their client/server applications over selected periods of time.

Performance data analysis and reporting can be automated. These activities can be scheduled to run periodically during the off-peak hours. Exception reporting on Unix systems is further simplified with a number of "top x" graphs which are particularly useful for environments with a very large number of managed objects, such as workloads, nodes, disks, interconnecting devices, and networking components.

DbPublish from DP-Tech Computers, Incorporated.   DbPublish is a complete reporting system consisting of the graphical user interface to generate 4GL programs. It is ideal for nonprogrammers. It can also be used by programmers to paint the page layout of the report and then incorporate the reporting logic into various applications.

The statistical interface enables users to generate business and statistical graphical output. Highlights of the product are as follows:

- *Open Systems report writer.*   The user can easily switch between database management systems. All reporting programs can be used. To change the database management system, simple two-shell variables must be changed.

- *Direct PostScript output.*   When executed, generates PostScript code. Eliminates the need for additional postprocessing through filters.

- *Support for flat files and DBMS.*   Allows users with flat files to use the language with the same ease and efficiency as those having a

DBMS. In addition, it supports variable-length records with field delimiters as well as fixed-length records with fixed-size fields.

- *Event-based language.* Two types of events are available. Input-based events are triggered based upon the main incoming data stream. Position-based events are triggered based upon the current print position.

- *Multiple-font support.* Change fonts at will. Print items with any font or in any size.

- *Support for color.* Supports the RGB (red, green, and blue) and HSB (high, saturation, and brightness) color models. Using these color models, the user can make reports colorful using a wide variety of color combinations.

- *Print images.* Using capabilities of the user's DBMS, images stored as binary data can be printed. Various image formats are supported, including TIFF and EPSF.

- *Images and text objects as table items.* Images and text objects can also be used as table items. This is particularly useful for aligning images and text items.

- *Highlighting of individual items.* Any item or an entire row or column can be highlighted. In addition to the special attributes (underline, outline, reverse, and box), color can be used to highlight a table item.

- *Figures and special-effect strings.* Functions are provided to draw geometric figures such as ellipses and rectangles. Parameters can be specified to fill them with different shades or colors. Also, text strings can be printed with special effects such as vertical printing, mirrored printing, and circular printing.

- *Run-time options and parameters.* Numerous run-time options are available. These include the option to print only the desired pages or to process only a specified list of records. Command-line parameters are also supported.

This product is extremely helpful in cases where the user is interested in customizing all reports. The customization effort is greater than with other products, such as SAS, but the level of sophistication is worth it.

Special instruments

Special instruments support specific LAN-management areas. Accounting management is supported in particular by two types of products: Software meters, and audit trail management tools.

Software meters. PC software vendors are particularly concerned about product licensing; they want to keep tight control over illegal copying of their software. Obviously, a vendor doesn't want to sell one copy of a product to a large company, only to have hundreds of employees copy it. On the other hand, it would be quite inefficient for the LAN manager to buy as many copies of the software as there are employees. At any time, it's unlikely that thousands, or even hundreds, of people need a given application. Vendors have devised software meters as a way of deterring illegal copying. Certain PC applications now come with built-in meters. A meter works on the same principle as a lending library. When a user starts an application, he or she checks it out of the license library and returns it when finished. If all copies are lent out, the meter returns a temporary denial.

The LAN manager may consider using meters to monitor and control software usage, as well as to provide users with enough copies without purchasing volumes of software. The LAN manager can also use the meter to keep usage statistics; this can assist "traffic engineering" of the software library.

Audit trail management tools. Audit trail systems are a key component of security management, although the function can be considered part of accounting management. Audit trail systems provide information on user activity on the LAN. Additionally, these systems can assist in billing management by providing the data needed to charge back usage.

For an audit trail system to be effective, it must provide LAN management with streamlined and useful information. The manager may wish to audit only certain users, operations on files with certain extensions or in certain subdirectories, certain types of operations, or certain servers. All file and directory creations, deletions, and renames may need to be reported. A system error log report, listing all system error messages to alert the LAN manager of potential problems, may be advantageous. A sophisticated audit tool must allow this management flexibility.

Most vendors provide some form of support for accounting management, but the level of sophistication is much lower than with SMDR Station Message Detail Record. Substantial future development is needed and expected in this area.

Segment-Management Products

In the case of managing segments, fault management functions and applications are targeted first. The role of hubs is increasingly important because they physically incorporate the cards for Ethernet, Token Ring, and FDDI. They serve as wiring concentrators and repeaters for all logical and virtual segments. PC LAN management solutions are part of this segment.

The following list of applications for managing intelligent hubs and concentrators represents currently available solutions:

3Com LinkBuilder Vision

3Com Transcend

AT&T/NCR StarLAN 10 Smart Hub Manager

Bay Networks Optivity

Bytex 7700 Series NMS

Cabletron Spectrum for Open Systems

Chipcom ONdemand NCS

Cisco Crescendo Manager

FiberMux LightWatch Open

Hirschmann StarCoupler Manager

IBM Hub Management Program/6000

LANNET (Madge) Data Comm. MultiMan

Network Solutions Cabletron MMAC Hub Views

Optical Data Systems LANVision

Raylan Network Manager

Sestel HubMan

Synernetics ViewPlex

Ungermann-Bass NetDirector for Unix

Xyplex ControlPoint

Each hub vendor tries to interact with management platforms. The integration level differs depending on the features and services the platform vendor supports. In case of the most popular platforms, there are many choices. It is up to the hub vendor to select the right ones. Due to the need to support multiple platforms, hub vendors are not expected to offer deep integration or to support many features. In case of Cabletron hubs, the integration is deep because the same company is providing a platform (Spectrum) with built-in management capabilities. In other cases, the responses may be very different.

Management functionality usually includes the following items:

- Central management of a certain amount of hubs.
- Management of Ethernet, Token Ring, and FDDI from a single management station.

- Maintaining a network map and displaying the physical and logical topology, including its hubs, servers, clients, routers, bridges, and other equipment.

- Maintaining a graphical view of the hubs and the current state of their components.

- Management and surveillance of each module and port in the networks; enabling, disabling, or toggling any port or module.

- Measuring key fault and performance indicators in Ethernets, Token Rings, and in FDDI. These indicators support real-time analysis on utilization levels, response time, and error statistics.

- Maintaining filters to reduce the number of messages and events sent to the management station. The same time alarms are triggered when certain conditions occur.

- Setting thresholds for key fault and performance indicators.

- Downline-loading firmware from the management station to change configuration, activate redundant links, and activate or deactivate data collection.

- Logging all alarm messages generated in the network or in its components for further analysis.

- Supporting security features to better control the access to station addresses. In case an unauthorized address appears, the management station is expected to turn off that port.

- Agent-to-agent communication within the hub supports information exchange via a communication backplane. This capability allows all hub information to be gathered, viewed, and configured by attaching a single SNMP manager to a single management card.

These functions are usually supported by the hub vendors. Special functions are provided by some of the vendors. Optical Data Systems has added optional hardware-based management and reliability features to its FDDI management capabilities. These features include the following:

- Preport monitoring provides the capability to learn each port's MAC address and detect when this address changes. In addition, it can detect MAC frame problems that are difficult to isolate even with the best FDDI protocol analyzers.

- Provides analysis of the traffic generated on each FDDI port.

- Detects which station caused a lost token.

- Detects "no token" MAC frames, which can be caused by hardware or software faults. With current technology, this condition can be detected on a ring only through a binary search where a two-tap logic analyzer is used to bound the fault domain; then human intervention is required to move the taps during the search. ODS can detect which port is causing this condition without human intervention.

- Detects when and which station on the port is stuck in beacon mode and can detect this beacon much more quickly than the 9 seconds taken by the RMT (Ring Management). As a result, faster recovery of the network is possible.

- Statistics logic includes programmable counters as well as other management support functions.

- Ring mapping determines which stations are connected into ports and is a valuable topology mapping capability that provides more accuracy than a software-based-approach algorithm.

- Network utilization counters allow network management to determine the approximate amount of network bandwidth consumed by attached stations. This feature can be valuable for per-port billing applications.

- FDDI stations can waste bandwidth by holding the token and not transmitting. ODS modules measure both transmit time as well as holding time to determine true network utilization.

- Four configurable counters can count frames of various types, including destination address, source address, frame length, frame control field, and selectable patterns occurring at selectable points within the first 256 bytes of the frame.

- Allows for the capture of the source address of beacon frames.

ODS has added sideband management access ports to the Ethernet, Token Ring, and FDDI management cards. The new auxiliary ports provide network managers with a convenient and consistent way to diagnose problems even when the network goes down. They can also be used for standard network maintenance such as software downloads without taking up bandwidth on the primary links. The Ethernet ports can be used to manage all cards in the hub, regardless of media type, via a single homogenous sideband network.

The characteristic that distinguishes the smart hub from a repeater is its ability to be managed—its "intelligence." One can construct a LAN without using smart hubs; however, the morass of cabling and the complexity of accommodating moves, adds, and changes to a hubless network makes that approach infeasible. Because manageability is such a key selling point for hubs in general, hub vendors direct great effort into enhancing the quality and integration of their management applications. Consequently, there are more applications for managing hubs than for any other type of network device.

Optivity from Bay Networks. The main function is the management for Bay Networks' smart hubs and routing/bridging modules. Optivity runs on SunNet Manager, HP OpenView, and NetView for AIX by using icon launching, "SuperAgent," Global Enterprise Management (GEM) applications as integration techniques.

Optivity collects hub, board, and port-level data, such as MAC-layer diagnostics, errors, and utilization information. Optivity also provides detailed ring and segment views, as well as real-time views of Bay Networks' LattisHub, LattisRing, or System 3000 concentrators, including active LEDs and configuration status. Optivity also includes an Auto-topology Plus feature, which employs a heuristic, recurring algorithm for dynamically creating and updating a hierarchical network map.

In addition to these features, there are several other aspects that make Optivity a unique product offering. On the Unix platforms (Sun-Net Manager, IBM NetView for AIX, and HP OpenView Unix), it supports distributed domain management by employing what SynOptics calls "SuperAgent" software residing in critical hubs throughout the network. Each SuperAgent uses polling to collect a wealth of data in a given domain (such as a single Ethernet segment) and processes that data locally, forwarding concise packages of information to the central Optivity application. Distributing intelligence to the SuperAgents scattered throughout the network helps to reduce traffic overhead and speed up the management process.

Network intelligence requires processing power, and Bay Networks supplies this in the form of *network control engines* or NCEs. An NCE is essentially a Sun SPARCstation residing on a Bay Networks' concentrator module. Since the NCE comes preloaded with Unix, many customers use NCEs to distribute SunNet Manager functions as well— such as collecting and processing data locally to avoid traffic overhead. NCEs also support HP NetMetrix traffic-monitoring and analysis applications. Customers may choose to run Optivity in centralized mode without NCEs. However, NCEs are required to support Optivity's distributed domain management capabilities.

Optivity and the SuperAgents form a foundation for Bay Networks' value-added "LattisWare" applications such as RouterMan, PathMan, MeterMan, and BridgeMan. For example, RouterMan displays all protocols and interfaces supported by routers on the network, including performance statistics. PathMan can determine and display the path between any two stations in the network to assist in troubleshooting.

Optivity also supports another class of applications, called Global Enterprise Management (GEM), developed by third parties. The first GEM applications available are NetLabs' Vision Desktop and Asset Manager. Both Vision Desktop and Asset Manager support the IETF Host Resources MIB and emerging Desktop Management Task Force

(DMTF) specifications. Asset Manager supports automatic collection of PC component data; Vision Desktop provides a graphical interface and can assist in monitoring software-licensing violations.

In order to help users with more complete solutions, the following applications are supported:

- MIBman is responsible for information collection from connected devices that may or may not support device-level MIBs.

- METERman depicts MIB data in graphical form to generate status and performance reports.

- TRENDman uses existing performance data to predict future performance.

- POLICYman evaluates thresholds and dynamically enables and disables ports of wiring hubs.

- FAULTman administers trouble tickets for tracking and resolving network problems.

- Bay Networks extends the scope of the manageability of hubs by offering LattisViews. LattisViews will run as applications on Polycenter, OpenView, and on NetView for AIX. The functions available represent a subset of those offered with LattisNet Manager under Unix.

Spectrum from Cabletron Systems.   This application offers new avenues by combining an SNMP-based management system and expert systems technology for managing enterprise networks. Spectrum uses inductive modeling technology, creating programming models that define the intelligence and interrelationship of each network element and build an object-oriented knowledge base. As a result, the product can correlate information such as multiple alarms for multivendor network elements to identify the cause of a problem and solve it. Spectrum is very user-friendly for this type of maintenance and for changing network configuration and its graphical mapping.

Cabletron integrates all products under INA (Integrated Network Architecture). The LANView network analyzer has been designed and implemented for Ethernet networks. LANView is applicable for continuous monitoring. Its principal features include the following:

- Multiprotocol support: ISO/OSI, DECnet, TCP/IP, XNS, Novell, Banyan, Appletalk

- Powerful filtering of the large amounts of data

- Capturing individual packets with packet tracing

- Built-in time domain reflectometer tests

- Support of network load generation

- Generating controlled network traffic to force a suspected problem to occur

- Built-in SNMP agent capabilities connected to SunNet Manager

The LAN Analyzer board has been licensed from Novell and is based on LANtern.

Spectrum is sold as a new enterprise network management system to integrate a number of vendors' products. To a certain extent, Spectrum may also be considered a platform. Spectrum offers an extremely flexible, extended architecture based on highly intelligent software modeling of each and every network element, including equipment, users, privileges, and much more. By adding new induction rules to its model-based reasoning scheme, Spectrum can even capture and systemize the knowledge and preferences of a network administrator.

The heart of Spectrum is the virtual network machine (VNM). The VNM embodies an intelligent, comprehensive model of the overall enterprise network and each of its subelements. The VNM is based on Cabletron's breakthrough inductive modeling technology. The company's reasoning-capable technology provides an extremely agile, adaptive, and automatic way to model and control complex entities with software; Spectrum is its first commercial application.

Inductive modeling embraces model-based reasoning—one form of artificial intelligence. It creates programmatic models of each individual subfunction of a larger entity. Each of these "molecular" subfunction models understands the attributes and behavior of its real-world counterpart, essentially defining its intelligence. These molecular models are context-aware, interacting with each other to self-adjust their behavior as other subfunction models change status, appear, or disappear. This adaptive integration is similar to some synaptic processes of the brain. Through these adaptive subfunction responses, large-entity system models exhibit some traits of inductive reasoning. They can follow a logical progression from symptoms and effects to conclusions and actions.

Through inductive modeling technology, the VNM models everything that makes up the enterprise network—every network interface card, cable, workstation, node, user application, bridge, or other connection, and more.

The device communication manager supplies protocol support, which includes SNMP, 802.1, CMIP, and ASCII. ASCII support enables nonstandard managed objects to send alarms to Spectrum. The graphical user interface offers many view levels and complex icons that enable it to create new views and to generate statistics. However, too many views may be difficult to learn and to use for an average help-desk person or LAN operator. Integrating NetVisualyzer will add considerable graphical and real-time network-monitoring capabilities to Spectrum. The combination represents the integration of passive monitoring capabilities with active control features.

Cabletron, Remedy, and Isicad have shown that Spectrum network management software, Remedy's Action Request System trouble ticket software, and Isicad's Command physical network management software can work together on a Sun workstation. With such a product's combination, alarm information identified by Spectrum can be fed into the Command system, which will locate the problem; and into the Action Request System, which will help the LAN administrator track and resolve the problem.

In conjunction with the Concert network management strategy from BT, Ungermann-Bass has delivered the Access/One management system, called **NetDirector**. The product is based on a client/server architecture and is designed to provide an open platform for the management of multiple-vendor devices in an enterprise LAN environment. It's distinguished by its use of an SQL database as its core repository of network data, allowing access to network data and control via standard APIs to off-the-shell applications to managers of managers. A CMIP interface has been demonstrated connecting NetDirector to Concert, completing enterprise management offered by WAN and LAN management components.

The architecture of NetDirector is modular to allow for the support of multiple standard MIBs; it currently supports XNS management protocols and SNMP, and will support CMIS/CMIP as well. It provides a powerful topographical mapping and user interface via Presentation Manager/Windows through which a network administrator can readily identify and isolate network faults and performance status.

NetDirector is deployed to manage large, LAN-based, enterprise networks that are built around the Access/One intelligent hubs and include a variety of third-party devices as well. Access/One has been very successful, as it offers a very broad range of desktop connectivity and internetworking capabilities, with Ethernet, Token Ring, and FDDI-based high-speed LANs. These capabilities include device concentration, terminal service, bridging and routing covering the spectrum of device, protocol, media, and speed requirements of the enterprise user. The LAN-based backplane of Access/One can be equipped with a high-speed switching-based backplane and with extensions to standard bus architectures allowing network service applications to be integrated into the managed hub environment. This capability is built into the infrastructure of current systems, allowing customers to migrate by simply inserting new modules. With this capability, LAN, MAN, WAN, and routing functions will be made far more efficient and manageable, and support of multimedia (voice, data, video) applications to the desktop will be possible.

Ungermann-Bass intends to enhance its platform by using the capabilities of Internet. The core is to embed Java applets into the hubs so the devices can troubleshoot problems without administrator intervention. This built-in intelligence, along with the automated nature of the tools, may reduce labor-intensive work. The Web page concentrates on status information to be reviewed by LAN administrators. The applets will maintain a set of policies determined by the LAN administrator. Applets are offered for LAN utilization and load balancing.

Also, **MultiMan** from Lannet (Lannet 1991) may be considered here as an alternative solution for multivendor LAN/WAN management. MultiMan is a powerful SNMP-based system that allows effective and optimal use of network devices and resources.

It allows enterprisewide monitoring, control, and administration of active network devices in the internetworking environment. The system is implemented under state-of-the-art X-Windows and OSF/Motif on a Unix platform, providing powerful, flexible, and realistic representations of internetworking hardware, configuration, and status.

The console requests, sends, or traps information from the internetworking devices, relating to the states, parameters, and option settings of each device. Management data is transmitted to the console on an interrupt basis when faults or critical events occur. This enables the system to continuously keep the network manager informed and to dynamically display changes and site modifications. When a fault in a managed device occurs, a visual alarm is immediately displayed, allowing the network manager to respond accordingly.

In particular, the following features distinguish MultiMan from other products:

- Auto-configuration through automatic recognition of manageable objects
- Multilayer management of hubs, bridges, and routers
- Support of multiconsole management, with regional or type-specific submanagers
- Support of both inband and outband management
- Diagnostics and tests without interrupting LAN operations

The manufacturer intends to integrate OSI-CMIP capabilities into a future version of MultiMan.

Hub market and network management alternatives are expected to boom soon. Many small companies are expected to enter the market with specific solutions, but network management capabilities will be limited to a general-purpose SNMP agent. This agent is expected to support certain indicators of MIB II and RMON.

Also, powerful players, such as AT&T, IBM, and DEC, will likely invest in this market due to its strategic importance and pressure from their major accounts. IBM has introduced its first active hub product, called **Controlled Access Unit** (CAU). The technological capabilities of this hub are limited, but IBM is strong in the area of network management offerings. The integration of hub management and NetView will be an interesting solution for many IBM users.

DEC has entered this market with **DEChub**, which offers modular expansion opportunities. Management of these hubs is supported by built-in SNMP agent software, leaving the door open for SNMP managers, perhaps DECmcc or third-party managers.

Hewlett-Packard competes in the hub market with **EtherTwist**, which is equipped with SNMP agent software. The recommended management uses OpenView Interconnect Manager, which runs under the Unix version of OpenView. Other innovative solutions are expected from electronic matrix switch vendors; the first example is **Maestro** from Bytex.

In hubless LANs, it's still very important to learn about server and client status. Agents residing in the workstation help to identify the configuration and generate events. The latest solutions offer SNMP agents for the workstations without the requirement of installing TCP/IP protocol stacks. This reduces the agent memory demand to a few Kbytes. In order not to lose management capabilities, security has to be tougher at the managed-objects (server, client, workstation, interface card) level. In summary, system vendors offer less hub functionality, but more integration with other managed objects using their own platforms or manager stations.

Details on Ethernim from Digital Equipment and LAN Network Manager from IBM can be found in (Terplan 1992).

Management of PC LANs

PC LANs are specialized solutions implemented by smaller user groups or departments. Principal implementation criteria are low cost, ease of installation, and transparent maintenance. They're generally built around the client/server model of computing. Products have been tuned for high performance—mostly in the MS-DOS area—within severe memory and processing power limitations. PC LANs were in the past rarely interconnected. As a result, the number of LAN management instruments was limited. Solutions focused on status supervision, fault determination, and very basic administration capabilities. Most of these functions have been incorporated into the LAN operating systems of market-leading companies.

Besides IBM, products from Novell, 3Com, and Banyan have dominated the market. Until recently, these dominating players have resisted opening their architectures and products to multiprotocol applications, interoperability, and to leading network management protocols, such as SNMP, CMOT, and CMIP. Other interesting products in the PC LAN area are StarLAN from AT&T and LocalTalk from Apple.

As a result of tremendous user pressure, leading companies have been reacting in the following ways:

- Offering gateways to TCP/IP
- Cooperative agreements (e.g., IBM and Novell, IBM and 3Com, Banyan and Novell)
- Support of SNMP over a short range
- Support of CMOT over a longer range
- Acquisition of monitoring products in order to immediately provide users with enhanced monitoring and management

The following PC systems and PC LAN management applications are currently shipping:

AIM Technology Sharpshooter

AT&T/NCR StarSENTRY LAN Manager Monitor

Axlan Administrator

Frye Utilities for Networks

Intel LANDesk Manager

McAfee's Brightworks

NetLabs Vision/Desktop

Peregrine Systems ServerView

Peregrine Systems StationView

Saber's LAN Management System

Symantec's Norton Administrator for Networks

Managing small clusters of PCs is relatively straightforward on a local level, maintaining consistency, uptime, and accountability across a vast complex of interconnected PC LANs is incredibly difficult and time-consuming—and therefore expensive.

Currently, most organizations employ two separate sets of products and strategies to tackle this problem: DOS/Windows-based utilities such as Novell NMS for managing the local LAN, and Unix/SNMP-based management systems for managing the internetworking highways that connect those LANs.

However, the need to support a more effective and efficient corporatewide management structure is driving a new trend toward products that will blur the distinctions between Unix- and Windows-based management. While there are relatively few Unix-based applications for PC systems and PC LAN management today, many established PC utilities vendors such as Frye are actively working on porting their existing applications to open management platforms.

Frye Utilities for Networks.   Frye takes a different approach from Intel and Symantec. The product components work together but most of them must be purchased separately. There is an IntroPack bundle that includes NetWare management, NetWare early Warning System, and LAN Directory for server management, alerts, and inventory, respectively. It does not, however, include distribution or metering.

The à la carte structure allows LAN administrators to choose from a comprehensive set of network management tools, but the components could benefit from increased integration and updated DOS-based interface.

The inventory program is accurate and offers comprehensive identification. But the query process needs to be simplified. LAN Directory has separate hardware and software databases, so performing queries that involve all personal computers of a certain type with specific software installed is a two-step process.

The product integrates inventory and software distribution well. When defining a distribution job, LAN administrators can select targets by user name or build a query on any inventoried component. The user can define distribution criteria, but the package must be assembled manually. For driver updates, it is not a problem, but for distributing a new Windows application it is. They can share Dynamic Link Library files with previously installed packages and may restart Windows halfway through the process. In this case, this product requires more effort from the LAN administrator in configuring out all the steps required for complete installation. Both "push" and "pull" distribution is supported. Basic software metering features are supported as well.

In summary, the strengths are as follows:

- Modular approach lets administrators pick only those components they need.
- Simple installation.

- Not stressful to the servers.

But two facts are considered as drawbacks by users:

- There is no Windows interface.

- Complete integration of tools is not possible in DOS environments.

LANDesk Manager from Intel. This product ships with 13 applications for managing NetWare networks, including inventory, software distribution, and license metering of server-based applications. It is fully aware of NetWare Directory Services (NDS). Users can manage NDS objects and containers directly and not just in bindery-emulation mode.

Administrators can install multiple management consoles to distribute management tasks. Each console is a network manager's workstation running Brequest, the Btrieve workstation terminate-and-stay (TSR) program, and the LANDesk applications. Because LANDesk Manager is licensed on a per-node basis, multiple servers count as additional nodes, which simplifies pricing for large organizations with many servers.

Administrators also need a system, dedicated as a probe, which looks at all the packets on its cable segment and relays information back to the server NLM, which can then graph network traffic in a variety of ways on a manager's console. Probes can be at least a 386 with 2 MB of random access memory and 20 MB of free disk space. Most important, they must have a network interface card (NIC) with promiscuous mode drivers, which pass every packet on the wire to the next higher layer of the protocol stack. While this distributed configuration is scalable for growing networks, it still represents a substantial hit on network processing, memory, and disk space resources for a small or midsize company. The LANDesk Manager central management server is not meant to be used for any other purpose but LANDesk—no application or user file services—because it suffers a big performance hit when managing the central Btrieve database.

The principal benefits of the product are as follows:

- Tools are organized around management tasks.
- Flexible organization of network components.
- Broad range of tools are included.
- Monitors such network health indicators as packet rates, utilization, and error levels.
- Fine-tunes network performance.
- Offers graphic views, real-time summaries of application-related traffic.

- Protects workstations from common, stealth, and polymorphic viruses.

- Redirects traffic to secondary printers if primary printers fail.

There are various applications among the 13 that help to integrate PC LAN management with enterprise management, and to assist with performance improvements and virus protection.

The SNMP gateway is a software module that links network management consoles to desktop PCs and other devices on the LANs through SNMP. The result is that the user can manage any device or workstation running on Novell NetWare LANs. The gateway implements a new host resource MIB for the desktop. From a network management console, the LAN administrator is able to manage PC LAN workstations below the NIC card level. The gateway resides as an NLM on NetWare file servers. It dwells between a network management console and network devices. The private MIB ensures that no other agents are needed for managing the desktops. Using this gateway, other Intel products such as StorageExpress and all members of the NetPost and NetPortExpress family can also be managed. As a network management station, HP OpenView for Windows can also be used. OpenView offers more platform services and more integration.

In order to troubleshoot traffic jams and to test and optimize network performance, LANDesk manager can be extended by the capabilities of NetSight Analyst and Traffic Analyst. This combination of applications can be characterized as follows:

- Displays a real-time summary of packet-level traffic on the LAN

- Monitors all protocol conversations between network stations

- Builds station logs for up to 512 nodes

- Sets alarms and, when integrated with LANDesk Manager, gets immediate notification of potential problems

- Displays address pairs to find out who is talking to whom

- Determines the source of faults by listening to network conversations

- Builds intelligent packet-filtering applications

- Defines capture, display, trigger, and alarm filters to pinpoint problems and test alternatives

- Simulates large loads to test different configurations

- Spots unauthorized access by filtering for strings and addresses that might betray unwanted activity

- Analyzes protocol information on segments

- Decodes packets, records conversations, creates station logs and analyzes segments throughout the enterprise

- Turns workstations into a dedicated remote agent for packet analysis

Virus Protect offers a comprehensive and complete solution by using scanning and rules-based trapping. Operating at both the server and workstation, these two defense systems continuously protect all points of entries.

The shortcomings of the product are as follows:

- Interfaces may confuse administrators.

- The core tools are considered not best of class.

- It requires substantial networking resources.

LANDesk Manager has been embedded into NMS from Novell, offering a more complete suite of management applications for Novell LANs.

Peregrine Systems ServerView. The main function is the centralized monitoring and control of Novell NetWare servers. The application has been implemented on HP OpenView by using menu bar integration.

ServerView monitors performance of Netware servers, printer performance, and network connectivity and activity. ServerView allows operators to monitor over 10 key performance indicators on distributed NetWare servers, including CPU load, number of connections, number of users attached, disk usage, movable and nonmovable memory, permanent memory, short-term allocated memory, and cache buffers. Users can set thresholds; alarms will be triggered when thresholds are exceeded. In addition, ServerView depicts real-time graphs of CPU load, number of users and connections, and disk usage.

ServerView can alert operators to fault conditions and critical server actions such as disk volume dismounts, NLM unloads, and modification of directory rights.

ServerView also supports configuration management by centralizing user administration tasks and server rebooting. ServerView supports editing of server configuration files including autoexec.bat, config.sys, and system login scripts. ServerView can also highlight user and group security privileges and conditions. ServerView can display the top 20 users of server disk space and evaluate each user to determine whether or not accounting limits have been exceeded.

Brightworks from McAfee Associates. Brightworks is a suite of tools that include inventory, software distribution, and software metering. It additionally includes real help desk software called LSC and graphical server information in the form of NetTune.

Brightworks' products are more comprehensive than Sabers' but they are not as accurate as the others in this category of PC LAN-management. Brightworks collects data about every conceivable device and software, but there is not a single field that does not require the user to scroll in order to see all the information. Every component tracked also has a comprehensive asset management screen backing it up so that the administrator can enter tracking tags as well as warranty and financial information.

Both push and pull distribution is supported, and by using complex scripts configuration file edits can also be distributed. All major functions of software metering are supported.

In summary, the strengths are as follows:

- Trouble ticketing for help desk is supported.
- NetTune offers server optimization.
- It is fairly well integrated.

But users must not ignore weaknesses in the following areas:

- Enterprise metering is not yet completely stable.
- Distribution tasks are too simple.
- Interfaces between modules need more optimization.

Peregrine Systems StationView.   The main function is the centralized monitoring of distributed DOS PC workstations. The application has been implemented on HP OpenView by using menu bar integration.

One of the first Unix-based applications for managing PCs is StationView from Peregrine Systems. StationView runs as an application on top of HP OpenView Network Node Manager.

StationView allows network management to remotely control system files such as netconfig and autoexec.bat. StationView's ability to retrieve inventory and configuration can save organizations time, particularly when upgrading hundreds of PCs to new software environments. StationView can be used to quickly determine if there is enough memory and disk space to meet the requirements. Performing the same functions using a Windows-based console may be infeasible, particularly in flat, bridged network configurations.

StationView provides an accurate picture of workstation components and configuration, including PC hardware and software inventory, loaded drivers and versions, memory and interrupt mapping, RSFs and AUTOEXEC, CONFIG.SYS, WIN.INI, SYSTEM.INI, and login files. It also displays status and configuration of printer servers and print queues and shows how each PC is configured for printing. StationView provides real-time status and alerts for all managed components and network connections. StationView can help isolate problems to the workstation, cable, network, or server; it detects incorrectly loaded drivers and configuration problems.

LAN Management System from Saber Software Corporation. Sabers' offerings include the extensive menuing, desktop control, and inventory features for DOS and Windows workstations and adds metering and software distribution functions to them. The products lack a clear approach to all the component modules. The installation program creates over 20 icons, but only the Console Manager, Manu, and Enterprise Application Manager (which is the metering component) are truly useful. The product suite is based on datasets, or database files, and the LAN administrator needs to know the name Saber gives to each of them in order to access any of the data. When the administrator wants to use the Console Manager component where the most useful tools are hidden, dataset names must be selected from a file list. The architecture of the product allows datasets to be stored on multiple servers and then consolidated by the console for enterprise management. This keeps unnecessary network traffic down while providing flexibility. On the other hand, this flexibility leads to complexity and serious usability problems.

The inventory functions support hardware only. Application scanning is available in the metering module. The hardware component identification is not nearly as comprehensive as the other products. The distribution module has a very powerful script builder. Even the scriptually challenged can write complex scripts. Every action is a guided button/click away. The English language is displayed on screen to represent script syntax and commands. The script builder also prompts users for comments during every step, which are recorded as remarks in the script. The finished script is in SaberBASIC. Both push and pull distribution is supported. The product can distribute configuration file edits. All basic software metering functions are supported.

In summary, the strengths are as follows:

- All the major network and desktop management tasks are covered.
- It offers a flexible architecture.
- The script builder feature is easy to use.

But this application suite needs improvements in the following areas:

- It lacks module integration.
- The product architecture is very complex.
- LAN administrators need a lot of training.

Norton Administrator for Networks from Symantec. This product offers an enterprise administration framework with an extremely easy-to-use interface, but it lacks comprehensive network monitoring. Norton Enterprise Framework (NEF) consolidates data from multiple servers back to the manager software running at the master site. File servers running this application pass data up a hierarchy and may be parents or children; both have in and out boxes where data is transferred on a configurable schedule, but each parent site must run the NEF manager and NEF sender/receiver (transfer) programs, while child sites do not. Changed information is compressed prior to transmission; no entire databases are exchanged across the user-defined hierarchy.

The product requires no NLM, which lets it run on almost any network operating system, including NetWare, LAN Manager, Windows NT, LAN Server, Vines, and also Pathworks.

The inventory feature is very simple to manage. Data can be accessed by machine or query for a set of components across all nodes. Every screen is printable or can be seen in formal reports. But it does not inventory file servers. Software inventory must be manually added to the central database. Hardware inventory can be collected while the server is down. Software distribution is well integrated with software inventory functions. When defining a distribution job, LAN administrators can select targets by user name or build a query on any inventoried component. Both push and pull distribution is supported. The WAN distribution option can establish distribution routes across multiple servers with minimal impact on the WAN traffic. Basic software metering functions are supported as well.

In summary, the strengths are as follows:

- It is simple and to the point.
- Multiple server support is well designed.
- It includes comprehensive reporting.

But its core components do not cover all LAN management functions.

PC SystemView from IBM. This system management tool offers LAN administrators of small-to-medium-sized LAN environments a multiplatform desktop solution. Management capabilities are provided for OS/2, NetWare, Windows, and DOS over various networks, such as TCP/IP, Netbios, IPX, and SNMP. PC and server performance can be monitored via the Internet. Any machine with a Web browser can turn into a PC SystemView management console.

Device-Dependent LAN Management Applications

In particular, interconnecting devices such as repeaters, bridges, routers, extenders, and switches are under consideration here. In many cases, the management applications are shared with hub applications. Both types of applications may run on the same platform incorporated into the hub.

The following applications for managing bridges, routers, and repeaters are currently available:

3Com Transcend

Cisco CiscoWorks

Con Ware Computer Consulting NEMA

Gandalf Passport

HP OpenView Interconnect Manager

RAD Network Devices MultiVu

Siemens-Nixdorf Bridge Management

Wellfleet (Bay Networks) Site Manager

Router management applications help simplify the task of configuring routers. Despite the inroads made by SNMP, the router configuration process is anything but standardized. Each vendor has its own unique approach to setting up its routers; some vendors put a lot of configuration and control information in SNMP format; others do not. Most support the TCP/IP TELNET virtual terminal emulation mode for configuration and control, as well as the Trivial File Transfer Protocol (TFTP) for downloading configuration data to the router. Beyond that, however, the methods of configuring differ widely.

Right now, most leading vendors have simplified the user interface for configuring an individual router. The use of graphical point-and-click interfaces has helped speed up the time it takes to configure a router. Many vendors provide management applications with improved editing capabilities, helping to simplify the task even further. Router vendors have also added safeguards in their management applications to minimize the impact of human error in the configuration process.

More and more network managers would like to see the router management application supported on the platform of their choice. That way, they can manage multiple types from one console rather than employ separate console for just the routers. Ideally, a router management application should be tightly integrated with the underlying platform as well. This is not the case today, as all router management applications are primarily launched from the platform menu, with little or no integration in event management and platform database.

The following briefly describes key characteristics of router management applications with two products.

3Com Transcend. The main function is the integrated management for 3Com adapters, hubs, and routers. The application is running on Sun-Net Manager, HP Open View, and IBM NetView for AIX by using menu bar integration.

In an effort to simplify the router configuration process even further, 3Com has introduced an architecture called *boundary routing*, which takes standard routing software for n-way local routing and extends the LAN interface portion over the wide area. The goal of this is to simplify routing software functions for remote routers, which are often located at branch offices where there is no technical support staff. 3Com Transcend takes advantage of boundary routing to simplify router management.

Transcend software obtains information from SmartAgent intelligent device agents embedded in 3Com adapters, hubs, and routers. 3Com SmartAgents localize polling and organize collected data to reduce bandwidth overhead of management data. SmartAgents are capable of correlating information from multiple 3Com devices to provide a more integrated view of network status and assist in creation of baselines for performance management.

Cisco CiscoWorks. The main function is the configuration, performance, fault, and security management for Cisco's routers. This application is running on SunNet Manager, HP OpenView, and NetView for AIX. The integration methods include icon launching from SunNet Manager map, command line integration possible with HP NetMetrix (traffic monitoring), and Remedy ARS (trouble ticketing).

CiscoWorks is a suite of SNMP-based operations and management applications for users of Cisco's routers. CiscoWorks includes significant enhancements for easing remote installation and router software management. In particular, it provides a group-editing feature. The CiscoWorks global command capability allows managers to specify a group of routers and apply common configuration changes or software updates to the entire group. In addition, the CiscoWorks menu specifically calls out frequently used commands, such as enable passwords, SNMP community strings, and access lists. CiscoWorks includes a feature for checking a router's configuration against information stored in an SQL database.

CiscoWorks provides an operations series of applications for day-to-day router monitoring and troubleshooting. In addition, Cisco offers a management series for off-line analysis of network traffic and trends. Together, these utilities help satisfy both real-time concerns of network managers and requirements for long-term planning and trend analysis.

CiscoWorks' operations series includes six major aspects:

Configuration File Management

Path Tool

Health Monitor

Environmental Monitor

Device Management Database

Security Management

In particular, CiscoWorks' Path Tool provides visualization of the actual path taken by the data; it detects interface changes much more efficiently than SNMP monitoring alone. The Management Series portion of CiscoWorks assists managers in achieving long-term goals of network management, such as historical trend analysis for determining the cost-effectiveness of transmission options, determining usage, identifying potential problem areas, and isolating chronic problems. A Data WorkBench feature is actually a Sybase report writer tool that allows administrators to create reports. These reports can display traffic through every router interface, including throughput and error rates, traffic peaks, and percentage of broadcast traffic versus total traffic.

CiscoWorks Blue with Native Service Point helps to improve the management of routed networks in SNA environments. Cisco routers are defined as physical units (PU) from a VTAM environment, using NetView for MVS. Developed with support from IBM, Native Service Point preserves the security features of the mainframe environment. It provides physical and logical maps to identify SNA and IP resources and determine which SNA PUs and LUs are located on which router ports. The result is less administration effort and more visibility for status, performance, and capacity management.

In order to lower the cost of monitoring remote LANs, most bridge and router vendors incorporate RMON agents into their devices. ILAN routers from Crosscomm contain an RMON agent that monitors traffic from up to 32 remote LAN segments and reports to a net management console on one of the segments. This implementation covers all nine Ethernet groups and four Token Ring groups. These applications have been developed by Protools (now part of Network General Corporation). Statistics for workstation traffic profiles can be generated as well. The processing work is carried out by coprocessors running in the background, with the result of no performance impacts on routing functions due to monitoring. Similar combination of RMON monitoring with mainline functions can be observed with hubs and also with switches.

LAN Performance Management Applications

RMON seems to be the basis of many performance-related applications for LAN components. The RMON indicators offer a rich basis for performance investigations. RMON probes, however, will not replace LAN analyzers and monitors. Table 5.3 shows the feature comparison of both types of instruments. The results of this table assume that RMON has been implemented with all standardized features. That is not always true; it depends on the manufacturer of the RMON products. The implementation is different, too. There are stand-alone probes or built-in probes, shipped with hubs, routers, bridges, or with servers.

The following list contains some of the traffic-monitoring products that are based on RMON probes:

Armon Networking with OnSite

Axon Networks with LANServant Manager

Concord Communications with Trakker

Frontier with NetScout Manager

Hewlett-Packard with Network Advisor

Hewlett-Packard with NetMetrix

Hewlett-Packard with History Analyzer/Traffic Expert/Resource Manager

Network Application Technologies with Ethermeter

TABLE 5.3   Comparison of RMON Capabilities with LAN Analyzers

Attribute	RMON product	LAN analyzer
Decoding all seven layers of known protocols	RMON2 only	x
Protocol independency	x	x
Use of colors at decoding	x	x
Transmission of decoded information in networks	x	x
Graphical presentation of indicators	x	x
Filtering various patterns	x	
Presentation of protocol distributions	RMON2 only	x
Recognizing traffic trends	x	x
Measuring the time difference between packets		x
Measuring the time difference between sessions		x
Overhead-free monitoring	x	x
Generation of packets		x
Insertion of packets		x
Testing		x
Automatic edition of generated packets		x
Measuring response time	x	
In-depth troubleshooting		x
Decoding of unusual protocols		x
Laboratory use in network design		x

Network General with Distributed Sniffer System

Wandel & Goltermann with IDMS Manager

Technically Elite with RMONPlus

OnSite from Armon.   Today's SNMP-based network management systems are great for basic information about a network's infrastructure—equipment failures, connectivity, and physical-layer issues. But it just doesn't give the details or logical information about applications and network utilities that users need to balance network operation.

Based on the RMON MIB standard, OnSite delivers detailed information for all segments in real time—the kind of information users need for more comprehensive fault diagnosis, planning, and performance-tuning than users can get with your network management systems alone. With OnSite, users can look at every segment, local and remote, just as if technicians were there. Because users have access to detailed information about each segment, users can find out exactly which resources are being used by specific workgroups and applications.

OnSite Management Software allows monitoring and analysis of multiple segments—over even the widest networks—from a central management station. The software integrates fully into all popular NMS hardware-software platforms and blends right into the NMS on-screen display. What's more, OnSite Management Software is modular to ensure flexibility and extensibility. Each module is a complete, ready-to-use application that processes data into concise information that's presented clearly in graphic windows based on the X Window System™ and OSF/Motif™. And OnSite applications select and process information intelligently—they learn what to look for and know how to analyze what they find.

OnSite delivers the modules that LAN managers need most to establish a special network's point of view. The alarm editor and learning tools automatically baseline network performance and alert operators when important network characteristics change. Segment statistics provides detailed remote monitoring information for every segment with trend analysis that allows tracking of performance, utilization, and errors over time. Host Analysis reports offer clear graphic displays that identify who's using the network, why, and for what types of "conversations." And when LAN managers have to find out exactly what's happened, protocol decoding gives a plain English account of dialogs on the network.

OnSite probes are second-generation network-monitoring devices. They eliminate the need for costly network analyzers while delivering intelligent analysis capabilities on every segment—Ethernet and Token Ring. Each probe is packed full of functionality and gives full

RMON implementation—monitoring all groups simultaneously—plus MIB extensions and true client/server interoperability. OnSite probes are highly reliable. And they're extremely cost-effective, so LAN managers can cover the entire network without a major investment in new hardware.

OnSite probes are available as stand-alone devices with up to four network interfaces. Each probe is based on a powerful RISC processor and 2 to 12 MB of RAM. There's also an OnSite software-only solution that users can install on any existing SPARC station™ to gain OnSite probe functionality without any additional hardware.

OnSite Manager provides tools for monitoring multiple segments and analyzing information gathered by OnSite probes or any other RMON-based probes. OnSite Manager functionality is packaged as software that integrates fully into popular NMS hardware-software platforms. It effectively extends the view of the network and allows observation of application data and protocols across the network.

Application-oriented software. Unlike SNMP "browsers," which simply display raw information, OnSite Manager software is application-oriented. Each module gives a complete, ready-to-use application that intelligently gathers and correlates RMON MIB attributes and presents the information graphically in a useful form.

OnSite Manager applications are automatic, expert tools with the built-in know-how to select, analyze, and display the RMON MIB information that's most important for understanding the network's behavior. They present the most relevant summarized statistics graphically—as pie charts, bar charts, and in color-coded matrices. The graphical user interface is based on the X Window System™ and OSF/Motif™. All applications are fully integrated into a network management platform and use the same, familiar interface—network map, database, and SNMP services.

OnSite modular applications. OnSite Manager provides a variety of modular applications for making use of information gathered by the RMON probes at each segment. Alarm tools give the ability to record and display alarms graphically on network maps. OnSite's interactive alarm editor provides automatic threshold settings for desired attributes. The users select the attributes they want to monitor. The learning tool then samples the segment to discover normal levels and automatically sets thresholds for issuing and clearing alarms. Users can accept the automatic baseline or adjust any thresholds to meet their specific needs.

With thresholds set, operators can run the network health tool to monitor all segments on the network. When an alarm is issued, you can track it down to the segment graphically, right on your network management map.

Segment Statistics show exactly how the network is being used. The application displays current, accumulated, and peak rates for all selected variables as pie chart displays showing network usage, packet destinations, and packet lengths. A line graph monitors key attributes in real time. There's also history collection allowing you to accumulate data on selected variables over time for performing long-term trend analysis. LAN analysts can expand or contract data to alter the view over time.

Host Analysis allows you to see who's using the network and analyze why and for what types of conversations. A bar chart representation displays all hosts on a selected segment for information such as packet bytes received and transmitted, errors, and multicast and broadcast packets. Using the RMON HostTopN group, users can limit tracking to the most active hosts only. Display options allow you to search for and filter information and to zoom into any host group. A color-coded host matrix displays traffic patterns between any host pair for instant identification of all active conversations on the network.

Filter, Capture, and Protocol Decoding is designed for situations where LAN managers have to find out exactly what's taken place on a particular segment. This application provides flexible filter tools that allow you to set up a number of channels for data capture. Users can supply a wide range of criteria, including triggers for initiating and terminating capture. Once captured, protocol decoding displays packet content in easy-to-understand English. Protocol Decoding interprets TCP/IP, DECnet, AppleTalk, XNS, Vines, SNA, IPX, ISO protocol suites (seven layers), and more. Filtering allows real-time monitoring of selected views for measuring and comparing traffic patterns.

To reduce network overhead, Protocol Decoding filter selection allows you to capture only those packets that are of interest. LAN analysts can measure any selection of network statistics in real time and plot specific events and views to see how they affect the network.

To complement and enhance the utility of RMON MIBs, Armon has added its own proprietary MIB extensions. These provide more intelligent information and reduce network overhead for increased efficiency. MIB extensions include support for higher-level protocol statistics, active search for station existence, accounting, and more.

Because networks differ in size and scope, OnSite Manager is available in two software configurations. Each configuration supports all OnSite modules. OnSite Manager base configuration is designed for networks requiring very few probes. Setup and reporting features are geared toward single segments.

When networks are large, viewing individual components alone is not always enough. OnSite global configuration provides users with the capabilities they need to perform operations for the entire network and integrate all information into a global network view. With the global configuration, all segments' statistics are available on a single graph. Host and Matrix include host information for the entire network. The intrasegment application correlates traffic between segments.

OnSite Ethernet probes second-generation devices that collect information from individual network segments and forward it to the manager. Each probe provides a full implementation of the RMON MIB RFC 1271 standard plus Armon proprietary MIB extensions. Probes are available in a variety of configurations to meet varied network needs. All are based on Intel™ i960TM RISC processors with 2 to 12 MB of memory to deliver exceptional performance characteristics.

OnSite probes are available as stand-alone devices or are rack-mounted with one, two, or four Ethernet interfaces, so that you can choose the probe combination that best fits your network configuration. Probes are proprietary hardware devices based on Intel i960 CA/CF processors operating at 25 to 33 MHz and i82596TM controllers for each interface to ensure linear scalability in everything. And because processor and memory resources are shared, multiple interface probes are fully adaptive to handle dynamic network characteristics with high reliability.

Because monitoring is most important when problems occur, OnSite Ethernet probes give redundant access features without the need for extra hardware. Out-of-band access is provided by a built-in backup modem connection. On multi-interface models, each interface provides automatic, in-band, redundant access. Armon also offers two unique solutions for special network situations. For noncritical segments that don't require simultaneous monitoring, Armon offers a 4:2 OnSite probe. This model provides four multiplexed Ethernet interfaces. At any time, two interfaces may be software-selected to provide MIB agent services for a single segment.

Armon's software-only solution, for Sun-based networks, allows you to gain OnSite probe functionality on any existing SPARCstation™ without any additional hardware. OnSite software probes can be installed and executed remotely. Under RMON, probes are "eyes and ears" on each segment through a variety of Management Information Bases (MIBs). Each OnSite Ethernet probe collects segment information for all RMON MIBs. These include the following:

Segment Statistics	Information that LAN managers need to quantify the operational effectiveness of your network. Statistics include packets, octets, broadcasts, multicasts, dropped packets, soft errors, packet distribution, and more.

History	Long-term historical data, based on users' specifications and OnSite built-in intelligence, for segment trend analysis.
Host Table	Collects information on each host discovered on the segment.
Host TopN	Sorted statistics that allow you to reduce network overhead by looking at only the most active hosts on each segment.
Traffic Matrix	Reporting on traffic and errors between any host pair for correlating conversations on the most active nodes.
Alarms	Reports changes in network characteristics based on thresholds for any or all MIBs that users define. This information allows you to use RMON as an effective proactive tool.
Events	Logging of events based on thresholds that users define. LAN analysts may use these to initiate functions such as data capture or instance counts to isolate specific portions of the network's traffic.
Filters	Definitions of packet matches for selective information capture. These include logical operations (AND, OR, NOT), so users can specify network events for data capture, alarms, and statistics.
Packet Capture	Stores packets that match filtering specifications. A slice option provides more efficient memory usage.

Armon proprietary MIB extensions for Ethernet. OnSite Ethernet probes give proprietary MIBs for additional functionality at higher-level layers. These include protocol type distribution for information on the percentage of resources used by specific applications, network types, and high-level filtering for more efficient use of probe resources. Other MIBs include active local polling of devices for isolating specific host problems.

OnSite probes are based on Wind River Systems3 VxWorks real-time operating system and Armon's proprietary engine that collects virtually all network traffic. This combination allows continuing development of new applications and additional MIB extensions. All software can be updated to the probe automatically, over the network.

OnSite Token Ring probes collect information from individual Token Ring segments and forward it to the manager. Probes can be connected to an SNMP/RMON manager over bridges or source-routed networks.

Each probe provides a full implementation of the RMON MIB RFC 1271 and 1513 standards plus Armon proprietary MIB extensions. The standard provides both general ring information and specifics for each station. Probes are available in a variety of configurations to meet varied network needs. All are based on Intel i960 RISC processors with 4 to 20 MB of memory to deliver exceptional performance characteristics.

OnSite probes are available as stand-alone devices or rack-mounted with one, two, or four Token Ring interfaces, so that you can choose the probe combination that best fits your network configuration. Probes are dedicated hardware devices based on Intel i960 CA/CF processors operating at 33 MHz. And because processor and memory resources are shared, multiple interface probes are fully adaptive to handle dynamic network characteristics with high reliability.

Because monitoring is most important when problems occur, OnSite Token Ring probes give redundant access features without the need for extra hardware. Out-of-band access is provided by a built-in backup modem connection. On multi-interface models, each interface provides automatic sideband redundancy.

Under RMON, probes are "eyes and ears" on each segment through a variety of Management Information Bases (MIBs). Each OnSite Token Ring probe collects segment information for all RMON MIBs. These include standard RMON groups—Segment Statistics (MAC and LLC), History, Host Table, HostTopN, Traffic Matrix, Alarms, Events, Filters, and Packet Capture. There are also Token Ring extensions, including Ring Station, Ring Order, Source Routing statistics, and Configuration groups.

Segment Statistics	Information that LAN analysts need to quantify the operational effectiveness of the network. Statistics include packets, octets, broadcasts, dropped packets, soft errors, packet distribution, and more. Statistics are at two levels: MAC for the protocol level and LLC statistics to measure traffic flow.
History	Long-term historical data, based on users' specifications and OnSite built-in intelligence, for segment trend analysis. Histories include both MAC and LLC statistics.
Host Table	Collects information on each host discovered on the segment.
HostTopN	Sorted statistics that allow you to reduce network overhead by looking at only the most active hosts on each segment.
Traffic Matrix	Reporting on traffic and errors between any host pair for correlating conversations on the most active nodes.
Ring Station Group	Collects general ring information and specific information for each station. General information includes ring state (normal,

	beacon, claim token, purge), active monitor, number of active stations, and more. Ring Station Information includes a variety of error counters, station status, insertion times, and last enter/exist time.
Ring Station Order	Maps station MAC addresses in their order in ring.
Ring Station Configuration	Allows probe to act as Token Ring LAN manager. Probe may get station configuration information and remove stations from the ring.
Source-Routing Statistics	In bridged, source-routing environments, the probe collects information, including number of frames and octets to and from the local ring, broadcasts per route and frame counter per hop.
Alarms	Reports changes in network characteristics based on thresholds for any or all MIBs that users define. This information allows you to use RMON as an effective proactive tool.
Events	Logging of events based on thresholds that users define. LAN analysts may use these to initiate functions such as data capture or instance counts to isolate specific portions of the network's traffic.
Filters	Definitions of packet matches for selective information capture. These include logical operations (AND, OR, NOT), so users can specify network events for data capture, alarms, and statistics.
Packet Capture	Stores packets that match filtering specifications. A slice option provides more efficient memory usage. And only OnSite Token Ring probes, with their proprietary hardware design, give users the CPU and memory resources to ensure effective use of all these MIBs for better network management.

OnSite proprietary MIB extensions for Token Ring. OnSite Token Ring probes give proprietary MIBs for additional functionality at higher-level layers. These include protocol type distribution for information on the percentage of resources used by specific applications, network types, and high-level filtering for more efficient use of probe resources. Other MIBs include active local polling of devices for isolating specific host problems. OnSite probes are based on Wind River Systems

VxWorks real-time operating system and Armon's proprietary engine that collects virtually all network traffic. This combination allows continuing development of new applications and additional MIB extensions. All software can be updated to the probe automatically, over the network. Due to the flexibility of combining Ethernet and Token Ring probes, the price/performance ratio is very favorable with this product.

In order to support enterprisewide traffic reporting, Armon has implemented NetReporter. This package generates preformatted and customized reports in either graphical or textual format. With this new extension, users can consolidate information and do aggregate and statistical analysis. The Unix-based application is a fully integrated add-on to OnSite Manager.

NetReporter uses a built-in collection mechanism to gather data from probes or embedded agents. It also generates preformatted and customized reports in either graphical or textual format. The Unix-based application is a fully integrated add-on to OnSite. It helps LAN managers to track network performance over time for long-term configuration and planning.

LANServant from Axon. These products are client/server tools that extend the reach of SNMP stations out onto remote Ethernet and Token Ring LANs. The LABServant Probe™ sits on the LANs; LANServant Manager™ software runs on the network management platform or as a stand-alone application. Together they provide a comprehensive, in-depth source of information not just on particular devices, but on the entire LAN segment or ring and everything attached to it.

Working with a complete set of information simplifies the job of keeping complex internetworks operating smoothly. It helps the user better understand how the stations and devices on the network are interacting and affecting the overall quality of the LAN service provided to end users. It enables the LAN managers to improve not only the technical management of the network, but its business management as well, by making informed decisions that minimize costs and maximize benefits from valuable LAN resources.

Running on network speed, AXON LANServant is one of the highest fully RMON-compliant LAN management solutions. Applications are available in the form of management modules. This enables the user to install or download just those capabilities required on the LANs. As the network requirements expand, modules can be added to address management issues beyond the scope of standard RMON data.

LANServant components are as follows:

- LANServant Manager.   This comprehensive tool lets the users view all the activity on the LAN segment and drill down to see how specific hosts and pairs of hosts are impacting it. The user can also set up LAN-specific tables, alarms, and filters on remote probes. Different probe functions can be driven in parallel by various management stations. Each station can be assigned one of four levels of access permission (from read-only to full configuration privileges).

- **LANServant Probe.** These measurement collectors capture data at network speed, ensuring that no packet is missed. They operate with multitasking, so the collection for trend analysis can continue uninterrupted while packets are being filtered and captured for troubleshooting. All 9 Ethernet and 10 Token Ring RMON groups are supported. The modules can be installed selectively to meet the requirements of individual LAN segments. Modules can also be downloaded from management stations for immediate short-term inspection of a particular segment or ring.

LANServant provides management platforms with snapshots of LAN activity, so polling can be performed less frequently. Reduced overhead on the network is particularly beneficial when there is a wide area link between the management platform and the LAN.

As LANs generate increasing traffic, tools that reduce LAN activity data into meaningful information and help MIS focus in on what is important are becoming an essential part of every toolkit. LANServant Manager can operate as an integrated tool on any of the leading open network management platforms or as a stand-alone application. Information from AXON management modules can also be exported to other management tools, databases, and applications.

At a glance, LAN managers can see activity levels and alarm locations across an entire LAN segment or ring, identifying hot spots and potential bottlenecks before they become major problems. AXON has designed LANServant Manager displays to make working with RMON data fast and intuitive.

AXON LANServant also provides powerful tools for identifying and solving network faults. Users can set up a wide range of rising and falling thresholds—based on the individual characteristics of each LAN segment or ring—that generate alarms or other events when crossed.

For troubleshooting, the LANServant Probe performs the function of a LAN protocol analyzer, capturing and decoding transmission packets or frames. LAN analysts can define very specific filters and nest them for even more precise matching. The probe uses these filter sets along with comprehensive error statistics to collect and transmit to the management station only relevant data. Decodes are provided for a wide range of protocols, including TCP/IP, DECnet, Novell NetWare, Banyan VINES, AppleTalk, SNA, and NetBIOS.

Because probes are permanently in place on the LAN and controlled by the central management station, there is no need to send staff to problem sites. Technicians can control the troubleshooting process directly rather than having to rely on trial-and-error testing and back-and-forth phone calls. If it is necessary to send staff out to repair equipment, they can be directed to the specific problem and equipped to complete the job in one visit.

Insight into usage trends can help organizations to optimize the use of current network resources and make informed decisions about allocating future resources and planning network growth. AXON's LANServant Probes support trends analysis by accurately capturing samples of network activity at user-specified intervals. LANServant Manager's graphical display provides a high-level view of the data and a fast path to the detail beneath trend lines. By analyzing peaks and valleys in a line graph, for example, LAN analysts can find out the dates and times when particular events occurred.

Virtually all mission-critical applications will soon be running on LANs. To ensure a high level of service, MIS will need an ever broader set of tools for such tasks as managing traffic between stations and accounting for LAN users of WAN bandwidth, measuring service quality, performance tuning, and capacity planning.

The LANServant Probe protects user investments by adhering to industry standards, which will evolve to encompass some of these requirements, and by operating at high speeds that can easily accommodate rising network traffic. High speeds are important to support management tools that extend beyond the current scope of RMON, requiring data capture and filtering at upper levels of the protocol stack. AXON also provides unique investment protection by enabling customers to incorporate new management modules into LANServant products without disrupting ongoing network management operations.

AXON's Network Data Engine™, which is incorporated into all LANServant Probes, has the capacity to create a virtually unlimited variety of tables from incoming packet streams. A DLM that computes statistics for accounting purposes, for example, could be installed while probes continue to capture data for trend analysis and to filter packets for troubleshooting. Users can choose which DLM they want to install on each probe, evolving management capabilities to match changes in the global network.

Figure 5.19 shows the client/server structure of LANServant. The probes are responsible for data collection; the manager controls the software distribution over the network, running on the probe and on the management station, as management modules that can be loaded independently.

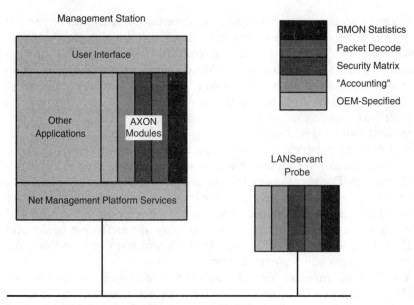

Management Station

User Interface

Other Applications

AXON Modules

Net Management Platform Services

RMON Statistics
Packet Decode
Security Matrix
"Accounting"
OEM-Specified

LANServant Probe

Figure 5.19   Distributed software structure of LANServant.

AXON's agent software running on the LANServant Probe provides the ability to install new functions at run time without disrupting ongoing data collection and packet filtering. This enables users to install just those functions that are needed on each LAN segment or ring and evolve probe capabilities as their network management needs grow. AXON's Extensible Agent and RMON Agent implementations rely on services of the SNMP Agent Library and the Network Data Engine (NDE). The SNMP Agent Library provides a complete framework for constructing an SNMP agent. The library is designed to make this task as simple and fast as possible. The Network Data Engine (NDE) is a data collection library. It can build and maintain the type of statistical tables required by the RMON MIB with a minimum amount of programming. The AXON agent also uses the communication services provided by AXON's Real Time Operating System (ART-OS). As these are provided by a standard socket interface, the agent is not bound to operate under ART-OS (Figure 5.20).

Each RMON group or similar application is implemented as two separate modules, an SNMP module and a data collection module. These are very loosely coupled, allowing the data collection modules to be interfaced to other SNMP libraries if required.

Each RMON group or similar application contains one or more control tables, each having a common set of objects (the index, owner, and status objects), as well as the group-specific objects. To ease the imple-

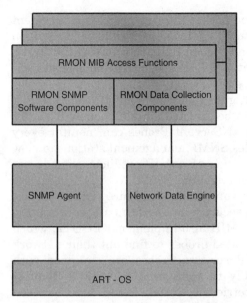

Figure 5.20   AXON Agent Software architecture.

mentation of the SNMP modules, an RMON Control Library has been constructed. This handles all access to the common objects as well as handling the semantics of RMON row creation and deletion. The whole system is highly modular and portable. It could be ported to other hardware platforms without difficulty.

LANServant Probe™ is the SNMP agent component of AXON's distributed LANServant system. The system's client/server architecture allows data capture and computation to take place in the most effective place—on the remote LAN. The probe is a high-speed, multitasking, passive hardware device which is continuously attached to the LAN. It monitors the entire segment and all the computers and devices on it, collecting activity statistics and valuable trend data, and initiating alarms based on parameters established by LANServant Manager™ or another RMON-compliant application. The probe also provides an efficient solution to the problems of troubleshooting remote LANs. It filters and captures packets with extreme precision based on complex user criteria. Running at network speed, it can accommodate high traffic loads without missing packets, yet is affordable enough to put on every LAN segment.

Various management functions can be installed on LANServant Probes to accommodate conditions on individual segments. Transient diagnostics can also be downloaded from management stations for immediate, short-term use.

High-speed data collection and packet filtering ensure management stations receive accurate pictures of LAN performance. Based on Intel's 80960 RISC processor and special collision counting hardware, LANServant Probes operate at network speeds. So no packets are missed, even as network traffic grows.

Probes can perform many different functions simultaneously and, if appropriate, these functions can be directed simultaneously from different management stations. LANServant Probes can monitor every host on the segment. This enables SNMP management stations to view older networks having devices, such as non-IP products, that do not incorporate network management agents.

AXON's Enterprise MIB lets you rapidly configure remote probes, assign multiple levels of access security, and perform all probe administrative tasks. The Enterprise MIB also implements BOOTP, which enables newly installed or relocated probes to find out their network addresses by querying BOOTP servers. Probes are equipped with serial interfaces that can easily be configured to work with most modems; so LAN analysts can retrieve LAN data even if links between management stations and probes go down.

AXON has implemented RMON Group 10 and all RMON Token Ring extensions, including complex Token Ring–specific error statistics such as Ring Beaconing Events. These extensions also include Ring Station tables, which show the host order on the ring, and provide host-specific Token Ring error conditions. Source Routing Tables identify packets that are local to the ring, are incoming or outgoing, or are simply passing through.

Based on Intel's 80960 RISC processor and special performance-enhancing Token Ring software, LANServant Probes operate at practical network speeds, so no important data is missed, even as network traffic grows.

Probes can perform many different functions simultaneously and, if appropriate, these functions can be directed simultaneously from different management stations.

Various management functions can be installed on LANServant Probes to accommodate conditions on individual rings. Transient diagnostics can also be downloaded from management stations for immediate, short-term use.

With AXON Dynamically Loadable Modules, the users can expand probe data collection capabilities as the network management requirements grow. AXON's Network Data Engine, incorporated into all LANServant Probes, allows new MIBs to be added easily while probes continue to perform existing tasks. AXON's Enterprise MIB lets you rapidly configure remote probes, assign multiple levels of access security, and perform all probe administrative tasks.

The Enterprise MIB also implements BOOTP, which enables newly installed or relocated probes to find out their network addresses by querying BOOTP servers. Probes are equipped with serial interfaces that can easily be configured to work with most modems; so the user can retrieve LAN data even if links between management stations and probes go down.

In order to support various management functions, LANServant incorporates a growing number of application modules. They focus on the following:

- Statistics management
- Packet decode management
- Traffic transmission module
- Enterprise communications analysis module

LANServant Manager works on a single platform along with applications from other vendors (e.g., to support trends analysis, trouble ticketing, performance evaluations, or to manage routers, hubs, and other networking devices).

LANServant Manager is integrated with the platform in the mapping, menu, and API levels. It makes use of platform services, such as naming, and provides the platform with traps for the display of alarms.

LANServant offers a rich set of reports on any or on a combination of RMON indicators. In addition, LANServant can export data to leading databases or to flat files to correlate data with other sources or to use other reporting capabilities.

LANServant can be extended by FlexiProbes that can monitor Ethernet switches. There are two versions: the first is capable of monitoring two Ethernet LAN segments; and the second is able to subdivide its functions into "talk only" and "listen only" alternatives.

RMONPlus from Technically Elite. Technically Elite Concepts has combined its network monitoring expertise, research, and technology with the SNMP-based RMON technology to produce the next step in network monitors called RMONPlus.

In particular, the RMONPlus Relational Matrix Group is valuable to generate matrix statistics with various indicators. RMONPlus collects interval statistic matrices based on relations. A *relation* is a set of fields defined in a network frame. Examples of relations are (source, destination, protocol) and (IPsource, IP destination, IP protocol). The set of data collected for a relation is called a *relation matrix*. For example, if the relation is (IP source, IP destination, NFS), then the relation matrix would be a list of all IP source/destination pairs and associated data for all NFS packets seen on the network. Relation matrices are sometimes called *traffic matrices* because data collected for relations such as the one in the example describe traffic patterns for the network.

RMONPlus supports relation matrix data collection on multiple relations simultaneously. The set of relations that are to be used for data collection is user selectable and dynamic.

RMONPlus allows the user to create and tailor new relations to be used to generate relation matrices. This flexibility allows the user to monitor just what is of interest, and may tailor the device to monitor events that may be unique to the user's network. For example, the user could create a relation that allows monitoring of an in-house protocol unique to that network.

RMONPlus will monitor all network protocols. This includes Apple-Talk, TCP/IP, DECnet, NetWare IPX, XNS, X Window, X.400, FTAM, Banyan Vines, Sun NFS, IBM, and others. Using the capability of User Definable Relations, any protocol can be described and monitored. This is not a fixed list but a dynamic capability of RMONPlus.

RMONPlus is able to look into the routed traffic on the network and build relation matrices showing the flow of information through the routed network. This ability is sometimes referred to as being able to "see" through routed networks.

RMONPlus can create relation matrices for peak and deviation events based on the traffic statistics collected over an interval. For example, the user may request to see the relation matrix for the 1 second when the number of broadcast messages peaked during an interval. Or the user may request to see the relation matrix for the 1 second when the number of packets seen on the network decreased the most. These matrices are controlled by the user.

The most important RMONPlus features are as follows:

- *User-definable statistics.* RMONPlus provides basic statistics such as number of frames, number of octets, and number of errors. RMONPlus also allows the user to define additional statistics based on data found in the packets. For example, if a type of packet on the network contained a counter, the user could create a statistic that was the sum of all the counters found in that type of packet. Or the user could create a statistic that was the count of the number of packets that had a particular bit set.

- *SNMP-compatible data compression.* RMONPlus relation matrices can consist of a lot of data per collection interval, especially on heavily used networks. RMONPlus has SNMP-compatible data compression built in. This allows efficient download, using SNMP, of matrix data to management stations with minimal impact on the network.

- *Accounting Integration.* RMONPlus can collect relation data that could be used to provide data on various accounting issues. RMON-

Plus can generate focused relation matrices. For example a relation matrix showing just the traffic from a set of workstations can be used to generate work-group accounting for those workstations. RMONPlus can also generate data useful in billing for server usage. For example a relation matrix showing all the NFS traffic to and from an NFS server could be isolated to a single matrix and all such network traffic billed to the requester of the service.

■ *Advanced memory management.* RMONPlus was implemented using advanced memory management in the device. The allocation of memory to various functions is user controlled with SNMP. None of the data tables have fixed limits to the amount of data that may be collected; rather, the limits are controlled by software and therefore may be managed with SNMP.

Technically Elite Concepts' RMONPlus Pod. The Technically Elite Concepts' RMONPlus Pod is based on the Intel i960 superscalar RISC processor and is designed to capture and process network frames in parallel. The high-speed components allow frames to be grabbed from the wire and processed in real time, giving accurate reports about the network even under high load conditions.

■ *In-band and out-of-band data access.* In addition to data access via SNMP over the network (in-band), RMONPlus devices can be configured to allow out-of-band, SLIP access to the data.

■ *Monitor multiple networks from a single device.* The RMONPlus device may be configured with multiple ports, and may be connected to and monitor more than one network simultaneously.

■ *Hub and router integration.* The RMONPlus agent can be integrated in various vendors' hub and router products. If the users are interested in having this unique product add value to the device, the vendor can help with this customization.

Device-Independent LAN Management Applications

Device-independent applications are expected to cover a number of different devices in the LANs by supporting principal management processes.

Asset management

Asset management is becoming the basis for efficiently supporting other management tasks, such as configuration, fault, and performance management. High-end products include the following:

Command 5000 from Isicad

Konfig from Autotrol

MountainView from Accugraph

Wireman from NHC Communications

Assetworks from Polycenter

MountainView from Accugraph. The main function of this product is cable management, physical asset management, and node-to-node connectivity analysis. The application is supported on the following platforms: SunNet Manager, HP OpenView, IBM NetView for AIX, Cabletron Spectrum, and NetLabs/DiMONS. Integration methods supported are menu-bar and event handling; also command-line integration with Remedy ARS and Legent Paradigm (trouble ticketing).

MountainView is a configuration management tool that integrates logical and physical network management with trouble-ticketing facilities to help automate management processes. MountainView integrates an advanced graphic modeler with a relational database management system (RDBMS-SQL), allowing users to create a complete model of the network's physical infrastructure.

Key components of MountainView include an advanced graphics modeler, integrated spreadsheet, RDBMS (SQL) link, integrated text editor, an expert system cable analyst module, and core MountainView application code.

MountainView relies on the underlying management platform (HP OpenView, IBM NetView for AIX) to perform device discovery. Optional MountainView modules can read information directly from SNMP MIBs, and use the LINK/TRANS function to load it into the relational database tables linked with the MountainView application.

Users can develop sophisticated hierarchies of physical drawings of network topology from existing CAD files or scanned documents. MountainView supports automatic attachment of any combination of drawings, audio files, raster images, or Unix programs. The expert cable analysis module supports cable routing and optimization analysis, and network traversal for cable tracing. It supports automatic grouping of path definition for trace correlation and report generation.

MountainView can be used to create dynamic models of the physical infrastructure and automate much of the input involved in tracking network asset data. Network inventory information tracked includes computer equipment, network protocol data, SNMP profiles, network TRAP data, maintenance information, connectivity data software revision levels and registration, and all aspects of cable plant, including validation on common cable types, management pairing assignments, and cable tracing with alpha data.

Using MountainView's LINK/TRANS function, users can automatically update equipment location changes and access changes from the underlying network management software. MountainView supports automatic port assignments of cable connections and report and work-order generation for monitoring moves/adds/changes.

Figure 5.21 shows the symbolic components of a network documentation system. The highlights of the components are as follows:

- *Physical design and management.* Using the system's sophisticated graphic capabilities, the user can design with an electronic model of user facility, including all network components. Then the attached database attributes give the user access to information on maintenance, capacity, connections, and more. On the screen, each component can exactly be located.

- *Cable management.* Cable length and type, and even wiring assignments, can be included in the electronic network model. Each attribute of the cable can be accessed and displayed.

- *Connectivity analysis.* The locations of nodes and their connectivity to other components is absolutely necessary to know. Accessing and displaying this information instantly help troubleshooting significantly.

- *Asset management.* All the communications assets in LANs are tracked with this system. The database can be accessed for price,

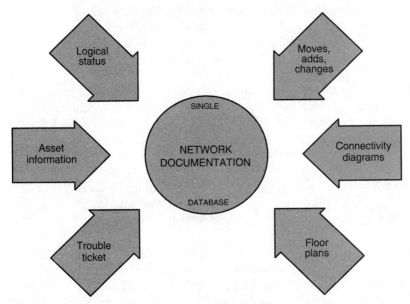

Figure 5.21   Network documentation with MountainView.

installation date, date of last move, and equipment assignments for all the networking components. This tracking system can also include furniture or any other item.

- *Management of adds, movers, and changes.* Integrated tools such as Accugraph's Equipment Modeler offer the ability to create graphics from the database. And it automatically updates drawings as database changes are made. Techniques such as autopopulation and data inheritance provide swift, effective information entry and maintenance.

- *Trouble-ticket integration.* The physical network management system also integrates popular trouble-ticket applications, such as Paradigm from Computer Associates and Actions Request system from Remedy. This allows network managers as well as users to solve problems quickly through faster access to detailed information.

Autotrol Konfig. The main functions are cable management and physical network and asset management. The application is supported on the following platforms: SunNet Manager, HP OpenView, IBM NetView for AIX. Integration methods included are menu bar, remote procedure calls (RPCs), some APIs, and also command-line integration with Remedy ARS.

Konfig tracks physical/wire/asset network configuration by documenting and displaying a detailed view of the voice, data, video, and environmental network. Using a relational database, Konfig builds intelligent relationships between active and/or passive network components and describes their association with the network.

Konfig uses menus and APIs to interface with SunNet Manager, HP OpenView, and IBM NetView for AIX. The API is used to issue SNMP requests and to receive SNMP responses. SNMP responses are stored in Konfig's SQL database.

Konfig includes a relational database for documenting network devices, their arrangement, connectivity, descriptions, and other attributes. A graphic engine depicts logical, physical, facility, and device views of the network on the screen. Advanced cable management functions allow users to represent and manipulate network connections at the circuit level. Konfig can trace circuit paths through bridges and cross-connects. Konfig supports a unique unambiguous identifier (UUI) for each object in the database; database integration with the underlying platform reduces the need to input data twice.

Isicad COMMAND 5000. The main function is cable management, physical asset tracking, and connectivity tracking. The application is supported on the following platforms: SunNet Manager, HP OpenView, Cabletron Spectrum, NetLabs/DiMONS, and Network Managers

NMC. Integration methods supported are menu bar, SNMP traps, and command-line interface with Remedy ARS (trouble ticketing).

COMMAND 5000 allows users to view everything from the entire network infrastructure down to the connectivity links between the smallest devices. COMMAND 5000 displays physical relationships between all elements on voice, video, LAN/WAN data, and security networks.

COMMAND 5000 tracks the inventory of physical network components, including workstations, cable layout, bridges, routers, and telecommunications equipment. Inventory data can include product descriptions, serial numbers, location, port numbers, and cable type. COMMAND can link CAD-based building layouts, floor plans, cable runs, trays, equipment layouts, etc., with database information such as circuit records, tray capacity, inventory data, and connectivity information.

Users can click on icons to obtain closer views or text from pop-up windows. By clicking on an inventory icon, users can call up database records on the displayed device. COMMAND 5000 tracks the cable pair, pathway jack port, patch panel, multiplexer, and every other device connected, as well as how they are connected.

Users can also initiate moves/adds/changes in near real time by making the changes directly on the graphical map—the database will be automatically updated upon the user's approval. COMMAND 5000 can automatically generate reports, schedules, work orders, audit histories, and bills of materials during moves/adds/changes. COMMAND 5000 can now automatically determine the best cabling configuration to support a new LAN station, and it can automatically create a work order to accomplish the job.

The COMMAND HelpDesk option, which is actually the Remedy ARS, can help automate troubleshooting operations by tracking problem histories and building an experience database for ongoing help desk management.

Isicad's new release of Comprehensive Network Management (CNM) is a suite of integrated software products for the management of network-related information. CNM provides customers with a scalable set of network management solutions for all levels of the corporation. This new integrated suite of products is a dramatic step forward in providing the market with network management tools that are less complex and therefore easier to use. The solution set provides for a centralized database of network information that can be accessed directly via Unix workstations or from remote field offices on a native Windows PC.

The product line offers solutions for companies with large networks that need to gain control of their Information Technology assets and maximize network availability. The COMMAND family provides a modular solution with appropriate levels of information distributed throughout the enterprise, from corporate headquarters to technicians in the field. Isicad now offers a solution at each level of the network hierarchy and for every level of network management and staff—keeping in mind the user's concern regarding overall cost and resource commitments.

The product family is based on COMMAND 5000 physical network management software. COMMAND 5000 is a graphics-based tool that illustrates the physical relationship between all elements contained on an enterprise network. Graphics are integrated with a relational database for network information, including assets, connectivity, and other information that can be gathered via integration with other network management software. COMMAND provides dramatically improved troubleshooting response time and proactive planning and management of network changes. This results in significant cost savings and increased network availability.

Comprehensive Network Management is the application integration of COMMAND, COMMAND HelpDesk, and logical management systems. With CNM, network administrators have a proactive approach to managing the physical and logical elements of the network as well as implementing and tracking service requests, all from a single management station. The applications share and update data, offering an automated process for companies attempting to maximize the effectiveness of their network management staffs and tools.

Figure 5.22 shows the principal components of the product.

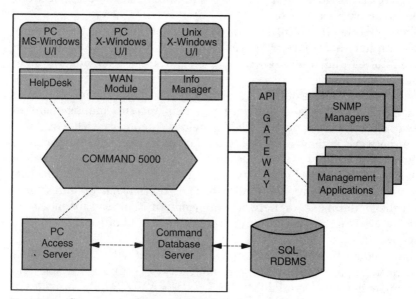

Figure 5.22 Components of Command 5000 product suite.

COMMAND Equipment Manager offers the foundation level of functionality for the rest of the product family. It is specifically designed for companies that want to track network assets and "high-level" connectivity—in other words, device-to-device relationships. The product provides a graphical view of this connectivity, giving the user a complete representation of the physical location of devices on the network. It includes the Move Manager module, which gives users an easy-to-use point-and-click capability to automate the process of making changes to the network. This graphical tool allows network operations staff to process changes to the network infrastructure quickly and efficiently, thereby decreasing budget expenditures and increasing end-user satisfaction.

The software integrates with leading SNMP management platforms and COMMAND HelpDesk. It also provides robust tools for network asset management with dynamic links to Oracle and Sybase relational databases. The product is specifically designed for customers who want to quickly document their networks and later take a phased approach to implementation by adding detailed levels of connectivity using the Connectivity Manager product.

COMMAND Connectivity Manager is an add-on module to the Equipment Manager product. It allows the user to detail and track connectivity down to the port and pin level. This level of detail is important in large-scale infrastructures where there are specific requirements to map:

- Device connections to specific hub ports
- Connectivity to the patch panel
- Services and applications that are provided to the desktop
- Detailed information on specific circuits down to the cable level
- Cable documentation and routing

This level of information is used for dynamically producing detailed work orders for managing moves, adds, and changes (MACs) to the infrastructure. For corporations that have a high level of "network churn," the ability to automate the MAC process provides a significant return on investment over a relatively short period of time. The system uses a more sophisticated version of the rules-based language that facilitates implementing corporate and industry standards for network implementation. This module contains a fully featured cable management system as well as all of the asset management tools. It is also the required base for the WAN Manager product.

COMMAND WAN Manager is an add-on module to the Connectivity Manager and is specifically designed for managing wide area network environments. It offers the unique capability to document links and circuits across the enterprise so that the user can quickly determine key information, such as

- Circuit ID
- Service-level agreements on all points of the circuit
- Service provider contact information
- Services and applications provided on the circuit
- Graphical view of circuit routing

Service provider contract information is easily accessed, allowing the user to determine the correct resource for troubleshooting over the WAN. This automated capability gives the network manager the ability to isolate specific problems and restore services faster. This is an extremely important capability that provides the end user with a means to build attractive payback (ROI) models.

This module also provides the capability to track bandwidth allocation in order to determine quickly if the network is over- or underutilized, thereby optimizing network utilization. The software can also track bandwidth allocation (by department and/or services) and bandwidth usage from network providers in order to produce accurate internal charge-backs. The bandwidth tool allows the user to fine-tune network capacity and in many cases reduce costs by canceling redundant or unnecessary circuits.

COMMAND Desktop Access specifically addresses the requirement to extend network management capability and control to remote and branch locations throughout the enterprise. COMMAND Desktop Access provides a solution set of common functions to be performed at the desktop, using a Microsoft Windows PC front end to COMMAND. This gives the local office the capability to make moves, adds, and changes; obtain circuit trace detail and asset and configuration information; and then easily transmit the changes back to the server. All field changes can be reconciled automatically with the drawings on a COMMAND workstation.

Field-office technicians or branch-office users can access remote COMMAND servers and make changes to the network without using the bandwidth necessary for conducting a remote X-Windows session or putting servers in field offices. For more site-specific functionality, the software offers a standard Windows interface such as Power Builder or Visual Basic. The prompts and menus are easy to customize and adapt to specific customer environments.

COMMAND HelpDesk is designed to automate network help desk and troubleshooting activities, dramatically improving response time and increasing network availability. COMMAND HelpDesk is a combination of problem and fault management applications and trouble-ticketing processes designed for seamless integration with Isicad's COMMAND product line and leading logical network management platforms.

COMMAND HelpDesk provides a workflow process designed to assist network users and technicians in reporting and resolving network problems. It assigns the problem to support staff, tracks its resolution, builds an experience database for ongoing help desk management, and notifies the requester when a service request is completed.

HelpDesk also provides problem escalation to meet guaranteed response times and attend to critical-level alarms. This ensures a consistent process for managing and resolving all levels of network problems.

COMMAND InfoManager is an object-oriented database front-end and report generator that makes managing large-scale network databases a much less tedious and time-consuming process. InfoManager is a true drag-and-drop environment that allows users to build screens, forms, and reports that link to Oracle and Sybase without having to write 4GL code. This functionality simplifies the whole process of database management and allows users to build screen forms and reports firsthand, eliminating the need for outside programming expertise.

The new technology provides users with a consistent database interface across platforms, greatly reducing training, implementation, and support issues. The product is distributed in three different formats: (1) InfoManager, which is the development environment, (2) ReportWorks, and (3) run time, which is bundled with COMMAND. Once forms and reports are built in InfoManager, they can be distributed across the network and accessed in the run-time version. The ability to now manage large-scale network databases without the requirement for 4GL programming skills greatly enhances the network operations staff's ability to deploy useful solutions faster and on a more wide-scale basis.

COMMAND ReportWorks is a subset of InfoManager which provides, as needed, on-the-fly report-generation capability. It is a GUI-driven product that allows ad hoc reporting without having to write any 4GL code. ReportWorks allows the creation of custom reports easily and quickly. This capability is extremely important to network staff who need to create numerous reports on asset, configuration, performance, etc., and don't have database programming skills.

Wireman from NHC Communications. Wireman tracks device location, using its object-oriented relational database to store physical and logical layouts. That means it can tell LAN managers not only an adapter's MAC address but also that the card is slotted into a workstation next to a potted palm on the fourth floor. Wireman is an SNMP manager in its own right, with its own MIB compiler. When used with Switchex and Shareit intelligent matrix switches from the same company, Wireman allows LAN managers to move devices without having to physically disconnect and reconnect them. All a manager has to do is simply drag an icon from one part of the network and drop it at another location. Changes are executed by sending an SNMP command to the intelligent switch, which changes the connections internally, eliminating the need for a technician to make the change manually.

Wireman documents the physical layout of the network. To do this, the package imports building blueprints and schematics, thus giving LAN managers the ability to view the network physically as well as logically. Both views are generated from a relational object-oriented database, which means that if the LAN manager changes one, the alterations are reflected immediately in the other. Wireman's graphical user interface guides LAN managers through the initial creation of the database. The package can automatically update the topology if SNMP-compatible probes and monitoring devices are plugged into the network.

There is a difference between Wireman and other products such as COMMAND 5000 from Isicad. Wireman runs stand-alone on a Windows machine rather than as an application on a management platform. This can be a drawback for managers of enterprise networks and is an issue that the company should address. But it is an advantage for smaller networking sites that cannot afford enterprise management software and expensive, high-performance Unix machines. Key features of this product are as follows:

- *Cable management.* Networks can be remotely reconfigured using simple drag-and-drop mouse techniques. Also, when NHC switch products are installed in the network, changes made at the Wireman console are automatically implemented in the wiring closet. For other changes, Wireman issues a Work Order that details the wiring change to be made manually. Wireman tracks work orders and trouble tickets by site, technician, and priority.

- *Automatic corrective action.* Wireman automatically implements user-defined scenarios based on SNMP-reported events and alarms. Corrective action includes unattended configuration changes, resegmenting the network, reassigning ports, and issuing SNMP commands to the other vendor's network equipment.

- *Node manager.* Users avoid direct interface with complex SNMP MIB variables by using node manager's graphical interface. Any variable or group of variables from one or more devices can be linked to a color screen icon. Instead of managing variables, users manage these objects by navigating through the network, clicking to retrieve description and status information, and issuing SNMP commands.

- *Logical and physical network integration.* By bridging together cable management and SNMP network management, Wireman offers more options for preventing downtime and restoring network service quickly when an outage does occur. For example, when SNMP reports very high traffic through a bridge, users on both sides of the bridge are suffering slow response times and lowered productivity. Wireman notifies the network manager and offers immediate solutions for resegmenting the network and keeping local traffic local.

- *Network views.* There are three different views offered by the product. The *geographical view* provides a reference of the network links between buildings. These links overlay a campus area, citywide, or national map. The *logical view* allows users to easily identify the computing resources allocated, such as mainframe ports, LAN segments, bridge, router, and hub connections, and server attachments. The *physical view* shows the network objects in their actual spacial layout in a building. Physical views contain the most detailed information about the network and are available to show horizontal cable distribution (workstations in offices on a floor plan), vertical cable distribution (the relationship of wiring closets), and wiring-closet details.

AssetWORKS from Digital Corporation.   From a central location using a single database, AssetWORKS automatically collects hardware and software configuration data, distributes applications and upgrades, and prints management reports. The user can manage remote and local software and hardware, no matter how dispersed and varied the network. All functions can be performed from a single console that uses a Windows graphical user interface, an easy-to-use tool that quickly increases the productivity. Inventory, software distribution, and reporting functions are completely integrated to quickly provide the information access and control that LAN managers need. For example, the user can, from a Windows NT station, drag and drop software packages to be installed on DEC OSF/1, Windows, SunOS, Macintosh, or MS-DOS systems. Then, when the upgrades are complete, the user can view the updated inventory information in a printed report.

These integrated capabilities result in better resource utilization, improved inventory management, more efficient upgrade planning, and enhanced service to the users. AssetWORKS is based on the System Management Server from Microsoft, and offers all the benefits of SMS, including administration capabilities at one or more sites throughout an enterprise network, remote maintenance, and troubleshooting. The other advantage is that the product supports an array of hardware and operating systems, including a variety of Unix-based systems.

Centralized management can be combined with local control for remote branches or departments. This allows users to delegate asset management tasks to business units. For example, a system management at a central site can distribute software to any networked desktop system, or the distribution can be performed from a local site server to desktop systems on the local LANs. With AssetWORKS, technology investments can be maximized:

- Redeploying assets as organizational and business needs change

- Managing the entire software upgrade process, from distributing client/server applications to updating inventory databases to reporting

- Understanding the total configuration needs, so the user can negotiate better volume pricing and service contracts

- Providing more effective support to the end users

Because the software automates routine configuration management and provides up-to-date information about assets, managers can always make the most informed decisions about using resources.

AssetWORKS gathers and maintains very detailed information about assets, such as machine, CPU, RAM, hard and floppy drives, hard disk partitions, controllers, servers, display types, users, groups, file systems, queues, and operating systems. For all installed software packages, the user can collect the product name, version number, publisher name, and directory location. License information can also be tracked. Data collection and database updates are done automatically over the network. The LAN managers can schedule the most convenient time to perform the data collection—when the user logs in to the server, during power on, or at a time the users specify.

Help desk, problem management, trouble ticket

Most of the tools available today provide extensive features that let help desk personnel resolve common problems within a short period of time. The addition of strong problem resolution features distinguishes today's products from yesterday's, which focused on recording and logging trouble calls. Most tools access a trouble database, a repository of solved problems. Depending on the power of the tool, there are the following opportunities for extracting the necessary information:

- Keyword search for well-defined problems

- Full text search in cases where the problem is not yet fully defined
- Case-based reasoning for problems defined and solved in the past

Help desk tools are also being fitted with application programming interfaces that enable them to be connected to other tools, such as asset management systems, electronic mail systems, fax servers, and interactive voice response systems. System integrators usually start with the integration of help desk tools into management platforms.

The following help desk, problem management, trouble-ticket applications are currently shipping:

Answer Computer Apriori

Clarity Incorporated Clear Logistics

Interference Corporation CBR2

CA-Legent Paradigm

NetLabs ServiceDesk

Peregrine Systems Cover/PNMS

Prolin Automation Pro/HelpDesk

Remedy Action Request System (ARS)

Scopus ProTeam

Software Artistry Expert Advisor

Vantive Corporation Vantive Help Desk

Vycor Corporation DP Umbrella

Apriori GT from Answer Systems, Incorporated. Answer Systems is on the forefront of problem resolution with its bubble up technology, which suggests the most likely problem causes are based on parameters that are unique to the caller, such as location, hardware, or network configuration. The tool also supports other problem-resolution technologies, such as index filtering, full text retrieval, and keyword searches. The user can store case and knowledge information in a proprietary Apriori database or a third-party database from such vendors as Oracle and Sybase. The product links to a variety of external systems, including electronic mail, network management tools, paging services, and automatic call distributors.

CBR2 from Inference Corporation. This product has very strong case-based reasoning technology. In fact, Inference Corporation is cooperating with many other companies by bundling this technology into other products' offerings. CBR2 has prepackaged knowledge bases for common Windows applications such as spreadsheets and word processors. Inference also sells CBR Express, an authoring tool for creating product- and user-specific knowledge bases. These knowledge bases can be spread across the enterprise on CD-ROMs, diskette, or via the Internet or dial-in servers, permitting end users to try solving their own problems before calling the help desk. CBR2 supports a wide range of SQL and relational databases. Integration with network management platforms is planned for future releases.

CA-Legent Paradigm.   Paradigm is a comprehensive problem management system. Paradigm models each critical phase of the problem management process; it supports a database capable of cross-referencing information on devices, trouble codes, status codes, priority classifications, and other key references. Using this database, Paradigm can associate several problems with a single device, correlating multiple events with a single trouble ticket; dispatch multiple actions through a single trouble ticket; relate multiple fields to a single reference on a form; associate service levels to a piece of equipment; and associate trouble codes with a type of problem

Paradigm filters raw events to detect suspicious patterns. Paradigm includes default filters, or users can customize or create their own filters to capture suspicious events before they cause major failures.

Paradigm immediately sends a message to appropriate personnel when a problem is recorded; it can also notify affected users to minimize phone inquiries or automatically dispatch customized E-mail messages (this requires an SMTP gateway). Audible alarms and pop-up applications are standard; users can add scripts to trigger pages, fax machines, and other notification methods.

Paradigm escalates unresolved problems based on user-defined priority levels and elapsed time. Paradigm maintains status until the trouble ticket is closed. It allows users to record successful repair strategies in "action templates" that operators can reuse to solve similar problems in the future.

Paradigm works with the underlying management platform to compile and maintain an inventory of network components, including MAC addresses, manufacturer names, service vendor names, phone numbers, and other device characteristics. The application maintains an accurate record of problems reported, actions taken, actual repair times, service staff performance, and other indicators that help users identify chronic problems and better evaluate how different brands of equipment meet specifications.

Paradigm allows users to track assignments and analyze help desk workload distribution. It can also track individual or third-party vendor performance. The product provides a full set of analytical reports for improving problem management, including resource failure and repair rates (MTBF/MTTR), vendor response time, and vendor loading. Paradigm supports a turnkey installation, including canned reports and sample trouble-ticket layouts. In comparison with competing products, Paradigm is less flexible than Remedy AR System; however, its predefined templates are preferred by some organizations that would prefer to have a trouble-ticket application preconfigured right out of the box.

Platforms supported are SunNet Manager, HP Open View, and IBM NetView for AIX. Integration is by filtering of event streams.

Remedy Action Request System (ARS). AR System is a combination trouble-ticket, help desk, workflow management application that runs on several major open management platforms. The product's modular, flexible design sets it apart from other other trouble-ticket applications that employ a more static, turnkey approach to problem management. ARS includes a "group engine" allowing it to be used as a work-flow tool—making it act like a trouble-ticket "spreadsheet."

ARS can be configured to automatically open up a trouble ticket once an SNMP trap is received from the management platform. ARS sends E-mail or a notification (such as a flashing icon) when an operator resolves an open problem. Users can browse through the ARS database to understand the status of requests submitted and potentially look up solutions, depending on the information that was previously logged. Users can generate a Query by Example to display similar problems and their resolutions and can add constraints to filter the results.

The customer can control the appearance and content of all ARS trouble-ticket forms and reports. ARS also supports creation of macros to automate responses to events. ARS includes a programmer's guide and an API. ARS has been integrated with several other third-party applications via command-line interface and Remedy's own APIs.

ARS creates a historical audit trail of logged problems. Users can make inquiries to the ARS database for problem analysis. No other trending or data analysis is supported, although data can be exported to other packages for that purpose. ARS includes a flat-file database and also supports hooks into several SQL databases including Ingres, Informix, and Sybase. Administrators can assign security privileges to each field on the ARS trouble ticket.

Remedy has integrated ARS with several other important applications, including Isicad's COMMAND 5000 and HP's NetMetrix. ARS employs a distributed client/server implementation. The modules communicate with each other using remote procedure calls. In order to support interconnected help desks, Remedy offers the Distributed Server Option. It means increased scalability to AR Systems by transferring management data, exchanging trouble tickets between two or more AR Servers. Data transfer is limited to single trouble tickets instead of complete tables. Also, users can specify which fields within the ticket travel to the target site. Update rights can be transferred as well, enabling any site to close a trouble ticket, not just the site that originated it.

Platforms supported are SunNet Manager, HP OpenView, and IBM NetView for AIX. Integration methods are SunNet Manager, HP Open-View, IBM NetView for AIX, Cabletron Spectrum, NetLabs/DiMONS, and AT&T StarSENTRY.

ProTEAM from Scopus Technology. Scopus develops and markets client/server-based customer information management systems that are flexible, scalable, and customizable. Scopus ProTEAM products enable the service, support, quality assurance, and sales organizations within a company to share critical information throughout all phases of the customer's relationship with that company. Scopus ProTEAM products include the following:

- SupportTEAM, for call tracking and technical support management
- QualityTEAM, a comprehensive system for tracking and managing defect resolution and quality assurance
- SalesTEAM that is a full-scale product- and sales-cycle management software, including modules for telemarketing, telesales, and field sales

The advantages reported by ProTEAM users include the following:

- *Heterogeneous client/server support.* The product runs in a client/server environment, with a combination of HP/UX, Macintosh, and Sun workstations linked to a Sun server running Sybase.
- *User-friendly interface.* The system presents users with an on-line. form to fill out; most fields have lookup values from which users can easily select. When the form is completed, the data is entered into the underlying database. All activity for each defect is recorded, allowing accurate tracking of historical data.
- *Flexible data manipulation.* Standard SQL can be used to access the data, perform ad hoc queries, and create reports. ProTEAM's open architecture and published API also provide broad connectivity to other products.
- *Extensibility and expandability.* Planned enhancements, including automating feedback to customers on problem status and automatic notification to management when a problem is critical and must be

fixed immediately, are made possible by ProTEAM's graphical work-flow automation and customization tools.

- *Worldwide information sharing.* The data replication server will also support the installation of additional servers at remote locations, providing real-time access to up-to-date information worldwide.

Scopus is working with many of its users to customize the product to specific needs.

Expert Advisor from Software Artistry.   Expert Advisor is a well-rounded tool that lets users customize it to their specific needs. But the product is delivered with a number of very useful features. The user gets source code and programming language with the product, which allows you to configure it to the size and number of users in the enterprise. The tool also has connectivity to E-mail, network management platforms, and mainframes.

Some of the strongest resolution technology is incorporated into this product. In fact, there are eight different technologies in the product, including a common problem database, hypermedia decision trees, and adaptive learning techniques. With an add-on product called Expert access, the user can export a knowledge base into a format that end users can employ. Software Artistry also sells Knowledge Paks, which contain knowledge bases for a number of popular products, such as operating systems and network equipment.

Vantive HelpDesk from Vantive.   The product is built around a comprehensive database of user, asset, and problem-tracking information. With this product, answers to problems are entered into the resolution database only once, allowing the user to capture and catalog solutions to problems as they are resolved. This establishes a comprehensive library of information and solutions that can be accessed and shared by everyone in the help desk organization. The result is that the knowledge of each help desk representative is leveraged throughout the company, giving users quick responses that are both consistent and accurate. Search options include the following:

- Keyword search of the resolution database
- Full text searches with Research Agent
- Case-based reasoning with access to CasePoint from Inference

By using Vantive Tools, the user can customize Vantive HelpDesk to meet specific needs without modifying source code or reprogramming. As the needs change, the application can change. Different groups of users can see entirely different screens and access entirely different capabilities. Elements that can be customized include the following:

- Look and feel of screens (e.g., labels, field names, layouts, default values, and buttons)
- Drop-down lists (e.g., product names, case status, impact levels, and error codes)
- Conditions for problem assignment, escalation, or insertion into to-do lists (e.g., classification, product, vacation schedules, vendors, organizational location, problem severity, and priority)
- Layout and generating procedures for reports

The product can be easily linked to many other applications using OpenLink features:

- Vantive ACDLink for integration to automatic call distributors
- Vantive CBRLink for access to case-based reasoning technology
- Vantive MailLink for specific integration with E-mail systems
- Vantive FaxLink for integration with on-line fax applications
- Vantive PagerLink for establishing a link to paging systems
- Vantive SourceLink for integration with source code systems

DP Umbrella from Vycor Corporation. DP Umbrella SQL for Windows is an asset and help desk management database that lets the user efficiently manage local area networks. The application monitors all aspects of hardware, software, and connectivity, including installation, assignment, and maintenance.

DP Umbrella SQL maintains integrated databases for systems, components, personnel activities, and tasks. Within each element of the database, the user can record very specific details. For example, the Components Module includes six tables to record administrative data, features, jack assignments, and information on the network topology, circuits, and ports.

When network users have problems, they call the help desk. DP Umbrella SQL's Help Desk Module lets operators deal with these calls quickly and efficiently. The operator listens to the caller's problem, then enters the symptoms into the database. DP Umbrella SQL matches the symptom with a cause and presents a solution. If the caller's problem is more complex, the help desk operator can issue a task or work order to different groups to execute the task.

The product consists of nine integrated modules:

- *Client.* This module allows the help desk operator to manage third parties, clients, or activities. This feature allows the application to be configured as an external help desk.

- *Components.* Use this module to organize all information on the system's hardware and software. For thorough tracking, the operator can break down a component into features or subcomponents. Components categories can be set up as subcategories for cross-references.

- *Contracts and vendors.* Use this module to track contract information such as pricing, effective and expiration dates, and maintenance coverage. This module includes predefined reports to use in contract negotiations and performance measurements. The LAN administrator can also use this module to classify vendors by the types of products and services they offer.

- *Help desk.* This module assists network administrators, PC managers, operations personnel, and end users in solving user's problems and ensures prompt response with its referral and warning system. This module lets the LAN administrator:

    Log, prioritize, and monitor calls

    Create historical files for equipment and users

    Issue and manage work orders

    Review records of calls

- *Jacks.* In addition to system hardware and software, the administrator needs to keep track of the system's wire and cable path. This is done through this module. It assigns IDs to each jack. The LAN administrator can define each jack in detail by its extension number, user, class of service, and the devices to which it is connected.

- *Personnel.* Use of this module helps to organize basic data for the users, including names, positions, departments, locations, and phone/fax numbers.

- *Purchase orders.* It creates purchase orders and requisitions for equipment, software, or features using the Purchase Order Module. The administrator can also receive partial shipments and place spare parts and unassigned items in the spare parts inventory.

- *Stock inventory.* This module is used to track equipment inventory and depreciation. Tracking monthly and yearly financial information such as costs, contracts, leases, and rents is also done in the Stock Inventory Module.

- *Systems.* Use of this module helps to set up new systems and to examine existing systems. A system is comprised of hardware and software components, the people who use those components, and the jacks that connect the components.

DP Umbrella SQL is an integrated database that keeps track of components, personnel, jacks, and wirepath information. The information is stored in a relational database and is available for LAN management staff. Components of this product are displayed in Fig. 5.23. Each piece of the network can be entered and maintained in the DP Umbrella SQL database.

With all this information entered into the database the help desk operator can use it to diagnose user's hardware, software, connectivity, and wirepath questions and requests. When the help desk takes a call from a user, all the information is available for the help desk operator to review. By using an Activity entry window, the operator can keep track of each call a user makes and maintain a complete history of calls from that user.

The product is very rich on various master codes, including those for administration components, class of service, features, manufacturers,

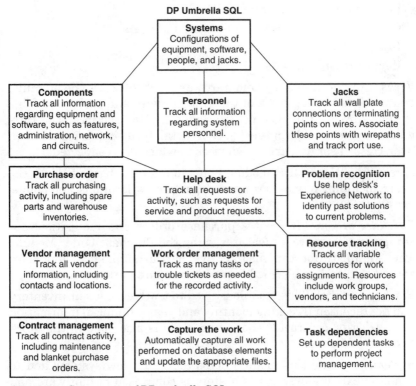

Figure 5.23   Components of DP umbrella SQL.

network, call types, problem causes, close conditions, resolution criteria, symptoms, locations, and personnel type.

DP Umbrella SQL has been successfully used to support help desk activities. The Help Desk Monitor provides a single window for reviewing caller-related information. This monitor allows operators to identify the caller, review the caller's previous call details, and determine if a new activity should be opened.

When end users have problems, they call the help desk. If a caller has a specific request for a new upgrade on hardware, software, network, changing location, or if a component needs work, the help desk assists in carrying out the task. The product ensures prompt response with its referral and escalation system. The help desk application is taking advantage of utilizing the database with various masks, such as caller profiles, resource profiles, and open tickets. It can be configured with E-mail applications. If so, when a call is closed, the application will send an E-mail message notifying the caller that the call has been processed and the problem resolved. E-mail can also be used for referrals.

The Expertise Viewer is a knowledge base of previously encountered situations, which assists the operator in working through user's questions and coming to a resolution. This extension gives the ability to review historical information regarding resources, symptoms, causes, and resolutions.

Security management products

Based upon the requirements addressed in Chap. 3 for security management, several powerful products will be evaluated here. This list is not complete by any means. In particular, in the area of virus protection, the reader may find a large number of solutions.

Antivirus from Central Point. In order to implement centralized virus management for NetWare, this product can be very useful. The following functions are supported for centralized security administration:

- Complete protection of servers.
- Central Setup enables centralized administration of virus scans and reports as well as virus signature updates on both clients and servers.
- Central Talk is a communication protocol that allows all Central Point utilities to exchange information such as alerts and control parameters.

- Central Alert supports the NMS alarm manager via SNMP, MHS, alphanumeric, and numeric pagers.

Antivirus offers advanced virus protection:

- Virus Analyzer detects unknown viruses without preinfection data.
- Library of over 2000 virus signatures for detecting known viruses.
- Real-time scanning of files read from and written to servers.
- Optional TSR programs continually and transparently monitor workstations.

The product supports NetWare 3.x and 4.x and SFT III servers, and scans DOS, Windows, Macintosh, and OS/2 files. It supports configuring NetWare Loadable Modules from an administrator's PC. The log-file viewer uses a spreadsheetlike format with movable, sizable columns, and lets you export data to other programs, including spreadsheets and databases.

TeleSec from E-systems.   TeleSec is the basis of the Secure Wide Area Network for the U.S. Defense Department. As companies move toward open systems, employees must exchange sensitive information outside their office via LANs and through public phone lines. The TeleSec Secure WAN combines encryption, authentication, and authorization mechanisms. The security of the TeleSec system can be quantified by the time demand needed to gain unauthorized access to it—it would require centuries. There are three basic elements of the system:

- *Access Controller.* It sits between the protected computer and its communications facilities and acts as a border guard, challenging each remote user in real time as the connection is attempted.
- *Access Terminal.* It is a circuit card placed within the remote user's PC, which acts as passport to identify the user to the Access Controller when the connection is attempted.
- *AuthCard.* It is a smart card that is the same size as a credit card, but it contains a microprocessor, memory, and a communications interface. The AuthCard has a built-in DES algorithm and contains electronic information that uniquely identifies the user.

Other features of TeleSec include the following:

- Implementation of the NIST-certified Data Encryption Standard (DES) engine for authentication and encryption. Positive authentication of a user's identity is established through use of the AuthCard and a personal identification number (PIN). The AuthCard is tamperproof and cannot be electronically penetrated or altered. After a programmable number of failed PIN entry attempts, the AuthCard will automatically disable itself. Authentication processing occurs through symmetric, encrypted, challenge-response protocols between the AuthCard, Access Terminal, and Access Controller.

- After successful authentication, the Access Controller correlates the user's service request against preestablished user profiles to determine access. These profiles are defined as a collection of rules and databases that are uniquely assigned to each authorized user. Applicable rule criteria may vary from a simple yes or no to a more sophisticated response based on time of day and frequency of access. The database is maintained by the system administrator from the security administration terminal.

- Uniquely designed automated key management. During authentication, the Access Terminal, AuthCard, and Access Controller become cryptographically synchronized. For applications that require protection of data during transport, the Secure WAN automatically and transparently establishes an encrypted data link, end to end, between the remote user and protected resource. Data is encrypted using DES.

- Secured access control for remote asynchronous WANs provides complete flexibility for communications managers looking for a network security system. The access-controlled, multiplatform system is based on modular construction. The point-to-point system can attach to a server, terminal, data storage device, or any hardware needing controlled access.

- Transparent mechanisms allow the user to operate using normal modem communications software packages.

- Physical tamper protection is effected by the combination of the Access Controller, Access Terminal, and the AuthCard.

This product can also be utilized to protect both WAN and LAN segments of the networks.

SecurID from Security Dynamics. Security Dynamics develops, markets, and supports software and hardware products that prevent unauthorized access to information on computers and networks. SecurID is a user identification and authentication technology. It positively identifies, then permits network and system access by authorized users, from both inside and outside the organization. It dramatically and cost-effectively enhances the security of existing networked systems without forfeiting user convenience, remote access, the power of networks, and centralized file serving. It also offers meaningful audit trails and other reports that ensure detection, easy management, and true user accountability.

The SecurID is an access control security token that is used to positively identify users of computer systems and networks. Used in conjunction with Security Dynamics' hardware and software access control modules (ACMs), the SecurID Card automatically generates a unique, unpredictable access code every 60 seconds. SecurID technology offers access security for a wide range of platforms in one easy-to-use package.

To properly identify and authenticate an authorized user, two factors are necessary. The first is something the user knows: a memorized personal identification number. The second factor is something unique that the user possesses: the SecurID Card. The changing number displayed on the card guarantees the user must have the card in his or her possession at the time it is used. Each card is programmed with a proprietary algorithm, which, in combination with unique parameters, assures that every number displayed is valid for only that user at that time.

To gain access to a protected resource, a user simply types his or her secret PIN, followed by the current access code displayed on the SecurID Card. Patented technology synchronizes each card with a hardware or software ACM. Authentication is assured when the ACM recognizes the card's unique code in combination with the user's secret PIN. The simple, one-step SecurID log-in results in the highest level of computer security provided by a token—it is also the easiest to use and administer. The ACM may reside at a host, operating system, network/client resource, or communications device—virtually any information resource that needs security.

An added level of security can be implemented with a SecurID PIN-PAD Card. This is especially appropriate for environments where a user's secret PIN might be compromised through electronic eavesdropping. Other uses include voice-based applications where the PIN could be compromised if spoken. The PINPAD card gives users who are accessing the network the option of sending an embedded combination of the user's secret PIN and SecurID card code over the line. Using the keypad on the face of the card, a user simply enters his or her PIN directly into the card, which generates a unique card code—the passcode. With the PIN incorporated and hidden within it, this passcode can be communicated without any exposure or potential for compromise.

Security Dynamics' family of hardware ACMs works in conjunction with the SecurID Card to protect the systems and networks from access by unauthorized users. Hardware access control modules add a vital layer of access security while maintaining log-on convenience.

They connect directly with any RS-232 asynchronous host and provide access through leased lines, dial-up modems, networks, X.25 networks, workstations, or terminals.

An integrated software-based security server, the ACE/Server centrally authenticates a user's identity and centrally manages user access to network resources via the Internet, a public gateway, remote dial-up modems, leased lines, workstations, terminals, PCs, or direct connections. The ACE/Server-protected network resource cannot be compromised by electronic eavesdropping and observation or by repeated password-attack schemes.

Figure 5.24 shows a typical structure with ACE/Server in operation. The benefits of this arrangement are as follows:

- Cost-effective access security solution for all TCP/IP networks.

- Operates on a variety of Unix platforms, establishing a protective perimeter around selected network-based nodes.

- Centralizes network authentication and security administration.

- Scalable for protection of additional users and workstations.

- Log-on procedures remain quick and easy.

- Audit trails and reporting assure true user accountability.

- Application Programming Interface (API) available for user customization.

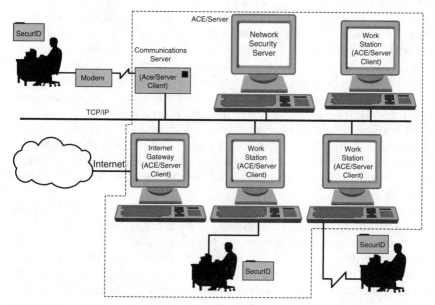

Figure 5.24   ACE/Server in operation.

- It may be used in conjunction with PC security software to add protection to data stored in the PC.

ACE/Client for NetWare provides enhanced access security for Novell NetWare environments. Used in conjunction with SecurID Card and ACE/Server, ACE/Client for NetWare protects the network from access by unauthorized users. Functioning as a client to the Security Dynamics ACE/Server, ACE/Client for NetWare requests remote users to provide valid user credentials before a log-in or an attach to a NetWare server is established. The credentials are then transmitted from the ACE/Client LNM to the ACE/Server for authentication. The log-in and attach process is simple and quick, and ACE/Server processing is transparent to the user.

ACE/Server software provides network security for Telebit's Net-Blazer product line of dial-up remote LAN access products. The software-based security server protects network data by identifying and authenticating users attempting access to the network. The SecurID-technology is also used by Bay Networks hubs, providing enterprise networks with advanced security features and passcodes that eliminate unauthorized access to corporate data. ACE/Server network security software also protects LANRover remote access products from Shiva Corporation.

Eagle Network Security Management System from Raptor. This product addresses the need for network security and overcomes the outstanding problems of less robust approaches such as packet filters. It is an integrated gateway system comprising a coherent security architecture. The Eagle solution can be configured to let selected sites have access to systems and network components while excluding all others. The Eagle solution runs on IBM, Hewlett-Packard, and Sun workstations. Because the Eagle security system is installed as a stand-alone solution, loopholes are eliminated. The first workstation of the Eagle is called the Gateway (Fig. 5.25). It has the responsibility of taking network traffic packets and handing them off to another network. Usually this means taking them from the Internet and putting them onto the local network (and vice versa). The Gateway opens packets, examines their content, and ensures that they cannot potentially damage the network.

Once the packets are checked for safety, the Gateway builds new ones with the same contents. Hence, only packet types for which there is construction code can be sent out from the Gateway. It is impossible to send unauthorized packet types because there is no code to generate them. This prevents "back doors." The new packets are sent out through an entirely separate network interface. By not sharing the

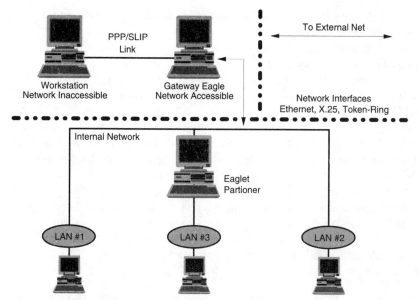

Figure 5.25 System architecture of Eagle.

input interface, it is impossible for undesired packet types to bypass the Gateway and get onto the network unchecked. When a user outside the network wants to use resources within the network, they must go through the Gateway box. Authorizing access is handled by the security administrator. The Eagle architecture has an added security dimension—separate authorization workstation that is connected to the Gateway box. The Authorization and Gateway workstations are connected through a special link that is not part of the network. This stops remote users from interfering with the authorization process. Only the security administrator can change the authorization file.

There is considerable flexibility in the permission process. The system administrator can specify that individual or entire groups of outside machines can use individual machines inside (or vice versa). They can specify times of day when service is permitted or denied. And they can ask to be alerted when certain requests are made, even if they are allowed. This feature is important, for example, in the case of a brokerage firm that would want to know every time a connection to them is made, regardless of the time of day.

In order to provide yet another level of security, the Eagle architecture includes a watchdog feature that constantly monitors the network. All unusual activity is logged, traced, and then killed. This whole process is called *active security* and differentiates the Eagle from passive security approaches.

The Eagle has rules that help it define suspicious activity. The Eagle quietly gathers information about where the attempted break-in is originating, how it got there, what the person appears to be trying to do, etc. This lets systems administrators find the perpetrator, and they have the reports and documentation to later prosecute them. The system also provides real-time notification of suspicious activity to a specified fax or beeper number.

Setting up the authorization file is easy. The default condition allows users to freely go outside to the Internet while allowing no one from the outside to come in. The security administrator can edit the default file to allow certain external access, but from the first minute that the Eagle is up, security is guaranteed up to the highest level. Every aspect of the Eagle is fail-safe, ensuring that security will not be compromised. The default condition for an outage of service is denial of service to users. Only when everything is operational can traffic move between the outside and inside users.

Other Eagle features include the following:

- *Spoofproof.* It is relatively easy for a system wizard to spoof machine addresses (i.e., pretend that the user's machine is a different one). Because the Eagle prevents access to the internal structure of the network, an outsider cannot determine which of the machines is down and pretend to be one of them in order to steal data and information.

- *Autochecking.* At random times the Eagle system gives itself a detailed physical examination, which includes computing an unforgettable metric of the state of its controlling software. If it has been changed in any way from the correct state, it will cease to function. This prevents an insider from patching the executable programs to let a cohort bypass the Eagle.

- *Encryption.* Similarly, the Eagle software self-encrypts and -decrypts to make it extremely difficult for someone to reverse-engineer it. The Eagle even checks the identification of the computer it is running on to protect the user.

The Eaglet was designed to meet the security needs of interdepartmental LANs. It offers the same security features as the Eagle, but sits inside the network and lets the user control which machines can talk to each other. The Eaglet uses the Authorization workstation of the Eagle for all of its access information. Hence, there is only one master file to maintain and secure, not multiple routers and bridges to administer and synchronize.

EtherGuard prevents people from entering networks through modems. When PCs with modems are heavily used in the organization, security breaches may increase significantly. EtherGuard works in conjunction with Eagle to match physical addresses on Ethernet boards to those authorized to access the network. If access is requested via a modem, EtherGuard refuses to return the Ethernet address. Therefore, if somebody is dialing in from off-site, access will be denied except to the immediate local area network of the caller. The strength of this product is simplicity. There is no way to avoid using the software, because the Eagle and the Eaglet will refuse to allow communication from machines that are supposed to be running EtherGuard and do not provide the secret handshake.

All three products of the Eagle family can be easily configured depending on the actual needs of the users.

Backup and disaster recovery products

Chapter 3 addressed the importance of backup systems and procedures for LANs. This fact has been recognized by many vendors. There are a number of products on the market with very different operating features. Important solutions include the following:

Arcada with BackupExec for Netware and for Windows NT

Cheyenne with ARCserve for Netware

Emerald Systems Corporation with Xpress Librarian

Epoch with Enterprise Backup

Legato with NetWorker

OpenVision with OpenV*NetBackup

Palindrome Corporation with Network Archivist

Symantec Corporation with Norton Enterprise

Sytron with ProServer

Usually, the products address the needs for NetWare or for Windows NT; it is rare that the same vendor addresses both. The products use different technologies for backup; all combinations of Chap. 3 are valid here, including the use of servers and/or workstations shared or in stand-alone versions as the backup machine. A couple of products are described in some depth.

BackupExec for NetWare and Windows NT. The software package for NetWare includes a NetWare Loadable Module (NLM) to run on a primary server and agents that run on a variety of workstations and servers. Network managers can use the software to configure backups from either a server or a workstation acting as a management console.

Backup Exec can run on SNMP-based platforms such as ManageWise from Novell and OpenView from Hewlett-Packard. Another management enhancement, called AgentView, lets LAN managers view BackupExec agents regardless of the network on which the computers hosting the agents run. The product also features an Agent Accelerator, an NLM residing on remote servers and compressing data to be backed up before it is sent over the network. This conserves valuable bandwidth.

It offers central administration of multiple backup stations in the Windows NT environment. Client software is offered for Macintosh and Unix clients. There are good notification capabilities, including Microsoft mail, MHS, and pager facilities. But the documentation and on-line help could be better. The installation requires some manual editing of system files. In certain cases when a backup operation is running, the user at the backup station cannot access other applications.

Other enhancements include the following:

- Full compatibility with Novell Directory Services as well as full backward compatibility to lower Netware versions

- A smart client technology that automatically backs up failing hard drives on Compaq workstations

- The ability to configure BackupExec to selectively reroute backups to alternate tape systems on the same or different servers in case the original tape system fails

ARCServe for NetWare and for Windows NT from Cheyenne.   This product is aimed at Novell users by providing support for 4- or 8-mm quarter-inch cartridge, digital linear tape autochangers that automatically change tapes in tape drives and optical storage. It can back up files from DOS, Unix, OS/2, and Apple. It provides unattended backup and scheduling that can be customized through an automated script generator. A parallel streaming feature enables users to perform simultaneous processing of file backup and restore operations on as many as seven storage devices attached to a single Small Computer System Interface adapter. In addition, it supports alerts via SNMP and electronic mail. It also supports Windows NT with fully automated installation, easy-to-add clients and with a good graphical user interface. The NetWare version is very fast; the Windows NT version is slow in comparison to other solutions.

The architecture for Reliable Managed Storage represents the company's effort to produce a consistent storage management solution across an enterprise network from the desktop to the mainframe. It is designed to give systems administrators a standard for data interchange, backup system reliability, and user interfaces. The architecture consists of basic services such as backup and restore facilities for Net-Ware and Windows NT, as well as advanced storage devices, including online database backup and hierarchical storage management. The strategy demands that the services be delivered on two computing levels. Cheyenne has the first tier of this strategy with its ARCsolo product line, a workstation-based suite of products. Under the second tier, the company offers services through its ARCserver products, design to back up servers running under various operating systems. For the high end of the enterprise, Hierarchical Storage Management products are offered.

Xpress Librarian from Emerald Systems Corporation.   This product is limited to NetWare environments. The product is workstation-oriented and offers strong support for autochangers and file migration to off-line storage. Besides the regular duties of changing tapes when they became full, Xpress Librarian also tracks which tapes contain files that have been migrated plus those in the tape magazine that are designated for backup. The graphical user interface makes the product easy to learn and use. It also offers a rich set of features for configuring backup and managing data for file restoration, migration, and grooming. Finally, it has a strong unattended backup feature that enables the software to automatically log on to remote servers, back up the files, and log off. Information on backed-up files is very detailed. Performance is decent even with workstations; encryption support is offered. But, the product does not support alert or status messages over the network. There is no facility for viewing the status of backup jobs, and installation involves a considerable amount of manual file editing. Customization can be difficult.

Enterprise Backup from Epoch.   This is a full-featured client/server backup and recovery system, which brings mainframe-class functionality, reliability, and flexibility to distributed computing environments. This single solution, which supports a variety of platforms, centralizes storage management activities to effectively reduce administrative overhead and costs. It uniquely combines both client- and server-level software to address today's backup/recovery requirements.

The product's client software, when prompted by the server, scans the local file system and sends to the server the files to be backed up. Server software manages client backups and provides central configuration, scheduling, and administration of the clients. Epoch Enterprise Backup's high-performance architecture easily scales to a range of network environments. It provides unattended, automatic backup and recovery services to stand-alone or networked Unix workstations and servers, PC clients, relational database management systems, and multiclient networks across the enterprise.

By completely automating backup functions, the product helps to increase organizational productivity. Administrators are relieved of time-consuming tasks, and spend less time managing the entire backup process for distributed, heterogeneous networks. The software supports flexible backup options, giving system administrators the freedom to select backup types and arrange backup schedules that meet their specific networking requirements. Administrative graphical user interfaces simplify installation, configuration, and maintenance. Recovery GUIs allow users to quickly and easily recover their own files or directories without the need of administrator intervention.

Figure 5.26 shows Epoch Enterprise's backup and recovery solution. The most important features of this product are as follows:

- High performance and scalability
- Intelligent schedule management, monitoring, and reporting
- Stable on-line backups
- Support of relational database management systems
- Quick and easy file recovery
- Complete and automatic volume management

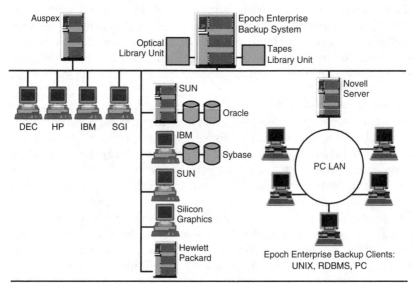

Epoch Enterprise Backup employs a two-tiered architecture for enterprise-wide backup and recovery. This single solution performs multiple, simultaneous backups of heterogeneous platforms, systems, and data formats.

Figure 5.26   Epoch Enterprise Backup.

- Flexible backup options
- Resilient to client and network failures
- Part of a comprehensive storage management strategy
- Support of multiple backup media

Additional products of the family support Hierarchical Storage Management (EpochServer) and management of inactive and active files in this storage hierarchy (EpochMigration).

NetWorker from Legato. This product shows exceptional strengths in its ability to support multiple operating systems and networking environments. As a client/server backup and recovery software product, NetWorker, transparently interoperates between Unix and NetWare platforms. It supports backup of most desktop platforms and can direct DOS, Unix, and OS/2 files to different storage devices.

Legato provides support for both server- and workstation-based backup systems that can support file backup and restoration processes simultaneously. The package is also working in a TCP/IP environment. It includes a disaster/recovery utility and supports multiple concurrent backup operations, which can write to single or multiple tape drives. It can issue alerts via E-mail and network broadcasts. Backed-up data can be encrypted. But all clients and servers must be individually defined to the backup station before they can be backed up. Relatively slow performance is reported for Windows PC clients.

The product is also able to back up Windows NT servers and workstations to NetWorker backup servers running Unix or NetWare. Hierarchical Storage Management Systems maintain server disk space by automatically migrating files by age, last access, and other rules to optical and tape drives, leaving behind placeholders so that users can recall data. The enhanced version of NetWorker lets clients access multiple data management functions: backup and recovery, archive, and eventually HSM services. Windows NT systems can be managed from a Windows NT station or any other NetWorker console.

OpenV*NetBackup from OpenVision. This product coordinates backup and recovery tasks. The product is capable of routing little-used files to departmental or central storage facilities to reduce the amount of data that requires backup. Users can back up distributed databases from Oracle while they are in use. The product is strong, with duplicating tapes for disaster recovery. It helps users eliminate downtime by handling backup and storage functions while systems are still on-line. OpenVision also supports the Enterprise Extension, which lets users back up data to a central storage system instead of to a local departmental server. It can work with other components of the application suite (e.g., OpenV*archive). The drawback of the suite is that it works only on Unix machines in TCP/IP networks.

Network Archivist from Palindrome Corporation.   This product is aimed at the network manager looking for advanced NetWare support. The server-based Network Archivist LNM runs as a NetWare Loadable Module, while the other version runs on DOS workstations. Both support SNMP for alerting and status surveillance. The NLM version supports Novell's Storage Management System specification.

Additionally, the packages back up NetWare and NetWare Directory Services files. Their other strengths include a rich set of backup maintenance, scheduling, and troubleshooting utilities and functions.

Norton Enterprise from Symantec Corporation.   This is the easiest NetWare-based product to install and use, rich in advanced features for backing up large, multiserver networks—the only NetWare package that supports job redirection and automatic distribution of backup processing across multiple backup stations. Clients and servers can be backed up automatically when added to the network. There is good backup speed in most cases, combined with the use of recycled older tapes.

But the backup speed is impacted by the automatic, full, byte-by-byte verification of backed-up data, which the user cannot disable or simplify. Subsequently, the software performs only slowly and exhibits some of the slowest restore rates, as reported by users about the performance.

ProServe from Sytron Corporation.   This is considered as the best-performing backup package for NetWare and Windows NT. In particular, in ease of use, ease of installation, and ease of configuration the product is superior to many others. Facilities for automatically installing client software are offered. The product is very flexible in terms of scheduling and verification options. It includes support for tape autoloaders and autochangers. But the performance of certain functions is much better for Windows NT than for NetWare. There is limited flexibility in using the program's integrated search facility. Alert messages warn the network administrator if problems are sent in broadcasting mode requiring more bandwidth than necessary.

Many changes are expected in this area. Products are getting more mature and will most likely be combined with others. The combination will show two faces:

- Tight connections to leading management platform products, such as OpenView, NetView for AIX, OpenVision, Solstice, and Spectrum

- Combination with other utilities, such as disaster recovery support, storage management support, help desk support, distribution and version control of software, security and virus surveillance, in order to build specific application suites for LAN administrators

Products for legacy management

In many cases, LAN segments must work together with other networking segments, including mainframes, wide area networking equipment, and facilities. Enterprisewide management requires the joint management of all managed objects. A few products are listed here that may help to jointly manage legacy equipment and local area networks.

Command/Post from Boole and Babbage.

OpenView needs support from applications especially in the area of legacy management and of managing non-SNMP devices. Command/Post is categorized as a typical platform extension application to ease the management of heterogeneous devices by using the technique of console emulation.

Functions of the product include message parsing and collection of alerts from multiple device types. Alerts are intercepted at the RS-232 port. Command/Post supports management of multiple types of SNMP and non-SNMP (legacy) systems through alert consolidation. Product features include the following:

- Message filtering
- Alert prioritization
- Manage translation
- Alert databasing

Command/Post also supports Service Point connection to NetView/ 390 and an SQL database. The operator interface is OSF/MOTIF. Command/Post intercepts alerts from printer ports (RS-232) or ASCII streams of multiple element management systems or devices, consolidating, processing, and displaying the messages on a single console. Message processing, or parsing, takes place in Command Post's Alert Logic Filter Editor (ALFE). ALFE removes control characters, translates tool-specific codes into meaningful information, and adds connectivity information. By knowing connectivity, ALFE can perform alarm correlation by analyzing multiple alarms and suppressing secondary alarms to highlight root causes.

A transformer routine scans device and element manager's message streams, looking for specific messages. Detection of these messages will trigger user-defined actions. Users can also specify alert filtering rules

to suppress low-priority messages. Command/Post supports a simplified menu-driven GUI and selective routing of alerts to operators and
supervisors. Command/Post's ALFE component can automatically
close outstanding alerts when restoral messages are detected.

Operators can also issue commands to element management systems via Command/Post's terminal emulation facilities. Each individual terminal emulator appears as a window on the Command/Post
screen. Command/Post supports VT100, 3270, and many other forms of
terminal emulation.

Command/Post comprises a Unix-based server and one or more
client workstations. X-terminals are supported for display only. Also
included is a communications server, a programmable interface device
manufactured by 3Com supporting conversion of RS-232 connections
to Ethernet.

EventIX from Bridgeway Corporation. EventIX is a software tool that is
fully integrated with and complements SNMP Network Management
Platforms such at NetView for AIX. It provides users, such as network
management staff, with an easy and time-saving way to develop network and system management solutions using the built-in features of
the SNMP Manager. Extending the reach of the SNMP Manager to fully
manage Legacy Systems (such as PBXs, modems, and X.25 switches) is
one such solution.

EventIX is designed to interact with a variety of network and system
environments, such as NetView for MVS, Legacy element management
systems and devices, SNMP Managers and Agents, X.25, and the Unix
operating system itself. By capturing events generated in each of these
environments, applications can be built to do the following:

- Filter, correlate, translate, and log these events locally or remotely.
- Initial actions, such as generating traps, sending NetView alerts,
  changing icon status on the console, or sending a Legacy Control
  command based on an SNMP SET.

EventIX is a set of tools that eliminates the need to write code.
Development is driven by an X-Window GUI with simple point-and-
click operations, so that sophisticated and complex applications can be
generated with minimal training. The EventIX product line consists of
the following:

- Development tools: Application Generator (AG), Extensible Proxy
  Agent Tool (EPA), Graphical MIB Builder, MAP Builder
- Network Interface Modules
- Event Detector

- Off-the-shelf applications, including gateway and function-specific applications

LegacyWatch from MicroMuse Limited. LegacyWatch integrates legacy systems with open management platforms such as NetView for AIX. Any systems that can be managed via a character-stream interface can be managed by NetView for AIX and LegacyWatch.

As Open Management Platforms become standards for managing open networks, it is necessary to manage older non-SNMP, nonnetworked devices through these same platforms. LegacyWatch is a software product that provides a gateway from the old to the new, allowing any device that is manageable from a character terminal to have its status and events integrated into NetView for AIX.

LegacyWatch makes a character-stream connection to the target device—usually using TELNET through a terminal server—and scans the messages that the device generates. LegacyWatch also can periodically conduct a dialog with the device to elicit messages. If a message matches an event condition, it is passed up to NetView for AIX, together with key information from the message. NetView for AIX maps the event onto the object that represents the device and displays it as a change in icon state.

Typical applications include the following:

- *Console management.* Monitor messages from computer consoles of any operating system and generate alarms from critical conditions.
- *Device management.* Manage non-SNMP devices, such as communications multiplexers and switches, via their control ports.

EView/Open for NetView for AIX from NetTech, Incorporated. EView/Open integrates graphical management of SNA resources integrated into NetView for AIX's GUI to give a total view of SNA- and SNMP-managed enterprise networks. VTAM SNA resources are automatically represented graphically and are color-coded according to their status and displayed hierarchically. This display makes it simple to view the status of the network and quickly locate the source of network problems. A GUI improves productivity by reducing the time that it takes to solve network problems.

EView/Open provides NetView functions on the workstation. Filtering alerts and alarms is also performed on the workstation level. Since most of the data processing is done on the workstation, EView/Open reduces expensive mainframe cycles consumed by network management activity as well as reducing network management's dependency on those resources. EView/Open Tools allow you to do the following:

- Perform equivalent downsized NetView functions
- Automatically represent SNA devices and their status
- Trigger platform automation actions
- Manage SNA resources
- Identify and depict current configuration of the SNA network
- View all SNA resources
- Filter alerts and messages at the workstation level
- Identify location and cause of a failure on the SNA network
- View multiple domain SNA networks in a single view
- Use an interface to a downsized problem management system
- Use an X-Windows interface to view SNA data
- Use menu-driven SNA operator commands

NetTech's logical-to-physical SNA correlation (LPC) process is an EView/Open option. The LPC option allows automatic physical-to-logical topology correlation for SNA physical units on LANs. This provides dynamic tracking of SNA devices' physical locations.

NetTech's problem manager interface extends IBM's mainframe Info/Manager high-level application programming interface (API) to the open system workstation problem manager application environment. The PMI option allows the capability to selectively transfer and update trouble-ticket reports to and from the mainframe and workstation problem managers.

Surveillance for uninterrupted power supply

Uninterrupted power supply (UPS) is a surge protection device that also has the capability of supplying clean power for a relatively short period of time in the event of a total power failure. Computer systems can use this short period of time to gracefully shut down all of its systems. If the desire is to protect just the electrical components in a router, wiring hub, digital modem, and dial-up modem units, then a simple surge protector is all that is needed. There are no disk drives to protect and no such thing as an orderly shutdown.

If the communication equipment is located adjacent to PC database servers or application servers, then it could use the same type of UPS, in addition to SNMP-agent software kept within one of the PCs. There are three different SNMP architectures for UPS systems, illustrated in Fig. 5.27. The initial configuration of the SNMP agent will require an IP address and subnet mask and the community names for read and write access, as well as the IP addresses of the management console for

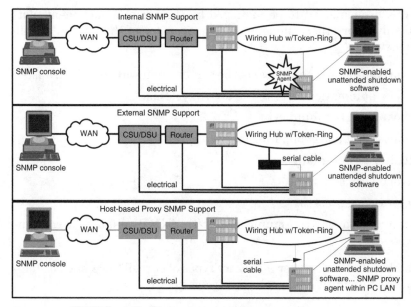

Figure 5.27 SNMP for controlling uninterrupted power supply.

sending alerts and traps. Software updates would be handled via the software-distribution software, and configuration changes would be handled by the management console. Each of the three methods of building an SNMP-based UPS has its advantages and disadvantages:

1. Alternative A: Internal SNMP support

   Advantages. It requires an internal PC within the UPS for initial configuration and booting.

   Disadvantage. Additional costs.

2. Alternative B: External SNMP support

   Advantages. Requires an inexpensive external PC with minimum hardware configuration.

   Disadvantages. External PC will require power outlet on the UPS. If UPS command is sent to power down, the SNMP agent will not work.

3. Alternative C: Host-based proxy support

   Advantages. Makes use of existing PCs in the installation.

   Disadvantages. If the PC crashes, the SNMP agent will not work and the management console would be unable to cold-boot the power cycle on the PC.

UPSs are expected to be managed by the same management platform suited for other components. The operator of the system can do the following:

- Invoke automatic shutdown of the servers, gateway, and file transfer.
- Invoke automatic reboot to the above systems.
- Invoke inverter shutdown.
- Monitor and notify of power loss.
- Monitor power quality.
- Invoke UPS self-tests.
- Record power losses.
- Conduct two-way communication with SNMP adapter for configuration.

Combination with other telemetry types of surveillance, such as temperature, humidity, and smoke, is always possible.

Systems Management

In particular in client/server environments, integrated management of servers, clients, and LANs are very important. This section is dedicated to the management and administration of systems components, including operating systems, peripheral devices, databases, and business applications.

Unix systems management

Among others, the following applications for Unix systems management are currently in use:

AT&T Computer Manager

Breakaway Software PICUS

Calypso Software Maestro Vision

CompuWare Eco Tools

Digital Analysis OSJEYE*NODE

HP OmniBack Link

HP OperationsCenter

HP PerfView

HP Systems Manager

IBM AIX Systems Monitor/6000

Landmark Systems Probe/Net

Network Partners, Incorporated, Trapper

Open Network Enterprises M.O.O.N.

Patrol Software DDS/Patrol Link

Unison Tymlabs Maestro

Unix Integration Services HeartBeat

The growing number of Unix systems management applications now being developed for or ported to SNMP-based management systems indicates the convergence of network and systems management. While many of the existing applications are currently less than comprehensive, the large potential revenues from a rapidly growing deployment of distributed Unix client/server environments are tempting these and other vendors to develop and enhance these products and the levels of integration they support.

Breakaway software PICUS.   The main function is to monitor multiple clients and servers in distributed Unix computing environments. This application has been implemented on NetLabs/DiMONS, SunNet Manager, HP OpenView, and IBM NetView for AIX. PICUS is integrated at the menu-bar level; it intercepts alarms from the management platform and feeds that information into the PICUS graphical user interface.

PICUS is designed to help systems administrators monitor complex networks of multiple clients and servers. The product itself has a client/server architecture. PICUS is available in two versions: (1) a server-based version, which supports system monitoring and configuration of a single Unix server and (2) a networked version, which allows administrators to monitor and configure a series of networked hosts and workstations. (See Fig. 5.28.)

PICUS is capable of monitoring Unix file systems, printers, ports, users, and user groups. File system monitoring includes tracking disk usage by file system, user name, and group name; alarms are triggered when user-defined thresholds are exceeded. PICUS also provides reports, such as disk usage summaries, disk utilization, and disk usage by user and group.

PICUS can make it easier for users to perform incremental or full backup on all disk partitions or on selected file systems. Because PICUS prompts operators for all necessary information to create the backup, operators do not need to know specific Unix backup commands. PICUS also includes a security module that includes native executables for checking security loopholes and logging threats in a file

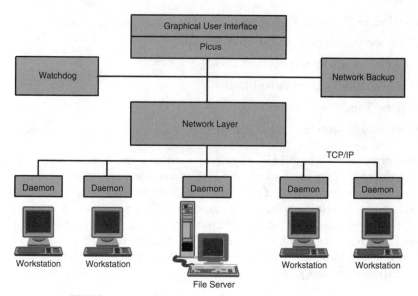

Figure 5.28   PICUS structure (Breakaway, Incorporated).

for later viewing. The product also allows operators to configure users, groups of users, TTY ports, or create custom printer modules.

Calypso software MaestroVision.   The main function is to monitor Unix (SunOS, SGI IRIX, IBM AIX, DEC Ultrix, HP-UX) and Windows NT workstations. This application has been implemented on Cabletron Spectrum. MaestroVision takes advantage of Spectrum APIs and inductive modeling technology to suppress secondary alarms and infer status of network components.

MaestroVision works in conjunction with Cabletron Spectrum to provide a highly graphic display of Unix and Windows NT system resources. MaestroVision automatically creates a model for each file system, CPU, and disk subsystem in the distributed computing network. Operators do not need to know primitive commands or manipulate text to monitor or configure computing system resources.

MaestroVision monitors and controls all processes running on the network. It graphically depicts CPU usage, RAM, applications, swap space, and local and remote file systems. MaestroVision allows operators to apply user-defined thresholds on activity levels and other metrics. Operators can also create administration groups to enforce organizational policies on groups of workstations.

MaestroVision's "process views" list all processes present on a system; operators can also obtain details on any single process by selecting that process from the list. Operators can also add, modify, or remove users from groups or workstations using MaestroVision. Operators can set thresholds on system components and applications. Version 2 of MaestroVision allows users to initiate actions off an alarm by triggering scripts, as well as to set an alarm based on more than one condition— such as CPU utilization greater than 90 percent for over two minutes.

HP OperationsCenter. The main function is to monitor Unix (HP-UX, HP-MPE, SunOS, and IBM AIX) workstations. The product is running on HP OpenView. For integration it uses menu bar; alarms from OperationsCenter are displayed on the HP OpenView map.

OperationsCenter is a distributed, client/server program that operates from a central management station and interacts with intelligent software agents installed on the managed Unix systems. The intelligent agents perform localized polling, collect information, and process it before forwarding pertinent information onto the central OperationsCenter or HP OpenView console. Agents use remote procedure calls (RPCs) to communicate processed information.

Operators define thresholds on systems parameters and set polling intervals at the central management console; this is automatically downloaded to the managed nodes. Polling ("monitoring service") is done locally at managed nodes to minimize network traffic overhead. Filter conditions can be specified at the managed nodes to further minimize traffic.

OperationsCenter includes a Workspace Manager feature allowing administrators to specify the managed nodes and message groups for which each operator is responsible. The Workspace Manager creates a specific task-oriented work environment for each operator.

The optional OmniBack application supports networked backup and restore. The optional Hierarchical Storage Manager application manages online storage for servers and client disks, supporting automatic and transparent migration of files between magnetic disks and optical disk libraries.

An optional HP OpenView Software Distributor application can verify installed software on remote target systems. Using Software Distributor, LAN administrators can build processes that monitor the integrity of software in remote locations. The product supports comprehensive packing, configuration, and removal of software throughout the network.

HP PerfView. The main function is performance tracking on Unix systems (HP-UX, SunOS). This application has been implemented on HP OpenView (through OperationsCenter). The integration methods are Menu-bar integration and alarms from PerfView appear on the HP OpenView screen.

HP PerfView tracks recent performance data for HP-UX and SunOS systems; PerfRX is a performance analysis tool for evaluating historical trends, load balancing, and problem diagnosis. HP PerfView includes two components:

1. Central analysis software (incorporating HP Network Node Manager)
2. Intelligent agents that reside on the managed systems

PerfView provides an umbrella for the HP GlancePlus stand-alone systems management utilities. It monitors the following performance factors across the network: CPU utilization; CPU queue depth and process wait information; number of processes; disk utilization (percentage peak activity disk queue depth and process wait data); physical and logical I/O rates; memory utilization; disk activity due to virtual memory management; swap utilization; network packet rate data; application utilization of CPU; disk I/O; and resources on which processes are blocked.

PerfRX provides historical trend analysis on transaction rates and response time, as well as parameters monitored by PerfView. This information can assist in workload balancing and capacity planning. PerfRX can display collected data in line, pie, or stacked graphs.

Unix systems security

At present, there is only one security management application shipping for use on open management platforms.

OpenVision OpenV*SecureMax. The main function is the centralized security management for distributed Unix systems (SunOS, HP-UX, AIX, Ultrix, and OpenVMS). This application is running on SunNet Manager and uses a menu bar as an integration technique.

OpenV*SecureMax allows an operator to access the security status of multiple workstations and servers from a central console and perform a detailed security audit, if necessary, and correct any security problems. The GUI leads the operator through a complete four-phase security management process. This process includes audit of overall security level, analysis of specific security risks, correction of identified security exposures, and monitoring of security-specific changes over time. OpenV*SecureMax can also generate reports for auditors or managers who may not be familiar with Unix technology. The product is also capable of producing a consolidated network report providing a single-line summary status for each monitored system.

OpenV*SecureMax assesses security for five major security categories: system files, networks, accounts, passwords, and file systems. An Audit Facility allows users to generate reports explaining security risks on specific systems as well as recommendations for correction. An Analyze Facility produces detailed reports on specific files and accounts with security exposures. By using the Correct Facility, operators can create customized shell script files to address security problems.

Users can create baselines using OpenV*SecureMax and compare them to future security reports. Baselines are stored in encoded, data-checked models. OpenV*SecureMax can monitor SunOS, Ultrix, HP-UX, and AIX systems. It is a read-only product that runs on the Unix operating system.

Electronic software distribution

Due to the large number of servers and workstations, it is no longer feasible to distribute software manually. This segment summarizes a number of alternatives, whereby the depot can be prepared on host computers (category A), on other servers (category B), or on workstations (category C).

Hewlett-Packard HP Software Distributor.   Product category is B.

Features
1. *Servers supported.*   HP-UX on HP9000 and SunOS; support for Novell NetWare; Microsoft LAN Manager. Support for AIX and Solaris.
2. *Clients supported.*   Clients supported include HP-UX and SunOS. Support for MS-DOS, MS-Windows, NetWare, LAN Manager, IBM AIX, and Solaris.
3. *Network operating systems / network protocols supported.*   TCP/IP, Novell NetWare, and LAN Manager.
4. *Software / hardware inventory.*   Administrators do not need to manually define each host in the host database if HP OpenView is installed. Software Distributor can obtain topology information about network nodes from HP OpenView, and administrators can click on nodes to indicate they are targets for distribution. However, this capability appears to be limited to TCP/IP nodes only, and it is not clear that the product supports grouping of targets for distribution using any flexible criteria. Software inventory reporting is not supported.
5. *Prerequisite and corequisite checking.*   Software Distributor can manage software dependencies, including software prerequisites and corequisites.
6. *Package creation.*   A single distribution depot can contain software packages for multiple platform types (distribution depots are

staging areas). Software Distributor has a flexible shell that allows for inclusion of pre- and postinstallation scripts.

7. *Distribution / installation.*   Supports both push and pull distributions. "Cascading" distributions (fanout) are supported in this manner: the depots (gateway staging areas) can copy a complete or partial package and then initiate local distribution over the LAN. This capability exists today for Unix clients. The fanout distribution mechanism is different for PC clients, and it requires a PC controller acting as the staging area.

8. *Scheduling.*   Administrators can schedule individual jobs or a combination of jobs for specific times.

9. *Version control.*   Packages are organized into products, subproducts, and file sets. The administrator can keep multiple versions of the same software in a single depot.

10. *Software licensing / metering and auditing.*   Not supported. A possible future feature, but no time frame given.

11. *Network management platforms supported.*   HP provides an interface from Software Distributor to HP OpenView Windows that gives administrators point-and-click capability to select target nodes for distribution. SNMP trap integration between HP OpenView and Software Distributor is not supported. However, HP is working on tight integration between HP OperationsCenter and Software Distributor. Currently, some customers are engineering their own interfaces to launch Software Distributor from OperationsCenter and to obtain status messages. Status information in HP OperationsCenter can be accessed from HP OpenView. However, HP OperationsCenter cannot manage DOS/Windows nodes—only HPUX, MPE, SunOS, AIX, and UNIXSVR4.

Product strengths.   Customers perceive a synergy between HP OperationsCenter, HP OpenView, HP AdminCenter, and HP Software Distributor—even though integration is more of a promise than a reality at this point. HP is effectively marketing Software Distributor as a standards-based solution by virtue of the product's influence on the forthcoming IEEE POSIX 1387.2 standard and its use of DCE RPCs.

VARs and systems integrators that have strong ties to HP are inclined to work with and push the product, even though it may not be the best on the market.

Product weaknesses.   HP Software Distributor does not include any leading-edge, object-oriented technology. It does not support OS/2 or Windows NT clients. The product is relatively new, and there are bound to be bugs.

IBM AIX NetView Distribution Manager/6000.   Product category is B.

Features

1. *Servers supported.*   IBM AIX RS/6000 POWERstation or POWER-server.

2. *Clients supported ("Change Control Clients").*   Any workstation capable of supporting OS/2 2.0 or higher, MS-Windows 3.1, IBM DOS 5.0.2 or higher, or MS-DOS 6.0 or higher, IBM AIX 3.2.3 or higher. NetView/DM Agents are also available for HP-UX. Support for SunOS and Solaris is also expected.

3. *Network operating systems / network protocols supported.*   TCP/IP Token-Ring, TCP/IP Ethernet, TCP/IP WAN (APPC for LU6.2) connectivity requires IBM's SNA Services/6000 software. Novell NetWare support is provided by NetView DM for NetWare.

4. *Software / hardware inventory.*   Automatic inventory is not supported. However, integration with NetView for AIX is supported and nodes defined in the NetView for AIX database are usable by DM.

5. *Prerequisite and corequisite checking (hardware, software).*   DM/6000 checks for disk space at both the server and client. Seven system software prerequisites are also checked.

6. *Package creation.*   IBM implements a proprietary method of defining packages, file sets, and bundles and moving them from one platform to another.

Using "installp" procedure from the AIX server, the executable package (including corequisites and prerequisites) is bundled by DM/6000. Users bundle pre- as well as postinstall scripts in a package.

DM/6000 allows grouping of clients into logical distribution lists. Data compression and translation is supported.

7. *Distribution / installation.*   Users can execute "install with activation," and the remote target machine will boot up with the latest code. DM/6000 supports both push and pull installation. Installation methods supported include installp for AIX, Configuration, Installation and Distribution (CID) for OS/2 or DOS, replication installation for client environments, and Disk Camera for Windows and DOS (update of system configuration files). Redirected software installation is also supported for NFS or AFS environments.

Remote unattended operations are supported for AIX clients and for OS/2 and DOS clients with CID-enabled applications. Rollback scripts may be included for AIX and CID-enabled distributions. File retrieval from client to server is supported in all environments.

8. *Scheduling.*   Support for scheduling and timing of software changes is supported.

9. *Version control.*   Change control is supported.

10. *Software licensing / metering and auditing.*   The product provides no intrinsic support for licensing/metering or auditing. However, IBM does resell Gradient's NetLS product for this purpose, and Net-

View DM/6000 and NetLS are packaged together as an option (not bundled).

11. *Network management platforms supported.* IBM NetView for AIX only. Currently, IBM provides a set of hard-coded status reports that go back to NetView for AIX. In the future, the user will be able to specify which messages are forwarded to NetView for AIX. Also in the future, DM/6000 will be able to access information about identified nodes stored in the NetView for AIX database and vice versa.

12. *Other features.* IBM is redesigning its DM product family using what it calls *portable code.* NetView for NetWare is the first product based on this portable code. This will enable IBM to roll out new features more quickly across its entire DM product line.

IBM provides upward scalability in its MVS-based NetView DM product. Customers are distributing software to over 10,000 workstations from a single focal point with this product. This may be attractive to organizations seeking to centralize software distribution. IBM is currently promoting a three-tiered architecture where MVS can control numerous AIX change control servers (which, in turn, distribute down to multiple clients). However, IBM plans to strengthen the AIX offering to provide better centralized control from the AIX platform.

Product strengths. IBM's NetView/DM family now supports a wide range of client environments, including the mainframe MVS and client/server systems (UNIX/AIX, HP-UX and SunOS, and Solaris; also OS/2, Windows, and DOS workstations) as well as NetWare LANs.

IBM has already persuaded scores of vendors to support its Configuration, Installation, and Distribution (CID) specification for remote unattended operations at DOS and OS/2 workstations. Competing software management packages that do not support this standard could be at a disadvantage.

Tight integration with NetView for AIX is attractive to organizations seeking to gain efficiencies across both network and systems management operations.

IBM has received a lot of favorable press concerning its DM products. Although competing products may be better, many users have not heard about them.

Product weaknesses. DOS clients require TSRs. Many users may see this as a limitation. Servers require RS/6000 hardware. Many users want the option of using a software management package on whichever hardware platform they choose.

Currently, NetView DM/6000 does not support the use of client profiles for large-scale distributions. This facility, called *distribution planning,* is now offered only on the MVS products. IBM is not using leading-edge, object-oriented technology. IBM has been bogged down by SystemView guidelines and the delay of CORBA.

Microsoft Hermes (Systems Management Server).   Product category is C.

Features

1. *Servers supported.*   Windows NT.
2. *Clients supported.*   Windows PCs. Macintosh clients can also be supported, but they must be manually installed within the SMS network.
3. *Network operating systems/network protocols supported.*   Primarily Windows NT, LAN Manager. Windows NT Sender service can be configured to use NetWare, NetBIOS, TCP/IP, and other LAN or remote access protocols.
4. *Software/hardware inventory.*   SMS will identify the hardware and software configurations of PCs as well as allow administrators to electronically distribute software to them. Inventory data is stored in Microsoft's SQL Server 4.2. Anything that can talk to an SQL Server database can make use of the inventory data. SMS will take advantage of DMTF technology to collect desktop inventory information in DMTF MIF format from those PCs that support that standard. Inventory data are collected at log-in. A Software/Hardware Inventory Collector (SHIC) program runs on each client, creating an inventory file. These files are collected by SMS file servers and converted into MIF format.
5. *Prerequisite and corequisite checking (hardware, software).*   SMS has the ability to check for user-specific prerequisites, such as disk space and software-version levels.
6. *Package creation.*   SMS will ship with an extensive list of applications (over 2000) that it will automatically recognize. Other applications will be flagged for the administrator's attention. Administrators can create scripts for different installation circumstances. These scripts can take into account departments, software installed, disk space, and other attributes.
7. *Distribution/installation.*   Software distribution can be set up as mandatory, optional, or a combination of push and pull, whereby an end user can refuse the update for a number of days, after which it becomes mandatory. Users are informed at log-in if a software update is scheduled.

   Administrators can use the drag-and-drop technique to designate a distribution to an individual PC or groups of PCs.
8. *Scheduling.*   The timing of distribution and of installation can be independently scheduled.
9. *Version control.*   Information not available.

10. *Software licensing/metering and auditing.* SMS can track how many applications are active on the network, but it does not perform software metering.

11. *Network management platforms supported.* No specific platforms supported. However, the existence of an SNMP agent built into Windows NT will allow SMS to forward traps to SNMP management systems.

Product strengths. This is from Microsoft, and it's the product everyone has been waiting for. Hermes will certainly change the whole outlook of desktop management, including software distribution to Windows NT environments. Microsoft is undisputably the dominant force in desktop PCs today.

Product weaknesses. This product is designed for Windows NT only. It is a departmental product, not an enterprisewide solution.

Novadigm Enterprise Desktop Manager. Product categories are A and B.

Features

1. *Servers supported.* DM:Manager originally supported MVS only. Now, EDM:Manager is available on AIX servers, HP-UX servers, and on Solaris. EDM:Administrator runs on OS/2, Windows, and ISPF 3270 systems. Support has recently been added for AIX. Support for HP-UX and for Solaris is provided as well.

2. *Clients supported.* OS/2, DOS, Windows, AIX, and HP-UX. Support for Macintosh and Windows NT is planned.

3. *Network operating systems/network protocols supported.* SNA (LU2 and LU6.2), Novell IPX, NetBIOS, and TCP/IP through gateways.

4. *Software/hardware inventory.* EDM includes an asset management facility for auditing the user desktop and reporting on hardware/software contents. Administrators can generate hardware/software inventory reports by user, workgroup, or department.

5. *Prerequisite and corequisite checking (hardware, software).* EDM establishes a two-way link before distribution, providing information about the physical attributes of the target workstations—checking memory, processor size and speed, and hard disk space—as part of the installation setup process.

EDM uses patented object-oriented technology that eliminates the need to maintain and update thousands of entries on various control lists. EDM provides desktop-driven application assembly that can take into account numerous differences at the client level, such as supported monitors, printers, and CPU memory configurations. This allows administrators to assign applications to individual users or workgroups by "connecting" them as related objects (EDM automatically decides "who gets what") according to user-established, centrally defined policies.

6. *Package creation.*   EDM allows administrators to deploy installation scripts (called *methods*), which are written in a REXX-like procedural language. Methods can check for current versions, corequisites, or run conversion processes. Administrators can define package Versions that customize the components of applications and assign appropriate contents for a variety of desktop configurations.

7. *Distribution / installation.*   EDM supports object-based transport management for network-efficient, object-based distribution of changes as large as entire directories or as small as single parameters.

By using an object-oriented transport process rather than a file-oriented process, EDM is able to distribute changes more efficiently. The object-oriented design permits encapsulation of files or application scripts into objects. EDM supports on-demand local assembly based on policies and user configurations. Administrators can build and maintain an enterprise model of relationships between users and applications.

EDM supports object-based installation/activation to install and activate versions of packages automatically as authorized.

8. *Scheduling.*   Scheduling is supported.

9. *Version control.*   EDM supports a change management facility that automates the process of identifying, packaging, delivering, and controlling versions of configuration updates to the desktop. EDM uses a "differencing" technology to synchronize changes automatically at the object level.

10. *Software licensing / metering and auditing.*   EDM does not support software metering.

11. *Network management platforms supported.*   Novadigm has recently ported EDM:Manager to AIX; this version can forward traps to IBM's NetView for AIX; also, any information in the NetView for AIX database can be accessed from EDM, although EDM cannot be launched from the NetView for AIX console.

12. *Other features.*   Novadigm Enterprise Desktop Manager has a three-tiered architecture: EDM:Manager, EDM:Administrator, and EDM:Client. EDM Manager is the enterprise server that configures applications and management policy relationships in a central object-oriented database repository that resides on an MVS mainframe. EDM:Administrator allows systems administrators to configure EDM: Manager and distribute management services to the desktop. EDM: Client is the desktop-resident facility.

EDM's object-oriented design also allows companies to enforce application and component inclusion and exclusion rules at the desktop level. In other words, EDM's object-oriented design and rules repository easily supports policy-based security. EDM can reuse existing RACF and NetView definitions; the product supports direct interfaces to existing security packages such as RACF, ACF/2, and Top Secret.

Product strengths. Novadigm EDM is designed from the start for enterprisewide (rather than just departmental) software distribution. The vendor has established an aggressive telemarketing campaign for the desktop market and OEM/VAR relationships for desktop platform/systems integrator channels.

According to Jim Herman of Northeast Consulting, EDM's tool's nature makes the product extremely open-ended and applicable for solving a broad range of systems management problems. Herman calls EDM "the greatest operations innovation since trouble tickets." Novadigm's object-oriented approach is different than Tivoli's. Whereas Tivoli Courier concentrates on modeling users and workgroups to support user administration, EDM focuses on modeling specific configurations of desktops using its "object differencing" technology. This allows administrators to handle thousands of differences in desktop configurations without the burdensome maintenance of control lists.

Product weaknesses. The original version of the product currently does not support a staging area. In the future, this feature will be supported for NetWare, OS/2, and Unix.

The mainframe-based version of the product is considered expensive.

The product requires significant effort to install; administrators must define the "policies" outlining the target systems and business requirements of each group of target systems. Some systems administrators may be put off by the esoteric object-oriented technology, as they must deal with schemas of objects to create the relationships between those objects. But the product lacks a set of canned interfaces to leading third-party systems and network management products— particularly HP OpenView.

DOS clients are TSRs; Windows clients are DLLs.

NetWare Navigator (part of ManageWise).   Product category is A.

Features

1. *Servers supported.*   Any NetWare 3.x or 4.x server. Does not support Unix workstations.

2. *Clients supported.*   Arly PC/XT/AT or PS12 or compatible. Available on OS/2 and Windows-based machines, too.

3. *Network operating systems supported/network protocols supported.*   Connectivity through most network operating systems.

4. *Software/hardware inventory.*   Not supported.

5. *Prerequisite and corequisite checking (hardware, software).*   Not supported.

6. *Package creation.* The ability to build packages is supported; however, the vendor declines to elaborate.

7. *Distribution / installation.* Store-and-forward operation. Stores files until workstation users are ready to receive them. PC- and dispatch-initiated transfer allows control at any point on the network. Supports automatic retry. PKZip data compression is supported. Supports fanout distribution.

8. *Scheduling*

Automatic event execution can automate a wide variety of tasks, including locking the keyboard, invoking Network Navigator for a software update or data collection function, and initiating full-screen applications such as Lotus 1-2-3, which cannot be automated by .BAT files. Also supports up to eight predefined processes.

Flexible schedule definition lets users define schedules by day, by week, by month, or for another period. Can be set individually or by group; can be set locally or centrally.

Automatic cold / warm booting supports automatic cold booting (including memory diagnostic check), warm booting (simulated Alt/Ctrl/Del), and other special functions.

Keystroke recording lets users easily develop command files that simulate PC keystrokes needed to carry out certain tasks. Can be developed and edited using any DOS text editor.

9. *Version control.* Information not available.

10. *Support for software licensing / metering and auditing.* Not supported by Navigator; however, Novell does resell Gradient's NetLS.

11. *Network management platforms supported.* Does not support any major network management platform at this time. But integration with NetView for AIX is planned.

Product Strengths. NetWare support. Navigator offers an integrated and badly needed extension to NetWare, and it also benefits from its close association with Novell. In addition to its association with NetWare, Network Navigator supports the widest range of hosting and communications options currently available. With the exception of AIX and AS/400 systems, most IBM platforms can act as the "dispatcher."

Some users consider Navigator's store-and-forward experience to be a strength. However, this technology is becoming outdated and does not support the complexities of enterprisewide distribution as well as newer, object-oriented models. While most suppliers use some variation of the store-and-forward approach as the technical underpinning, Annatek, who is the designer of the product, has been at it the longest and, in fact, based its original business on store and forward.

Product Weaknesses. Navigator does not yet target Macintosh and Unix workstations, nor can it act as host on either of these platforms. Novell has had programs in development for several years to change this situation but has yet to announce any product.

The major uncertainty concerning Network Navigator is the change in design philosophy. If it is eventually subsumed under NetWare, Network Navigator may lose its strength of wide platform and communications configurability. More important, many of the capabilities pioneered in its mainframe-centric versions may not transfer easily to the client/server environment. Novell states that it is its intention to make the product line functionally equivalent and scalable. However, Novell's decision to sell Navigator to another company casts doubt on the product's long-term viability. Also, the product is second-generation—its inability to account for desktop differences and lack of comprehensive packaging support make this a questionable choice for enterprisewide distribution.

Tivoli Courier.   Product category is B.

Features

1. *Servers supported.*   SunOS, HP-UX, Solaris, Motorola Unix SVR4.

2. *Clients supported.*   SunOS, Solaris, HPw, Motorola Unix SVR4, PC/DOS, PC/Windows NetWare.

3. *Network operating systems/network protocols supported.*   Supports FTP and NFS for copying Tivoli TME agents to DOS/Windows, NetWare, and Unix clients.

4. *Software/hardware inventory.*   A limited capability. While Courier keeps track of all software distributed, it does not support discovery of hardware/software attributes of clients on the network. Courier will discover and identify a node once the Courier agent is loaded. However, it cannot provide anymore information about that node.

5. *Prerequisite and corequisite checking (hardware, software).* Tivoli's support for prerequisite and corequisite checking is weak, according to users. Pre- and corequisite checking can be done, but it requires some finagling on the user's part. According to Tivoli, this can be done as a preinstall script, but it is not a product feature.

6. *Package creation.*   Batch file package describes a set of files and directories. Courier allows administrators to specify which subscribers (set of hosts) is to receive each file package. Administrators can also create nested file packages whereby a file package is added as an entity of another file package. Nested files may contain instructions about data in the nested files. Nested file packages also allow administrators

to run different pre- and postinstallation scripts for different portions of a single distribution.

Courier supports the ability to modify file packages as text files (import/export). Administrators export the file package to a text file, modify it using a text editor, and then import it back into Courier. This may be useful for long lists of files or nested file packages.

Courier supports pre- and postinstallation shell scripts as well as C programs and Perl scripts (and NLMs on NetWare servers, or .BAT, .EXE., or COM files on DOS and Windows clients) before or after the distribution, during a commit operation or after removing the old software.

7. *Distribution / installation.* Using Courier's "commit" feature, administrators can distribute new software days in advance of the actual upgrade. The commit program creates symbolic links between the new software and the users directories, and it removes those links to activate the new software.

Courier supports definable "domains of influence" or policy regions to help regulate who gets what.

Courier supports fanout distribution, allowing users to route a single copy of software across the gateway using a remote machine as a local distribution point to multiple targets. Administrators can fine-tune this process to control the percentage of network bandwidth used for distribution and to determine which machines will serve as distribution points. When distributing copies of software to multiple target machines, Courier performs the distribution in parallel.

Also, Courier does not use the store-and-forward method at interim distribution locations (multihop distribution), which requires that the gateway machine at each interim site have enough memoxy/disk space to handle the distribution. Instead, Courier uses a "dataflow distribution" process whereby packages flood through intermediate sites instead of collecting and being forwarded.

Any Unix machine in a Tivoli Management Region can be a source host, from which distribution of file packages occurs. Administrators can compress file packages before distributing them. Administrators can also specify backup paths for files that are overwritten on the target machine.

8. *Scheduling.* A flexible scheduling feature is provided.

9. *Version control.* Versions of software are tracked.

10. *Software licensing / metering and auditing.* Not supported. Tivoli is working with third parties to provide this capability in a future release.

11. *Network management platforms supported.* Tivoli Enterprise Console only. Integration between Tivoli Enterprise Console and IBM NetView for AIX is currently under development.

12. *Other features.*   Security is supported via Tivoli's Sentry application. To perform an operation within Courier, the administrator must have the required authorization from Tivoli's Sentry security mechanisms. In general, the "senior" role is required to create and edit file packages and validation policies. The "admin" role is sufficient for viewing file package profile properties and distribution file packages to subscribers.

Product strengths.   The product's leading-edge, object-oriented technology allows for a great margin of extensibility. The product is extremely flexible and open, providing many options for packaging and distribution, such as nested file packages, fanout distribution, dataflow distribution, and various pre- and postinstallation programs as well as scripts. Security options are comprehensive.

Product weaknesses.   Courier lacks software/hardware inventory support. It does not currently interface to any network management systems to obtain this data. Also, the product does not support software metering or file versioning. Courier does not allow administrators to create distribution plans based on nonsystem attributes such as geographic location or department. Courier does not support IBM AIX, OS/2, or NCR environments.

Tivoli's support for prerequisite and corequisite checking is weak, according to users. Pre- and corequisite checking can be done, but it requires some finagling on the user's part.

Software metering products

Software license metering is still a relatively underdeveloped area of LAN management. Manufacturers of software distribution packages or management applications suites offer solutions. There is no standard way of managing licenses. The users are expected to define their metering programs, which applications they want to meter, and how many licenses they own.

The following products offer software metering capabilities:

- NetView/DM with NetLS from IBM
- ManageWise from Novell
- LANDesk Manager from Intel
- Norton Administrator for Networks from Symantec
- Frye Utilities for Networks from Frye
- LAN Management System from Saber
- Brightworks from McAfee Associates

Usually, the following criteria are used to evaluate metering solutions (Marks 1995):

- Application—server-based
- Application—client-based
- Permissive metering
- Lockout option
- Queueing users until licenses are available
- Overflow logging
- License pooling across servers

Based on (Marks 1995), the application suites offer the following capabilities. Setting up metering is very similar with all of the products. In LANDesk Manager and Frye Utilities, the user selects which executable codes should be metered from a directory listing. Norton offers for the same purpose a master software list. For all three products, the LAN administrator can define suite licenses by selecting multiple executables for one application name. The users then inform the metering program how many licenses they own. They also specify whether users who were denied access should be placed in a queue until a license is available, whether any privileged user gets access even if it violates the license count, and which users should not be allowed access to the application.

If the license count is exceeded, an entry is made in the metering log file. Alerting features are either built-in (LANDesk, Frye) or can be scripted (Norton).

Brightworks offers metering as an NLM. The steps of setting up individual and suite licenses are easy to follow. This product is strong with logging and reporting features.

Saber metering offers solutions for all metering requirements. The procedures are complex to set up, but they work. Metering is new to this application suite and, as a result, it suffers less from inherited interface problems. In particular, performance tracking, lockouts and user's queueing are functioning well. There are similarities to Brightworks in terms of using the "set" command to collect statistics. But, Saber offers fewer reporting features.

Applications and database management

The management of applications directly impacts the productivity of users. This is particularly true with new client/server systems with distributed applications. Before deciding about the right strategy and tools, the following questions are important to ask (Carnese 1994):

- Are LAN operations automatically notified when applications encounter critical errors?
- Can applications dynamically respond to changes in environment?
- Why is the application's key transaction now taking substantially longer than usual?

Application management is the ability to observe and modify an application's internal state, if necessary. Monitoring database management systems errors encountered by an application, notification is necessary for the application to bring down the DBMS in order to diagnose the problems. Status indicators and actions to notifications may be very similar to other managed objects. Application management is absolutely necessary to ensure the desired level of business system availability. In other words, all mission-critical software must be managed. This applies whether software is internally or externally developed. Open and distributed systems present a far more complex environment than systems that are proprietary and centralized. Detailed knowledge and control of applications are critical for problem diagnosis and dynamic reconfiguration. Today the consequences of insufficient application management can be characterized as follows:

- No centralized point of observation of application-generated errors
- Difficulty in analyzing history of application events
- Lack of ability to dynamically change system configuration
- Lack of knowledge of what is happening from application and end-user perspective

Key applications management functionality includes the following:

- Information logging
- Event distribution
- Process monitoring
- Performance logging

Information logging is the basis for all other activities. Functions and requirements concentrate on the following items:

- API for message generation from all application processes
- Messages categorized by process type, subsystem, and severity
- Messages tagged with user request identifier, allowing correlation of system events with user behavior
- Dynamic modification of logging levels by subsystem and by type of process

- Tools for searching historical and event type repositories
- Single point of observation for all messages
- Centralized repository for all logged messages, enabling reporting and analysis
- Centralized repository for all message types—as a growing knowledge base for operations staff
- Ability to forward log files for noninstrumented processes
- Ability to filter log messages for automated notification and integration with other applications, with trouble-ticketing systems being the first target

Event distribution is an intelligent function concentrating on routing the right information to the right place at the right time. Functions and requirements are as follows:

- APIs for any process to generate events and for the registration for notification of subsets of events.
- Potential scope of event notification may mean a chain of functions.
- Notification examples are manyfold (e.g., notify communication servers that the host is down, notify application servers to log off DBMS, notify desktop applications to refresh local cache of application data, notify subset of processes to change logging levels, reconfigure transaction distribution mechanisms to accommodate node unavailability or network overload).
- General target is 24×7 service with the need to keep running processes informed of changing system state.

Process monitoring keeps track of the complicated internal chain of functions that may not be fully understandable to users. Functions and requirements concentrate on the following:

- Verification of viability of all processes required to provide service to users is critical for distributed systems, since many critical processes will not have users attached to them because they run in the background.
- Provide notification of process failure and be able to restart processes automatically if software fails.
- Allow configurable actions in the event of process failure.
- Process monitoring examples include the monitoring application servers for catastrophic failure due to application logic error, monitoring print spooler in remote offices, and monitoring communication servers for host connectivity.

Performance logging is the basis of optimizing the configuration and/or applications against each other. Functions and requirements concentrate on the following:

- Collecting performance statistics based on application-defined activities
- Collecting performance statistics at dynamically modifiable granularities
- Association of performance data with user requests, subsystems, and managed nodes
- Examples of performance indicators: time per group of SQL statements, count of services provided by individual nodes, and I/Os required for device management
- Analysis of data using customizable analysis programs

Application management may cause a volume problem due to the high number of applications and the number of indicators to be managed for all of them. In terms of the right policy, the following trade-offs must be carefully considered:

- *Polling versus eventing.*   Polling may cause high overhead. Eventing is more attractive for situations where the alarm state does not affect information gathering.
- *Connection versus connectionless distribution.*   Connection-oriented is more attractive as message volumes increase.
- *Self-describing messages versus anticipated-structure messages.* This is a trade-off between message volume and accessibility of message detail.
- *Blocking versus nonblocking messages.*   This is a trade-off between performance and reliability.

E-mail application management

Concrete application management examples are shown with E-mail systems.

The dominant LAN E-mail vendors are developing management capabilities for their applications to give network managers increased control of their messaging systems. In particular, Lotus, Microsoft, and Novell try to incorporate their solutions into existing and new management platforms.

Improvements are needed for the following reasons:

- Users want general information about their mail load so they can plan for more capacity. They also want to know how long messages must be stored and how much space needs to be allocated.

- Users want to know the actual status of the mail exchanged between various locations in order to troubleshoot problems.

- Some organizations need to bill those generating the most mail activity, either inside or outside the organization. It may also identify mail abuse.

Figure 5.29 shows the principal monitoring locations in E-mail systems, indicating the management station, the server, and the workstations. The solutions today offer individual features; standardization of management is still far away.

Lotus is offering NotesView and cc:MailView to help users to collect and process message information. cc:MailView provides a centralized view of an entire messaging network and helps administrators identify and correct problems. The administrators see a display of routing connections and directory exchange topologies that include LAN and mobile users. A graphical component, MailMap, displays post offices as icons and color-codes problems. MailAlert is a warning subsystem that notifies administrators of actual and potential problems based on preset thresholds.

NotesView and cc:MailView run on HP OpenView software management platform. Both Hewlett-Packard and IBM are concentrating on

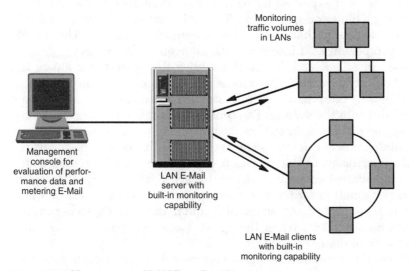

Figure 5.29   Management of LAN E-mail applications.

SNMP-based solutions for their management platforms. The functions include error tracking, counting E-mail messages, directory synchronization, updates, and exception reporting.

The Microsoft Exchange Server that is X.400-based logs all significant events, controls how much logging takes place, and monitors how much data has been accumulated. It is also possible to integrate with Windows NT performance monitor for server tuning and monitoring.

GroupWise from Novell combines E-mail, group calendaring, and task management features.

Patrol from BMC Software.   Patrol is an event-driven management product for the distributed computing environment. It simplifies systems management by providing an integrated, easy-to-use graphical user interface to an organization's computers, resources, databases, and applications. It frees database and systems administrators from the administration tasks as it oversees and automatically administers all the important software systems in the organization. Patrol is a graphical front end to an entire enterprisewide information system or to just a collection of workstations and servers. The console shows all the components of a distributed system as icons. The color of icon represents the status of the application. For instance, a crashed database will cause the corresponding database instance icon to flash red. Because Patrol displays all systems and applications simultaneously, it is easy to determine the overall status of the corporate information system.

Patrol was architected to be open, flexible, and extensible with loadable libraries of expertise for widely used databases and applications providing a plug-and-go solution. The architecture consists of a console and remote agents that reside on each managed processor. The console is the component that interacts with all agents and drives the graphical user interface. It is a set of modules that together manage the Patrol object hierarchy. The console can operate as an authoring station, allowing administrators to customize Patrol and incorporate new knowledge into the system. The console maintains a dialog with various server processes, known as *agents,* one on each remote processor. This dialog is event-driven, so no network traffic needs to be generated until a specific event that causes a state change occurs on a managed processor. Patrol communicates with each agent using TCP/IP. The agent is a small program that runs on each managed server or workstation. Its job is to discover, monitor, and manage any system running in that environment. When the agent is started the first time, rules about how to discover applications, databases, and key resources are sent from the console to the agents for execution. The agents automatically apply these rules and report back to the console the status information about each discovered module.

Integration of LAN Management Functions and Instruments

There is an obvious trend in the industry to reduce the number of different management systems. Platforms are very helpful to accommodate multiple management applications. Leading platforms were discussed in Chap. 4. Most of them are able to integrate LAN management functions and instruments up to a certain degree. Practically all products can be considered as integrators.

However, when enterprise management is the target, Unix-based standard platforms or special platforms such as NetExpert are at an advantage. In large organizations, a hierarchy of integrators may be implemented. The integrators are communicating with each other using standard or proprietary protocols.

Even the best management platforms and their integrated applications may fail in enterprise environments for the following reasons:

- *Difficulties in correlating events when they are generated in different domains.* Most management systems cannot correlate alerts or suppress secondary alerts across the enterprise network if the source of the alert is in another management system's domain. It is also true when multiple OpenView-based management systems are used in combination for enterprise management.

- *Prioritizing alerts across domains.* Most management systems cannot prioritize alerts across the network because the alert may belong to another copy of the management system or a different vendor's management system. Also in this case, advanced expert-system applications are required to be implemented. The first applicable examples are addressed in Chap. 8.

- *Multiuser capabilities.* Today's network management platforms provide limited multiuser support. Oftentimes, users in different geographic locations must coordinate their activities by sending bitmapped files—usually in XWindow format—across the network. This can drive the bandwidth demand high. Distributed operating systems with controlled handshaking can solve this problem.

- *Displaying a networkwide map.* In large networks deploying several copies of a management system or different management systems, each system owns parts of the network and is not aware of the nodes belonging to another management system's domain. Map consolidation is a very difficult problem. Building maps manually is not helpful because their maintenance is getting very complicated.

- *Displaying networkwide events.* In large networks, deploying several copies of a management system or different management systems, each system cannot display events occurring in another management system's domain. It is related to the previous observation; if maps can be correlated, events can drive the right segment on the map with the result of icon changes in shape, color, size, and performance.

- *Integration of databases.* A network's collective store of historical data and assets is typically scattered across multiple types of relational database management systems and flat files in different management applications. Accessing this data may require the use of several different database front-end tools. Of course, a physically distributed but logically integrated database would be the ideal solution. Vendors have been dealing with this problem, but without a satisfactory ultimate solution.

Practically all leading platform vendors are dealing with these drawbacks. The solution approaches are different. Some of the vendors license code from Seagate/NetLabs; others contract independent software vendors; still others try to solve these problems with internal resources.

Event correlation and management

In large networks with multiple management domains, it is not uncommon for a device failure in one domain to affect nodes in adjoining domains. But if each domain is managed by a separate manager, it becomes difficult to suppress secondary alarms from different domains. Managing cross-boundary nodes that overlap into two management domains is also problematic. But perhaps the most pressing problem with using multiple copies of today's management platforms is that it is impossible to achieve a networkwide view of real-time events. It is a list that is not only filtered and prioritized, but also one that identifies the cause of the fault and the management system reporting the fault as well. IBM, Hewlett-Packard, and SunSoft are aware of the limitation in their existing products, and they are developing new releases to address these shortcomings. In particular, HP and SunSoft have licensed technology from Seagate that is designed to enhance the polling and alert-handling process. This technology is embodied in the NerveCenter application, which implements the concept of conditional-state alarms to support a highly configurable polling mechanism. Without conditional-state alarming, users are restricted to setting a threshold on a simple yes/no basis—that is, has the MIB variable value exceeded a certain value? In a variety of cases, such as transient port failures and temporary spikes in Ethernet CRC errors, it is insignificant if a threshold is exceeded only for a few moments—because the problem goes away.

In these situations, it is more appropriate to generate an alert only if the MIB value remains above the threshold for a specified time period, or if the threshold is exceeded a given number of times within a specified time period. Also, it may be desirable to generate an alert when the MIB value comes back down to normal.

Conditional-state alarm facility can support this level of flexibility in event handling. However, one drawback of sophisticated alarming facilities such as NerveCenter is that the network administrator must think through many types of scenarios and then configure the system accordingly in order to take full advantage of the application's capabilities. Also, while the existing NerveCenter application can be used with OpenView, integration between the two does not yet exist. And it cannot be used with the widely installed SunNet Manager. Even future versions will support alarm handling for only one vendor's management system at a time.

To address these and other limitations in the alarm-handling capabilities, platform suppliers and integrators may use applications from third parties. One example is Netcools/OMNIbus from Micromuse. Implemented as an information bus from management platforms, it supports alarm distribution among multiple management platforms, including OpenView, SunNet Manager, and NetView for AIX. The core components are software applications called *probes* that collect events, an ObjectServer for processing and storing events, and gate software that exports processed information to other ObjectServers or network management systems.

A software probe connects to each management system and registers itself for user-specified events. When it receives event data, the probe reformats the event as an "Object Server Alert Object" and forwards it to the appropriate ObjectServer. The stream of Object-Server Alert Objects from one or more probes continually updates the ObjectServer's in-memory data store of all managed objects. More important, the ObjectServer applies user-defined rules during the update operations to filter out secondary, repetitive, and noncritical alarms.

According to Micromuse, ObjectServer filtering rules can be easily configured or modified, rather than preconfigured according to complex scenarios. Also, an optimal Automatic Extension feature allows the ObjectServer to start up scripts or processes to automatically respond to user-specified network events.

Finally, the product supports applications called *gates* that transfer the processed event data to an external application for displaying to the user. What the user sees as a result is a filtered, prioritized view of all events across the network in one screen called the EventList—so named because color-coded events are displayed in a scrolling list.

Network administrators can redefine filters to create multiple Event-List clients, enabling, for example, each operator accessing the system to see his or her own list with the appropriate event priorities and filters. The EventList can be used to reprioritize alarms or to assign problems to other operators.

Netcool/OMNIbus has several advantages over NerveCenter and over other existing alarm facilities, including the following:

- It integrates alarms from multiple management systems into a single view.

- It requires little configuration to automatically start gathering data.

- It can be used to distribute alert information from existing management systems to operators across the enterprise.

- It supports a high-performance, distributed object server.

Another alternative is the use of NetExpert from Objective Systems Integrators as an umbrella manager to coordinate multiple Unix-based domain managers.

Integrating network visualization

Today, multiple copies of OpenView can share map data only by sending XWindow files over the network—a process that is very expensive in terms of bandwidth. Future versions will be able to share map data more efficiently. Even at that point, however, OpenView users will not be able to share maps with other vendors' management platforms.

Similarly, sharing topology data is awkward and inefficient among multiple copies of SunNet Manager or NetView for AIX. IBM is developing new technology for supporting map sharing. Release dates have not been made public at this time.

SunNet Manager supports a third-party developed application, called Cooperative Consoles, that creates a single object repository among multiple copies of SunNet Manager. However, the product has had limited success. Most SunNet Manager customers are waiting to see how well Encompass will handle map sharing.

Map sharing can be solved by another product, called MapSynch, from Bridgeway. Even when the new products are out, applications like MapSynch will be required to facilitate map sharing between different vendors' management platforms.

Organizations deploying multiple management platforms or multiple copies of the same management platform have a tough job maintaining up-to-date network maps. While all leading SNMP management platforms support discovery of IP devices on the network, the automatically generated maps are typically crowded with icons and difficult to interpret. Invariably, the network administrator must customize the main maps and submaps in order to make them useful.

This customization process involves a lot of time. Today's management platforms do not support the ability to easily copy this customized data from one system to another, or even back to the system itself after a total rediscovery of the network.

MapSynch is designed to synchronize object database and network topology functions across dissimilar platforms. MapSynch currently supports both OpenView and NetView for AIX. The product reads the object database and topology map of the source SNMP network manager and then overwrites overlapping objects and attributes found in the destination SNMP manager's database and map. It also supports a second mode of operation, whereby only changes to the database and map are examined and compared, and any new information from the source is copied to the destination. Bridgeway recommends that customers perform the initial full synchronization weekly, with synchronization changes done on a daily or hourly basis.

MapSynch is also useful for recopying customization back onto a network map in the event of system failure or after a complete rediscovery. It saves the entire map verbatim (all X and Y coordinates) and then paints it back verbatim when the user specifies. It automatically generates an audit trail on all synchronization operations.

MapSynch gives customers with multiple management systems the capability of replacing disjoint, inconsistent maps with a single, complete network map or consistent set of submaps. It can also help dissimilar SNMP platforms to act as backup topology stores for each other in the event of failure.

In less advanced cases, there is a way of manually building maps. Products, like GrafBase, NetWiz, and Best/Vizualizer support this process. This alternative is very time-consuming and is not recommended for integration.

Synchronization of databases

Today, management data describing the network is stored in multiple databases or files. For example, CiscoWorks supports a Sybase relational database describing router configurations. Concord Trakker supports an Ingres database for storing traffic statistics. OpenView stores certain types of data in an Ingres database. And IBM NetView for AIX supports Oracle, Sybase, Informix, and DB2. In addition, many applications, such as Action Request System from Remedy, store data in a flat file and support export to different relational databases.

On occasion, it is necessary to reach into these different databases to produce comprehensive asset or historical reports. For example, an organization may want to develop a report, listing the value of all information technology assets, using data from CiscoWorks, Optivity from Bay Networks, and COMMAND 5000 from Isicad. Another example is a report on the maintenance history of various network devices, also requiring information stored in multiple relational databases. But creating reports using data from different network management databases can be cumbersome and very time-consuming.

In the future, there may be a single management repository, where management data from all types of applications and systems is fed into standardized format. However, until that day comes, administrators must still maintain multiple management databases.

Database synchronization and integration are very difficult tasks. Many client/server systems show similar weaknesses with synchronization. In many cases, a sort of directory service is implemented on top of databases by various applications.

Third-party applications are now emerging to address this problem. The Cooperative Reporting application developed by DeskTalk Systems has been used by customers in the SunNet Manager environment. For OpenView users, Isicad now offers the Info Manager application to ease the task of addressing multiple relational databases. This product is a point-and-click application builder capable of transparently handling interactions between multiple types of relational databases. Info Manager supports simultaneous update, access, and reporting from different vendors' relational databases.

It allows users to leverage the data from multiple management applications without having to create a true, single management repository. It is an object-oriented database front-end and report generator that allows users to build screens, forms, and reports that link to Oracle and Sybase without having to write 4GL code or use tools such as Oracle Forms and Accell SQL. Support from Ingres and Informix are planned. In addition to the Info Manager development environment, Isicad offers an ad hoc report generator called Report Works, which is actually a subset of Info Manager. A run-time version of Info Manager is also bundled into COMMAND 5000.

Selection of LAN Management Instruments

In order to select the right instrument, prior to making a decision, both the selection criteria and products must be carefully evaluated. To do so, use the criteria listed in the following section.

Functional criteria

Functional criteria focus on LAN management functions, integration capabilities, and conformance to standards.

Support of configuration management. Configuration management is a set of mid-range and long-range activities for controlling physical, electrical, and logical inventories, maintaining vendor files and trouble tickets, supporting provisioning and order processing, managing changes, and distributing software. Directory service and help for generating different network generations are also provided.

Support of fault management. Fault management is a collection of activities required to dynamically maintain the network service level. These activities ensure high availability by quickly recognizing problems and performance degradation, and by initiating controlling functions when necessary, which may include diagnosis, repair, testing, recovery, workaround, and backup. Log control and information distribution techniques are also supported.

Support of performance management. Performance management defines the ongoing evaluation of the network in order to verify that service levels are maintained, to identify actual and potential bottlenecks, and establish and report on trends for management decision making and planning. Building and maintaining the performance database and automation procedures for operational control are also included.

Support of security management. Security management is a set of functions to ensure the ongoing protection of the network by analyzing risks, minimizing risks, implementing a network security plan, and monitoring success of the strategy. Special functions include surveillance of security indicators, partitioning, password administration, and warning or alarm messages on violations.

Support of accounting management. Accounting management is the process of collecting, interpreting, processing, and reporting cost-oriented and charge-oriented information on resource usage. In particular, processing of SMDRs, bill notification, and charge-back procedures are included for voice and data.

Support of LAN design and planning. Network planning is the process of determining the optimal network, based on data for network performance, traffic flow, resource use, networking requirements, technological trade-offs, and estimated growth of present and future applications. Sizing rules and interfaces to modeling devices are also parts of the planning process.

Integration capabilities. These capabilities include the ability of interfacing different kinds of products that use proprietary or standard architectures.

- *Multivendor capability.* Ability to integrate other vendors' products.

- *Space covered that needs integration.* WAN, LAN, MAN; private, public; logical, physical; processing and networking components; data and voice.

- *Depth of integration.* Physical terminal level, protocol conversion, full integration.

- *Conformance to standards.* Including support of CMISEs from OSI and TCP/IP management capabilities (SNMP).

- *Electronic Data Interchange.* Used for improving communications with customers.

- *Peer-to-peer to other network management systems.* Capability of interconnection to other vendors' network management systems using advanced communication techniques.

Database support. Repository support summarizes information about integrity across network management functions, what sort of data is included in the repository, and the techniques used. The criteria are as follows:

- Static and dynamic support
- Relational or object-oriented techniques
- Integrity across network management subsystems
- Performance

Database support includes the capability of defining and maintaining MIBs and their variables. MIB public contains only generic, or non-implementation-specific objects that the Internet working group has determined as essential to managing components. From this minimal set of objects, all other variables specific to a product and to an implementation can be derived. These variables constitute the private branches of MIBs. The support of the public branch is absolutely necessary; the content of the private branch is negotiable.

Operational criteria

The operational and maintainability criteria focus on the product's installation, performance, and use. These criteria provide support of judging a product's applicability to the user's environment apart from its functionality and conformance to standards.

Ease of installation. Most products are user-installed software, meaning that the users are responsible for software installation. Ease of installation means the use of automated or semiautomated procedures assisted by high-quality documentation.

User interface. The user interface defines the quality level for presenting network-related information, and characterizes the flexibility of changing product features:

- *Platform.* Hardware and software that refer to the actual machine and operating system that perform the management tasks.

- *Presentation services.* Features that characterize what level of user support is needed from the network management workstations, including graphics, zooms, windowing, business graphics combined with text windows, colors keyed to content, automated generation of network pictures, standardized commands, and information reports.

- *Programmability.* Defines the language supported for customizing and value-added functions.

- *Main memory and disk storage capacity.* Defines the resource capabilities that may influence configuration, generation, and sizing.

Performance. Performance of a network management system may be defined as its ability to effectively process large amounts of requests and responses in an acceptable manner. Performance also includes the demand of using as little as possible bandwidth to exchange network management-related information. Distribution of LAN management functions may help in this respect. In order to guarantee improved service, multiple workstations may be installed, each of them serving certain users or certain applications.

Reliability. Because the LAN management product provides the focal point of controlling and monitoring the LANs, the product should be robust enough to minimize LAN crashes. If the management product fails, it should not affect the LANs being managed in any way.

Security. The security criteria focuses on access control and authentication for using the product, its database, and its communication connections. *Authentication* means to determine the identity of the requester, while *access control* is determining whether the requester has the authority to issue a given request. A different level of access is desirable.

Scalability. This criteria refers to use in larger and more complex LANs than the original environment. It means that the product should handle higher volumes of information, use more sophisticated maps, be able to partition the complex network, and provide for manager-to-manager (product-to-product) communication if necessary.

General purchase criteria

Besides the functional and operational criteria, other more general criteria must be used to evaluate the merits of the network management product. These criteria embed purchase conditions.

- *Customer support.* Differentiates manufacturers on the basis of product customization and whether they provide consulting services.

- *Development kit.* Help for design, development, and implementation.

- *Customizing.* Ability to tailor applications.

- *Consulting.* Service provided by the manufacturer for supporting, planning, configuring, sizing, and testing the network management system.

- *Costs.* Includes all components of purchasing, implementing, and operating the product.

- *Availability of products.* Indicates which features are applicable now and in the near future and how easy the migration will be. Installation records and efficiency of use on many networks may be included as well.

- *Documentation.* The existence of well-organized and easily readable documentation is essential to installing and maintaining a network management product. State-of-the-art techniques, such as the use of hypertext may be considered.

- *Training requirements.* Because the skill level of LAN management personnel varies from enterprise to enterprise, training requirements are essential. Questions about type of training, duration of training, and technical level of training must become part of the evaluation process.

- *Financial stability.* The business environment and financial viability of the vendor is evaluated here. In certain cases, this criterion receives a lot of attention and a high weight.

Table 5.4 summarizes the criteria for selecting LAN management products.

In order to facilitate the selection process, I have provided three tables. Table 5.5 identifies leading products, their managed objects, such as bridges, FDDI-nodes, DQDB-nodes, servers, routers, LAN hubs, extenders, repeaters, adapters, and processors, and network management capabilities. Table 5.6 shows physical and logical interfaces, support of leading network architectures, support of new net-

TABLE 5.4   Network Management Systems'
Evaluation Criteria

Functional criteria
- Support of configuration management
- Support of fault management
- Support of performance management
- Support of security management
- Support of accounting management
- Support of LAN design and planning
- Integration capabilities
- Database support

Operational criteria
- Ease of installation
- User interface
- Performance
- Reliability
- Security
- Scalability

General purchase criteria
- Customer support
- Costs
- Availability
- Documentation
- Training requirements
- Financial

working services, such as fast packet, SMDS, and B-ISDN for the same products. Finally, Table 5.7 summarizes LAN management capabilities, such as protocols supported, element manager, integrator, and support of integrators for the same product.

LAN Monitoring and Performance Reporting as a Third-Party Service

Not everybody wants to equip the whole network with monitoring instruments, because processing measurement data would require significant human resources. They turn to companies who offer measurement, reporting, and planning services. International Network Services with its NETracker is exactly the solution many users are looking for. The company provides performance monitoring and provides information for proactive fault management.

INS NETracker works within the Internet Network Management Framework and relies on the SNMP protocol and the manager/agent model. Currently, the system uses SNMP to obtain performance information from wiring hubs, routers, and RMON agents.

Many vendors have developed private MIBs that support their equipment in ways that go beyond the capabilities supported by the

TABLE 5.5 Products/Capabilities Matrix

Company	Product	Wiring Hub and Repeater	Router	Bridge	Extender	Brouter	Terminal Server	File Server	Print Server	Processor	Cable and NIC	FDDI Node	D&DB Node	Concentrator	Multiplexer
Advanced Computer Communications	ACS 4800 Network Management System	x	x	x		x	x							x	
Applied Computing Devices	ACCs Network Knowledge Platforms	x	x	x		x	x	x	x		x		x	x	x
AT&T	StarGroup Router Manager Systems Manager		x							x					
BICC Data Network	ISOview	x		x									x	x	
Bytex Corp.	ATS 1000		x	x		x	x	x	x		x		x	x	
Bytex Corp.	Maestro NMS		x	x		x	x	x	x		x				
Cabletron Systems	LANView, Spectrum	x	x	x	x	x	x	x		x	x		x	x	
Chipcom	Online NCS		x	x		x	x	x							
Data General Corp.	Eye*Node, AViiON		x	x		x	x	x	x		x	x		x	
Cisco Systems	NetCentral		x												
David Systems	ExpressView	x	x	x		x	x								
Digilog	LANVista	x	x	x		x	x	x							
FiberCom	ViewMaster	x	x	x		x	x	x	x	x			x	x	
Fibermux	Lightwatch	x	x			x	x	x	x	x			x	x	
Fibronics	FX 8510-Interview	x	x	x			x				x				
General DataComm	Mega*Bridge		x	x											
Halley Systems	ConnectView		x	x			x	x							
Hewlett-Packard	OpenView	x	x	x		x	x	x	x		x		x	x	

Company	Product	1	2	3	4	5	6	7	8	9	10	11	12	13	14
Hughes LAN Systems	MONET	x	x	x	x	x			x			x		x	x
Infotron-Dowty	LANSpan		x	x		x									
IBM	LAN Network Manager	x		x							x				
	LMU/2	x		x							x				
IBM	AIX NetView/6000		x	x		x									
Intercon	WatchTower						x	x	x	x					
Micro Technology-Lexcel	LANCE	x	x	x		x	x								
NCR Corp.	Star*Sentry		x	x		x	x		x						
Network Resources	MultiGate Manager	x	x			x		x						x	
Newbridge	8001 LAN Manager	x	x			x		x						x	
Proteon	OverView		x	x		x	x	x	x			x		x	
Racal Milgo	CMS Express	x	x	x		x	x							x	
Silicon Graphics	NetVisualyzer								x		x				
Sun Connect	SunNet Manager	x	x	x				x						x	x
SynOptics	Lattisnet Network Manager	x	x	x	x	x	x	x		x	x	x		x	
Timeplex	Time/LAN 100 EMS	x	x	x		x			x			x		x	x
Ungermann-Bass	Net Director	x	x	x	x	x	x	x	x	x					
Vitalink	WAN Manager		x	x		x	x			x					
WANG	PC LAN Network Manager		x			x	x	x	x						
Wellfleet Communications	SNMP-NMS		x	x		x					x				
Wollongong Group	WIN Management Station	x	x	x		x	x	x		x		x		x	x
Zenith	Enterprise Network Manager		x	x		x									

TABLE 5.6 Products/Interfaces Matrix

Company	Product	OSI	Ethernet	Token Ring	Token Bus	X.25	TCP/IP	FDDI	D&DB	IPX	NFS	Kermit	NetBios	LLC 1,2	SNA	DCA	DNA	DSA	Fast Packet	SMDS	ISDN	B-ISDN
Advanced Computer Communications	ACS 4800 Network Management System		x			x																
Applied Computing Devices	ACCs Network Knowledge Platforms	x	x	x		x	x			x	x				x		x					
AT&T	StarGroup Router Manager		x	x																		
	Systems Manager		x	x			x	x														
BICC Data Network	ISOView		x	x			x	x														
Bytex Corp.	ATS 1000		x	x			x						x	x								
	Maestro NMS		x	x			x				x		x	x								
Cabletron Systems	LANView, Spectrum		x	x		x	x			x					x							
Chipcom	Online NCS		x	x		x	x			x	x											
Cisco Systems	NetCentral		x	x				x														
Data General Corp.	Eye*Node, AViiON		x				x															
David Systems	ExpressView		x																			
Digilog	LANVista		x	x		x	x	x		x	x											
FiberCom	ViewMaster		x	x	x			x														
Fibermux	Lightwatch		x	x	x																	
Fibronics	FX 8510-Interview		x					x														
General DataComm	Mega*Bridge		x	x		x	x															
Halley Systems	ConnectView		x																			
Hewlett-Packard	OpenView	x	x	x		x	x	x			x				x							

Company	Product									
Hughes LAN Systems	MONET		x	x	x					
Infotron-Dowty	LANSpan	x	x							
IBM	LAN Network Manager			x	x		x	x	x	
IBM	LMU/2		x	x			x	x	x	
Intercon	AIX NetView/6000	x	x		x					
Micro Technology-Lexcel	WatchTower	x	x	x	x					
NCR Corp.	LANCE	x	x	x	x		x	x	x	
	Star*Sentry	x	x	x	x					
Network Resources	MultiGate Manager	x				x				
Newbridge	8001 LAN Manager	x								
Proteon	OverView	x	x	x	x					
Racal Milgo	CMS Express	x	x							
Silicon Graphics	NetVisualyzer	x	x	x	x					
Sun Connect	SunNet Manager	x	x	x	x	x				
SynOptics	Lattisnet Network Manager	x	x	x	x					
Timeplex	Time/LAN 100 EMS	x	x	x	x					x
Ungermann-Bass	Net Director	x	x	x	x					
Vitalink	WAN Manager	x	x	x	x		x			x
WANG	PC LAN Network Manager	x	x	x	x		x	x		
Wellfleet Communications	SNMP-NMS	x	x	x	x		x	x		
Wollongong Group	WIN Management Station	x	x	x	x					
Zenith	Enterprise Network Manager	x	x	x	x					

TABLE 5.7   LAN management capabilities

Company	Product	Protocols Supported	Element Management	Integration	Support of Integrators
3Com	ViewBuilder	SNMP	Yes	No	NetView
Advanced Comp. Comm.	ACS 4800 NMS	SNMP (SNMP Res.)	Yes	Yes	Concert
Applied Computing Devices	ACD Network Knowledge Platform	CMIP, NMVT DECnet, CMOT, SNMP CMOL	Yes	No	NetView, DECmcc Accumaster-Integrator OpenView
AT&T	Computer Manager	Proprietary	Yes	No	NetView, Accumaster-Integrator
	StarGroup Manager	OSI	Yes	No	NetView, Accumaster-Integrator
	StarGroup Router	OSI	Yes	No	NetView, Accumaster-Integrator
	System Manager (NetLabs)	CMOT, SNMP	Yes	Yes	
BICC Data Networks	IsoView	CMIP, SNMP	Yes	Yes	Accumaster-Integrator, DECmcc, OpenView, SunNet Manager
BIM	Netcortex	SNMP	Yes	Yes	
Bytex	ATS 1000	IEEE 802.5 MAC Frames			
	Maestro NMS	SNMP	Yes	No	NetView
Cabletron	LanView	Proprietary	Yes	No	
	Spectrum	CMIP, SNMP DECnet, NMVT	Yes	Yes	NetView, Accumaster-Integrator, DECmcc
Chipcom Corp.	Online NCS	SNMP (SNMP Res.)	Yes	No	
Cisco Systems	NetCentral	SNMP	Yes	No	SunNet Manager
Codex Corp.	9800 SNMP Processor	SNMP (MIT)	Yes	Yes	
Concord	Trakker	SNMP	Yes	No	SunNet Manager
Data General	Eye*Node	SNMP (SNMP Res.)	Yes	No	
	AViiON	SNMP, CMIP	Yes	No	
David Systems	ExpressView	SNMP (Epilogue)	Yes	No	
Digilog	LanVista	Proprietary, NICE DECnet	Yes	No	DECmcc
Digital Equip.	DECmcc TCP/IP	Proprietary, SNMP	Yes	Yes	DECmcc

TABLE 5.7   LAN management capabilities (*Continued*)

Company	Product	Protocols Supported	Element Management	Integration	Support of Integrators
Digital Equip.	DECmcc Ultrix	Proprietary, SNMP	Yes	Yes	DECmcc
Fibercom	Viewmaster	SNMP (Carnegie)	Yes	Yes	
Fibermux	Lightwatch	Proprietary, SNMP (SNMP Res.)	Yes	No	Accumaster-Integrator, OpenView, NetView, SunNet Manager
Fibronics	FX-8510 Interview	SNMP	Yes	No	NetView
Gandalf	Access Manager	SNMP (NetLabs)	Yes	No	NetView, Accumaster-Integrator
General Datacom	Mega*Bridge	SNMP	Yes	No	NetView
Halley Systems	ConnectView	Proprietary	Yes	No	
Hewlett-Packard	OpenView Bridge Manager	SNMP (Carnegie, MIT)	Yes	Yes	OpenView
	OpenView Hub Manager	SNMP (Carnegie, MIT)	Yes	Yes	OpenView
	OpenView Interconnect Manager	SNMP (Carnegie, MIT)	Yes	Yes	OpenView
	OpenView NM Server Manager	SNMP (Carnegie, MIT)	Yes	Yes	OpenView
	OpenView Network Node Manager	SNMP (Carnegie, MIT)	Yes	Yes	OpenView
Hughes LAN Systems	Monet	SNMP (Epilogue)	Yes	Yes	NetView, Accumaster-Integrator
IBM	AIX NetView/6000	SNMP	Yes	Yes	NetView
	LAN Network Manager	NMVT, CMIP	Yes	No	NetView
Infotron (Dowty)	LANSpan	Proprietary, SNMP	Yes	No	NetView, Accumaster-Integrator
Interlan	WatchTower	SNMP	Yes	No	
Lannet	MultiMan	SNMP (MIT)	Yes	Yes	NetView
Micro Techn. Lextel	Lance	SNMP (PSI)	Yes	Yes	DECmcc, NetView Accumaster-Integrator
NetLabs	DualManager	SNMP, CMIP CMOT	Yes	Yes	
NCR Corp.	Star*Sentry Manager	CMIP, NMVT CMOT, SNMP	Yes	Yes	Accumaster-Integrator, NetView, DECmcc

TABLE 5.7   LAN management capabilities (*Continued*)

Company	Product	Protocols Supported	Element Management	Integration	Support of Integrators
Network Managers	NMC 3000	SNMP, CMOT	Yes	Yes	NetView, OpenView, DECmcc
Network Systems Corp.	SNMP Manager	SNMP (SNMP Res.)	Yes	No	
Network Resources Corp.	MultiGate Manager	Proprietary	Yes	No	
Newbridge	LAN Manager	SNMP (SNMP Res.)	Yes	No	NetView, Accumaster-Integrator
Northern Telecom	LANScope	SNMP	Yes	No	NetView
Novell	LANtern NMS	SNMP (Carnegie)	Yes Yes	No Yes	NetView NetView
Objective Systems Integrators	NetExpert	CMIP SNMP	Yes	Yes	NetView, DECmcc, OpenView
Proteon	OverView	SNMP	Yes	No	NetView
Retix	5025 Network Management Center	SNMP, CMIP (Epilogue)	Yes	No	SunNet Manager
Silicon Graphics	NetVisualizer	Proprietary	Yes	No	Spectrum
SynOptics	Lattisnet	SNMP, NMVT (Epilogue)	Yes	Yes	NetView, SunNet Manager, DECmcc, OpenView
Teknekron	NMS/Core	Proprietary	Yes	No	
Timeplex	Time/LAN	SNMP	Yes	No	NetView, Accumaster-Integrator
Ungermann-Bass	NetDirector	SNMP	Yes	No	NetView, Concert
Vitalink	WAN Manager	SNMP (SNMP Res.)	Yes	No	DECmcc
Wang Labs	PC LAN Network Manager	Vines	Yes	No	
Wellfleet Comm.	SNMP-NMS	SNMP	Yes	No	DECmcc, SunNet Manager
Wollongong Group	WIN Management Station	SNMP (PSI)	Yes	No	
Zenith	Enterprise Network Manager	SNMP	Yes	Yes	

standard MIB-II. Currently, Cisco MIBs are used to monitor the processing load and memory utilization on Cisco routers. Other private MIB monitoring implementations are being developed for NETracker.

In addition to SNMP-gathered information, the system also uses two non-SNMP mechanisms to gather performance data. Resource uptime is measured using ICMP echoes (PING) and ICMP echo replies. Any IP device, usually IP hosts, that can respond to a PING can be monitored. An intelligent platform, referred to as an *INS meter*, placed on one of the client's LAN segments will periodically PING client-specified hosts and record the results. The mechanism will give an indication of the reachability of the host, which is a function of the host's condition and the network path to the host.

Response times to IP hosts are determined using ICMP echoes (PINGs) and echo replies. PINGs and their replies are timed and these times are used to determine the round-trip transit time from the INS meter to the host. Because most IP hosts implement the ICMP echoes and replies at low levels in the operating system (Unix kernel), the response time is normally not affected by application load on the host. Therefore, this is a good measure of true network delay.

Figure 5.30 shows the NETracker system in operation.

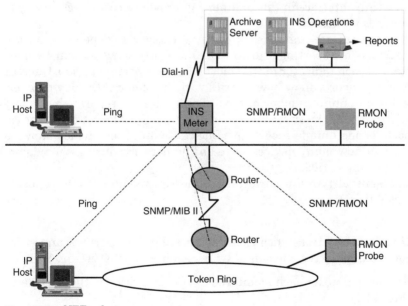

Figure 5.30   NETracker arrangement.

The system consists of one or more INS meters that are connected to one or more client LAN segments. These meters have INS-developed software that communicates with the SNMP agents and IP hosts, collects performance data, analyzes and consolidates the data into hourly statistics, and uploads this data daily via a dial-out modem connection to an INS server at an INS location that maintains current and archived data.

Database applications create weekly and monthly reports from the information on the INS server. These reports are printed and delivered to the client on the following day. INS considers each resource monitored as an element. Typically, an element is either an IP host being monitored for uptime and response time, a router interface, or a Cisco router CPU and memory. NETracker utilizes both MIB and RMON entries for the performance evaluation. RMON probes see all traffic on the LAN segment. Utilization and error reports based on RMON as the collection device reflect the total traffic and total errors on the segment.

When data are collected via MIB-II, the utilization and error information applies to a particular interface on the device, which is typically a router, but could be a bridge, hub, or switch. Router interface statistics provide a good indication of traffic entering and exiting the LAN and can be useful in sizing routers and WAN links and in determining the effects of reconfiguring the local LAN. Error information collected from a LAN interface in this manner can provide a cost-effective way to monitor LAN health.

The reports are organized into three categories depending on the time frame for reporting. Current Detail reports show an hour-by-hour history of each indicator for the most current reporting period. Current Summary reports show how metrics varied by hour of the day, on average, for a definite number of days. The Historical reports show daily statistics for the most recent 91 days. Included in the set of Historical reports is one unique report, the Device Count report, which shows a history of how many devices were on the network during each day of the reporting period.

The general types of performance metrics monitored and reported are as follows:

- Uptime of resources, such as file servers, database servers, and interconnecting devices, measured by responding to PINGs (Fig. 5.31)

- Response time for each monitored device in relation to the INS meter (Fig. 5.32)

- Utilization of Ethernet and Token Ring segments

Average Uptime (%)

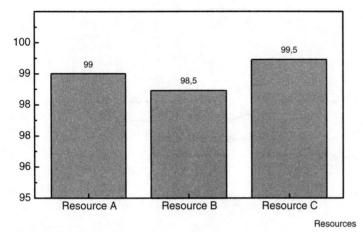

Figure 5.31 Uptime of resources measured by responses to PINGS.

- Utilization of WAN links from the perspective of in- and outgoing traffic of routers (Fig. 5.33)
- Distribution of protocols to determine bandwidth occupancy by applications (Fig. 5.34)
- Errors and events

Response time in ms

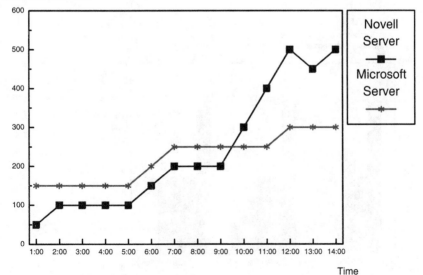

Figure 5.32 Response time in relation to the INS meter.

WAN utilization rate (%)

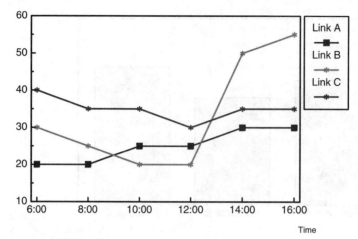

Figure 5.33   WAN utilization measured by router traffic.

- Collisions
- Distribution of frame sizes
- Communigrams for top traffic transmitters and receivers
- CPU utilization of routers to highlight saturation levels; proactive view of load peaks and their impacts on routers to help avoid crashes and discarded traffic (Fig. 5.35)

Protocol Distribution by principal
nodes representing LAN segments (%)

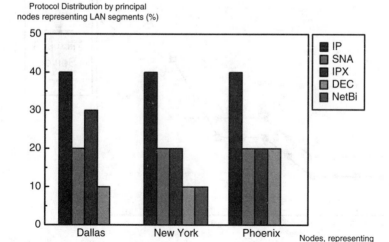

Figure 5.34   Distribution by protocols.

CPU utilization (%)

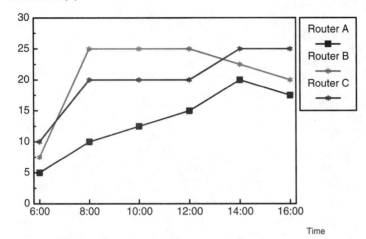

Figure 5.35   Utilization of Cisco routers.

This way of outsourcing performance monitoring and report generation off-loads network management staff from these activities for a
reasonable fee. But performance-related data are managed outside the
company, making ad hoc reporting, trending, and capacity planning
very difficult.

Summary

The instrumentation of LAN management is becoming more visible.
Also, the number of alternatives is increasing, making implementation
easier, but selection more difficult.

Instrumentation trends may be summarized as follows:

- LAN management requires a combination of tools.

- Most manufacturers implement SNMP agent capabilities into their
  products, offering both public and private MIBs.

- Some manufacturers also offer SNMP manager capabilities, including the management of third-party agents.

- Platforms are getting more popular; some of them will support
  SNMP, CMOT, and CMIP capabilities.

- Most vendors will offer gateways to leading network management
  integrators, such as OpenView, NetView for AIX, NetExpert, Spectrum, NetView for MVS, Polycenter, and Solstice.

- There is more cooperation between vendors of LAN-related products
  in the area of LAN management.

6

Design and Planning of LANs

LAN design and capacity planning is the process of determining the optimal local area network, based on data for networking and internetworking requirements, technological trade-offs, existing and estimated traffic flows, current resource use, and estimated growth of present and future applications. Sizing rules, and information export/import are considered parts of the planning process. The most important functions are as follows:

- Determining and quantifying current workload and resource use

- Estimating future user demand, volume by communication form, location, and user groups

- Design and sizing of servers, communication facilities, and workstations, including backup disaster and recovery plans

- Implementation of local area networks, including wiring plans, conformance and stress testing, tuning, paralleling existing and new LANs, and cutover

- Selecting the right technology in terms of throughput, cabling, access technique, topology, and media

Local area network design and planning don't receive enough attention. In most cases, they're an afterthought, usually considered a continuation of LAN tuning work. LAN design and planning are understood in only a limited sense. It's understood as the installation of the infrastructure. After introducing the basics of the LAN design and planning process, this chapter will address the principal functions and design criteria. Instrumentation will also be analyzed in some depth, with particular attention to modeling instruments.

The Process of LAN Design and Capacity Planning

Figure 6.1 shows the basic steps in the design and capacity planning process. In the first step—assuming LANs are in operation—the current workload is identified and quantified. Measured and modeled results may help to calibrate modeling instruments and determine communication overhead. Step one offers as a final result the quantified resource demand by application, workstation, and users.

Step two deals with estimating and quantifying future load. This step starts with identifying locations for LAN segments and their components, respectively. Also included are activities that determine user

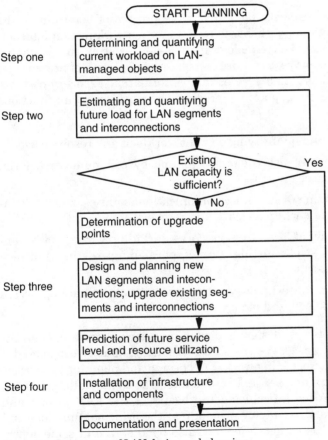

Figure 6.1   Basic steps of LAN design and planning.

requirements for communication services by communication form, volume, and application. Step two offers as a final result the quantified resource demand by application and user. For new LANs, step two is the entry point into the design and planning process.

Step three addresses the design of new LAN segments, upgrades, cabling plans, and internetworking components. To optimize design, various criteria, such as performance, availability, and cost, are considered. Also, backup and recovery plans need to be elaborated in this step. Step three offers as a final result the complete design of local area networks, including their components with sizing specifications and emergency procedures. Step three provides information to be included in requests for proposals to vendors.

Step four includes sending out requests for proposals, evaluating their responses, selecting products and vendors, physically installing the infrastructure and LAN components, preparing operations and conversion plans, conformance, feasibility and stress testing, and, finally, the cutover to a completely installed and tested LAN. This chapter concentrates on steps two and three. However, recommendations are also provided for steps one and four.

The ultimate goal of LAN design and planning is to meet service-level agreements using optimal resource capacity at a reasonable cost. LAN optimization can be viewed as a process of balancing design factors to attain the best LAN configuration within the constraints of such factors as transport, service, performance, and cost indicators. During the design and optimization process, when one factor is held constant, the interaction of the others must be quantified, since each indicator, when held constant, affects all the others.

Figure 6.2 shows a simple example illustrating the interaction of the indicators mentioned. The first diagram displays cost as a function of the expected level of availability; the performance indicator—number of collisions—is kept constant (CSMA/CD access method is assumed). Redundant cabling may improve availability by increasing cost. The same is true for backup. The overall load is assumed to remain constant, and user behavior is not expected to change significantly. The second diagram shows the relationship between availability and number of collisions while cost is kept constant. Cost may represent the total bandwidth considered for the LAN segment. Requirements for increasing availability may mean separation of the bandwidth into parallel channels supporting production and offering backup. Finally, the third diagram displays the number of collisions as a function of cost while availability is constrained. As shown, the number of collisions may be significantly reduced by increasing bandwidth migration from baseband to broadband.

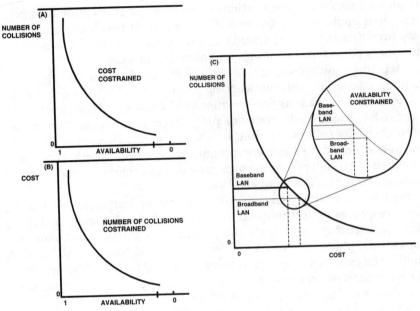

Figure 6.2 Interaction of planning indicators.

Design and Planning Functions

This section summarizes the principal functions of designing and planning of LANs.

Determination and quantification of current workload

The principal goal is to determine resource demand by application, by user, or by both. Resource demand means bits and bytes when considering transmission resources, and it means the processing demand for all kinds of servers. Resource demand may be measured by LAN analyzers, which were addressed in Chap. 5. Resource demand may be determined by sampling the use of LAN resources. In order to break down global resource use, volume indicators have to be collected as well. In this case, continuous monitoring is required. Examples of continuous monitoring are all the RMON probes supported by vendors such as Hewlett-Packard, Axon, Armon, Technology Elite, and distributed LAN monitors from companies such as Network General, Concord Communications, and Hewlett-Packard.

There is another way (as indicated in Chap. 5) to collect, process, and report performance data. NETracker is a good example for this solution. In addition to continuous monitoring and periodic reporting, databases may be turned over to the customer to conduct capacity planning and modeling.

Workload volumes have to be collected in representative time periods. If monthly and weekly volume are fairly constant, then the representative day should be chosen. The concept of the busy (peak) hour is helpful in designing LANs. This refers to a continuous period of any day when the intensity of traffic is at its maximum. The busy (peak) hour is a statistical tool that allows the system planner to accommodate and engineer for peak traffic and avoid long delays during WAN peaks. There are two common ways to determine the busy hour: time-constant busy hour, and bouncing busy hour.

After aggregating individual load components by user and by application, computed and measured results have to be compared. For deviations, multiple reasons should be evaluated. Examples are as follows:

- Data that's too global for workload projection
- Underestimation of contingency workload
- Overestimation of the impact of data compression and compaction
- Forecasting errors for the workload volumes
- Planning errors in terms of selecting the base month, week, or hour
- Resource capacities not accurately estimated
- Underestimation of overhead
- Inaccurate estimates for the resources
- Wrong selection of quantities
- Wrong characterization of application groups and communication forms

In most cases, a combination of reasons apply. After several LAN planning cycles, the most probable causes for the deviation become easier to identify. This process helps to do the following:

- Increase the visibility of applications and their resource demand.
- Quantify typical volumes by application and user.
- Choose the right instruments for planning-related data collection.
- Identify resource demand components that can't be allocated to workload groups.
- Verify computations of LAN resource demand.

Estimation and quantification of future workload

This function should start with identifying locations for LAN segments and their components, such as servers, interconnecting devices, and workstations. This activity usually involves drawing maps based on information that's usually submitted. With existing LANs, the inventory or configuration database could serve as the basis. Other functions have to address the collection of service-related, workload-related, and volume-related information. In LANs, communication no longer means simply transmitting data between various locations. Figure 6.3 gives an overview of how to start identifying desired or existing services (e.g., E-mail, voice mail, teleconferencing) with network traffic requirements. Table 6.1 defines all cells of Fig. 6.3. In the first phase, users identify the services they want to implement during the planning cycle. In the second phase, users are expected to identify volume ranges for the services they're requesting. As a result of these phases, the separation into cable-oriented LANs and PBXs may be very clearly identified.

LAN designers and planners have to identify the quantities of each service item. To determine the individual resource demand on transmission facilities, Tables 6.2 and 6.3 are very helpful. These tables represent only general guidelines, but at least some resource demand ranges by user and by application may be determined.

Consolidation of the workload means to aggregate the resource demand from (1) current locations and current applications/services after growth factor adoption, (2) current locations and new applica-

Input \ Output	Video	Data	Voice	Facsimile
Video	Television 1	Radar analysis 2	Surveillance system 3	Freeze frame video 4
Data	Computer aided design videotex 5	Data processing 6	Voice response credit author 7	Hard-copy terminal 8
Voice	Voice-actuated system 9	Voice compression and storage 10	Phone voice mail 11	Voice-actuated system 12
Facsimile (word & fixed image)	Computer aided design videotex 13	Pattern recognition 14	Voice response (output) 15	Document transmission 16

Teleconferencing: 1,9,10,11,16
Computer aided design: 5,6,8,13,14
Credit author: 10,11,14,15,16
Videotex: 5,6,11,13

Figure 6.3 Matrix of user needs.

TABLE 6.1   Categories of Users' Needs

1. *Television:* Video-Video with expected quality and bandwidth
2. *Radar analysis:* Video-Data for military applications, in particular
3. *Surveillance system:* Video-Voice for supervising installations including alarm and alert management
4. *Freeze-frame video:* Video-Fax for transmitting information framewise
5. *CAD videotex:* Data-Video for information distribution
6. *Data processing:* Data-Data for processing information
7. *Voice response credit author:* Data-Voice for output processing or decision making results
8. *Hard-copy terminal:* Data-Fax for displaying and storing data displays on paper
9. *Voice actuated system:* Voice-Video, using voice as a trigger for displaying and distributing information
10. *Voice compression and storage:* Voice-Data for storing voice-based information in computing systems
11. *Phone, voice mail:* Voice-Voice for straight or delayed transmission of voice
12. *Voice actuated system:* Voice-Fax, see item 9
13. *CAD videotex:* Fax-Video, see item 5
14. *Pattern recognition:* Fax-Data for analyzing word or fixed images using data output for results
15. *Voice response:* Fax-Voice, whereby voice output will be triggered by Fax
16. *Document transmission:* Fax-Fax for serving office automation in particular

TABLE 6.2   Resource Demand by Communication Forms

Communication form	Application area	Throughput rates
Data	Low volume	4.8 Kbps
	Medium volume	
	(Data entry, word processing)	9.6 Kbps
	Line printer	19.2 Kbps
	High volume	
	(Data enquiry, laser printer)	64–256 Kbps
	Net server/hosts	100 Kbps–20 Mbps
Voice	Digital voice	32 Kbps
	Analog voice	64 Kbps
	Store and forward	8–32 Kbps
Image	OCR	2.4 Kbps
	Facsimile	9.6 Kbps
	Compressed graphics	64 Kbps
	Noncompressed graphics	256 Kbps
Video	Freeze-frame	64 Kbps
	Compressed motion	400 Kbps–1.5 Mbps
	Noncompressed motion	30 Mbps
	Digital video	30 Mbps
	Television-grade color video	92 Mbps

TABLE 6.3   Resource Demand
by Typical Messages

Message type	Volume (bits)
Color picture	2,000,000
Television picture	1,000,000
Short phone message	1,000,000
One-page document	200,000
Newspaper picture	100,000
One-page document (coded)	10,000
Typical interoffice memo	3,000
Typical telegram	2,000
Transaction inbound	500
Transaction outbound	1,500
Airline reservation	200
Fire alarm	40

tion/services, (3) new locations and current application/services after growth factor adoption, and (4) new locations and new application/services.

The aggregated results have to be extended by overhead figures, by contingency workload reserves, and by the pent-up demand. The results of this function may be summarized as follows:

- Realistic concept of user requirements
- Realistic range (not precise value) of resources demand broken down by location, application/service, and user
- Consideration of contingency workload elements for backups and emergencies
- Phased plan for implementing new applications on LAN segments

Design, planning, and sizing LAN components

The previous step has provided the consolidated workload and its aggregated resource demand for all significant LAN resources. Those are, in most cases, communication facilities and servers. This consolidated demand has then to be compared with existing or ordered resources. In this comparison, practical capacity limits have to be considered instead of theoretical throughput limits. For communication facilities, peak throughput limits can be determined by stress testing. Industry standards indicate the following:

- Ethernet with CSMA/CD—up to 40 percent use
- Token Ring—up to 80 percent use

- FDDI—up to 85 percent use
- ATM—close to 100 percent use

The remaining part can't be used due to the inefficiency of the access control mechanism, frame/message sizes, and physical layout of the LAN segments.

Due to greater throughput demand, it is often better to migrate to higher-speed local area networks. There are many choices open to the LAN manager, including FDDI, switched 10-Mbps Ethernet, shared or switched 100-Mbps Ethernet, 10/100-Mbps switched Ethernet, or ATM. Chapter 2 gives a short description of each. Table 6.4 compares these alternatives from the planner point of view using the following criteria:

- Compatibility with category-3 UTP cable
- Compatibility with category-5 UTP cable
- Usability of installed internetworking components
- Availability of the technology
- Implementation in backbones
- Implementation for work groups
- Support of multimedia communications
- Fail-safe operations
- Support of virtual LANs

In interconnecting LANs, the same or similar rules apply as for wide area networks. Due to use ceilings, unscheduled downtime, and overhead, portions of the bandwidth can't be used for productive traffic. Depending on the communication protocols, the practical limit is between 50 and 70 percent.

There are several methods to increase efficiency. Data compaction and compression help to eliminate meaningless code (e.g., blanks) and use fewer bits for the most frequent characters. Spoofing is helpful to keep remote sessions alive when main sessions are broken or are too slow, saving the repeated transfer of characters to session reestablishment.

The ultimate goal of internetworking LAN segments is to economically connect local area networks to each other and to an enterprise's various information sources. The interconnection strategy depends on many factors, including the level of distributed processing, traffic concentration by sharing communication resources, and the availability of networking services.

Despite the fact that processing power and databases are now gradually becoming distributed, investment in central resources will

TABLE 6.4 Comparison of High-Speed LAN Alternatives

High-speed LANs criteria	FDDI	10-Mbps switched Ethernet	100-Mbps shared Ethernet	10- to 100-Mbps switched Ethernet	ATM
1. Compatibility with category-3 UTP cable	Not yet, technically too expensive.	Yes. Benefits due to usability of existing cabling.	Not yet available. In the future possible, but will require concentrated technical effort.	Support is yes with 10-Mbps connections; no with 100-Mbps connections.	No for 155 Mbps; eventual support for 25 to 51 Mbps.
2. Compatibility with category-5 UTP cable	Yes.	Yes.	Yes.	Yes.	Yes.
3. Usability of installed internetworking components	Additional FDDI interfaces and software for translational bridges and multiprotocol routers are required.	Connecting to existing bridges and routers is possible without software and hardware changes or replacements.	New Ethernet interface and new internetworking software is required.	100-Mbps switching hardware is required in hubs; no software changes are required because CSMA/CD is in use.	Usability of installed internetworking components. Additional ATM interfaces and software for translational bridges and multiprotocol routers are required.
4. Availability of the technology	Available and proven technology.	Available and proven.	First products are available.	First products are available.	Stand-alone and modular switches are available.
5. Implementation in backbones	FDDI is a proven solution for backbones with high availability, fail-safe capabilities, and manageability. Well suited for internetworking buildings as part of a hierarchical backbone structure. Performance is, however, somewhat limited; not well suited for multimedia.	Not recommended due to limited filtering, incomplete security, and firewall support.	Not recommended due to short distances; limitations to workgroup areas.	Good combination with 10 Mbps for users and 100 Mbps for servers; routers increase efficiency because they can be used in existing Ethernets. Disadvantage is the limited fail-safe capability.	Best solution with great scalability and manageability.

6. Implementation for work groups	Good performance, but at high price. Device adapters must be replaced; new hub and router interfaces and software are necessary.	It offers application-specific performance improvements but can cause performance bottlenecks when multiple users want to access servers simultaneously.	Good performance improvement, but no cost and technological benefits in comparison to other high-speed technologies such as FDDI.	This combination saves existing investments while improving performance by offering dedicated 10-Mbps access to users and dedicated 100-Mbps access to servers.	Offers high-speed connections with variable speeds and bandwidth.
7. Support of multimedia communications	Video and voice can be transmitted in compressed form. HDTV or other bandwidth-hungry applications can easily saturate the bandwidth when many users are using them simultaneously.	Very limited to compressed video and to very few users.	Video and voice can be transmitted in compressed form. HDTV or other bandwidth-hungry applications can easily saturate the bandwidth when many users are using them simultaneously.	With 10 Mbps in work groups combined with 100 Mbps to servers, multimedia applications can also be supported. But professional applications such as HDTV require more bandwidth.	Well suited for all communication services.
8. Fail-safe operations	Good results due to double rings, particularly in combination with hubs supporting dual homing.	At this moment, no redundant paths are supported. Support is offered by spanning tree algorithm.	At this moment, no redundant paths are supported. Support is offered by spanning tree algorithm.	At this moment, no redundant paths are supported. Support is offered by spanning tree algorithm.	Excellent redundancy; use of multiple paths, automated establishing of backup paths.
9. Support of virtual LANs	No.	Yes.	Yes.	Yes.	Yes.

remain substantial over the next few years. Those resources have to remain accessible to LAN segments.

Depending on the LAN locations—few large sites or many small sites—existing communication facilities may be used, or new ones may have to be provisioned. In the latter case, transmission costs need to be included in the budget.

The internetworking decision depends to a large extent on the availability of networking services within the corporation or, in a broader sense, in the geographical area of the LAN segments and processing entities. These services include leased lines, virtual networks, and circuit, packet, or frame switching.

The LAN designer and planner faces several alternatives: centralized processing and support of a few LAN sites, distributed processing and support of a few LAN sites, centralized processing and support of many smaller LAN sites, or distributed processing and support of many smaller LAN sites.

With centralized processing and support of a few LAN sites, there are no basic changes to the existing hierarchical network. LANs are gatewayed to the central or remote communication controller. In most cases, private networks are in operation. But, it's highly unlikely that the same physical channel is shared between internetworked LAN traffic and traffic supported by proprietary protocols.

With distributed processing and support of a few LAN sites, it would be desirable to use the same LAN operating systems. The solution is the use of open or at least de facto standards. When migrating to a standard, the common denominator is usually found with TCP/IP, XNS, or NFS. The best solution is to link the local LANs to a premise backbone, and then to network the backbones via current private network facilities.

With centralized processing and support of many smaller LAN sites, the overall star topology will remain. LANs are gatewayed to the central or remote controllers or concentrators. In most cases, virtual networking services are used to internetwork the LAN segments with the central processing entity.

With distributed processing and support of many smaller LAN sites, each LAN segment works relatively independently from the other. Standards for the operating systems would be advantageous, but are not a prerequisite. Information exchange is occasional; most likely support is via frame relay with public/private packet switching.

Although FDDI or DQDB could cover larger metropolitan area distances, the majority of interconnected LANs will involve a remote bridge or router connection. Whether to choose bridges or routers will depend on the type of internetwork traffic, and on the overall network configuration.

In general, routers are the best choice for applications in which the interlinked network connects many independent networks that occasionally exchange information with each other. In such cases, the intra-LAN traffic is considerably higher than the inter-LAN traffic. Local LAN administration is required. TCP/IP internets are good examples of those applications. When traffic volumes are higher and more directed, local LAN administration is not required, and bridges offer better performance. Bridges allow support of multiple operating systems and protocols, a critical requirement not met by routers.

Corporations with highly distributed geography dedicated to distributed processing will find routers the best solution for interconnection. Routers allow local control of LANs and offer a more flexible network, with future high growth and change in mind.

Table 6.5 compares the most important attributes of bridges and routers from a LAN designer perspective. It's assumed that the differences will disappear as more brouters appear on the market.

Usually, the decision of whether to use the spanning tree or source routing algorithms for bridging networks is beyond the LAN design and planning activity. But, depending on the standards and products selected, the impact of the algorithms has to be quantified by the designer and planner. Spanning tree may cause some performance bot-

TABLE 6.5   Comparison of Bridges and Routers

Attributes	Bridges	Routers
Function	Device for offering connectivity at layer 2 between various access protocols and media	Device for offering connectivity at layer 3 for networks with the same protocol at layer 3 and higher
Traffic volumes	High	Low to medium
Directed traffic	Good	Fair
Multiple protocols	Not sensitive	Sensitive
Address interpretation	Fast	Fair
Flexibility	Fair	High
Robustness	Fair	High
Management capabilities	Fair	Good
Route selection and path optimization	Not supported	Supported
Address analysis and filtering	Yes	Yes
Combination with wiring hubs	Yes	Yes
Backup and alternate routes support	Weak	Strong
Number of devices required	High	Moderate
Number of hops	Fair	Fair to good
Costs	Low	High

tlenecks unless the WAN portion of the interconnection is sized correctly or unless vendors provide additional features for bandwidth increase and load balancing among available channels. But spanning tree would not cause electronic storms or flooding of the interconnected LAN network. In the case of heavily meshed and bridged LANs, source routing may seriously degrade overall performance and impact all applications using the same WAN connection. While source routing broadcast messages are small—generally only 30 to 40 characters—their numbers can significantly increase the load on communication facilities connecting remote bridges to each other. Worst-case considerations are summarized in Table 6.6.

Table 6.6 takes the theoretical bandwidth as a basis. Practical examples from Travelers, Incorporated, show that the saturation level is reached earlier. LAN designers and planners have to limit the hop count by not sacrificing alternate routing capabilities. As the table shows, the maximum number of messages increases exponentially with the number of hop counts.

These facts require building partitioned mesh networks with limited numbers of connections to each other. Practical examples show that corporations are unlikely to build bridged networks with so many connections to each other, increasing performance risks due to source routing overhead. When a number of parallel connections is required, routers may be implemented instead.

Other consideration for planners include the following:

- Use of boundary routing

- Use of LAN switching to increase bandwidth for servers or for bandwidth-hungry applications

- Use of virtual LANs to offer more flexibility if moves or changes are necessary

- Consideration of new internetworking technologies

- Use of remote LAN extensions

- Use of wireless connections

TABLE 6.6   Source Routing in a Meshed Network

Number of nodes	Maximum number of broadcast messages per connection request	Line utilization			
		9.6 Kbps	56 Kbps	128 Kbps	1.5 Mbps
5	5	14%	2%	1%	0.1%
6	16	46%	8%	4%	0.3%
7	65	184%	32%	14%	1.1%
8	328	929%	159%	74%	5.8%

- Consider collapsed backbones or distributed backbones in the local area

The results of the technology diffusion will show the following changes during the second half of the present decade:

- Business applications move from LAN internets to switched LANs.
- Technical applications move from switched LANs to ATM.
- Research applications will use more bandwidth for ATM reaching the gigabit range.

Basically, there are three alternatives to carrying the traffic of inter-networked LANs:

1. Physical and logical connections of network architectures serving other applications; SNA, DNA, DCA, Expand, and so on could be chosen. This solution requires that gateways be at the locations of the LANs to be connected. Both the gateways and the communication links may become the bottlenecks.
2. Separate LAN-LAN internetwork using bridges, routers, or brouters for directing the traffic between the LAN locations. By selecting adequate bandwidth, performance bottlenecks are unlikely.
3. Encapsulation technology, where TCP/IP is carrying the traffic for all other protocols. This is the preferred alternative today. Performance bottlenecks from earlier applications could be successfully eliminated. IBM's solution—DSW—seems to play the role of a de facto industry standard.

Recent surveys show that approximately 25 percent choose solution 1, 35 percent choose solution 2, and 40 percent solution 3. Solutions 2 and 3 are more expensive due to the dedicated nature of the communication links.

In sizing servers, certain server computation cycles are used for administration that can't be allocated to any particular station or application. Factors such as overhead, downtime and queuing at high-use levels reduce the practical server utilization limit to 75 to 85 percent.

RAD is enhancing its routers to handle SNA and LAN protocols, including SDLC, NetBios, and LU 6.2, using a new combination of routing/bridging schemes. The protocols are transmitted at the MAC layer, but the bridges exchange information in order to find the best path through the network. The new technique, called shortest-path first (SPF), is replacing source routing. In terms of bandwidth utilization, using SPF is more economical than encapsulating protocols into TCP/IP packets.

Figure 6.4 shows how upgrade points can be identified for LAN resources. With new design, this consideration starts at the upgrade point. This figure offers a generic view that's applicable for all LAN managed objects.

The design stage is accomplished in a hierarchical manner:

1. Designing and sizing LAN segments at floors

2. Designing and sizing building distribution systems

3. Designing and sizing premise (campus) distribution systems

4. Designing and sizing LAN interconnection facilities

Design includes the wiring concentrators and wiring connections to the network interface cards in the servers and stations. Figure 6.5 shows the result of the "logical" design, indicating Ethernet and Token Rings at the floors, Token Ring for connecting floors, and FDDI for the campus backbone. The same logical topology is mapped into the "physical" layout, as shown in Fig. 6.6.

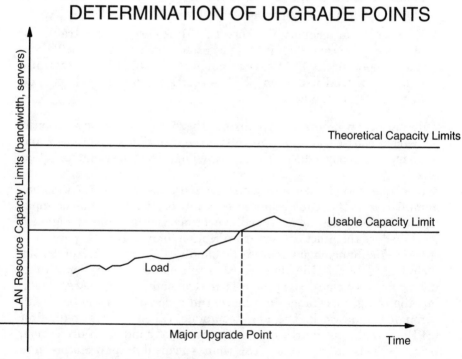

Figure 6.4 Upgrade points for LAN resources.

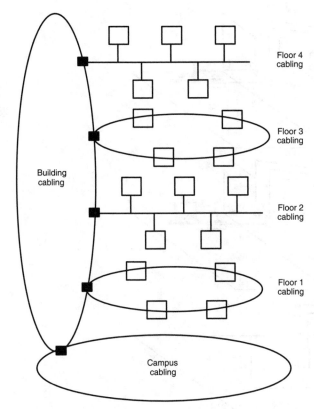

Figure 6.5   Results of logical network design.

In order to improve fault tolerance of hub topologies, redundancy needs to be planned very carefully. Hubs may be networked by using the tree, ring, or bus topology. Figure 6.7 (Lannet 1991) shows the three structures, indicating a decision point for redundant links with an "R." It's assumed that Ethernet transceivers are equipped with redundant link connections. In the event of any link or hub breakdown, the network is still fully functional.

Figure 6.8 (Lannet 1991) shows a ring solution with redundant links. The media of this arrangement could be copper or fiber. Figure 6.9 (Lannet 1991) offers a full fault-tolerant network. Synchronous Ethernet is assumed due to the number of hubs traversed between stations on the maximum path. Part of the aim of designing and planning is to provide management access to the hubs. Either outband access has to be guaranteed to each of the hubs, or parts connecting backbone hubs must be retained in a manual (nonmanageable) mode.

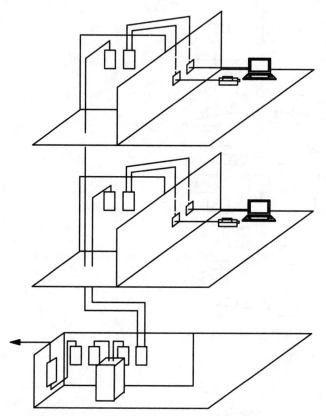

Figure 6.6   Results of physical network design.

In planning and implementing LANs, the question of power supply must not be ignored. There are two options: (1) online uninterrupted power supply (UPS) or (2) a standby UPS. As part of the design process, careful consideration is needed to determine which components need special protection. The availability of inexpensive UPSs makes protection of each managed object attractive, but the planner should make sure not to sacrifice quality for price. UPSs only stop electrical transients from the wall outlet, and they don't provide protection against the potentially harmful transients—surges and spikes—that enter into peripheral pacts via the cables connecting components, such as hiring hubs, concentrators, adapter cards, modems, and principal servers with other LAN segments or CPUs.

LAN cables act like antennas, attracting all forms of transients: secondary lightning hits, electrostatic discharges, and equipment power transients. Switching and environmentally caused transients may enter into the connected equipment part and bring expensive circuitry down.

R = Reserve

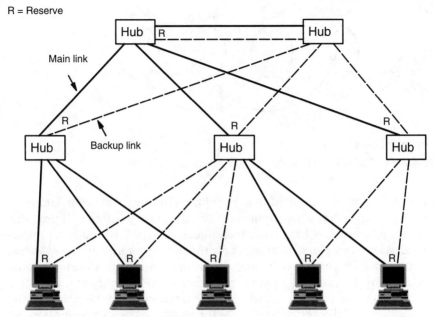

Figure 6.7 Full tolerant tree topology with hubs.

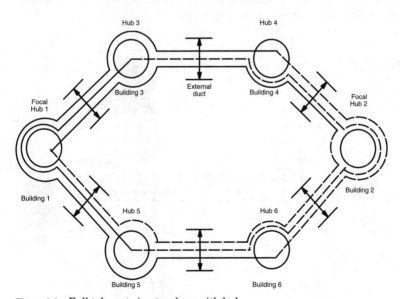

Figure 6.8 Full tolerant ring topology with hubs.

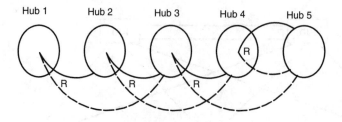

Hub 1   Hub 2   Hub 3   Hub 4   Hub 5

R = Reserve

Figure 6.9   Full tolerant bus topology with hubs.

UPSs may be configured in a distributed or central manner. Opinions vary on which is the best approach. The ultimate solution will probably be a combination of both basic techniques. Figure 6.10 shows an implementation example, with support for the file server and all the attached nodes. Ideally, a smart UPS offers monitoring and auto-shutdown capabilities. In the event of a power breakdown, the software will initiate a countdown and proceed with an orderly termination of the program and a shutdown of the system to ensure the protection of all information. An intelligent UPS also adjusts for overloaded, defective, or aging batteries and closes down critical programs before the batteries are exhausted. Links to wiring concentrators are expected.

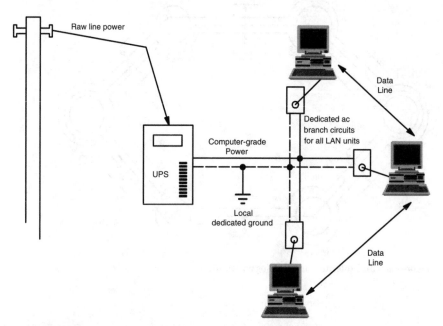

Figure 6.10   Uninterrupted power supply for key LAN components.

For each planning phase, several criteria have to be considered. Those criteria may be grouped as follows:

1. Transport-oriented criteria
   a. Fairness: all stations have the same rights to transmit.
   b. Priority of transmission: certain frames/messages may be transmitted in an expedited manner.
   c. Flexibility: reconfiguration of station without interrupting operations.
   d. Expandability: additional stations may be connected without interrupting operations.
   e. Connectivity: any-to-any connections have to be supported.
   f. Throughput rates: practical throughput limits between stations, which may be supported independently from the overall traffic in the LAN segments, or in the LAN interconnecting segments.
2. Service-oriented criteria
   a. Throughput rates: practical throughput rates that may be offered to users.
   b. Elapsed time: transmission time of frames/messages within the LAN segment or in the interconnected LAN environment.
   c. Access delay: elapsed time between transmission intention and actual "control" of transmission devices.
   d. Use: dynamic indicators showing the ratio between offered and supportable traffic.
   e. Performance in saturation: metric for quantifying how rapidly congested traffic can be accommodated and serviced.
3. Quality-oriented criteria
   a. Availability: LANs are expected to be available when users want service.
   b. Reliability: metric to characterize the ability of individual objects to sustain service; usually MTBF (mean time between failures) is used as an indicator.
   c. Maintainability: metric to express the ability for detecting, determining, and eliminating problems; usually MTTR (mean time to repair) is used as indicator.
   d. Accuracy: LANs are expected to offer error-free transmission of frames/messages.
   e. Data security: this indicator offers the transmission of frames/messages without the risk of being read or manipulated.
   f. User friendliness: handling of applications has to be as simple as possible; usually help functions, front ends, and menus are offered and implemented.
4. Cost-oriented criteria
   a. Installation costs: one-time costs to implement the LAN segment or segments.

  b. Operational costs: recurring cost of operating the WAN segment or segments.

  c. Maintenance costs: recurring cost of preventing maintenance activities.

Cabling selection is very important to ensure good economics and reasonable performance at the same time. The demarcation lines between technologies can't be drawn very easily.

The competition between media still exists, but the following trends can be observed:

- Unshielded twisted pair—category-5—is leading the broadest applications in local area networks with continuously increased upper bandwidth limits.

- Shielded twisted pair for special high-speed applications where unshielded twisted pair is not recommended due to radiation.

- Optical fiber for very high speed, in most cases for LAN backbones in metropolitan and campus areas.

- Coaxial cables are no longer under serious consideration for LANs; but they may play a role for interconnecting LANs using services from cable television suppliers.

- Wireless technology for special buildings, remote LANs, and as a backup alternative for local area networks.

Besides technological feasibility, cabling costs have to be evaluated very carefully. Cable costs per foot are approximately 10 times higher for optical fiber than for unshielded twisted pair; for wall plates, this ratio could be as high as 40. In case of comparing typical installations, the ratio is decreasing to 2 to 3. The installation cost per station is approximately $900 with unshielded twisted pair, and $1800 with optical fiber (Mier 1991).

Shielded twisted pair is between those prices. Outside the United States, prices are much different. Examples of how some of the criteria interact with each other were discussed earlier in this chapter.

Implementation of local area networks

Implementation is the planning and execution of all activities related to upgrades or new installations. Activities are partly clerical and partly technical.

Requests for proposals. Companies ask vendors for specific information on products. This information is then used to select facilities and equipment, interconnecting devices, WAN communication services (optional), wiring solutions, and interrupted power supply components. Potential suppliers are expected to detail the products' functions, price, availability, support, security, and conformance with international standards.

Selection and weighting criteria. Selection criteria, and the priority weighting of each criterion, should be determined prior to evaluation. For weighting criteria, the preference matrix technique is very useful. Rather than comparing each criterion against all others at the same time, the preference matrix compares only two criteria at a time (Terplan 1991b). Expert systems may be used as well for configuring complex networks, considering a fairly large number of design alternatives.

Operational manuals. Operational manuals should be prepared based on guidelines from planning steps. They will describe how the LAN is going to be used. An operational manual is extremely useful in helping someone to understand what he or she is supposed to accomplish in the operational control and administration areas. In particular, standards and procedures for the following areas may be included: problem determination and LAN management, version control of server software, fallback or failure planning, inventory control and name management, financial analysis and budgeting, configuration and management, change management.

Conversion plans. Assuming that you're dealing with a complex interconnected LAN, whereby the operation of the larger organization may be impaired once the network has broken down, it's quite unlikely that the network will be implemented without careful scrutiny. It will more likely need a step-by-step approach, perhaps running parallel, doubling volumes and operation for a certain period of time. That means that the old network (most likely a hierarchical structure with a powerful host computer) should remain operational until the new one has been thoroughly tested and proven. These functions involve plans detailing the necessary products to be installed and time frames for the development of standards and procedures, education, and installation management.

Prototyping. When the user has custom engineering and/or custom software development, he or she is expected to take responsibility for testing by using prototypes of the network. Based on the testing results, the principal requirements may or may not be met. If not, the capacity planner must go back to step 2 in order to do more planning, and the engineering effort must continue. The whole planning process is strongly iterative (in other words, previous phases and steps within the phases may be repeated many times). When the functionality and/or the service requirements are not met, there are several alternatives to be implemented: Return to the planning phase and include more alternatives; return to the optimization and modeling phase and evaluate additional alternatives within the original hardware or software capabilities; tune the prototype, evaluate the results, and decide on further actions. This procedure may be observed again in Fig. 6.1 as part of the overall capacity planning methodology.

Backup and recovery plan.   Due to the reliability behavior of a complex LAN, it's not a matter of whether the LAN(s) will break down as much as when. When the LAN does fail, LAN operational control must be ready with a preconceived action plan. Contingency and recovery planning become key elements of operating a LAN with on-line service. Since the various components are relied upon so heavily by the users, it's essential that there are predefined plans for restoring service in the case of adverse circumstances. The two plans required follow.

Contingency plan.   A contingency plan must deal with ways for temporarily reconfiguring to overcome individually failing LAN components and allow for continued operation during the time taken to resolve the problem. Each operational level of the network should be considered in this plan and a full range of automated and manual methods included. There will be some situations that can be handled by network operations alone through dynamic reconfiguration; others will require a combination of automated and manual steps to be performed both centrally and remotely. Contingency plans should prescribe the various combinations of these steps and should also define alternative procedures in the event that the primary method is unworkable. Examples of situations that should be addressed in the plan include handling of the following situations: a failing cable; a failing regional concentrator, node, gateway, router, or bridge; a failing communication server; a failing wiring hub; a failing power supply; an errant application or system program.

Any significant change in the LAN components will require that the contingency plan be reevaluated and updated as appropriate. The addition or deletion of hardware or software components in the LAN could have an impact on the alternatives available in contingency planning. The impact of such changes should be reflected in the contingency plan. "Dry run" testing of the plan should be used to verify its workability and to train the LAN staff in the identified methods. The complexity of the contingency plan becomes a reflection of how well the components are isolated from one another. The network should be designed to minimize the impact of network failures. Such a network will result in fewer variables to be considered in the contingency plan and perhaps simplify modeling if the independence also applies to the component's functionality. In this respect, segmentation by using local and remote bridges may contribute to lower vulnerability.

Recovery plan.   The recovery plan differs from the contingency plan in that it defines methods available to restore either a single component of the network or the entire network to operational status. The recovery plan should contain detailed procedures to be used in returning the component back to service. Topics that should be covered in this plan include preferred approach, acceptable alternatives, critical steps to be performed (along with their priorities), personnel responsibilities, and target deadlines. The plan should take into account the fact that system failure may result from equipment malfunction, natural disaster, fire, and sabotage, as well as from other, unforeseen causes. Therefore, the identified procedures must be able to deal with single components all the way up to the entire network. Procedures developed as a result of the recovery planning process should become a permanent portion of guides for LAN operational control. To the extent possible, the recovery plan should also be tested to familiarize personnel with the effort involved and to validate the plan's effectiveness.

Examples of issues that should be covered in the recovery plan are the following:

- Emergency procedures for the recovery of critical items such as on-line files and programs
- Assignment of responsibilities to human resources
- Who should be contacted first in the escalation procedure
- Recovery procedures for operator errors that destroy files and programs
- Recovery from application software failures on servers
- Availability of backup computer facilities
- Recovery from power failures
- Implementing continuous backup systems
- Availability of backup power
- How to diagnose the problem
- Off-site storage of duplicates of customer-sensitive information
- How to guarantee LAN security
- How to inform customers about anomalies

Cutover scheduling. Based on the conversion plan, implementation usually takes several steps. The best way is to phase in implementation by location or application. The cutover must be prepared with great care and should be accomplished overnight or over a weekend to give time for debugging. For extensive debugging, test transactions are expected to be ready for trial runs. These could be the same transactions used previously in the prototyping phase. They may be generated and composed as part of the remote terminal emulation.

Stress testing. LAN design and planning are iterative processes. Using remote terminal emulation for existing subsets of communication networks (e.g., for prototypes) is a promising technique for reducing the time requirements for designing and modeling. A remote terminal emulator is an external, independent driver that's connected to the system and LAN under test via standard communication interfaces. The emulator generates messages and transactions for the network under test, based on a set of representative scripts defined by the user's application.

Using this technique, not only the functionality but also the service-level requirements can be evaluated. By attempting to use as many of the new LAN facilities as possible, the chances of identifying potential bottlenecks are significantly improved. Operations and communication networks personnel must be trained to face all eventualities before actual cutover. Help desk, administration, and technical support personnel should be prepared as well. As a result, tuning activities may be initiated. Examples include placement of bridges or routers, splitting LAN segments, consolidating LAN segments, changing the logical sequence of stations, upgrading and downgrading servers, reallocating stations to servers, and many others. Links to performance management are options. CPM and PERT techniques are useful in timing the cutover.

Paralleling actual volumes and cutover. It's recommended that actual volumes and transaction types be emulated as closely as possible prior to cutover. The new LAN and the old LAN (or old procedures) should work simultaneously for a defined period of time. If results are satisfactory, service levels are met, and personnel are properly trained, complete cutover may be executed.

Modeling, Design, and Capacity Planning of Local Area Networks

Recently, designing LANs has been a more or less intuitive process. Due to the price of products and human time requirements, users were not really eager to design and size local area networks. Connectivity and compatibility items were much more highly prioritized than properly sizing the servers and properly determining the bandwidth required for satisfactory performance. But load and local area networks are increasing, topologies are getting more complex, and performance is being evaluated more critically.

LAN design tools is a fairly new product area. There are many wide area network design tools on the market, but few address the LAN design marketplace. Outside of design guidelines provided by vendors, which are usually not available to users, there are only a handful of tools that can be purchased for in-house planning and ongoing network management. The present obstacles of using such tools are as follows:

- There's no budget for such tools.
- They require a computer that may not be part of the installation.
- Performance information is required but is not available.
- They require monitoring instruments that may not be part of the installation.

In order to evaluate products, the following criteria should be considered (Datapro NS30 1990c): system requirements, input data requirements, control parameter extensions, technology used, applicability of live data, postprocessing, animated displays, and maturity of product.

System requirements. The processing power should be enough to meet needs of simulation techniques, which can be very extensive for large segments or interconnected LANs. At least an EGA display is generally required for PC-based systems. However, some of the design systems are based on more powerful platforms, such as Sun Microsystems workstations.

Input data requirements. This includes which data the user should provide prior to starting a what-if evaluation. Input parameters may be grouped by LAN segment and interconnecting parameters. Modeling parameters may be classified into two groups: LAN parameters and internetwork parameters.

LAN segments parameters are sizes (average packet and message sizes), protocols (lower-, middle-, and high-level), application and network operating systems, measure of LAN power and its background load index of average workstations on a local LAN, and number of workstations on a remote LAN.

Internetwork parameters are network architecture; bridge, router, and gateway transfer rates; lower-level protocol on the interlink; number of hops between two LANs; background load on links between LANs.

Control parameter extensions.   Users may be interested in changing or extending modeling to new operating systems, unsupported protocols, and to new transmission media. This criterion checks on the openness of the modeling process. Also, programmability may be included here.

Technology used.   The answers here impact the accuracy of modeling results. Queuing equations allow for quick evaluations of expected performance ranges. Complex simulation allows modeling in greater detail, and guarantees much higher accuracy. Some products combine both techniques.

Applicability of live data.   Once the LAN is running, LAN analyzers (see Chap. 5 for more details) may be used to collect actual traffic data. Some performance models can read in this collected data and use it to augment the modeling capabilities. It helps model calibration and validation. Also, the effects of growth may be observed more accurately.

Postprocessing.   The right presentation form helps to interpret modeling results. It's extremely important to reexamine the modeling results without completely rerunning the model. Graphics and colors help to better understand the results.

Animated displays.   This capability allows designers and planners to get a feel for the impact of certain modeling parameters, such as queuing delays at congestion points or collisions in certain LAN segments. Some products provide both a step mode and an automatic mode in support of this type of visual display. In many circumstances, this graphical support accelerates the evaluation process by highlighting potential performance bottlenecks.

Maturity of product.   It's extremely important to collect implementation experiences from other users. Most products are recent developments, and just a few products are based on mature products that have been around in the WAN area for many years. Also, the integration of existing solutions for LAN segments and for interconnected LANs would be a positive sign of maturity.

Modeling design and capacity planning for LANs can no longer be separated from other networking segments. The vast majority of LANs are interconnected over MANs and WANs. Suboptimal design solutions for LANs don't help to control and stabilize overall performance and operating costs.

Modeling, design, and capacity planning always starts with the intelligent interpretation of measurement results if such results exist. Chapter 5 showed a number of performance reporting examples. Performance visualization, including workload profiles, service indicators, and utilization figures help to understand how the networking segments perform. The use of RMON probes means a real breakthrough in this area. Based on these results, modeling packages help to answer what-if questions in terms of changing the workload profiles, network configurations, networking parameters, or a combination of them. It does not make any difference to the planner whether the modeling package is using analytical, emulation, or simulation techniques.

A brief review of existing products for modeling individual and interconnected LANs follows.

BESTnet from BGS. For companies with strong IBM presence where SNA is the internetworking solution, this tool can help to model and optimize performance. The modeling part consists of BESTnet Boundary and BESTnet MSNF. The modeling part uses accurate and up-to-date configuration and workload data collected by Capture. The actual data are collected in VTAM and in the network and are merged together to guarantee unique visualization of the configuration, its load, and utilizations.

Modeling is supported for SNA sessions with Token Rings, SNA-sessions over X.25, and SNA sessions across SNI gateways.

This product gains more importance when SNMP data are to be transferred over SNA sessions.

COMNET III from C.A.C.I. COMNET III is an off-the-shelf model that predicts the performance of LANs, MANs, and WANs. This product is capable of modeling the following technologies: X.25, ISDN, SS7, Frame Relay, Cell Relay, FDDI, SNA, TCP/IP, DECnet, CSMA/CD, token passing, polling, radio, and satellite networks.

The network topology is defined by nodes and links. They can be organized hierarchically into subnetworks. Nodes perform processing functions and contain parts for connecting to links. Ports provide input or output buffering and processing. A link is a physical transmission facility connecting parts on two or more nodes.

The library of node objects includes a generic node model as well as specific configurations for modeling computer groups, routers, and ATM switches. The library of link objects includes point-to-point, CSMA/CD, CSMA, Token Ring, FDDI, token bus, polling, and ALOHA models.

A node has a list of commands that it can execute. The command library includes process data, read file, write file, transport message, answer message, and setup-session objects.

Sequences of these commands are associated with application sources attached to a node. Applications can be scheduled to occur according to an interarrival time distribution or contingent on satisfaction of an incoming message requirement.

The network workload can also be produced by attaching message sources, response sources, session sources, or call sources to a node. A message source produces applications that execute a single transport command; a response source executes a single answer command. A session source executes a setup command, which establishes a session. Once a session is established, a series of messages is sent for the duration of the session. A call source is used to model circuit-switched traffic.

Messages are transported from source to destination using transport, routing, data link, and medium access control protocol objects. Transport services are provided by the source and destination nodes. The transport service breaks a message into packets at the source node and reassembles the packets into a delivered message at the destination node. The packets are transported by an end-to-end transport connection. A node selects an outgoing port for a packet using a routing protocol. For subnetworks that use connection-oriented routing, packets follow the path established at session setup time. The data link service at the port creates frames out of incoming packets and then uses the medium access controller at the port to contend for the link. Physical layer services are provided by links.

Users can add their own variations to any of the object libraries of nodes, links, traffic sources, protocols, and distributions by copying an object and changing its parameters or by developing a new object. Adding objects by changing parameters requires no programming; developing a new object requires a minimal amount of programming using MODSIM II.

Particularly for LANs, the following reports are provided:

- LAN statistics, including packet/frame transfer time, transit time, system waiting time, overhead percentages, throughput rates, message losses, and interarrival distribution diagrams

- Client statistics, showing queue lengths, waiting time, and eventual blocking

- Server statistics, concentrating on queue lengths, waiting time, blocking, and storage utilization

- Link statistics, including expected utilization rates and throughput

NetSolve from Quantessential Solutions. NetSolve focuses on interconnected LANs. It is a wide area network modeling software that contains several WAN pricing and design applications. The upper limits of the product are 250 switching locations with a maximum of 25,000 switch-traffic routes.

NetSolve has a modular structure; it starts with simple point-to-point pricing and performance calculations and ends with Mesh Designer. Mesh Designer contains a set of modules that automate mesh network design and optimize the key criteria of price, performance, and reliability. Standard features include billing ratios, the ability to create custom tariff and point-of-presence databases. Net-Solve can interact with COMNET III from C.A.C.I. After Mesh Designer is used to produce a least-cost LAN interconnection model, the model file can be exported to COMNET III, allowing analysts to evaluate the performance of the model. The result is optimal WAN performance at reasonable costs.

Autonet from network design and analysis corporation. Autonet consists of planning and operational tools (Fig. 6.11).

The majority of planning tools help with optimizing the interconnection of LANs. In particular, the following targets are followed by the company:

- Design and maintenance of cost-effective network
- Effective use of networking resources
- Identifying billing errors

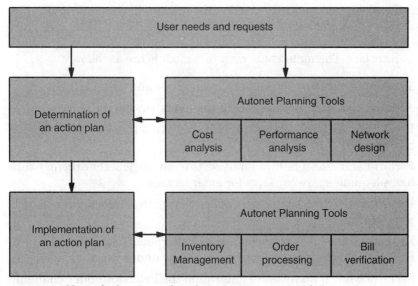

Figure 6.11 Network planning and implementation process with Autonet.

- Building a contingency plan
- Optimizing network performance
- Connecting the models to change management
- Connecting the models to asset management

Performance-1 provides performance analysis for WANs and LANs using analytical modeling techniques with the convenience of a Windows graphical user interface. The WAN component includes a queueing model for most known WAN protocols. The LAN component is based on a discrete time analysis model. Both Ethernet and Token Ring are supported. The main goals with this module are as follows:

- Evaluate the impact of increased traffic by performing a sensitivity analysis.
- Analyze the performance of the existing network using indicators such as response time and resource utilization.
- Determine the maximal allowable traffic for facilities and equipment.
- Plan future growth to optimize network design.
- Evaluate LAN performance for Ethernets and Token Rings to ensure ideal operating conditions.

Performance-3 is a comprehensive performance analysis tool for multiprotocol networks comprised of LAN-to-LAN connections and WAN transmission facilities. By entering the network topology, equipment specifications, and workload profiles, the model will generate application response times and network utilizations. Link and node failures can also be simulated to create robust networks using the Windows graphical user interface. The main goals with this module are as follows:

- Determine network bottlenecks in facilities and in equipment.
- Achieve high accuracy and quick results to review.
- Predict future performance problems to avoid stressed utilization of resources.
- Perform and model failure analysis to evaluate whether the network has adequate spare capacity for emergencies.
- Import traffic data from LAN probes that gather information on network traffic.
- Evaluate local LAN performance in Ethernets, Token Rings, and in FDDIs to ensure ideal operating conditions under various load mixes.
- Perform what-if analyses to determine the behavior under changing configurations and workload conditions.

Autonet in combination with special LAN modeling tools can support an enterprise modeling solution.

OPNET from Mil3. OPNET is a comprehensive software environment for modeling, simulating, and analyzing the performance of communication networks, processors, and applications, as well as distributed systems. OPNET presents an advanced graphical user interface that supports multiwindowing, makes use of menus and icons, and runs under X-Windows. Supported platforms include widely used engineering workstations from Sun, HP, DEC, IBM, and Silicon Graphics.

Graphical object-oriented editors for defining topologies and architectures directly parallel actual systems, allowing an intuitive mapping between a system and its model. Its hierarchical approach simplifies the specification and presentation of large and complex interconnected LANs.

The process editor provides a powerful and flexible language to design models of protocols, resources, applications, algorithms, queueing policies, and other processes. Specification is performed in the Proto-C language, which combines a graphical state-transition-diagram approach with a library of approximately 300 communication- and simulation-specific functions. The full generality and power of the C language is also available.

OPNET simulations generate user-selected performance and behavioral data. Simulation results can be plotted as time-series graphs, scatter plots, histograms, and probability functions. Standard statistics and confidence intervals are easily generated, and additional insight can be obtained by applying mathematical operators to the collected data. The product provides an advanced animation capability for visualizing simulation events. Both automatic and user-customized animations can be displayed interactively during or after a simulation. Animations can depict messages flowing between objects, control flow in a process, paths of mobile nodes, and dynamic values such as queue size or resource status.

OPNET provides open system features, including interfaces to standard languages, the ability to take advantage of third-party libraries, an application program interface, access to databases and data files such as those generated by network analyzers, and PostScript and TIFF export for desktop publishing.

Modeling technology is based on a series of hierarchically related editors that parallel the structure of actual networks. The usual approach is to start at the wide area and end in process models of selected nodes.

Node objects are created to represent the various communicating sites of a network. Each node belongs to a class that defines its internal structure and its attributes. Attributes can be either built-in or user-defined properties of node models. Attribute examples include the processing speed of a switch, the buffer capacity of a gateway, and the traffic-generation rate of a workstation.

Nodes communicate with each other via various communication links. All versions of OPNET support fixed-position nodes with point-to-point and bus links (e.g., Ethernet LANs). In addition to these, OPNET Modeler/Radio supports mobile and satellite node communications over radio links. Link models are used to account for delays and transmission-error rates. Each type of link model can be customized, if necessary, to fit particular applications. Models of local or metropolitan area networks can be created within the context of a subnetwork. They can be designed to contain any combination of node and link objects deployed within their local coordinate systems. Communication links can be defined between subnetworks to form internetworks on a larger scale. Subnetworks can contain other subnetworks to form unlimited network hierarchies.

The Process Editor combines a powerful state-transition-diagram representation with an extensive procedure library to support rapid development of process models. Since protocol and algorithm specifications are often defined using these diagrams, this development environment gives the modeler a critical head start in transforming specifications into operational models.

The Analysis Tool provides a graphical environment to view and manipulate data and statistics collected during the simulation. It supports the evaluation of complex network performance and behavior. Standard and user-specified probes can be inserted at any point in a model to collect data and statistics. Simulation output collected by probes can be displayed graphically, viewed numerically, or exported to other software packages. In addition, results from a series of simulation runs can be automatically collated into a single OPNET output file, facilitating sensitivity analysis. OPNET graphs can be printed in color or black and white on PostScript output devices. Graphs can also be exported using standard TIFF or Encapsulated PostScript formats for placement in desktop publishing packages. Using menus, network variables can be inspected and compared in a multiwindow environment that includes time-series plots, histograms, probability and cumulative distribution functions, scattergrams, and animated displays of process model execution.

Typical performance indicators include the following:

- Response time and its distribution
- Transfer delays in nodes
- Communigrams between selected stations and applications

- Bandwidth utilization
- Packet length distributions
- Throughput of interconnecting devices
- End-to-end delay analysis (Fig. 6.12)

Data exports can help you to use other tools (e.g., SAS to validate OPNET models with measurement data collected by RMON probes or other monitors).

BONeS network modules from the AltaGroup. The BONeS network modeling modules are a comprehensive set of libraries of network devices and applications. They offer engineering expertise to help users achieve instant productivity in network design and planning. Using the appropriate BONeS network modules allows you to do the following:

- Determine the effect of additional traffic in existing configurations.
- Evaluate the impact of new applications before the software is purchased or upgraded and installed.
- Determine when to upgrade LAN segments to different protocols or higher speeds.
- Configure interconnections with various types of routers.
- Size WAN links and plan for link failure.
- Optimize WAN capacities and determine current and projected bandwidth requirements.

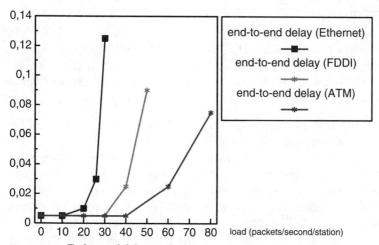

Figure 6.12   End-to-end delay analysis.

- Do client/server studies to determine the hardware capacity required at the server for the requisite number of users as well as the impact of the additional traffic on the network.

- Analyze router performance and experiment by simulating various hardware interconnecting devices and trying out various routing protocols.

The BONeS network modules can be used with the BONeS PlanNet simulation engine for plug-and-play simulation using standard components. When used with the BONeS Designer engine, the user can develop new modules or make detailed adjustments to existing network modules. Simulation of the network results in plots of various performance metrics such as delay, utilization, and throughput. These plots can be used to make decisions on the WAN, MAN, and LAN design.

LAN segment modules are used to model network segments using specific network protocols. When a traffic generator is attached to the network segment, packets are generated in accordance to the specified LAN protocol, and packet transmission is simulated with one of these modules. Each module acts as a bus or traffic concentrator with traffic modules connected to represent user nodes. LAN segment models include the following:

- Token Ring with 4 and 16 Mbps with early token release.

- Ethernet represents the standard Ethernet—10-Base5 with the CSMA/CD family of protocols.

- 10-BaseT module models the behavior of 10-BaseT with the CSMA/CD family of protocols.

- 100-BaseT module models the behavior of 100-BaseT with CSMA/CD family of protocols.

- FDDI module models the high-speed token-passing protocol that operates over fiber media. FDDI includes a complex capacity-allocation scheme to accommodate both bursty and stream traffic consisting of synchronous (voice and real-time video) and asynchronous (typically data packets) portions.

Table 6.7 summarizes the input parameters and output results for each of the local networks modeled.

Figure 6.13 shows the segmentation need for an office Token Ring beyond a certain number of attorneys (Jarzwinski 1993) for two 4-Mbps Token Rings. Also new applications (e.g., imaging) could be modeled using PlanNet. Figure 6.14 shows the result, with an earlier stress point of approximately 30 attorneys. This early warning of performance bottlenecks helps to plan for additional capacity. Additional capacity means segmentation or higher bandwidth or a combination of both.

TABLE 6.7   Input and Output Parameters for Modeling LANs

LANs	Ethernet	10-BaseT	100-BaseT	Token Ring	FDDI
Input parameters					
Segment/ring length	x			x	x
Mean cable length	x	x	x		
Repeated signal distance		x	x		
Propagation delay	x				
Target token rotation time					x
Priority thresholds T_Pri					x
Synch allocation/node					x
Buffer size/node (frames)				x	x
Hardware latency				x	x
Label	x	x	x	x	x
Collect statistics	x	x	x	x	x
Output parameters					
Delay	x	x	x	x	x
Packets/sec	x	x	x	x	x
Collisions/sec	x	x	x		
Transmission attempts per packet	x	x	x		
Bits/sec	x	x	x	x	x

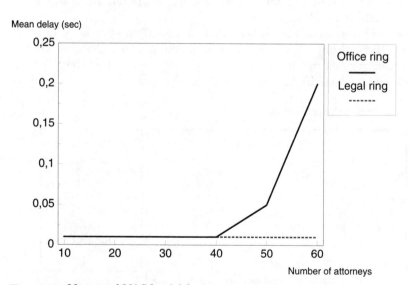

Figure 6.13   Mean total MAC-level delays.

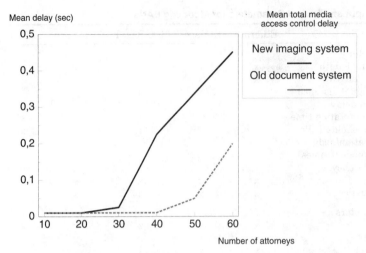

Mean delay (sec)

Mean total media
access control delay

New imaging system

Old document system

Number of attorneys

Figure 6.14   MAC-level message delays on office ring.

Figure 6.15 shows simulated results for FDDI supporting various types of applications. The results include the combination of synchronous and asynchronous traffic. The aggregate bandwidth demand is approaching 80 Mbps at peak.

BONeS interconnect modules assist in identifying bottlenecks, evaluating throughput of interconnect components, and discovering the impact of various routing protocols and spanning tree bridge configurations. The router library consists of two components:

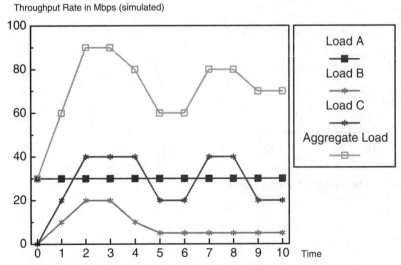

Throughput Rate in Mbps (simulated)

Load A

Load B

Load C

Aggregate Load

Time

Figure 6.15   Simulated results for FDDI utilization.

1. *Multiprotocol router with vendor-specific parameters.*   This represents a bridge/router that can be used to connect LAN segments to each other or to a WAN. This module supports Apple ARP, DECnet, Novell IPX, OSPF, RIP, and XNS protocols. To allow users to support other routing protocols, there is a generic routing protocol available. Using these features, users can add other routing protocols to the module by specifying the protocol characteristics. The multiprotocol router also supports spanning tree bridging. It models the performance characteristics of approximately 20 router devices, including those from 3Com, Cisco, Chipcom, DEC, IBM, Proteon, Vitalink, Wellfleet, and Xyplex. The performance characteristics used for modeling the devices are obtained from published benchmarks of the vendors. The multiprotocol router consists of two types of components: processors and ports. Data is received/transmitted via the ports, and the processors make routing decisions. Statistics can be collected for the ports and/or the processors.

2. *Single-protocol router.*   This is a streamlined version of the multiprotocol router and is optimized for ease of use. This module supports only one routing protocol. The vendor-specific performance parameters are not available with this module.

The bridge module models the spanning tree algorithm. It consists of two types of components: processors and ports. Data is received/transmitted via the ports, and the processors make bridging decisions. Statistics can be collected for the ports and/or for the processors.

Table 6.8 lists the input parameters for single-protocol routers, multiprotocol routers, bridges, and the output results that may be plotted and listed or exported to other reporting applications.

Other modules support WAN modeling and traffic generation for applications running under TCP/IP, FTP, NFS, and NetBIOS.

NetReview design service from IBM.   IBM has packaged the design and modeling tools into a consulting package. This package contains the following modules:

- *Traffic survey.*   This module analyzes data extracted directly from the network components, and it will report exactly what is happening in the network, revealing bottlenecks or potential problems.

- *Cost optimization.*   Even in a network with a technically sound design there are still many choices to make that have significant cost impacts; for example, decisions for which service to use from which suppliers, which devices to use where in the network, and use of more centralized or distributed structures. This module produces cost-optimal data and voice or integrated traffic network solutions

TABLE 6.8   Input and Output Parameters for Modeling Routers and Bridges

Interconnecting device	Single-protocol router	Multiprotocol router	Bridge
Input parameters			
Bidge ID		x	x
Memory size	x	x	x
Number of processors	x	x	x
Vendor-specific router		x	
Latency parameters	x	x	x
Protocol priority		x	
Load balance WAN link?	x	x	
Bridge by port		x	
Route protocol by port		x	
Costs by port	x	x	x
Maximum transmission unit by port	x	x	x
Subnet, network, and domain names	x	x	
Label	x	x	x
Collect statistics?	x	x	x
Output parameters			
Delay	x	x	x
Packets/sec	x	x	x
Bits/sec	x	x	x
Utilization and throughput	x	x	x

that deliver the correct levels of service to support business requirements while minimizing the investment in communication facilities and equipment.

- *Backbone design.*   This module considers traffic volumes, performance, and availability requirements and produces an optimal backbone design and routing strategy for the networks.

- *Performance simulation.*   This module allows you to project network design into the future and analyze its probable performance. Simulation provides maximum reassurance that the design choice will keep the networks future-proof.

- *Design consultancy.*   In addition to the preceding modules, network design specialists are available on a daily consulting basis to help users with network design problems using various types of instruments from IBM and from third parties.

This professional services package is very IBM-oriented. The input parameters are populated by IBM network monitors or application packages. IBM does not offer specific modules for LAN design and monitoring. The package is limited to SNA backbone design and performance prediction and is useful in cases where SNA is used as the LAN interconnection architecture.

NetMaker from Make Systems. NetMaker is an object-oriented suite of tools for designing, simulating, and analyzing internetworks. It allows users to visualize network data incorporating simulation of specific vendors' devices and tariffs from specific carriers. The product is a Unix-based client/server software package that helps managers design their networks, judge how specific equipment or services will affect their installations, predict the need for new equipment, services, or bandwidth—and foresee potential performance bottlenecks.

Users can populate the database by adding premade templates, loading log files from network devices, and importing files that define characteristics of various pieces of equipment (Jander 1994). All applications, menus, and graphics are melded together seamlessly and transparently to the end user.

In addition to parameters about network devices, NetMaker can channel other types of data into its reports and displays, including an optional database of tariff information for both dial-up and leased lines from carriers such as AT&T, MCI, and Sprint. Users also can plug in any other tariff information they have on hand.

NetMaker supports various multiplexers and routers that interconnect LANs. Make Systems connects the modeling device to monitors from Frontier Software Development and Concord Communications. The monitors will load the database with accurate performance data on service and utilization indicators.

NetMaker includes six core applications. The Visualizer is a prerequisite for all other applications. It furnishes the graphical user interface, a network map, assorted report templates, and network device templates. The Planner works with plug-in libraries to perform network simulation, predicting the behavior of networks using parameters for specific equipment. The Analyzer gives managers a clue as to what will happen if specific connections or devices fail. The Accountant supplies the tariff data that is integral to many NetMaker reports. The Designer exports information from the Accountant to explore alternative network topologies. The Interpreter analyzes traffic in router-based internetworks.

All the applications work together behind the scenes, contributing functions to one another. For instance, if a department is planning to move to a new location, a manager might query the package about new bandwidth requirements and the associated costs; to display the answer entails the teamwork of the Planner and Accountant applications. To present a report about reducing costs while still fulfilling users' bandwidth needs, the Designer and Accountant applications work in concert. Administrators can call up a network map and click on an icon that represents a network device or connection. They can drag that icon to an open management report to bring up detailed information about the item. Users can edit this data and run new analyses to predict what might happen if, for example, more bandwidth is added to a network connection. Managers can obtain information about the most cost-efficient type of carrier services to use with particular vendors' devices.

NetMaker offers the combination of simulating a variety of equipment and a decision-making tool at a reasonable price.

NetMaker XA features a new software module, called INET Designer, that enables users to evaluate the performance implications of existing and proposed network designs by modeling the behavior of multiprotocol routers. When combined with other modules, INET Designer allows users to evaluate tariffing and optimize the capacity of WAN links.

Coronet Management System from Coronet Systems. Coronet Management System is a software suite that automatically identifies the specific applications in a network and denotes their bandwidth consumption and response time. The three Windows-based packages of the system not only monitor LAN traffic without requiring specialized probes or hardware, but also automatically identify the applications generating that traffic.

With Coronet's SingleView, Super Monitor, and Quick Model software, network troubleshooters can diagnose and pinpoint application-layer problems on Ethernet and Token Ring LANs for a range of network protocols, including TCP/IP, IPX, LAN Manager, Appletalk, DECnet, and Vines (Jander 1995). Along with spotting performance problems, the Coronet packages can help network managers determine the throughput needs of specific applications, which can make network planning easier. The package runs either as a stand-alone monitor or as part of ManageWise from Novell. SingleView and Super Monitor are the core components of the management suite. SingleView functions as the management console. It uses SNMP to discover network devices—including workstations, servers, bridges, and routers—in a multisegment internetwork, and it generates a network map of those devices. Super Monitor serves as the monitoring device at strategic points throughout the network. It turns the host PC into a management agent that listens in on LAN traffic and sends back data to a SingleView console. The software monitors the so-called conversation path between specific clients and servers, showing exactly which applications are running on a particular segment, where they are coming from, and how much bandwidth they are consuming. Super Monitor also gauges related response times for each application. Super Monitor does not have to be placed on every server or workstation on the LAN to monitor application traffic. Instead, network managers can deploy the software on workstations situated near key network gateways on LAN segments, such as next to routers, servers, or bridges.

Super Monitor uses the PC adapter card as its point of entry into the network. The software resets the adapter to what Coronet calls *promiscuous mode,* which enables Super Monitor to capture all the packets traversing the LAN for analysis. Packets captured by the monitor go through several different analyses. First, Super Monitor looks at the port configurations, or port bindings, associated with specific applications. Network applications such as Notes from IBM-Lotus or Oracle database management system from Oracle incorporate unique port bindings into the network protocol, and these port bindings identify the application to the network operating system. By reading the port bindings, the monitor can identify which applications are responsible for captured packets. Users can configure port bindings for custom applications.

Super Monitor also identifies LAN traffic with specific applications by tracking open-file requests on NetWare IPX LANs. These requests are included within IPX packets sent from clients to servers; when Super Monitor decodes the packet, it reads the application name from the open-file request. In addition to decoding the packets it captures for analysis, the monitor can analyze files of packet data captured by protocol analyzers made by Novell and Network General. Data gathered by distributed Super Monitors is forwarded to the network manager's SingleView console. The information is stored in a database at the console for use by Quick Model, the third component of the package. Quick Model contains a variety of rules that are applied to captured data to perform what-if analyses.

This unique combination of an application monitor and modeling package is very much needed. With this product, the criticality of component outages can be quantified. In addition to physical and logical views, application views can also be displayed. Based on accurate data, the modeling part helps to make short-term decisions about configuration changes in the LANs.

Optimal Performance from Optimal Networks Corporation.   Optimal Performance imports real network topology and traffic collected by network monitors such as Expert Sniffer Network Analyzer and Distributed Sniffer System from Network General to automatically create an accurate model of the networks. Using a high-performance engine designed specifically for network analysis and simulation, this product then analyzes the dynamics of the networks.

With an analysis of performance, the product delivers specific problem-solving recommendations that address common operational decisions. Based on the optimization criteria that the user specifies, recommendations are made on the following:

- LAN segmentation
- Hub partitioning
- LAN switch deployment
- Optimal server and workstation positioning
- Optimal application positioning
- Capacity requirements for WAN links
- Survivability of bridges, routers, switches, and WAN links

The predictive what-if capability lets the user evaluate proposed network designs and changes before financial committments are made. The product simulates all seven layers of the OSI reference model to ensure a realistic and accurate reflection of a network's design and performance. The software's event simulator gives the user an animated picture of the proposed network, making it easier to understand its operation. Optimizing the existing network and providing previews of future designs and changes, the product saves time and money and delivers an optimal return on investment.

Optimal Performance analyzes the networks in order to make specific optimization recommendations. The user sets the goals that govern the analysis of the network to determine the recommendations. Optimization goals include LAN segmentation constraints, utilization thresholds for LAN segments and WAN links, and whether the positioning of servers and applications should be based on achieving the least average delay for all clients or minimizing overall network traffic. The user defines specific optimization settings for how he or she wants to tune the networks to focus on areas of greatest interest.

With a model of the network and the optimization goals, Quick Analysis and Event Simulation are the modules of analysis. A Quick Analysis reviews network traffic using computational methods to produce a set of recommendations and reports. An Event Simulation will characterize timing-dependent qualities of traffic flow and network capacity. The user can view the traffic dynamics of the model and monitor activity on segments, bridges, routers, Ethernet switches, and WAN links. For in-depth analysis, the user can capture operational details of any model element and analyze its performance following a simulation run. Event Simulation allows you to receive both optimization recommendations and detailed, time-dependent performance analysis.

Optimal Performance offers comprehensive reports, traffic matrices, and graphs. Included are reports on optimization, survivability, traffic, and network performance. Following an event simulation, the user can also generate various statistical graphs. The reports enable the network managers to present a business case for network changes and major investments to nontechnical managers with data, graphs, and easy-to-understand reports.

Figure 6.16 displays a traffic matrix of segments' traffic. It can also be broken down into a traffic matrix between workstations in the LANs.

Further reports include the following:

- Each recommendation for a LAN segment includes a summary of its configuration, its performance, and the utilization objectives for optimization.

- If the recommendation is to split a LAN into two or more segments, the workstations and servers to be attached to each segment are specifically listed. The user can use the report as an action list for changes that should be made to a network's configuration.

- The optimal segment for a server or an application is specified, and the relative performance improvements on every other segment are listed. Recommendations for the optimal positioning of a server provide its traffic load and optimization setting. Similarly, recommendations for the optimal positioning of an application identify the number of clients, the total number of messages transmitted and received, and its optimization setting.

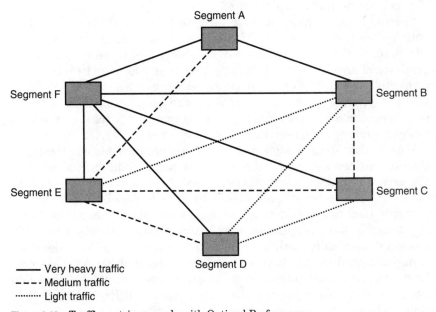

Figure 6.16   Traffic matrix example with Optimal Performance.

- For WAN links, recommendations define specific bandwidth requirements to achieve a desired utilization. A summary identifies the connections of a WAN link, as well as its utilization in each direction of a connection.

An optimization report provides a summary of recommendations for LAN segmentation, the optimal positioning of servers, workstations and applications, and the capacity requirements for WAN links. Optimization recommendations for LAN segments include the splitting of some segments and the replacement of others with higher-speed alternatives in order to achieve specified goals for utilization.

With this product, it is easy to change a network design. Starting with a model of the existing network, the user can make changes to evaluate their impact and automatically implement recommendations. LAN segments, workstations and servers, bridges, routers, Ethernet switches, WAN links, and applications can be added, moved, deleted, and reconfigured. Point and click on the icon for a LAN segment and change it from Ethernet to an FDDI segment. Select a server and move it from one segment to another. Change a network protocol or routing protocol and determine the impact. Add an additional T1 link, or select a WAN link and temporarily disable it. Increase traffic generated by a client/server application and see the change in end-to-end response times and the demand on network capacity. Evaluate changes to the model of the network before the changes are actually implemented.

Specific recommendations help LAN designers and planners to find optimal solutions. They can also perform what-if analysis to simulate the changes the software has recommended and to analyze how the proposed changes would affect factors such as traffic and routing patterns and the ability of the network to survive a major breakdown. Using a graphical interface and drag-and-drop operations, network managers can add, move, delete, or reconfigure LAN segments, nodes, bridges, routers, switches, links, and applications.

When evaluating design and planning products, LAN managers should consider the issues of how the network model is created, how the network traffic is characterized, and which platforms the applications run on. The managers should be sure to find out whether the products they are considering perform event simulation or not. With event simulation, an application will simulate each step of a network process dynamically, such as setting up a call over a WAN, allocating bandwidth, and taking down the link. In contrast, other products perform analytical modeling and rely on static routing tables, so they do not give a complete picture of actual network utilization or reflect changes that occur dynamically on the network.

LAN modeling tools have matured, particularly those that are PC-based. LAN segments can be adequately modeled now; the real void is the lack of products composing models for interconnected LANs.

Summary

Designing and planning LANs are activities that are usually still limited to the infrastructure. Performance metrics and service indicators are not included. For LAN segments that have a limited geographical area and stable workload and user profiles, change is not expected soon. However, when LAN segments have to be interconnected, serving a wider user base and occasionally including wide area networks, more objective design and planning are urgently needed. In particular, in cases when LAN segments are extending or replacing the traditionally hierarchical networking structures, users are very familiar with service-level agreements, including service and use indicators. In terms of the planning process, there are many similarities between LAN and WAN design and planning. LAN modeling tools have matured, but offer little for interconnected LANs. For improving planning quality, the LAN designer and planner are expected to combine various models from both the WAN and LAN area.

LAN design and optimization tools run on a wide variety of processors, from minicomputers to powerful mainframes. At the low end are tools such as SoftBench (Internetix) and NetMod (University of Michigan), both of which estimate feasibility and performance without going into detail at the LAN protocol levels. At the high end, there are simulators that emulate and simulate a lot of the details of protocols, access methods, and LAN configurations. This category includes SES (Scientific and Engineering Software, Incorporated), Lannet and Network II (C.A.C.I.), Lansim (Internetix), BONeS (Comdisco) and Optimized Network Engineering Tools (MIL3).

Performance of LAN interconnecting devices can be predicted by NeTool (Make Systems), which simulates specific vendors' bridge, router, and brouter devices using an approach similar to computer-aided engineering. Performance of individual software applications running on specific LANs can be modeled by QASE (Quantitative Aided Software Engineering from Advanced Systems Technologies, Incorporated). This product uses computer-aided engineering technology as well.

LAN Management Organizational Structure

LAN management functions are assigned to various people who are hired and educated to manage LANs. The same is true of the instruments addressed in previous chapters; typical groups of instruments are used by certain organizational units of the enterprise. The LAN management organizational structure is not yet mature, but installation and operation do seem to be clearly segregated from each other. At the moment, the following human resources can be identified. A LAN management supervisor is responsible for supervising design, planning, installation, and operation. Reporting to the LAN manager (LM) are two supervisory functions consisting of experts in the following areas:

- Supervisor for LAN design, planning, and installation (DS)

    LAN designers and planners (DP)

    LAN installer (LI)

- Supervisor for LAN operations (OS)

    LAN client contact point operator (CC)

    LAN operator (OP)

    LAN administrator (AD)

    LAN performance analyst (AN)

    LAN security officer (SO)

Table 7.1 shows an organizational chart of a hypothetical LAN environment. If WANs and LANs are going to be managed together, there will be some overlap. Otherwise, interconnecting devices such as bridges, routers, and gateways represent demarcation lines between the WAN and LAN management organizations (refer to Chap. 1, Fig. 1.1). These components are expected to provide information to both management entities. Sharing responsibilities between the management entities depends on the environment and its service expectations. In any case, it's recommended to use outband communication techniques between those entities to ensure management capabilities when objects, segments, or communication links have broken down.

Table 7.2 shows the clearly defined responsibilities for each human resource involved in LAN management. As can be seen, there are overlaps in the functions each group/person is responsible for. In order to identify the right instruments for each LAN management group, Table 7.3 displays the allocation of typical instruments. This table represents the most likely allocations.

The number of human resources needed to execute LAN management functions depends on many factors, such as the number and educational level of users, the number of workstations to be managed, the number of servers to be managed, the number of interconnecting devices to be managed, the geography of and distances within LAN segments, the density of station and servers, the communication media used, the availability of instruments for continuous monitoring, the availability of instruments for troubleshooting, the skill levels of the LAN management group, and the level of support from the control (WAN) network management organization.

Table 7.4 summarizes the number ranges that may be applicable in a typical LAN environment. This table uses two different numbers for the server/station ratio: one server for thirty workstations, or two servers for seventy workstations. Furthermore, both stand-alone LANs and internetworked LANs are considered.

The assumptions on which this table is based include:

1. Geographical distances not exceeding a typical campus of approximately two miles in diameter.
2. Skill levels of the LAN management staff are average.

TABLE 7.1   Organizational Structure of LAN Management

LAN manager	
Supervisor for design, planning, and installation	Supervisor for operations
LAN designers and planners LAN installer	LAN client contact point operator LAN operator LAN administrator LAN performance analyst LAN security officer

TABLE 7.2 Allocation of LAN Management Functions to Human Resources*

Human resources management functions	LM	DS	OS	LD	LI	LC	LO	LA	LP	LS
Configuration management										
Inventory and topology service				x				x		
Change management	x	x	x	x	x		x	x	x	x
Naming and addressing				x				x	x	
Cabling management								x		
Backup and archive			x					x	x	x
Directory services	x	x	x					x		
Fault management										
Status supervision	x		x			x	x			
Fault detection and alarming			x			x	x		x	
Problem determination and isolation			x				x		x	
Diagnostics, backup, repair, and recovery			x				x		x	
Disaster recovery										
Dynamic trouble ticketing	x		x				x		x	x
Tests			x						x	
Performance management										
Defining performance indicators	x	x							x	
Performance monitoring									x	
Tuning of local area networks									x	
Modeling and performance optimization	x	x							x	
Reporting of performance	x	x	x						x	

TABLE 7.2 Allocation of LAN Management Functions to Human Resources* (Continued)

Human resources management functions	LM	DS	OS	LD	LI	LC	LO	LA	LP	LS
Security management										
Identifying the sensitive information to be protected	x									
Analyzing threats and defining security indicators	x									
Reviewing and analyzing the security framework	x									x
Selection of security services									x	x
Implementing security management services									x	x
Securing the LAN management system									x	x
Accounting management										
Determining resource usage	x	x						x	x	
Software licensing	x	x						x	x	
Billing	x	x						x		
Bill verification								x		
LAN administration										
LAN documentation	x	x	x	x	x	x	x	x	x	x
User administration								x		
Software distribution							x	x		
LAN maintenance							x	x	x	
Design and planning										
Strategic planning	x	x								
Capacity planning		x							x	
Analyzing trends		x		x					x	
Logical and physical design		x		x					x	
Contingency planning		x		x					x	
Installation					x					
Testing					x				x	

* The following abbreviations are used: LM, LAN manager; LD, LAN designer; LI, LAN installer; LC, LAN client contact point; LO, LAN operator; LA, LAN administrator; LP, LAN performance analyst; LS, LAN security officer; DS, LAN design supervisor; OS, LAN operations supervisor.

TABLE 7.3 Allocation of LAN Management Instruments to Human Resources*

Human resources management instruments	LM	DS	OS	LD	LI	LC	LO	LA	LP	LS
Management platforms	x		x						x	
Databases	x	x	x	x	x	x	x	x	x	x
Backup utilities		x		x					x	
Diagnostic tools			x						x	
Analyzers			x				x		x	x
Monitors			x				x		x	
RMON probes			x				x		x	
Emulators				x					x	
Modeling tools	x	x		x					x	
Simulators		x		x					x	
Metering tools	x							x		x
Software distribution								x	x	
Asset management	x				x			x	x	
Trouble ticketing	x		x			x	x	x	x	x
Security auditing								x		x
Document managers	x	x	x		x	x	x	x	x	x
Reporting software	x	x	x		x	x	x	x	x	x
MIB tools		x						x	x	x

* The following abbreviations are used: LM, LAN manager; LD, LAN designer; LI, LAN installer; LC, LAN client contact point; LO, LAN operator; LA, LAN administrator; LP, LAN performance analyst; LS, LAN security officer; DS, LAN design supervisor; OS, LAN operations supervisor.

TABLE 7.4   **Quantification of Human Resources Needs**

LANs	Stand-alone		Networked	
Number of segments	30 segments	30 segments	30 segments	30 segments
Server/client ratio	1 to 30	2 to 70	1 to 30	2 to 70
Total number of servers	30	60	30	60
Total number of clients	900	2100	900	2100
LAN manager	1*	1	1	1
Supervisor for LAN design, planning, and installation	1	1	1	1
LAN design and planner	1	2	1	2
LAN installer[†]	1	3	2	4
Supervisor for operations	1	1	1	1
LAN client contact point	1	2	1	2
LAN operator	2	2	2	3
LAN administrator	1	2	2	3
LAN analyst	1	2	2	2
LAN security officer	1	1	1	1
Total human resources demand	11	17	14	20

* All numbers in FTEs (full-time equivalents).
† Not a continuous activity.

3. Instrumentation.
   a. Console emulation for the LAN help desk
   b. Relational database for administration
   c. LAN analyzers for LAN client contact point (for use by analysts and installers)
   d. Unsophisticated modeling tools for LAN designers and planners
4. LAN segments and LAN interconnecting devices provide raw data for both WAN and LAN management.
5. Basic LAN services include spreadsheet applications, E-mail, printing, and connections to other LAN segments or to mainframes.

It is not easy to determine the number of support persons needed to administer servers, clients, and the wide and local area networks. The following example is based on a business unit with approximately 5000 employees and approximately 200 researchers. This business unit supports research, manufacturing, and sales activities. Support is local; connections to corporate IS do not require substantial equipment and facilities.

There are 25 servers, 50 intelligent workstations for knowledge workers, 250 printers, and approximately 1000 networked PCs. The company is using structured cabling, and the servers and workstations are properly allocated using intelligent hubs. It is assumed that segmentation using bridges is well tuned. The ratio between servers and clients in the LAN segments varies by the departments that are supported by the LANs. There are no virtual LANs yet in use.

The estimated number of the support staff can be computed as follows:

Activity	Basic demand	Factor	Total demand
1. Central server			
Coordination	1	1	1
One Unix version	0.2	5	1
Network Operating System	0.2	3	0.6
Special processor	0.5	1	0.5
Systems programming	0.5	2	1
Operating servers	0.5	1	0.5
Administration 500 users	0.5	2	1
Maintenance of databases	0.2	2	0.4
Subtotal			6
2. Planning and purchase for servers and clients			
Coordination	1	1	1
$1 million investment	0.2	2	0.4
License supervision	0.2	8	1.6
Systems maintenance for 500 equipment	1	3	3
Subtotal			5
3. Support for clients			
One operating system	1	1	1
Coordination and consulting	1	1	1
Administration for 500 clients	0.5	3	1.5
One application package	0.2	5	1
Support for databases	0.5	2	1
Feasibility and connectivity supervision	0.5	1	0.5
Subtotal			7
4. Operating the LANs			
First 500 connections	1.5	1	1.5
Second 500 connections	1	1	1
Planning and segmenting	1	1	1
Connectivity to backbone	0.5	1	0.5
Management tools	2	1	3
Subtotal			6
Grand total			24

The factors are installation-dependent. In other words, they are determined by the volumes of installed equipment and facilities.

In this environment, 24 persons are required to support the LANs and the systems. This number indicates FTEs (full-time equivalents), not considering training, sickness, vacation, and any other unforeseen time spent outside the organization. Usually, 30 to 50 percent must be added to meet the realistic human resources requirements; the final result is then between 32 and 36 persons. These calculations and the actual human resources expenses greatly impact the budget required for networks and systems management. In all evaluations and surveys, human resource expenses are higher than hardware, software, communications, and infrastructure expenditures.

The Gartner Group has done several studies and found the following results for three very typical LAN environments:

Environment 1
  One site
  20 clients
  One PC-based server
  Purchased applications
  One LAN administrator
  Basic systems and LAN management

  Annual cost per client = $ 10,160.00

Environment 2
  Five remote sites
  200 clients
  One work group server per site
  One mid-range enterprise server
  One purchased application
  Five end-user support staff
  10 application developers
  Basic systems and LAN management

  Annual cost per client = $ 13,270.00

Environment 3
  250 remote sites with server
  5000 clients
  Legacy and new enterprise servers
  55 application dialog types
  Centralized management
  83 end-user support staff

  Annual cost per client = $ 9,680.00

Tables 7.5 to 7.14 summarize the human resources profiles for each LAN management organizational unit, including the manager of the group. Each profile includes a job description, responsibilities, interfaces, qualifying experiences, training requirements, and compensation ranges.

The process of creating or expanding the LAN management staff is complicated by a number of factors. Here are the most important ones: scarce technical resources, no standard job descriptions and responsi-

TABLE 7.5   Profile of a LAN Network Manager

Job description: Allocation and coordination of work in the area of LAN design, planning, installation, and operations.

Responsibilities
 1. Allocates work to staff
 2. Coordinates work among staff members
 3. Resolves problems between staff members
 4. Selects instruments
 5. Oversees all functions
 6. Works out processes and procedures
 7. Reviews staff performance
 8. Assists in evaluating LAN performance
 9. Supervises planning and change management
10. Sets priorities for work orders
11. Schedules installation work
12. Consults on which applications may be ported to LANs
13. Provides vision
14. Provides overall architectures for LAN management

Interfaces
 1. Network manager
 2. LAN designers and planners
 3. Users
 4. Vendors
 5. Group leaders

Qualifying experiences
 1. Some know-how of LAN applications, servers, workstations, LAN media, and internetworking alternatives
 2. Communication and negotiation skills
 3. Some know-how of LAN management tools
 4. Decision-making skills
 5. Project management experiences
 6. People management skills
 7. B.S. or B.A. degree expected

Training
 1. Continuing education toward a B.S. in business administration
 2. Overview courses on LAN technology
 3. Overview courses on LAN instrumentation

Compensation: $65–$75 K

---

bilities, few specific academic training programs, rapidly changing LAN technology, short career paths, and few upward mobility alternatives.

These factors complicate the hiring process by making it very difficult to write job descriptions and analyze candidates' background materials. The following is a list of recommended criteria when hiring LAN management staff.

Identify team members.   Table 7.1 gave an overview on functions to be supported for managing LANs. Depending on the size of LANs, the human resources demand may be computed (Table 7.4). After subtract-

TABLE 7.6   Profile of Planning and Design Supervisor

Duties
1. Identifies events requiring response from the planning and design group
2. Develops a strategy for producing the required response
3. Assigns priorities to the projects to be completed
4. Monitors the progress of each project
5. Prepares the migration and installation plans
6. Establishes education program for staff

External job contacts
1. Other supervisors within the network management organization
2. Network manager
3. Vendors
4. Business planners of the larger organization

Qualifying experience and attributes
1. In addition to managerial skills, good understanding of the current environment and how changes in that environment may affect the network
2. Good understanding of the principles of network design and of communication hardware and software
3. Training in administrative management

Compensation: $50–$60 K

TABLE 7.7   Profile of Network Operational Control Supervisor

Duties
1. Staffing is adequate.
2. All documentation needed by the planning groups accurately created.
3. Installation time schedules are met.
4. Required network changes and modifications are performed and are properly coordinated with user, vendors, programmers, and operating personnel.
5. All problems reported by users through the Client Contact Point are satisfactorily resolved.
6. Prepares reports documenting the effectiveness of the operations group.
7. Establishes educational program for staff.

External job contacts
1. Other supervisors within network management
2. Customers
3. Network manager

Qualifying experience and attributes
1. Knowledge of the communications system software used and the operator facilities used to control it
2. Knowledge of communications hardware
3. Experience with hardware network-diagnostic aids
4. Experience with software network-diagnostic aids
5. Knowledge of problem-determination process
6. Training in administrative management

Compensation: $45–$55 K

TABLE 7.8   Profile of a LAN Designer and Planner

Job description: Technically oriented activities resulting in an optimal LAN configuration within reasonable budgetary limits.

Responsibilities
1. Reviews user needs
2. Quantifies user needs
3. Evaluates current LAN utilization
4. Evaluates technology
5. Conducts LAN design
6. Sizes principal LAN resources
7. Models LANs, and evaluates modeling results
8. Writes specifications and operational manuals
9. Helps in selecting LAN instruments
10. Presents funding to management in a clearly understandable manner

Interfaces
1. LAN network manager
2. Users
3. Vendors
4. LAN analysts
5. Other designers and planners from the WAN area

Qualifying experiences
1. Detailed knowledge of LAN applications
2. Detailed knowledge of LAN components, such as servers, workstations, media, access methods, protocols, interconnecting devices, and interconnecting networking alternatives
3. Some background in statistics
4. Communication skills
5. Patience in pursuing planning projects
6. B.S. or B.A. degree expected

Training
1. Continuing education toward a B.S. or M.S.
2. In-depth courses on technology
3. In-depth courses on LAN modeling
4. Overview courses on LAN instrumentation

Compensation: $50–$60 K

ing the available staff from the total demand for each activity, the demand on new hires can be quantified.

Recruit candidates. Advertisements, conferences, headhunters, and individual contacts to colleges, universities, and other companies help to find candidates to be interviewed.

Establish interview criteria. Guidelines and evaluation criteria have to be set prior to starting the interviews. In order to keep investment for both parties low, written applications must be filtered carefully. Occasional phone conversations may fill existing gaps. Invitations to personal interviews should be sent out to candidates whose applications match the expectations.

TABLE 7.9   Profile of a LAN Installer

Job description: Based on accurate specifications, installation of LAN segments, interconnected WANs, and LAN management instruments.

Responsibilities
1. Tests LAN components prior to installation
2. Installs LANs
3. Conducts integration tests
4. Maintains and coordinates subcontractors and their data
5. Assists in problem determination
6. Activates and deactivates LAN segments
7. Customizes LAN test instruments
8. Interprets and reviews LAN configuration documentation
9. Conducts stress tests
10. Assists in writing troubleshooting checklists for LAN help desk operators
11. Maintains LAN database

Interfaces
1. Vendors
2. Suppliers
3. Users
4. LAN designers and planners

Qualifying experiences
1. Detailed knowledge of LAN components to be installed
2. Knowledge of LAN software
3. Detailed knowledge of LAN media, their testing, and their measurement
4. Detailed knowledge of test instruments

Training
1. Continuing education toward an engineering degree
2. In-depth briefings on new LAN hardware and WAN media
3. Updates on LAN test instruments

Compensation: $35–$45 K

Hire properly qualified candidates.   Hiring has to be for mutual benefit, and not just to fill the job. Future turnover can be avoided this way.

Assign and/or reassign responsibilities.   Static job descriptions should serve as a guideline only. Within this framework, more dynamic descriptions with rotation in mind are necessary.

Institute performance evaluations.   Periodic reviews are most widely used. If possible, upward performance appraisals should be agreed upon as early as possible in the team-building phase.

Promote openness and handle complaints.   In order to emphasize team spirit, opinions (even complaints) must be encouraged on behalf of LAN management supervisors. The employees must have the feeling that their comments and suggestions are handled at the earliest convenience of managers.

TABLE 7.10   Profile of Client Control Point Operator

Duties
1. Network supervision
   Implements first-level problem-determination procedures
   Maintains documentation to assist customer in terminal operation
2. Problem logging
   Uses procedure guide for opening trouble tickets
   Reviews change activities log
3. Problem delegation
   Determines problem area
   Assigns priorities
   Distributes information
4. Additional duties when support desk activity is low
   Data entry for configuration and inventory
   Summary of active problems for problem coordinator
   Entering change information for change coordinator
   Monitoring of security
   Generating management and technical reports
   Recommends modification to procedures

External job contacts
1. Customers
2. Vendor representatives
3. Problem and change coordinators of network administrator
4. Network operation and technical support
5. Network administrator for trouble tickets
6. LAN administrator

Qualifying experience and attributes
1. Familiarity with functional applications and terminal equipment
2. Training in personal relationships
3. Clerical rather than technical
   Data-entry skills
   Problem-determination know-how
4. Sensitivity to customers
   Understanding of their business needs
   Pleasant telephone voice
   Language know-how

Compensation: $30–$35 K

Resolve personnel problems quickly.   In order to avoid tensions within the LAN management organization, problems must be resolved for mutual benefit as quickly as possible. The reward system must provide opportunities to do so. More often, visibility of how the reward system works resolves problems almost automatically.

Institute systematic training and development programs.   Systematic education should include training for LAN management functions, LAN management instruments, and for personal skills. A curriculum in coordination with vendors and educational institutes would guarantee high quality and employee satisfaction.

TABLE 7.11   Profile of a LAN Operator

Job description: Accepting and prediagnosing user calls and monitored events in order to properly solve problems.

Responsibilities
1. Supervises LAN operations
2. Registers troubles identified by users and monitors
3. Opens trouble tickets
4. Implements procedures for "tier 1" problem determination
5. Invokes corrections
6. Solves problems, depending on priorities, to central network management center or to peer help desks
7. Communicates with users
8. Communicates with vendors
9. Activates and deactivates local area networks
10. Generates reports on network problems
11. Closes trouble tickets
12. Reviews documentation of change management
13. Sets priorities for problem diagnosis
14. Registers security management problems

Interfaces
1. Users
2. Vendors
3. Central client contact point operators
4. LAN administrators
5. LAN analysts
6. LAN installers

Qualifying experiences
1. Some knowledge of applications, servers, and workstations
2. Very good communication skills
3. Background in dealing with trouble-ticketing systems
4. At least one year's experience with LANs
5. Know-how of instruments that help monitor LAN status and performance
6. Experience judging which problems need escalation
7. Negotiation skills
8. Some knowledge about how to execute changes
9. Experience handling powerful workstations

Training
1. Continuing education toward a college degree
2. In-depth courses on LAN instrumentation
3. Course on interpersonal communication skills

Compensation: $30–$35 K

Regularly interface LAN management staff with LAN users. In order to promote mutual understanding of working conditions and problems, both parties should exchange views and opinions. The level of formality may vary from very informal to very formal; in the second case, written service-level agreements are evaluated.

Evaluate new technologies. As part of the motivation process, LAN management renovation opportunities must be evaluated continuously.

TABLE 7.12   **Profile of a LAN Administrator**

Job description: An administration-oriented specialist that combines clerical and project control capabilities.

Responsibilities
1. Administers LAN configuration, including logical, electrical, and physical attributes
2. Maintains LAN database
3. Maintains vendor data
4. Coordinates planning and executing changes
5. Administers names and addresses
6. Defines and supervises authorizations
7. Maintains trouble tickets and trouble files
8. Coordinates complex problem solving
9. Helps to establish powerful security policy
10. Organizes data export and import with central database

Interfaces
1. LAN client contact point operators
2. Users
3. Vendors
4. LAN analysts
5. LAN installers

Qualifying experiences
1. Know-how of applications, servers, workstations, cables, and internetworking devices
2. Experience with inventory management
3. Some experience with project management
4. Some communications skills
5. Detailed knowledge of database or file management systems in use
6. Experience handling powerful workstations

Training
1. Continuing education toward a B.S. in business administration
2. In-depth courses in the area of inventory management
3. Project management courses

Compensation: $35–$45 K

This process includes new management platforms, new technologies of LAN processing and internetworking, feasibility of new and existing solutions, new monitors, change in supporting de facto and open standards, simplification of management processes, changes in the offerings of leading manufacturers, and monitoring the needs of LAN users. Thus, enrichment of lower-level jobs may easily be accomplished.

In order to keep the LAN management team together, expectations of employers and employees must match to a certain degree. Table 7.15 shows a sample of expectations on both sides. The individual-organization contract is termed *psychological* because much of it is often unwritten and unspoken. There are several reasons why this may be so:

TABLE 7.13 Profile of a LAN Analyst

Job description: A technically oriented specialist to measure, interpret, analyze, and optimize LAN performance.

Responsibilities
1. Conducts LAN-tuning studies
2. Executes specific LAN measurements
3. Designs and executes performance and functionality tests
4. Defines performance indicators
5. Selects LAN management instruments
6. Surveys performance needs of LAN users
7. Maintains the LAN performance database
8. Generates reports
9. Maintains the LAN baseline models
10. Sizes LAN resources
11. Customizes LAN instruments
12. Analyzes workload and utilization trends
13. Prepares checklists and processes for LAN help desk
14. Helps install LAN management instruments
15. Specifies and documents LAN configurations

Interfaces
1. Vendors
2. Users
3. LAN designers and planners
4. LAN administrators
5. LAN client contact point operators
6. Other companies

Qualifying experiences
1. Detailed knowledge of media, protocols, access methods, servers, bridges, brouters, routers, gateways, wiring hubs, interconnecting alternatives, and LAN network operating systems
2. Detailed knowledge of LAN measurement, and management instruments
3. Some know-how of LAN modeling instruments
4. Communication skills
5. Some experience with project management.

Training
1. Continuing education toward a B.S. degree
2. In-depth briefings on new technology
3. Updates on LAN management instruments

Compensation: $50–$60 K

- Both parties may not be entirely clear about their expectations and how they wish them to be met. They may not want to define the contract until they have a better feel for what they want.

- Neither of the parties are aware of their expectations. For example, organizations are hardly able to define loyalty.

- Some expectations may be perceived as so natural and basic that they're taken for granted (e.g., expectations of not stealing and an honest day's work for a day's pay).

- Cultural norms may inhibit verbalization.

TABLE 7.14   Profile of Security Officer

Duties
1. Evaluates security risks
2. Supervises security in real time
3. Decides about actions against penetrator
4. Helps evaluate surveillance logs
5. Helps in elaborating on security plans
6. Supervises the security of the network-management system
7. Manages passwords
8. Helps to select instruments

External job contacts
1. Security auditor
2. Security analyst
3. Customers
4. Vendors of security-related instruments
5. Other companies

Qualifying experiences and attributes
1. Has knowledge of customer information flows
2. Has knowledge of security impacts for the larger organization
3. Has a superior personal record
4. Ability to make decisions rapidly
5. Has some communication skills
6. Has in-depth knowledge of security-related instruments

Compensation: $35–$45 K

At a given time, there will be some relatively fulfilled and unfulfilled expectations; however, each party has to have a minimum acceptance level of fulfillment. If either party concludes that the fulfillment of its needs is below this minimum level, it will view the contract as having been violated.

Turnover in LAN management can be very disadvantageous for maintaining service levels to end users. Corporate and business units management should try to avoid overaverage turnover by implementing rewards to satisfy employees. Gaining satisfaction with the rewards given is not a simple matter. It's a function of several factors that organizations must learn to manage.

TABLE 7.15   Expectations in the Employer/Employee Contract

Expectations of the individual	Expectations of the employer
1. Compensation	1. An honest day's work
2. Personal development opportunities	2. Loyalty to organization
3. Recognition and approval for good work	3. Initiative
4. Security through fringe benefits	4. Conformity to organizational norms
5. Friendly, supportive environment	5. Job effectiveness
6. Fair treatment	6. Flexibility and willingness to learn
7. Meaningful or purposeful job	and develop
	7. No security violations

The individual's satisfaction with rewards is, in part, related to what's expected and how much is received. Feelings of satisfaction or dissatisfaction arise when individuals compare their input (knowledge, skills, experience) to output (mix of rewards) they receive.

Employee satisfaction is also affected by comparisons with other people in similar jobs and organizations. People vary considerably in how they weigh various inputs and outputs in that comparison. They tend to weigh their strong points such as certain skills or a recent performance peak more heavily. Individuals also tend to correlate their own performance compared with the rating they receive from their supervisors. The problem of unrealistic self-ratings exists partly because supervisors in most organizations don't communicate a candid evaluation of their subordinates' performance to them.

Employees often misperceive the rewards of others; their misperception can cause the employees to become dissatisfied. Evidence shows that individuals tend to overestimate the pay of colleagues doing similar jobs and to underestimate their colleagues' performance.

Finally, overall satisfaction results from a mix of rewards rather than from any single reward. The evidence suggests that intrinsic rewards and extrinsic rewards are both important and that they can't be directly substituted for each other.

Rewards mean motivation. To be useful, rewards must be tied as closely as possible to effective performance. Success factors of motivation are: employees must believe in effective performance; employees must feel that the rewards offered are attractive; employees must believe that a certain level of individual effort will lead to achieving the corporation's standards of performance.

Rewards fall into two principal categories: extrinsic and intrinsic. *Extrinsic rewards* come from the employer as compensation, benefits, job security, training, promotions, effective LAN management instruments, and recognition. *Intrinsic rewards* come from performing the task itself, and may include job satisfaction, sense of influence, quality of environment, and quality of assignment. The priority of extrinsic and intrinsic rewards depends on the individual person. The following list tries to give a frequently seen priority sequence.

Compensation. Payment is still the most important motivation factor. Organizations try to use a number of person-based or skill-based compensation techniques combined with the dependence of sales revenues of the larger organization, if applicable. Pay is a matter of perception and values that often generates conflict.

Benefits. Benefits take special forms, depending on the employer's business (e.g., company car, life insurance, lower interest rates, housing). The cost of benefits at companies can be as high as 30 to 40 percent of pay dollars.

Job security. Seniority with job assignments is a very valuable management practice, particularly when the economy is stressed. Job security policies include retirement plans, options for early retirement, and agreements of nonlayoff. Job security packages are more advanced in Europe and Japan than in the United States.

Recognition. Recognition may come from the organization or from fellow employees. The periodic form of recognition is the performance appraisal conducted by the supervisor. A relatively new form, the so-called upward appraisal, is considered a form of recognition. It's difficult because most managers don't want to be evaluated by their subordinates. For the subordinates, it's a forum to articulate ideas for improvement.

Career path and creation of dual ladders. In order to keep motivation high, managerial and technical assignments must be compensated equally. Promoting technically interested persons into managerial positions may not have the desired results; these persons are usually high in affiliation motivation and low in power motivation. Helpful activities include career counseling and exploration, increased company career opportunity information, improving career feedback, enhancing linear career, slower early-career advancement, and enrichment of lower-level jobs with more challenges.

Effective training. This type of motivation helps to keep the specific and generic knowledge of the employees at the most advanced level. Three to six weeks of training and education per annum is considered adequate in the dynamically changing LAN management environment.

Quality of assignments. Job descriptions are expected to give the framework for expectations. But dynamic job descriptions may help to avoid monotony and promote job rotation. The help desk, LAN administration, and LAN analysis may be rotated periodically.

Use of adequate tools. Better-instrumented LAN environments facilitate the jobs of the LAN staff, increase the service quality to LAN users, and improve the image of the LAN management organization. At the same time, persons working with advanced tools are proud of their special knowledge and of their employer. They're highly motivated to continue with the company.

Realistic performance goals. As part of dynamic job descriptions and job rotation, realistic performance expectations may help to stabilize the position of the LAN management team. Management must find the balance between quantifiable and nonquantifiable goals. Average time spent on trouble calls, response time to problems, time of repair, and end-user satisfaction/dissatisfaction are examples for both types of goals.

Quality of environment. This is more or less a generic term expressing the mix of LAN-related instruments, pleasant working atmosphere, comfortable furniture, adequate legroom, easy access to filing cabinets or to hypermedia, acceptance of opinions on shortcomings, and team spirit.

Employee control. Despite high team spirit, individuals need certain levels of control that can be determined only by managerial skills. Depending on the person, use positive or negative motivation, or a combination of both.

The preceding list has concentrated on key motivation alternatives only. There are many more. In order to find the optimal combination for individual LAN installations, a human resources management audit is recommended.

Partial outsourcing may become very interesting to users in small and midsize organizations that want help linking their LANs. But they are not willing to turn over everything to the outsourcers. The same type of LAN interconnecting service may become attractive to larger organizations that want to reduce operating expenses. Offers are available now, but service definitions are still missing. The result is that it is very difficult to compare interconnectivity services.

The most advanced services provide LAN-to-LAN connectivity, network management, and LAN administration, as well as custom design of special applications. Advanced services provide off-the-shelf LAN-to-LAN management options in which the supplier administers the internetwork and its equipment. Modest interconnectivity services offer transport services for LAN-to-LAN-connections in the wide and metropolitan areas.

In order to compare and differentiate service offers, the following elements should be evaluated (Heckart 1995):

- *Which types of LANs could be connected to each other.* A matrix could represent this connectivity, as shown in Table 7.16.

- *Which LAN protocols are supported.* This is a sensitive issue and a real differentiator among outsourcers. Protocols include AppleTalk,

TABLE 7.16   LAN Connectivity Matrix

From	To	4 Mbps TR	16 Mbps TR	10 Mbps ethernet	100 Mbps ethernet	FDDI
4 Mbps TR						
16 Mbps TR						
10 Mbps Ethernet						
1000 Mbps Ethernet						
FDDI						

DECnet, IPX, LLC2, Netbeui, Netbios, SNA, Vines, and TCP/IP. Outsourcers with multiprotocol support are definitely preferred.

- *Local access options.* The access could be switched or dedicated. Many outsourcers support both options.

- *Which equipment is supported.* Interconnection may include bridges, modems, routers, extenders, DSU/CSUs, and multiplexers. The outsourcer is unlikely to be able to support all types of equipment. This is a real differentiator. If the company does not use equipment yet, the outsourcer will install its preferred equipment from its preferred vendor. It would guarantee good knowledge and good support. The location of equipment can be on-premise or off-premise.

- *WAN transport technology and bandwidth.* Depending on the contract with the outsourcer, the selected WAN transport technology and bandwidth may be important. Technologies include frame relay, private lines, packet switching, wireless services, SMDS, or ATM. In terms of bandwidth, many outsourcers offer T3 rates that are not inexpensive.

- *Professional services.* Many outsourcers offer more than just transport services. Professional services include WAN design, network reengineering, network optimization, LAN addressing and naming, wiring optimization, service configuration, setting up LAN-to-LAN routing tables, router management, WAN and LAN monitoring, training, and education.

The depth of outsourcing agreements is different. Figure 7.1 shows the two basic alternatives of LAN interconnectivity services. The basic service offers transport only; the managed service does include transport services and the management of networking equipment.

In case of total outsourcing, LAN interconnectivity is becoming an important part of it. LAN interconnectivity services are offered by, among others, AT&T, Cable & Wireless, CompuServe, Infonet, MCI, Sprint, Teleport, and Wiltel.

When considering outsourcing LAN management, customers are investigating the feasibility of farming out LAN management functions. Before deciding for or against outsourcing, the following criteria should be evaluated very carefully (Terplan 1992):

1. In the first step, present costs of LAN management equipment, communications, and people have to be quantified. Basically, LAN management costs can be subdivided into the following categories:

   Hardware, including server and clients

   Software, including operating systems for servers, clients, and for the networks, and business applications

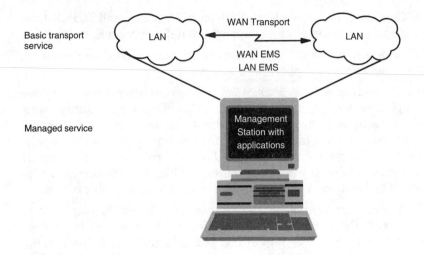

Basic transport service

Managed service

EMS = Element Managed Service

Figure 7.1 LAN interconnectivity services.

Communications, including the LAN segments

Infrastructure, including cabling and hubs

Management, including platforms, element management systems, monitors, analyzers, and management applications

Human resources

2. Full analysis of all existing processes, instruments, and human resources in order to decide which functions may be considered appropriate for outsourcing. Considering outsourcing is a good excuse for auditing present operations and addressing areas that need improvement. The result of considering outsourcing may be insourcing. Analysis by internal or external analysts may result in substantial savings in operating expenses (30 to 40 percent), in staff reduction (25 to 50 percent), and in a network budget's stabilization.

3. Determination of the company's dependence on network availability, indicating highest levels by critical LAN applications. The company should include the key indicators into the service contract; many times, vendors will fall short from the very beginning, not being able to guarantee the target availability levels.

4. Determination of the service grade required by users and applications. Perhaps the outsourcing company should even be solely dedicated to the user company and not share its resources among multiple clients.

5. Security standards and risk levels may prohibit a company from allowing third-party vendors to gain access to the network and to its carried traffic.

6. Because the business may need to concentrate its main energy and resources on its own business, it may simply not be a practical priority to it to build a sophisticated LAN management system and organization.

7. Availability of LAN management instruments may facilitate the decision. If the company had to invest substantial amounts into instrumentation, outsourcing should be favored; if not, outsourcing may still be considered, but with a lower priority.

8. Availability of skilled LAN management personnel is one of the most critical issues; most frequently, it's the only driving factor for outsourcing. Not only the present status, but the satisfaction of future needs has to be quantified prior to the outsourcing decision.

9. Stability of environment and growth rates has serious impacts on the contract with the vendor. Acquisitions, mergers, business unit sales, and application portfolio changes need special and careful treatment in vendor contracts.

10. Consideration of the intention to offer value-added services to other third parties needs to be made. In certain corporations, the underused bandwidth of communication resources may be used for offering "low-priority" services to third parties who can't afford to build a network on their own (e.g., point-of-sale applications).

11. The ability to construct good outsourcing contracts is one of the key issues. The length of outsourcing contracts—often seven to ten years—means that the wording of the contract is extremely important. Adequate legal support is required from the very beginning.

12. Consideration of the philosophy of a company's LAN management approach, including consideration of whether to use horizontal or vertical integration, centralization, automation, and/or the use of a network management repository, should be in concert with the offer and capabilities of the outsourcer.

The final decision of the right outsourcing partner depends on the networking environment and the budget for third-party network management. Summarizing the expectations, outsourcers are expected to meet the following requirements:

- Financial strength and stability over a long period of time
- Proven experience in managing domestic and multinational networks

- Availability of a powerful pool of skilled personnel
- Tailored LAN management instruments that may be used exclusively for one client or shared between multiple clients
- Proven ability of implementing the most advanced technology
- Outstanding reputation in conducting business
- Willingness for revenue sharing
- Fair employee transfers

The user community is still divided. There are strong opinions against outsourcing LAN management. Frequently used arguments are: LAN management can easily be handled by in-house staff; outsourcing involves losing control to "unknown" third parties; problems can be solved cheaper in-house; business is better known by in-house staff; in-house staff is more responsible and more easily motivated. It seems likely that LAN maintenance functions will be farmed out at first. In summary, it's many times easier to build than to keep the LAN management team.

Chapter

8

Future Trends for Managing LANs

Local area networks and interconnected local area networks are becoming mission-critical to many corporations who need to provide the end user with computing power, support client/server structures, supply bandwidth for integrating communication forms and databases, support better service levels, decrease risks due to fatal outages of focal point resources, and speed up application design cycles.

LAN technology shows a number of dynamic changes. In terms of expectations, keep attuned to the following developments: Ethernet and Token Ring technologies will stay and will be enriched by switching that offers more bandwidth to individual servers, users, and applications; fast LANs and MANs will penetrate the market rapidly; in terms of media, twisted-pair may penetrate new areas when radiation reduction techniques are more effective; wiring hubs will take on the responsibility for being the local management entity, incorporating both physical and logical management; wireless LANs will be used for certain environments and applications, particularly as a backup alternative, but they will remain limited, and a major breakthrough is not expected soon; due to higher flexibility, routers and brouters will take implementation away from bridges, particularly in complex and geographically widespread environments; with bridges, the spanning tree technique or its enhanced versions will most likely be preferred to source routing algorithms. However, new source routing algorithms seem to be more efficient and may delay this process; interconnecting devices will house multiple functions, integrating the capabilities of a multiplexer, router, packet switch, and eventually of a matrix switch; from the management point of view, these devices will offer a multifunctional, integrated element management system, representing attributes of distributed element management; interconnecting LANs technology will show a number of alternatives; and fast packet (frame and cell relay), SMDS, B-ISDN and T1/T3 services seem to be the most popular ones.

LAN management has always been concerned with minimizing costs and improving operator efficiency. Various factors will make these goals more challenging in the near future:

- *Growth of LANs.* Enterprise networks continue to expand, both domestically and internationally. In particular, the number of interconnected LANs will grow substantially. In the LAN management control center, this growth adds to the volume of status and alarm data that an operator must monitor and analyze. LAN instrumentation must allow operators to easily and comprehensively monitor the large interconnected LANs, determine the troubles, and rapidly focus on a magnified portion of the network. At the highest level of monitoring, a several-hundred-segments network must be reduced to a graphic display with well-designed icons and symbols for key network elements.

- *Switched LANs and virtual LANs.* These will require dramatically new management and measurement techniques. Either special maintenance ports, built-in monitoring techniques, or low-price RMON probes will meet this challenge. But, altogether, instrumentation costs may go up again.

- *Continuous operations.* Most enterprise networks will operate continuously around the clock. The challenge for network management system vendors is to maintain operators' attention and focus their activities on the most relevant actions in emergencies.

- *Automation.* LAN management systems must begin to automate routine functions by improving their capabilities for automated decision making. Thus, LAN administrators can focus on traffic analysis, trend analysis, and planning.

- *Multimedia and multivendor networks.* Proprietary designs, separate workstations, dissimilar operator interfaces, and unique command structures can prevent LAN operators from becoming experienced users in all LAN management products they operate.

- *High cost of reactive LAN management.* The majority of monitors and management systems support reactive techniques instead of proactive ones. Instruments are not yet powerful enough to perform real-time trend analysis on parallel, seemingly unrelated, information streams.

The success of LANs and interconnected LAN management will depend on three critical success factors: (1) a well-organized set of LAN management functions, allocated and assigned to instruments and to human skill levels; (2) proper instrumentation, with the ability to extract integrated information, to export and import it, to maintain databases, and to provide analysis and performance prediction; and (3) personnel who understand their job responsibilities and possess the necessary qualifying skills.

Over a long period of time, it will remain valid to expand LAN management processes to include configuration, fault, performance, security, accounting management, LAN administration, and LAN design and capacity planning concerns. Naturally, functions will be constantly added and deleted, depending on actual user needs. However, a core with standard functions and features will remain.

The key is how applications are going to be developed and implemented for the six principal LAN management functional areas. The following trends are very likely.

Configuration Management

Recommendations for managed objects and their must-and-can attributes will be widely accepted by users. They will slowly convert existing fragmented files and databases into a more integrated structure. More graphics are expected for supporting inventory and configuration management by a meaningful combination of a relational database and computer aided design. Object-oriented databases will be used in combination with relational databases. The migration will be smooth; existing products will not be replaced overnight. The tools of prime interest will address asset and configuration management while at the same time offering flexibility and distribution up to a certain extent. More integrity is expected between configuration and fault management via autoconfiguration features that will be offered by various vendors.

Fault Management

In order to accelerate problem determination and diagnosis, new trouble-ticketing applications are expected. They will provide the flexibility of entering, exporting and importing trouble tickets, using advanced electronic mail features. The same systems will simplify the trouble-ownership question. More automation is expected, where examples from mainframes will show the directions; NetView with REXX extensions or Solve: Automation with NCL applications will embed LAN automation procedures into existing WAN-automation solutions. Existing and new monitors will be equipped with polling and eventing features or with a combination of both. Fine-tuning polling and eventing will help to reduce the overhead in communications channels.

Further add-ons will include expert systems and special applications for diagnostics in the hubs. State-of-the-art management applications, such as NerveCenter from Netlabs, will be implemented as an intelligent SNMP manager in many management platforms.

Performance Management

Performance data are expected to be ported from the MIBs of LAN management stations into existing performance databases, such as SLR, SAS, and MICS. For a more comprehensive LAN performance evaluation, more help is expected from LAN operating systems; vendors will offer alternatives but not necessarily by external and internal monitoring capabilities. Performance evaluation is going to be made easier by continuous and distributed monitoring in practically all LAN segments using RMON probes.

RMON2 will extend the present capabilities of monitoring into the application layers, offering a better basis for modeling and capacity planning.

Security Management

Security management in LANs will definitively get a face-lift; there will simply be too many mission-critical applications on LANs. Companies will try to find the optimal combination of organizational, physical, and logical protection; authentication and authorization are becoming equally important. Within a short period of time, a breakthrough is expected with using biometrics as the basis of authentication. Virus detection and removal will remain very high on the priority list.

Accounting Management

Accounting management will receive higher priority treatment due to the high cost of interconnecting LAN segments. In addition, as a preparation for evaluating outsourcing, LAN managers will try to estimate the costs of LAN ownership.

Software metering will regulate the use of software packages. This will become the basis of charge-back to users and of negotiation of service agreements with software vendors. The intelligent use of metering information will help enterprises to reduce the expenses for software licenses. Multinational companies may take advantage of time zones and provide access to applications by following the sun.

LAN Administration

The importance of LAN administration will increase in the future. Due to the large number of components in LANs, the control of hardware and software versions, the distribution of software without impacting production, and the professional management of changes will determine effectiveness.

User administration is expected to receive more attention and more utilities to simplify the use of LANs. But most of the features will incorporate some sort of authentication check in order to avoid security violations. More advanced tools are expected for the help desk as well.

Corporatewide centers of excellence will take over the present role of help desks. Very powerful tools will support the human resources in troubleshooting, change management, order processing, and in answering various types of questions. The basic tools under consideration will be stepwise extended by knowledge packs to be provided by the manufacturers of LAN components.

When expanding and redesigning processes, several innovative design principles must be considered (Herman 1991b):

- *Information sharing.*   Information must be made available to anyone who can effectively use it to perform their work. Sharing captured knowledge will avoid having to rediscover problems and changes.

- *Responsibility of individuals.*   The responsibility for the quality of process execution should lie with a single individual. That person should also be responsible for the integrity of the data they create or update. This way, additional integrity checks may be eliminated.

- *Simplification.*   Processes should be performed in as simple a fashion as possible, eliminating all steps that don't clearly add value.

- *Stratification.*   After defining levels of process complexity, the lowest level is the primary target for automation. In future steps, process experiences have to be used to derive from the highest level to the lowest possible level and to continue automation.

LAN management standards will help in accelerating the implementation of functions and in selecting future proof instruments. Specific management application areas that are supported by system management functions and by common management information service elements (CMIP) have been clearly defined by ISO groups. Their implementation in LANs, however, depends on how de facto standards perform. OSI network management may include LAN management, but the estimated overhead scares away both vendors and users. Similar definitions for the management dialog have been provided for the

TCP/IP environment (SNMP). Users have turned to SNMP, and hope to have found a common denominator for at least a number of years. For standardizing the manager-agent dialog, the following items have to be carefully considered (Herman 1991a).

How will the management information be formatted and how will the information exchange be regulated? This is actually the protocol-definition problem. How will the management information be transported between manager and agent? The OSI standards are using OSI protocol stack, and the TCP/IP standards use TCP/IP protocol stack. In both cases, the management protocol is defined as an application-layer protocol that uses the underlying transport services of the protocol stack. What management information will be exchanged? The collection of management data definitions that a manager or agent knows about is called the *management information base*. MIBs have to be known to both.

In terms of SNMP, the following trends are expected. SNMP agent-level support will be provided by the greatest number of vendors. This support is coming very soon. SNMP manager-level support will be provided by some vendors who most likely will implement on a well-accepted platform, leaving customization and the development of additional applications to vendors and users. Leading manufacturers with network management integrator products such as NetView for AIX, NetExpert, OneVision, and OpenView will enable vendors to link their SNMP managers to the integrators. Competition for SNMP manager products and platforms will be significant over the next few years. The MIB private areas are expected to move slowly to the public area and support heterogeneous LAN management on an SNMP basis. The RMON MIB will bridge the gap between the functionality of LAN management systems and analyzers with rich functionality. It defines the next generation of network monitoring with more comprehensive network fault diagnosis, planning, and performance-tuning features than any current monitoring solution. It uses SNMP and its standard MIB design to provide multivendor interoperability between monitoring products and management stations, allowing users to mix and match network monitors and management stations from different vendors.

SNMPv2 will be implemented with or without the security features. Also, RMON implementations will consider RMON2, and desktop management will most likely be supported by SNMP proxy agents. These agents will be responsible to convert MIF (Management Information Format) into MIBs before or during transmission to the SNMP manager.

The number of SNMP-based managers and objects is increasing. It's not easy to decide which product is best suited to the customer's environment. To help to select, the following items will become important.

Which LAN management functions are supported by the agents and manager(s)? Which security features are supported? Which non-LAN objects and services can be managed. Which platforms are supported. Is the product helpful for determining any LAN troubles? Is the product able to determine whether the managed object is operating at its potential? Is the product helpful in assessing whether the LAN is operating at its best performance capabilities?

As more LAN management application software gets written, it's important to define standardized APIs so that the software can be easily ported to different platforms and so that software developed by different vendors can be easily combined on a single platform. The platforms provide a standardized environment for developing and implementing applications, and they also separate management application software from the usual system-level services. Users and vendors do not have to deal with the details of protocols, data definitions, user interfaces, and presentation services.

On the basis of platforms, it's expected that independent companies will offer network and system management applications designed to provide real multivendor solutions while taking advantage of the system-level services of platforms. This way, vendors can concentrate on their specific hardware and software, and users can focus on the customization and fine-tuning of LAN management applications.

In order to provide supervision of LAN segments, there will be more continuous monitoring supported by inexpensive sensors residing in each segment. At least at the beginning, they will communicate with their master monitor using proprietary protocols. In such environments, both eventing and polling structures and inband and outband transmission options may be implemented. In addition to fault management, structures may also support performance management by distributing analysis capabilities to remote sites. In order to maximize the uptime of LAN segments, outband channels are preferred as carriers of LAN management information. Depending on budget limits, outband channels may be dedicated or switched. Not only the independence from communication facilities can be guaranteed, but also the power supply for the sensor is supplied to the sensor residing in the managed object. Health-check recording doesn't stop when the managed object breaks down.

Monitoring devices may become part of network management structures. These devices expand the capability of managed objects to provide status and performance indicators. The structures of the future may follow one of the following three basic alternatives:

- *LAN integrator.* Hierarchical LAN management structure with a network management service station in the middle. This station supervises all the managed objects through polling and eventing techniques. A typical example is an arrangement of an SNMP manager and SNMP agents. A LAN-specific example includes the central manager of Cabletron with the product Spectrum.

- *Manager of the managers.* Hierarchical LAN management structure with a network management service station in the middle. This station supervises LAN element management systems that are responsible for managing a family of managed objects, such as hubs, segments, routers, and bridges. In this case, investment in an installed base can be preserved. The interfaces are well defined, but the number of managers will probably not be reduced. Typical examples are NetView, NetExpert, MAXM, Spectrum, and OpenView. A LAN-specific example is from Bay Networks using the network control engine as an element manager for reducing the SNMP message volume and polling overhead.

- *Management platform.* In this case, system services and clearly defined application programming interfaces are provided by the suppliers, enabling other vendors to develop, implement, and port applications. Typical examples are NetView for AIX, NetView for Windows, OpenView, SunNet Manager, Spectrum, NetExpert, OneVision, NMC Vision, ISM, Tivoli Enterprise Environment, Integration Systems Manager, Unicenter, and Command/Post. Most of the companies are not eager to offer products for the element management system level. The main goal is to offer integration capabilities.

Completely new technologies for supporting various LAN management functions are likely. Examples may include: smart or intelligent SNMP agents to reduce polling overhead; manager-to-manager dialogs for distributed environments; hypermedia and hypertext for the help desk; training, and problem sectionalization and design; voice annotation of trouble tickets and voice messaging; optical storage for documentation and raw LAN analyzer data; storage of graphical images for assisting trouble storage at remote/local LAN help desks; intelligent user interfaces with flexible customization features; and expert systems for fault isolation and diagnosis.

In the future, progress is expected in the following areas:

- *Graphical user interfaces.* Progress has been made with various tools, including X-Windows (low-level window manager running on Unix), OpenLook (high-level graphic toolkit from Sun), Motif (high-level graphic toolkit from DEC and HP), and GMS (Graphics Modeling Systems for providing graphics routines for all the others). As a result, GUIs can draw complex network diagrams that allow an operator to view the status of hundreds of network nodes and elements simultaneously. Within a short period of time, operators can focus on particular managed objects. In addition, the animation of icons, along with digital speech processing, can attract an operator's attention to a problem.

- *Expert systems and neural networks.* In order to support proactive LAN management, many measurements have to be taken at different points in the LAN segments and at interconnecting devices. These measurement results must be correlated and analyzed in real time. Figure 8.1 shows the combination of both tools. The neural network is a fundamentally new form of computer processor to collect and correlate high volumes of measurement data and to provide appropriate input to the rule-based expert system. Unlike traditional processors, neural networks are trained to recognize patterns by running simple data through them. They can also process many inputs simultaneously. In managing local area networks, neural networks can correlate multiple measurement data streams against preprogrammed measurement data ranges that will cause network faults unless corrected proactively. The output from the neural networks is then used by the rule-based expert system to select a corrective action.

- *Distributed element management.* Managed objects are equipped with enough processing power to manage their own environment, to self-diagnose, and to initiate status reports to the network management center. This trend supports the implementation of robust OSI-based network management standards in the future.

- *Database technology.* LANs are expected to be modeled as objects. Objects interact by sending messages between each other. The called object (e.g., any network element) executes the processes prescribed in the message against its attributes (configuration data and status), and reports the results back to the calling object (e.g., network management station). Object-oriented databases are supporting this type of dialogue with high efficiency. For some applications, they offer considerably better performance than relational databases.

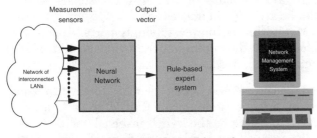

Figure 8.1 Combination of neural networks and expert systems.

   LAN switching technology can practically challenge all well-proven solutions to monitor, supervise, and manage LAN segments. Shared LANs are controlled by hubs, which provide connections to clients, servers, and interconnecting devices. All parts of the hub are connected to the same LAN segment with the result that all ports have access to all the traffic as it passes the LAN segment. Monitoring and managing devices attached to a port can monitor all the traffic on that LAN segment. Using switching technology to increase bandwidth, lower latency, and improve flexibility between particular servers and clients, the ports of a LAN switch are connected to a switching matrix that provides point-to-point connections between any two ports. Each port can practically function as a separate LAN segment. Using this solution, there is no shared-media point of entry that would allow you to monitor all traffic in the switch.

   Present solutions are technologically immature (e.g., port mirroring, roving port mirroring, or built-in features) or prohibitively expensive (e.g., port monitoring by RMON agents). Still, these are the core technologies for future solutions. These methods can be summarized as follows (Newman 1995):

Use of a Y-cable. The simplest measurement method is to insert a Y-shaped cable that links the switch, the node under test, and a protocol analyzer. This method is commonly used with WAN analyzers. But even WAN-monitor vendors are leaving this technology for more flexible ones.

Benefits. Y-cables are simple and relatively inexpensive, and they even can be attached in midsession—most LAN protocols will keep a session alive for the time needed to insert the Y-cable.

Disadvantages. Monitoring is limited to single ports. Fiber Y-cables require precisely aligned optical splitters.

Use of a minihub. The minihub offers a few Ethernet ports and creates a shared-access medium from which traffic can be monitored. Any hub with at least three ports, one for the hub, one for the end station, and one for the analyzer, will do the job.

Benefits. Minihubs are inexpensive and easy to use. As with Y-cables, they often can be attached in midsession.

Disadvantages. Monitoring is limited to single ports. A crossover cable must be used to connect the minihub to the switch so that cabling pin assignments remain unchanged.

Use of monitoring ports on LAN switches. Some switches come with a special port that allows an attached analyzer or RMON probe to observe traffic on other ports. Depending on the switch involved, monitor ports can capture traffic from one other port only, or from all ports on the switch. Roving port monitoring goes beyond port monitoring by using the switch's internal capability to create a roving RMON probe, whereby statistics are gathered on port segments at specified intervals.

Benefits.   Monitor ports offer a built-in method of traffic measurement by external devices. Roving port monitoring may save costs by using one probe for many ports.

Disadvantages.   Some monitor ports view traffic from only one other switch port at a time. On devices able to copy traffic from all ports, the monitor port may become flooded and drop measurement data. Roving port monitoring does not offer full visibility due to discontinuous monitoring.

Use of SNMP statistics to measure traffic.   Virtually all switch vendors include SNMP MIB II agents in their switches, and these gather basic data such as port status and the number of packets flowing through each port. Switch vendors are working on new MIBs to offer more opportunities of monitoring, evaluation, and capacity planning.

Benefits.   Built-in SNMP offers a quick, inexpensive, integrated way of checking the status of each switch port. There are an increasing number of applications and services to further process and report raw MIB data.

Disadvantages.   SNMP by itself offers very limited traffic measurement capabilities, such as number of packets sent to and from a port. Getting an accurate picture of network traffic usually requires more detailed reporting on statistics such as frame size, network utilization, and protocol distribution. The need for special applications is still there, requiring human and financial resources.

Use of RMON agents at each switch port.   Many switch makers see RMON as the most promising way to gather detailed traffic information.

Benefits.   RMON is a full-blown monitoring tool, offering useful measurements and capture capabilities on a wide array of data link statistics. RMON2, expected to be adopted soon, will incorporate key network-layer management data such as protocol distribution statistics. ASIC (application-specific integrated circuits) offer cheaper and faster probes, making this technology available at reasonable prices.

Disadvantages.   RMON agents add cost and complexity to the switch. On switches with CPU architecture, processing RMON data can affect the switch performance. ASIC is still a very new technology and has not yet been widely used in everyday applications.

Some combination of these technologies will help to meet the challenges due to switching and due to the implementation of virtual LANs.

The distribution of human responsibilities will follow the same path as the functions of LAN management. Depending on the size of LAN segments, and their interconnection, staffing will vary greatly. In terms of LAN management teams, two subjects have to be remembered: building the team and keeping the team together. These require considerable managerial skills. The LAN area supervisors will report to the LAN manager, who may also be the WAN manager, who may report to the information system manager or the chief information officer of the corporation. In a completely decentralized environment, the LAN manager most likely reports to business unit management.

LAN management directions may be summarized as follows. There will be integration of LAN-element management systems by a platform, SNMP manager, or with a manager of managers. In very complex and interconnected LANs, multiple integrators may be implemented. These integrators will use standard protocols for peer-to-peer communication.

There will be integration of LAN and WAN management, first by SNMP, then by CMIP; dual support is expected by integrators and platform providers. This step of integration will take place in multiple steps; in the case of MANs and interconnected LANs, the integration speed is expected to be higher. The integration is expected to be demand-driven.

Expect more centralized LAN management that will centralize control but distribute certain functions. In particular, monitoring, filtering functions, and reactions to routine messages will be distributed to remote sites. The practical implementation may follow OSI standards or hierarchical SNMP standards.

Due to limited human resources, automation of routine LAN management functions is absolutely necessary; support is expected by providers of integrated WAN/MAN management solutions. Automation packages may migrate to expert systems that can be used off-line and then on-line, off-loading LAN management personnel from routine tasks.

There will be implementation of more powerful databases as support for the LAN management stations, which will consolidate many templates from various LAN and WAN MIBs. Object-orientation is obvious, but relational databases will not lose their importance, particularly not for fault management.

Expect a slow move to outsource LAN management functions. The decision making will depend on the country, industry, and on the importance of LANs for critical applications. WAN network management outsourcing is expected to provide positive and negative examples.

The expenses of managing LANs and interconnected LANs will increase due to the demand for constantly improved service levels and enhanced management capabilities. The LAN management market is expected to face a serious shakeout; only products and companies with the best responses to strategic direction demands will survive. These directions mean better integration of management applications into the platforms or the availability of tightly integrated application suites.

LAN management is expected to take advantage of Internet opportunities. This may happen in two ways: managed object level or manager level. In the first case, management-related information (e.g., fault, performance, and accounting data) is collected within the object and stored in a Web home page instead of or in addition to MIBs. This page is accessible over the Internet by management terminals that usually use a powerful browser. When these home pages are accessed, transmitted, and processed depends on the polling frequency determined by the owner of the management terminals.

In the second case, processed management–related information is stored in a Web server next to the management station. Authorized users are able to access and retrieve these pages. In this case, the emphasis is on distributing performance-related information over the Internet.

Security firewalls are required in both cases. Recent progress with a new interpretative language, called Java, allows the presentation quality of results to be substantially improved. Java applets are developed and deployed in the Web pages; if requested they are downloaded to the client, where they execute automatically. Local modules may be used in addition to the applets.

Using the Internet will give alternatives to LAN managers, but it is not going to replace existing management protocols and applications.

Abbreviations

ACD	automated call distributor
ACSE	association control service element
ANSI	American National Standards Institute
ARP	Address Resolution Protocol
ARPA	Advanced Research Projects Agency
ARPANET	ARPA computer network
AS	autonomous system (connection between IGP and EGP)
ASN.1	Abstract Syntax Notation One
ATM	association transfer mode
AUI	attachment unit interface
BHCA	busy hour call attempt
B-ISDN	Broadband ISDN
BU	business unit
CAD	computer aided design
CATV	coaxial community antenna television
CAU	controlled access unit
CCITT	*Commitee Consultatif International Telegraphique et Telephonique*
CLNP	Connectionless Network Protocol
CMIP	Common Management Information Protocol
CMISE	common management information service element
CMOL	CMIP over logical link control
CMOT	CMIP over TCP/IP
CMS	cable management system
CSMA/CD	carrier sense multiple access/collision detect

CSU	channel service unit
CSV	comma separated value
CU	call Unix (remote session)
DAP	Data Access Protocol (DEC)
DARPA	ARPA of DoD
DAS	double attached station
DEE	data circuit-terminating equipment
DDN	Defense Data Network
DME	Distributed Management Environment (from OSF)
DNA	Digital Network Architecture (DEC)
DQDB	dual queue dual bus
DSA	Distributed Systems Architecture (Bull)
DSAP	destination service access point
DSU	data service unit
DTE	data terminal equipment
EDI	electronic data interchange
EGP	Exterior Gateway Protocol
EMS	element management system
ETN	electronic tandem network
FADU	file access data unit
FAT	file allocation table
FCS	frame checksum
FDDI	fiber distributed data interface
FDM	frequency division multiplexing
FIFO	first in first out
FOIRL	fiber-optic interrepeater link
FOMAU	fiber-optic medium attach unit
FSK	frequency shift keying
FTP	file transfer protocol
GGP	Gateway Gateway Protocol
GNMP	Government Network Management Profile
GOS	global operating system
GUI	graphical user interface
HDLC	High-level Data Link Protocol
IAB	Internet Activities Board
ICMP	Internet Control Message Protocol
IEEE	Institute of Electrical and Electronic Engineers
IETF	Internet Engineering Task Force

IGP	Internet Gateway Routing Protocol
IIVR	integrated interactive voice response
IMP	interface messages processors
IP	Internet Protocol
IPX	internet packet exchange
IS	intermediate system (ISO for IP-router)
ISDN	Integrated Services Digital Network
ISN	initial sequence number
ISO	International Organization for Standardization
LAN	local area network
LAT	Local Area Transport Protocol (DEC)
LED	light-emitting device
LLC	logical link control
LM	LAN manager
LMU	LAN management utilities
LM/X	LAN manager on Unix
MAC	media access control
MAN	metropolitan area network
MAP	manufacturing automation protocol
MAU	media attachment unit or multiple access unit
MIB	management information base
MIS	management information system
MO	managed object
MTA	message transfer agent
MTBF	mean time between failures
MTOR	mean time of repair
MTTD	mean time to diagnosis
MTTR	mean time to repair
MTU	maximum transmission unit
NCB	Network Control Block (IBM–NetBIOS)
NCE	network control engine
NCP	network control program
NCL	network control language
NE	network element
NetBIOS	network basic input-output system
NFS	Network File System (Sun)
NIC	network interface card
NMF	Network Management Forum

NMM	network management module
NMP	Network Management Protocol
NMS	network management station or network management system
NMVT	network management vector transport
NOS	network operating system
NVT	network virtual terminal
OSF	Open Systems Foundation
OSI	open system interconnected
OTDR	optical time domain reflectometer
PAD	packet assembler disassembler
PBX	private branch exchange
PDU	protocol data unit
PC	personal computer
PCM	pulse code modulation
PHY	physical layer (FDDI)
PIN	personal identification number or positive intrinsic negative
PING	packet internet grouper
PLS	physical signaling
PMD	physical-medium-dependent
PSM	product-specific module
RFC	request for comments
RFS	Remote File System (AT&T)
RMON	Remote Monitoring standard for SNMP-MIBs
RODM	resource object data manager
ROSE	remote operating service element
RPC	remote procedure call
SAS	single attached station
SDH	synchronous digital hierarchy
SFD	start frame delimiter
SGMP	Simple Gateway Monitoring Protocol
SLIP	IP over serial lines
SMAE	systems management application entities
SMAP	specific management application protocol
SMF	systems management function
SMFA	specific management functional area
SMB	Server Message Block (IBM—NetBIOS)

SMI	structure of management information
SMDR	station message detailed recording
SMP	Station or Simple Management Protocol (FDDI)
SMTP	Simple Mail Transfer Protocol
SNA	Systems Network Architecture (IBM)
SNI	Systems Network Interconnected (IBM)
SNMP	Simple Network Management Protocol
SNP	Sub Network Protocol
SPF	shortest path first
SPX	sequenced packet exchange
SQE	Signal Quality Error (Heartbeat)
SRB	source routing bridge
SSAP	source service access point
STA	spanning tree algorithms
TB	token bus
TCP	Transmission Control Protocol
TDM	time-division multiplexing
TDR	time domain reflectometer
TFTP	Trivial File Transfer Protocol
TLI	Transport Level Interface (AT&T)
TR	token ring
TTRT	target token ring rotation time
UA	user agent
UDP	User Datagram Protocol
ULP	Upper Layer Protocol
UPS	uninterrupted power supply
VNM	Virtual Network Machine
VT	virtual terminal
VTAM	Virtual Telecommunication Access Method (IBM)
WAN	wide area network
XNS	Xerox Network Services

Appendix

B

Bibliography

Applied Computer Devices. Network Knowledge Tool Implementation Manual, Terre Haute, Indiana, 1992.

Aaron, S., Chartoff, M., Reinhold, B. Putting an end to swivel shuffle, *Network World*, July 5, 1993, p. 35–42.

AT&T. Premises Distribution System, Product Implementation Guide, Basking Ridge, N.J., 1989.

Autrata, M. Technologies and support in the OSF/DME offering Network & Distributed Systems Management '91, Washington, D.C., September 1991.

Axner, D. H. Tools for analyzing LAN performance, *Business Communication Review*, August 1991, pp. 46–52.

Banyan Systems Inc. VINES System Guide, Westborough, Mass., 1991.

Bapat, S. OSI Management Information Base Implementation, Integrated Network Management II, Washington, D.C., 1991.

BICC Data Networks. ISOLAN Product Guide, Westborough, Mass., 1990.

BIM. Netcortex Operational Guide, Bruxelles, 1992.

Birenbaum, E. RMON Agent Gets the Goods on Remote LANs, *Data Communications*, April 1994, p. 45–46.

Bloom, G. An End to Cable Chaos, *Telecommunications*, February, 1990.

Boell, H. P. *Lokale Netze (Local Area Networks)*, McGraw-Hill Book Company GmbH, Hamburg, Germany, 1989.

Brady, S. Management User Interfaces, IEEE Network Management and Control Workshop, Tarrytown, N.Y., 1989, pp. 329–334.

Brigth J. The smart card: An application in search of a technology, *Telecommunications*, March, 1990, pp. 63–68.

Bytex Corporation. Maestro—Intelligent Switching Hub, Product Guide, Southborough, Mass., 1991.

Cabletron Systems. LanceView Product Guide, Rochester, New York, 1990.

Cabletron Systems. Spectrum Product Guide, Rochester, New York, 1991.

CACI, Inc. SIMLAN II Local Area Network Analysis Product Guide, La Jolla, California, 1990.

Carnese, D. Managing distributed applications, Independence Technologies, White Paper, Freemont, Calif., 1994.

Carter, E. H., Dia, P. G. Evaluating Network Management Systems: Criteria and observations, Integrated Network Management II, Washington, D.C., 1991.

Case, J. D. SNMP: Making the Standards work in today's heterogenous networks, ComNet '92, Washington, D.C., 1992.

Chiong, J. UNIX can play a key role in Network Management, *Computer Technology Review*, Winter 1990, pp. 29–33.

Cisco Systems. NetCentral Product Guide, Santa Clara, California, 1991.

Collins, W. The reality of OSI management, *Network World,* October 9, 1989.

Comdisco Systems, Inc. BoNes Product Guide, Foster City, California, 1991.

Concord Communications, Inc. Trakker LAN Monitor Product Guide, Marlborough, Mass., 1991.

Cooper, J. A. The Network Security Management. *Datapro Research Corporation,* NM20-200, Delran, N.J., 1990.

CrossComm Corporation. Understanding LAN Bridge and Router Performance, Technical Note, 1990.

CrossComm Corporation. IMS Reference Guide, 1990.

Datapro Research Corp. An Overview of Simple Network Management Protocol, NM40-300, pp. 201–207, Delran, N.J., 1990.

———. A look at Selected LAN Management Tools, NM50-300a, pp. 701–708, Delran, N.J., 1989.

———. AT&T's Unified Network Management Architecture, NM40-313, pp. 101–114, Delran, N.J., 1989.

———. Cable Management Systems: Overview, NS60-020, pp. 101–107, Delran, N.J., 1992.

———. DEC Enterprise Management Architecture' Datapro Research Corp. OpenView's Architectural Model, NM40-325, pp. 101–107, Delran, N.J., 1989.

———. IBM AIX NetView/6000, NS30-604a, pp. 201–203, Delran, N.J., 1992.

———. IBM LAN Network Manager. NS30-504b, p. 101, Delran, N.J., 1990.

———. IBM SNA and NetView, NM40-491, pp. 101–108, Delran, N.J., 1989.

———. LAN Design Tools. NS30-202c, pp. 301, Delran, N.J., 1990.

———. Managing local area networks. Accounting, Performance and Security Management, NM50-300b, pp. 501–509, Delran, N.J., 1989.

———. Managing local area networks. Fault and configuration management, NM50c-300, pp. 410–412, Delran, N.J., 1989.

———. Network Management of TCP/IP Networks: Present and Future. NM40-300, pp. 101–108, Delran, N.J., 1991.

———. SNMP Product Guide, NM40-300, pp. 301–316, Delran, N.J., 1990.

———. SNMP Query Language, NM40-300, pp. 401–404, Delran, N.J., 1991.

———. Synernetics Viewplex LAN Management Tools. NS05-864, p. 101, Delran, N.J., 1991.

———. The LAN troubleshooting Sequence, NM50-300, pp. 101–106, Delran, N.J., 1989.

Dem, D. P., Till, J. Monitoring LANs from a distance, *Data Communications,* McGraw-Hill, November 1989, pp. 17–20.

Digilog, Inc. LANVista Product Guide, Montgomeryville, Pa., 1990.

Digital Equipment Corp. LAN Traffic Monitor, Product Guide, Cambridge, Mass., 1989.

Fabbio, R. WizardWare: An Overview, Network & Distributed Systems Management '91, Washington, D.C., September 1991.

Feldkhum, L. *Integrated Network Management Systems,* Elsevier Publisher, 1989, IFIP Congress, pp. 279–300.

Feldkhum, L., Ericson, J. *Event management as a common functional area of Open Systems Management,* Elsevier Publisher, 1989, IFIP Congress, pp. 365–376.

Ferguson, R. The Business Case for Network Management, Distributed Systems & Network Management Conference, Washington, D.C., 1991.

FiberCom. ViewMaster Product Specification, Roanoke, Va., 1991.

Fisher, S. Dueling Protocols, *BYTE,* March 1991, pp. 182–190, San Francisco, 1991.

Fischer International Systems Corp. Watchdog PC Data Security Product Guide, Naples, Fla., 1991.

Fortier, P, J. *Handbook of LAN Technology,* Intertext Publications, McGraw-Hill, Inc., New York, 1989.

Frederick Engineering. FECOS Users Guide, Columbia, Maryland, 1991.

Galvin, J. M., McClogbrie, K., Davis, J. R. Secure Management of SNMP networks, Integrated Network Management II, Washington, D.C., 1991.

Gambit Inc. GamOptics System 9000 Product Guide, Yokneam, Israel, 1991.

Gilbert, E. E. Unified Network Management Architecture Putting it All Together, *AT&T Technology,* vol. 3, number 2, 1988.

Gilliam, P. A Practical Perspective on LAN Performance, *Business Communications Review,* October 1990, pp. 56–58.

Goehring, G., Jasper, E. Network Management in Token Rings, *Datacom,* Special Edition, October 1990, pp. 44–52.

Heckart, C. Carriers extend a LAN interconnectivity hand, Network World, January 9, 1995, p. 35–42.

Herman, J. Enterprise Management Vendors Shoot It Out, *Data Communications,* McGraw-Hill, November 1990, pp. 92–110.

Herman, J. A New View of OpenView, *Network Monitor,* vol. 5, no. 3, March 1990, Boston, Mass.

Herman, J. Net Management Directions—Architectures and standards for multivendor net management, *Business Communication Review,* June 1991a, pp. 79–83.

———. Net Management Directions—Renovating how networks are managed, *Business Communication Review,* August 1991b, pp. 71–73.

Herman, J. The Suite Smell of Success, *Business Communications Review,* April 1995.

Herman, J., Lippis, N. The Internetwork Decade, *Supplement to Data Communications,* McGraw-Hill, January 1991, pp. 2–32.

Herman, J., Weber, R. The LAN Management Market, Northeast Consulting Resources, Boston, Mass., 1989.

Hewlett-Packard Company. HP OpenView Network Manager Server, Palo Alto, California, 1989.

Hewlett-Packard Company. HP ProbeView Product Guide, Palo Alto, California, 1989.

Hewlett-Packard Company, HP OpenView, NM Server Technical Evaluation Guide, Palo Alto, California, 1989.

Howard, M. LAN Management Assessment, IDG Network Management Solutions, April 1990, Anaheim, California.

Huntington, J. A. OSI-based net management, *Data Communications,* March 1989, pp. 111–129.

Huntington, J. A. SNMP/CMIP market penetration and user perception, Interop 1990, San Jose, Calif., October 1990.

Huntington-Lee, J. Inventory and Configuration Management, *Datapro Network Management,* NM20-300-101, Delran, N.J., October 1991.

Huntington-Lee, J. Systems Management Server extends its reach with ISV appl, *Network World,* August 7, 1995, p. 6L–8L.

Infonetics, Inc. The Cost of LAN Downtime, 1989.

Infotel Systems Corp. LAN interconnecting technologies, Course Material, 1990.

International Business Machines, Inc. IBM Token Ring Problems Determination Guide, Document SY27-0280-1, 1988.

Internetics. Product Guides for Softbench, LANSIM and LANAI, Upper Marlboro, Maryland, 1991.

Intratec Systems, Inc. Telecommunications Facilities Management System, Product Guide, Dallas, Tex., 1991.

Industrial Technology Institute. Metasan Product Implementation Guide, 1991.

Isicad, Inc. Command Implementation Guide, Anaheim, Calif., 1991.

Jander, M. A Bundle of Systems Management Tools, *Data Communications,* December 1993, p. 41–42.

Jander, M. An On-Screen Decision Maker, *Data Communications,* April 1994, p. 49–50.

Jander, M. LAN Analysis: The View from Layer 7, *Data Communications,* March 1995, p. 47–48.

Jarzwinski, A. Applying Simulation to Network Planning, *Network World,* May 17, 1993, p. 33–35.

Johnson, J. T. LAN Management: More than Monitoring, *Data Communications,* December 1994, p. 133–134.

Kauffels, F.-J. *The Future of LANs* (German), Datacom, Bergheim, Germany, 1994, p. 1–79.

Krall, G. SNMP opens new lines of sight, *Data Communication—LAN Strategies,* McGraw-Hill, March 1990, pp. 45–54.

LAN Magazine. The Local Area Network Glossary, New York, 1989.

Lannet, Inc. MultiMan Product Guide, Huntington Beach, California, 1991.

Leinwand, A., Fang, K. Network Management–A practical perspective, Addison-Wesley Publishing Company, Inc., Menlo Park, California, 1993.

Lerner, S., Bion, J. The Well-Managed LAN, *LAN Magazine,* June 1989, p. 78–89.

Linnel, D. Enterprise Client/Server Management, TTI Workshop in Washington, D.C., October 1994.

Lo, T, L. Local Area Networks for Managers, CMG Transactions, Summer 1990, Chicago, pp. 31–40.

Marks, K. Tools for the network handyman, *Network World,* May 22, 1995, p. 63–70.

Martin, J. *Local Area Networks,* Prentice-Hall, Englewood Cliffs, New Jersey, 1991.

Micro Technology. LANCE Product Guide, Anaheim, California, 1991.

Mier, E. Testing SNMP in Routers, *Network World,* July 1991.

Mier, E., Mier, D., Smithers, R. Product Testing LAN Backup Software, *Communications Week,* May 15, 1995, p. 63–75.

Mier, E., Mier, D., Yocom, B. Product testing SNMP Managers, *Communications Week,* February 13, 1995, p. 55–61.

Mil 3, Inc. OpNet Product Implementation Guide, Boston, Mass., 1991.

Miller, H. *LAN Troubleshooting Handbook,* M&T Books, Redwood City, Calif., 1989.

Miller, M. Net Management Platforms on the move, *Network World,* October 17, 1994, p. 55–68.

Morrison, W. *Ethernet LAN Management: NMCC/VAX ETHERnim,* Integrated Network Management, Elsevier Science Publisher, IFIP 1989.

Mouttham, A., Frontini, M., Griffin, J., Lewin, S. *LAN Management using expert systems,* Integrated Network Management, Elsevier Science Publisher, IFIP 1989.

Musthaler, L. The Trouble with Help Desk Selection, *Network World,* February 20, 1995, p. 35–40.

Nance, B. Managing Big Blue, *BYTE,* March 1991, pp. 197–204.

Nance, B. LAN Tune Up, *BYTE,* August 1991, pp. 287–299.

NetLabs, Inc. DualManager Product Implementation Guide, Los Angeles, 1991.

Network General Corp. Sniffer Network Analyzer Product Family User's Guide, Menlo Park, Calif. 1991.

Network Management, Inc. LANfolio Product Guide, New York, 1990.

Network Managers Limited. NMC 3000 Product Specification and Implementation Guideline, Guildford, United Kingdom, 1991.

Newman, D. LAN switches leave users looking for trouble, *Data Communications,* March 1995, p. 103–108.

Novell, Inc. NetWare Management Functions, San Jose, California, 1990.

Novell, Inc. LANAnalyzer and LANtern Product Guide, San Jose, California, 1991.

Nuciforo, T. What a computerized cable management system should do, *Business Communications Review,* July 1989, pp. 22–26.

The OSF Distributed Management Environment, White Paper, Cambridge, Mass., 1991.

Objective Systems Integrators. NetExpert-Product Description, Folsum, Calif., February 1992.

OSI/Network Management Forum. Forum 002—Application Services, Bernandsville, N.J. OSI/Network Management Forum.

   Forum 003—Objects Specification Framework, Bernandsville, N.J. OSI/Network Management Forum.

   Forum 006—Forum Library of Managed Object Classes, Name Bindings and Attributes, Bernandsville, N.J.

Patterson, T. Evaluating LAN Security, Network World, October 21, 1991, pp. 47–52.

Penrod, P. LAN Backup Systems, *Network World,* February 14, 1994, p. 45–50.

Presuhn, R. Considering CMIP, *Data Communication—LAN strategies,* McGraw-Hill, March 1990, pp. 55–66.

Remedy Inc. Action Request System—Product Description, Sunnyvale, Calif., September 1991.

Quintrel Corp. CableTrak Communication Facilities Management Software, Cedar Rapids, Iowa, 1991.

Rhodes, P. D. *LAN Operations*—A Guide to Daily Management, Addison-Wesley Publishing Company, Inc., Reading, Massachusetts, 1991.

Robertson, B. Name Services—The Key to Large Network Management, *LAN Technology,* October 1990, pp. 42–50.

Rose, M. T. Network Management is Simple: you just need the "right" framework, Integrated Network Management II, Washington, D.C., 1991.

Rothberg, M. L. Cable Management Systems, *Datapro Reports on Network Management Systems,* NS60-020-101. Delran, N.J., March 1991.

Saal, H. The Protocol Analyzer—A Multipurpose Tool for LAN Managers, *LAN Technology,* M&T Publishing, Inc., June 1989.

Saal, H. LAN downtime: Clear and present danger, *Data Communication—LAN Strategies,* McGraw-Hill, March 1990, pp. 67–72.

Saen, H. LAN Network Planning and Design, IBM-IEC, La Hulpe, Belgium, 1991.

Sanghi, S., Chandna, A., Wetzel, G., Sengupta, S. How well do SNMP and CMOT meet IP router management needs?, Integrated Network Management II, Washington, D.C., 1991.

Scott, K. SNMP brings order to chaos, *Data Communication—LAN Strategies,* McGraw-Hill, March 1990, pp. 24–30.

Scott, K. Taking care of Business with SNMP, *Data Communication—LAN Strategies,* McGraw-Hill, March 1990, pp. 31–44.

Security Dynamics. Access Control and Encryption Product Family Guide, Cambridge, Mass., 1991.

Spider Systems, Inc. Spider Multi-Segment LAN Monitoring and Analysis Products, Burlington, Mass., 1990.

Stallings, W.: SNMP, SNMPv2, and CMIP—The Practical Guide to Network-Management Standards, Addison-Wesley Publishing Company, Reading, Massachusetts, 1993.

Sturm, R., Weinstcck, J. Application MIBs: Taming the Software Beast, *Data Communications,* November 1995, pp. 85–92.

Sun Microsystems. SunNet Manager Product Guide, Mountain View, California, 1990.

Swanson, R. H. Emerging technologies for network management, *Business Communication Review,* August 1991, pp. 53–58.

SynOptics Communications, Inc. Lattisnet Product Guide, Santa Clara, California, 1990.

SynOptics Communications, Inc. Network Control Engine Product Guide, Santa Clara, California, 1990.

Teknekron Communication Systems. NMS/Core Product Guide, Berkeley, California, 1991.

Terplan, K. Effective LAN Management, Technology Transfer Institute, Seminar Documentation, Santa Monica, Calif., 1991a.

———. *Communication Networks Management,* Prentice-Hall, Inc., Englewood Cliffs N.J., 1991b.

Terplan, K. *Effective Management of Local Area Networks,* McGraw-Hill, New York, 1992.

Terplan, K., Huntington, J. *Applications for Distributed Systems and Network Management,* Van Nostrand-Reinhold, New York, 1995.

Theakston, A. LAN resilience and security, *Insight IBM,* Xephon Publication, August 1991, United Kingdom, pp. 15–21.

Tjaden, G. S. The Allink Approach to Management Systems Integration, Network & Distributed Systems Management '91, Washington, D.C., September 1991.

Tschammer, V., Klessman. Local Area Network Management Issues, *Datapro Research Corporation,* NM50-300, Delran, N.J., 1989, pp. 100–108.

VandenBerg, Chr. MIB II extends SNMP Interoperability, *Data Communications,* McGraw-Hill, October 1990, pp. 119–124.

Vollmer, T. Network design: trends and solutions (German), *Datacom Magazine,* October 1994, November 1994, and January 1995, Bergheim, Germany.

Weil, J. What You Can Do with a Network Analyzer?—Network Management Solutions, Anaheim, Calif., 1990.

Weissmann, P. T. Automated Problem Management, *Technical Support,* vol. 5, number 10, August 1991, Technical Enterprises Inc., Milwaukee, Wis.

Index

ABOUT THE AUTHOR

Kornel Terplan is a telecommunications expert with more than 24 years of international consulting experience in the areas of network and systems management, benchmarking, outsourcing, and performance optimization. His clients include AT&T, Walt Disney World, BMW, Salomon Brothers, Siemens, IBM, and many other companies. Dr. Terplan has written numerous conference papers and technical articles, and is the author of 12 books, including *Benchmarking for Effective Network Management,* and the forthcoming *Hewlett-Packard's OpenView: A Practical Guide,* both available from McGraw-Hill.